Developmental Psychology

Theron Alexander
Temple University

Paul Roodin
State University of New York College at Oswego

Bernard Gorman
Nassau Community College

Developmental Psychology

D. VAN NOSTRAND COMPANY
New York   Cincinnati   Toronto   London   Melbourne

To Marie Bailey Alexander—T.A.

To Harry and Blossom Roodin—P.R.

To Dale Wendy Gorman and Betsy and Leanne Gorman—B.G.

Cover photo by Dianne Baasch.

Frontispiece by David Strickler/Monkmeyer Press Photo Service. Photo on page 178 by Mary M. Duncan. Photo on page 266 by Diana Blanchard. Photo on page 354 by United Press International.

D. Van Nostrand Company Regional Offices:
New York   Cincinnati

D. Van Nostrand Company International Offices:
London   Toronto   Melbourne

Library of Congress Catalog Card Number: 79-65547
ISBN: 0-442-25212-9

Published by D. Van Nostrand Company
135 West 50th Street, New York, N.Y. 10020

10   9   8   7   6   5   4   3   2   1

Preface

Developmental Psychology provides an integrated approach to the study of child and adolescent development. The authors have combined a thorough orientation to research with an awareness of the wonder and uniqueness of the developmental process. The focus of human development—the individual infant, child, or adolescent—always holds the center of attention.

The authors aim throughout to present a research-based text, while at the same time emphasizing developmental theory. The book stresses how to apply the major developmental theories—cognitive, psychoanalytic, learning, and ethological—to the understanding of development.

Developmental Psychology is divided into six parts. Part I, Basic Foundations of Development, introduces the study of development historically and theoretically. The chapters in this part describe the historical basis of human development research and the four major theoretical approaches, seeking to place modern theory and research in historical perspective.

Part II reviews prenatal development and development in early infancy. Heredity, embryonic and fetal development, birth, and maternal health and nutrition are discussed. Also explored are the capabilities of infants (with emphasis on the extensive current research in this area) and physical growth during infancy (with discussion of the concept of "normal" development and individual differences among infants).

Part III covers cognitive development, the beginnings of language, and social development in later infancy and toddlerhood. The authors discuss major theories of language acquisition and Piaget's research on cognitive development. The discussion of social development in infancy includes early social interaction, attachment, and problems of institutionalized infants.

Parts IV and V are devoted to development in early and middle childhood. Each part includes chapters on intellectual, cognitive, personality, and social development in the respective stages. Sex differences in early development are given particular emphasis. In addition, the treatment of early childhood includes a further study of language acquisition emphasizing the development of children's syntactical proficiency and the relationship between language and thought. Part V, on middle childhood, includes a chapter on moral development, including psychoanalytic, social-learning, and cognitive development views of this topic and concluding with a discussion of research on moral development.

Part VI covers development during adolescence. One chapter deals with physical and social development during this period, with particular emphasis on current theoretical explanations of adolescent behavior. Sexual development is also covered at length. The final chapter, Cognitive Development, Identity, and Experience, discusses problems that face all adolescents: identity formation, moral development, political awareness, vocational choice, and problems of alienation.

In the discussions of all developmental processes, the authors aim to integrate theory and research in human development with an understanding of developmental processes from the child's point of view. The emphasis is on practical application of theory and research. *Developmental Psychology* is thus appropriate for courses on childhood and adolescence in departments of education, home economics, and nursing, as well as psychology.

The authors have attempted to write a text that is above all engaging to its audience. An outline of contents precedes each chapter to facilitate learning. Brief summaries and lists of suggested readings are provided at the end of each chapter. Tables, graphs, drawings, and photographs illustrate the text. The authors have prepared an extensive Instructor's Manual that includes test items for each chapter.

The authors acknowledge with appreciation the suggestions and comments of the following people, who reviewed the manuscript during its development: David Brodzinsky, of Douglass College; Peter DePaulo, of Saint Joseph's College; Edward Fahrmeier, of the University of Maryland; Jeanette Haviland, of Livingston College; Manuel Leon, of the University of California at Los Angeles; Tony Lutkus, of Rutgers University; Cathleen McClusky, of West Virginia University; Neil Salkind, of the University of Kansas; Sally Sternglanz, of the State University of New York at Stony Brook; Tom Trabasso, of the University of Minnesota; and Michael Walraven, of Jackson Community College.

The authors wish to acknowledge the contributions of Joan Dennision and Beverly Pfund, who typed part of the final manuscript; their colleagues, including Gilbert Voyat and Alden Wessman; and students and former professors, for their ideas, thoughts, questions, and comments.

Contents

Basic Foundations of Development

Prenatal Development and Early Infancy

3

Infancy and Toddlerhood

4

Early Childhood

5

Middle Childhood

Adolescence

Developmental Psychology

BASIC FOUNDATIONS OF DEVELOPMENT

Historical and Methodological Foundations of Human Development Research

THE HISTORY OF THE CONCEPT OF HUMAN DEVELOPMENT

The Concept of Human Development

In this book we shall explore the processes that shape human development from the moment of conception through the years of infancy, childhood, and adolescence. We shall use a variety of disciplines to help us in our explorations. We shall borrow concepts from biology and medicine, psychology and education, and sociology and anthropology.

Why might you, the student, find the study of human development rewarding? You might study human development to investigate the origins of our behaviors. We know that some people are typically shy while others are outgoing; some people strike us as highly intelligent while others seem to be quite dull; and some people seem to be highly concerned with social rules and morality while others behave in lawless, sometimes antisocial ways. How and why did these people get to be the way that they are now?

As we observe ourselves and others, we may notice that at different points in the lifespan, people act in characteristically different ways. We might ask ourselves if there are different life "stages" that can be found at different ages. If so, what can we expect to find in each stage? Are the behaviors that we see in each stage learned or are they due to some underlying biological processes? Are these behaviors influenced by society? Alternately, are they created by some complex interaction of biological forces, personal learning histories, and social forces? Can we skip stages; that is, miss them entirely or perhaps accelerate people rapidly from one stage to another? As we proceed in the study of human development, we will confront these questions again and again.

As humans, we are concerned with value issues. We often question whether things or events are good or bad, pleasurable or painful for us. In looking backward and forward in our lives, did we and will we like the results of what we have seen and what we will see? In studying human development, we might obtain some clues as to how the quality of life may be changed for better or for worse in ourselves and in other people. Since we know that the lives of many people are often plagued by sickness and misery, this notion of a better life goes far beyond mere academic discussion.

Everyone who reads this book was once a child. Most readers, we suspect, are young through middle-aged adults. Some of you will be entrusted with the care of infants and adolescents. How then can we gain both an understanding and some practical knowledge of the ways in which the quality and meaning of human life can be made more valuable?

Finally, on a purely intellectual level, to be able to understand the factors that determine the development of an individual human life is a goal that easily ranks with such goals as understanding the atom or exploring the mysteries of the physi-

Figure 1-1.   Everyone who reads this book was once a child. (United Nations photo by Marcia Weinstein)

cal universe. Studying human development can be a rich and rewarding intellectual enterprise.

When and where did we get our current scientific ideas about human development? Many of our modern concepts of human nature, our values concerning individuality, childhood, and our need to study behavior hardly existed before the

Twentieth century. Some of these concepts are still undergoing change in our present society, and many of them are not shared with other societies. With variations and overlappings, the growth of our modern scientific concepts of human development can be roughly traced to the following historical stages:

1. The rise in Western Europe of our distinctive concept of human dignity and individual worth—roughly from the time of the ancient Greeks to about 1600 A.D. and beyond.

2. The rise (mostly in Northern Europe) of a community of scientists, a scientific approach to nature, and a scientific method of study—about 1600 to 1780.

3. The rise of modern European and American images of childhood as a distinct, sensitive, and important period in the life span. These notions developed about 1900 (by which time child labor regulations had largely established these concepts in law).

4. The rise of a modern science of human behavior—starting about 1900 and still growing.

In the next two sections we shall review these stages, and in following sections we will present an overview of scientific methods as they apply to the study of human development.

Some Pre-Scientific and Early Scientific Views of Human Nature and Development

Our views of human nature and of the dignity of individuals have been inherited from Western European ideas that slowly evolved from Hebrew, ancient Greek, Mediterranean, and Northern European sources. Out of the lore of priests and storytellers, the wisdom of prophets and philosophers, European experience was shaped into some distinctive cultural attitudes and traditions concerning individuality and childhood that are still influential today. One early belief about human nature and behavior concerned the notion of "humors," or vital fluids. According to this idea, behavior and temperament depended upon the proportion of four fluids in the body: blood, black bile, yellow bile, and phlegm. Remnants of this ancient idea remain today in our language when we say that a person is in an *ill humor.* Also, we sometimes refer to a cheerful person as being of *sanguine humor,* meaning that the person has "high color" (lots of blood) and is therefore sturdy and in good spirits or optimistic. Another early belief is the medieval idea that mental illness could be accounted for by the presence of evil spirits or devils in the body. A cure for such "possessions" depended upon exorcising the spirits. Such ideas about temperament gradually gave way to present scientific concepts about human development and behavior.

Traditional and Medieval Views.   In the late middle ages, the rise of trading towns and cities made these centers of growth favorable to kings, whose governments needed bureaucracies. These bureaucracies were provided by the church's clergy, who trained in the newly formed universities. Thus, the universities provided new avenues for individuals to change and improve their lives. At the same time, improvements in agriculture and technology allowed a greater survival rate and set the stage for an increased appreciation of the individual's chances to achieve greater human potentials (Morris, 1972).

In medieval times, children who were seven years old or older were considered to be miniature adults, and they were given nearly full adult responsibilities. For example, at seven or so they were usually apprenticed to a tradesman. Academically inclined children could even be sent to a university on a level comparable with adult scholars. Thus, in the medieval universities the new interest in human potential and individual worth was encouraged. Students in these universities were expected to pursue the newly revived classics in order to acquire a view of the world similar to that contained in the ancient Greek and Roman teachings about human nature and social virtue. They used this classical material to help them to clarify and define what the role of humankind and of individual people should be in what seemed to be an expanding universe (Hale, 1971). This movement, commonly termed "humanism" in its early phases, became the rebirth, or renaissance, of interest in new knowledge, which gave the name *Renaissance* to the entire era.

One of the greatest scholars of the early Renaissance was Erasmus, who grew up in commercial Rotterdam but moved and worked freely among scholars and friends everywhere in Western Europe. He was widely admired in his time for his defense of the dignity and liberty of the human spirit, his stress on rational systems for discovering truth, and his pursuit of these values in opposition to traditional systems of unquestioning belief in established ideas (Phillips, 1967). Erasmus pub-

Figure 1-2. Erasmus of Rotterdam, 1466–1536? (Photo by the Bettmann Archive)

lished and lectured widely in important centers of learning throughout Europe. His personal style and rigorous methods won admiration and widely promoted his most important themes, namely, that the human mind should be free to pursue rational inquiry wherever it leads, and that the goal of expanding human knowledge will be achieved by allowing freedom and respecting the dignity of individuals (Thompson, 1965).

These themes became the basic conditions for the growth of new knowledge that produced such sciences as astronomy, physics, engineering, chemistry and, eventually, biology and medicine. The new faith in rational investigation also provided the basis for social sciences such as political science, sociology and, finally, psychology. With the growth of these sciences, the needs and characteristics of children and adults in relation to their environments, their social and their political organizations, became topics of scientific study.

The Scientific Revolution and the Enlightenment.   The Scientific Revolution in the physical and natural sciences began in mathematics and astronomy and eventually spread to physics. Physics, as developed by Isaac Newton and others, produced new insights that astonished the world shortly before 1700. It reinforced other technological knowledge and shaped ways of thinking about the world and human behavior. The effort to be scientific had a profound influence on thinkers of that time and later, as is revealed in the works of John Locke (1632–1704) and his successors.

The Scientific Revolution produced a breakthrough in medicine and biology with the discovery that blood moves in living bodies through a recirculating system. The knowledge that body parts could be "systematic" inspired efforts to investigate every sort of life system, and classifying and discovering systems and studying their interconnections became major aspects of the discipline of biology.

By the end of the seventeenth century there were two major movements that shaped the Western world. One was a philosophical movement called *The Enlightenment:* a movement that believed humanity could be perfected through the forces of reason, logic, and the scientific method which were rapidly evolving during that time. The spirit of the Enlightenment was an exciting one because it was hoped that the forces of reason would free people from the superstitions, inertia, and ignorance of the past (Brinton, 1950). The other major movement of this period was more practical: industrialization. As new technologies were developed and new political organizations formed, small factories began to rise, and the age of the individual craftsman, the small farmer, and the shopkeeper slowly started to shift toward the age of mass production and mass culture.

Philosophers of the Enlightenment and early Industrial Age, influenced by the sciences of physics or biology, produced early theories about the processes of human learning, growth and development, as well as about social and political processes (Merton, 1968). Let us briefly examine the views of some of the most influential thinkers of the Enlightenment period, who wrote about human behavior and human developmental processes. We might very simply classify Enlightenment philosophers as inheritors of: (1) the physical-science tradition, representing "empiricism," or (2) the biological-science tradition, representing a kind of "naturalism." Both traditions were ultimately blended in modern psychology, though they still represent distinct and separate influences on modern thinking.

The Empirical Tradition: John Locke and His Successors.   The English philosopher John Locke (1632–1704) worked during the early Enlightenment era when discoveries of the new physical sciences were rapidly changing old views of the world. His ideas represent some of the most useful and characteristic values of scientific thought. Among these values are the attempts to remain objective, neutral, and dispassionate about competing ideas and to be tolerant, yet rigorous and precise, in measuring the merits of one idea against another. These attitudes were reflected strongly in his notion that the mind must approach new experiences as if it were a fresh tablet of clay, ready to be molded and formed with impressions originating from outside. Locke's concept that the human mind was a *tabula rasa,* or "blank slate" (Locke, reprinted 1969), sharpened issues then and later among theorists of human behavior (Aaron, 1971; Lamprecht, 1928).

The "blank slate" was a kind of theoretical explanation and not a physical description of the mind, since little or nothing was known then about the workings of the human brain or its structures. Since no real, innate capacities of the brain could be proved, Locke assumed that the blank tablet brain must be the natural condition of humans at birth. Locke therefore believed that most, if not all, human mental activity resulted from receiving, storing, and processing impressions after birth. Locke believed that childhood represents a time when the brain is most impressionable and least cluttered with earlier impressions. In other respects, Locke believed that a child's learning process is identical with an adult's. In keeping with the ideas of his time, he tended to view children as impressionable small adults. Children were worthy of special attention, as discussed in his classic "Thoughts Concerning Education," mainly because they were such clear models of what the human being could or should be.

Locke's philosophy was further developed about a half-century later by the Scottish philosopher, David Hume (1711–1776) (Aiken, 1948; Cavendish, 1969; Hume, 1758). Hume was skeptical about the reliability of human observations and believed that people can, at best, form imperfect views of what might or might not actually be happening in the physical world. Hume tried to show that no kind of connection between any two observed events (such as similarity between two events or cause and effect sequences) can ever really be proved in the outer world itself. Hume believed that such connections occur only in the human mind, which has a natural and a habitual tendency to connect impressions and form associations in ways previously shown by Locke. Hume's view of the associating power of the mind was echoed by other philosophers and built into a philosophical system called *Associationism,* which had important influences on later British and American psychological theories about behavior (Selby-Bigge, 1967) and especially influenced later theories of learning and memory.

The Naturalist Tradition: Rousseau and the Life Scientists.   While the Empiricists, such as Locke and Hume, were stressing what the mind could do with impressions received from the outer world, other thinkers focused on the inner working of the mind and were influenced by new ideas in biology and medicine. These thinkers were interested in qualities that living beings show in any environment during growth—qualities that living things are born with and which seem to unfold from within in a natural development process. This interest was strongly expressed in the social and philosophical writings of the Swiss-French moral philosopher, Jean-Jacques Rousseau (1712–1778), whose name is associated with the beginnings of the Naturalistic view of human nature. Rousseau is known for some of the earliest writing on childhood as an especially sensitive and significant formative period in human development. Rousseau's work on human development (notably in his book *Émile,* 1762), followed by that of Heinrich Pestalozzi (1746–1827) and Friedrich Froebel (1782–1852), founder of the kindergarten movement, formed an influential body of writing that emphasized the importance of childhood (Heafford, 1967; Lawrence, 1969). Rousseau held a view that contrasted sharply with the views of Locke and Hume. First, he thought that the human child is born "naturally good," and that this goodness will appear during development provided that the child is given emotional security and is not hindered by the corrupting forces of society. From the idea that "civilization is corrupting," Rousseau built a theory of the need for political liberty, which probably influenced the architects of the French Revolution.

Some other influential concepts were added to the naturalist tradition by Immanuel Kant (1724–1804), a German philosopher who was slightly younger than Rousseau. Kant's principal work, *Critique of Pure Reason* (reprinted 1963), was aimed somewhere between the empirical and naturalistic positions (Greene, 1957; Friedrich, 1949; Smith, 1968; Blakney, 1960). Kant believed that all ideas and behaviors are built up empirically from sensations of the outer world. On the other hand, he also believed that the mind has apparently inborn patterns of perceiving and thinking that filter, direct, and organize incoming sensory impressions. This higher level of the mind discovers *schemas,* or patterns or categories, in sense perceptions and forms a succession of impressions according to rules built into the mind. It should be noted that Kant's work strongly influenced modern developmental theorists such as Piaget, whose work we shall examine later.

Meanwhile, a quite different aspect of naturalistic thinking developed through scientific work in biology and reached a climax in Charles Darwin's (1809–1882) explanation of evolution. This theory demonstrated that living creatures became what they are through a long biological selection process in which each species came to have certain qualities, or features, that helped it to survive (Thompson, 1968). These selected qualities were more often passed down to later generations. Characteristics that were better suited to survival allowed more individuals to stay alive long enough to reproduce, while characteristics that hindered survival tended to be reproduced by only a few individuals and so were "selected out" of the species. In evolutionary theory individual behavior or learning was relatively unimportant, except as it expressed a best-adapted use for those innate, genetically inherited features that helped the species survive over many generations. Evolutionary theory inspired biologically-oriented thinkers to search for behaviors that were dependent upon inborn survival instincts. The concept of instinctual, innate

Box 1-1
Two Voices on Childraising: John Locke and Jean-Jacques Rousseau

John Locke, 1632–1704.
(Photo by Bettmann Archive)

Jean Jacques Rousseau, 1712–1704.
(Photo by the Bettmann Archive)

On the Value of Training Children

The great mistake I have observed in people's breeding their children has been, that this has not been taken care enough of in due season: that the mind has not been made obedient to discipline, and pliant to reason, when at first it was most tender, most easy to be bowed. (p. 20, No. 34)

Everything is good as it comes from the hands of the Maker of the world but degenerates once it gets into the hands of man. Man makes one land yield the products of another, disregards differences of climates, elements and seasons, mutilates his dogs and horses, perverts and disfigures everything. Not content to leave anything as nature has made it, he must needs shape man himself to his notions, as he does the trees in his garden. (p. 11)

On the Naturalness of Feelings

Crying is a fault that should not be tolerated in children; not only for the unpleasant and unbecoming noise it fills the house with, but for more considerable reasons, in reference to the children themselves; which is our aim in education. (p. 40, No. 111)

Love childhood. Look with friendly eyes on its games, its pleasures, its amiable dispositions. Which of you does not sometimes look back regretfully on the age when laughter was ever on the lips and heart free of care? Why steal from the little innocents the enjoyment of a time that passes all too quickly? (p. 33)

On Rewards and Punishments

Rewards, I grant, and punishments must be proposed to children, if we intend to work upon them. The mistake, I imagine, is that those that are generally made use of, are ill chosen. The pains and pleasures of the body are, I think, of ill consequence, when made the rewards and punishments. . . . (p. 32, No. 54)

On fact there is never any need to inflict punishment as such on children. It should always come to them as the natural consequence of their bad conduct. In the case of lying, for example, you need not punish them because they have lied, but so arrange that if they lie they will not be believed even when they speak the truth, and will be accused of bad things they have not done. (p. 45)

Sources: Locke quotes from Greven, P. J., Jr. *Child-Rearing Concepts, 1628–1861: Historical Sources.* Itasca, Ill.: Peacock Publishers, 1973. Chapter 3: John Locke's, *Some Thoughts Concerning Education* (1690). Rousseau quotes from Rousseau, J. J. *The Émile of Jean-Jacques Rousseau.* Trans. ed., William Boyd. New York: Teacher's College Press, 1956. Reprinted with permission of the publishers. Photos by Bettman Archive.

behavior was adapted to the study of human behavior by a number of pioneering psychologists such as William James (1890) and William McDougall (1908; 1914).

Charles Darwin was also one of the first biologists to pursue the idea that we can learn more about the human species through increased knowledge of the developmental years. Darwin believed that the stages of child development reflected the earlier phases of human evolution. Furthermore, Darwin published careful observations of his own child's development in a biographical sketch (1877) and thus provided a model for the biographical method which was influential with a number of later researchers.

The Late Nineteenth Century.   The end of the nineteenth century saw the first real beginnings of a science of psychology, as researchers discovered more reliable, objective methods of observing and describing human behavior. In America, developmental psychology grew partly because the concern with childhood that emerged during the nineteenth century finally reached the level of official political concern, expressed in child labor and welfare laws. Developmental psychology also grew because, in the era of rapid social change at the turn of the century, there was an interest in the best role for the family in rearing children.

In this atmosphere, a number of pioneering developmental psychologists received considerable public support and professional recognition. At Johns Hopkins University, G. Stanley Hall established the first psychological laboratory in America, and his efforts toward objectivity proved influential. To record behavior, Hall used a kind of questionnaire that was an improvement over the early subjective observations from biographical, autobiographical, or simple descriptive techniques. Later, as President of Clark University, Hall invited Sigmund Freud, Carl Jung, and other famous psychoanalysts to give a series of lectures in 1905 and, thus, introduced psychoanalysis to American psychology.

Figure 1-3. G. Stanley Hall, 1846–1924. (Photo by the Bettmann Archive)

Human Development in the Twentieth Century

Developmental Psychology in the Early 1900s. At the turn of the twentieth century, many forces were working to create the need for a new scientific understanding of human development. By 1900 the United States, Canada, and most of Europe were already engaged in an age of industrial development that included mass production, mechanization, and new patterns of ownership and labor. As industry grew, several social changes occurred that had a direct bearing on human development research.

Children were used as cheap sources of labor, often working from dawn to dusk in mines and factories. To justify the need for child labor laws, reformers often relied upon research that indicated that such harsh working conditions were damaging to the physical and mental health of children (Sears, 1975; Senn, 1975).

New work patterns forced many people to leave farms and rural villages for larger towns and industrial cities. With large population shifts into the cities, there were increases in juvenile delinquency. In response, many researchers searched for the roots of delinquency in childrearing practices. By 1920 many psychologists, psychiatrists, and social workers were being trained to guide and redirect wayward children and adolescents (Sears, 1975).

As industrial technology increased, agricultrual technology also flourished. Farmers were learning about selective breeding of plants and animals and were trying new methods of growing healthy crops and animals. People began to wonder if similar scientific principles could be applied to the growth and development of children. Not surprisingly, some of the first large-scale child development laboratories were developed at colleges and universities that also had agricultural pro-

Figure 1-4. In recent years, childhood has been viewed as a developmental stage. One hundred years ago, however, children often were considered to be miniature adults and employed in factories, mines, and shops. (Photo by Diana Blanchard)

grams. Among these were the State University of Iowa, which opened its first laboratory in 1917 (Sears, 1975).

As society became more complex, the need for highly educated people became more pressing. People began to see in education an important route toward economic advancement and self-improvement. At the turn of the century, most Western countries started to pass laws requiring compulsory mass education for at least young children. In the United States, for example, in the 1870s only about 57% of children between the ages of five and seventeen were enrolled in elementary schools. By 1910, however, this figure had risen to about 74% (Sears, 1975).

The rapid increase in sheer numbers of children attending school made several problems apparent. One problem concerned the fact that not all children were equally educable. Consequently, methods had to be devised for detecting children who had potential learning difficulties. In France, for example, two young psychologists were asked in 1904 to develop intelligence tests that would detect children with special educational needs. Today, the original intelligence test developed by Alfred Binet and Theophile Simon has gone through many revisions but is still one of the most widely used individual intelligence tests. One of Simon's protégées, the Swiss psychologist Jean Piaget, has revolutionized modern concepts of cognitive development—the study of how thought, memory, and perception develop in children.

Psychologists and educators also started to ask questions about the conditions under which learning could take place. Many psychologists were actively exploring problems of memory, learning, and conditioning. Among them were the Russian psychologist and physiologist Ivan Pavlov (1928), the American psychologist and educator Edward Thorndike (1913), and the German psychologist Hermann Ebbinghaus. Because the study of learning encompasses the formation of habits, attitudes, values, prejudices, and fears, as well as the acquisition of school subjects, many modern developmental psychologists have followed in the footsteps of these pioneering learning theorists to explore the roles that learning plays in human development.

The school of thought known as *behaviorism* has had a major influence on modern psychology. The founder of behaviorism was the American psychologist John B. Watson, who strongly believed that most complex human behaviors could be best examined from the standpoint of learning and conditioning. At the core of his approach was Watson's attempt to show how the findings of research on animal learning could be applied to human learning. In addition to books and articles intended for other psychologists, Watson wrote popular books and articles on childrearing in which he claimed that desirable behaviors in children could be created in much the same way that laboratory animals were trained (Watson, 1928a, 1928b). Although Watson's notions are now considered oversimplified and sometimes harsh, behaviorism has encouraged hundreds of experiments on learning and conditioning in children.

Today, we place great faith in the discoveries and techniques of modern medicine. A century ago, however, medicine was a very primitive field. By 1900 medicine was being established as a science, with new discoveries on the nature of infectious diseases, genetics, the techniques of X-rays, anesthetic and antiseptic surgery, and the role of nutrition on growth. For professionals concerned with human development, these medical discoveries provided promise for improving and understanding human growth and development. Many studies were conducted, for example, on the physical growth of children. Some of the earliest textbooks and handbooks of child development contained elaborate descriptions of physical factors in development but had fairly little to say about psychological factors (Sears, 1975). Parents were starting to turn (as they often do today) to pediatricians and other physicians for childrearing advice. Many popular books, some highly useful and some quite bizarre, were rapidly published to give parents the latest scientific advice on the best methods of raising children.

Although he had earned a Ph.D. in psychology under G. Stanley Hall, Arnold Gesell went on to study medicine at Yale University. While still a medical student, Gesell organized the Yale Clinic for Child Development in 1911. A firm believer that many children's behaviors were programmed by evolution, Gesell felt that by carefully observing children he could discover when certain biologically determined behaviors would unfold. Over the next thirty years, Gesell and his colleagues made thousands of observations of children and published many books giving detailed descriptions of the average ages at which many behaviors appeared. Although modern developmental psychologists would disagree with Gesell's theory, many of the methods that he developed for observing children and infants are widely used

Figure 1-5. As a result of psychoanalytic explorations, we are now more aware of the forces that produce friendship, aggression, and other important interpersonal behaviors. According to psychoanalytic theory, the friendship between these youngsters may have consequences for their later personality development.

today. His books are still popular among both laymen and professionals, and his tables of expected ages for children's behaviors have formed the basis of many pediatric examinations (Senn, 1975).

Medicine left another important legacy—the field of psychoanalysis. Psychoanalysis, as developed by Sigmund Freud (1905, 1923), emphasized some notions that have guided modern research projects. One important idea was that adult personality patterns have their roots in childhood experiences. Another concern was the importance of understanding the effects of early patterns of attachment between infants and parents on later psychological and social development. With its strong emphasis on motivation, especially sexual and aggressive, psychoanalytic theory paved the way for research on sex-role and gender development, achievement motivation, and aggression. Because psychoanalysis was originally, and still continues to be, a method of psychotherapy, it paved the way for further understanding of the causes and treatment of children's emotional disorders.

While psychoanalytic theories and techniques met many strong challenges, the influence of psychoanalysis on child development theories, research projects, and childrearing practices can be easily seen. The writings of psychoanalysts such as Sigmund Freud, Anna Freud, Erik Erikson, John Bowlby, Melanie Klein, Susan

Isaacs, and David Levy have formed a large amount of the literature in clinical child psychology.

The 1930s.   The 1930s presented child development researchers with a number of problems. When the Great Depression increased poverty, researchers became more interested in the effects of poverty, cultural differences, and social class on the development of personality traits and intellectual abilities in children. Government agencies and private foundations such as the Rockefeller Foundation, sponsored the establishment of many special child research centers in or near universities and medical centers. Many of these centers are still operating today. In addition, the social welfare concerns of the 1930s were revived in such "Great Society" programs of the 1960s as Project Head Start and VISTA, which attempted to eliminate the conditions for poverty through compensatory education (Sears, 1975; Senn, 1975).

The 1940s.   During World War II several new concerns arose. Although many child psychologists and psychiatrists were drafted into military service, those researchers who remained behind attacked such problems as the effects of family separation on the development of infants and older children. As we shall see in Chapter 6, there are still many questions to be answered about the processes of attachment and separation and their roles in personal and social behaviors.

Post-World War II.   At the end of World War II, the return of veterans to the universities and the post-war "baby boom" made child development a thriving field. We will see how much of our knowledge about human development has undergone a tremendous change during the past forty years. In fact, it is nearly impossible to stand back and catalogue the recent discoveries in human development research.

An important trend in current developmental psychology is the amount of research being done in the area of infancy. Previously, infancy had been relatively ignored because of the technical problems that arise when researchers attempt to study subjects who cannot understand instructions, are not always alert, and cannot verbally tell researchers about their behaviors. New and creative advances in research methods, however, have turned infancy into a highly exciting field that produces hundreds of research reports each year.

There has been a large increase in research into children's cognitive development. Behaviorists such as Watson discouraged psychologists from studying thoughts and feelings because these behaviors were considered too unreliable for scientific researchers to study, but new research methods and new theories of cognition have encouraged researchers to examine problem-solving, memory, perception, and creativity in children and infants. The pioneering work of such cognitive development researchers as Jean Piaget (1970), Heinz Werner (1948), Jerome Bruner (1964), Lawrence Kohlberg (1969), and Jerome Kagan (1971) have inspired many new discoveries that allow us to get a closer look at the child's mind. Many of these findings can be applied to educational and child-raising practices.

Finally, we should mention another modern trend: ethology. Although there is no single definition, ethology is generally the study of animal behaviors in their natural habitats. Ethologists are especially interested in behaviors that are species-specific. Species-specific behaviors are relatively inborn behaviors that have evolved in order to aid in the species' survival (Hess, 1970; Lorenz, 1957 a, b; Tinbergen, 1951).

Charles Darwin had suggested that many human behaviors had developed through an evolutionary process, but it was not until about thirty years ago that researchers had started to actively examine the role of inborn biologically-based behaviors. It now appears that many infant behaviors are so well-developed at birth or shortly afterwards that it would be difficult to explain their origins with learning theories. Instead, it would appear that these behaviors are at least partly inborn.

In the later parts of this book, we will see how many of these historical traditions and modern trends have appeared and reappeared, as we discuss the development of language, thought, perception, and social behaviors. In the next sections of this chapter, we will look briefly at research methods that have been used to gather the kinds of information needed for a modern science of human development.

SCIENTIFIC RESEARCH AND HUMAN DEVELOPMENT

The Nature of the Scientific Method

When we conduct psychological research, we essentially examine relationships among variables. By a *variable* we mean anything that can be measured and that has more than one value. For example, *body weight* is a variable because we can measure it and because there is a range of values for body weight. Similarly, *room lighting* can be a variable as we can measure room illumination and can also assess varying degrees of brightness. The psychologist picks some characteristic of behavior as a variable and then examines how other variables influence this behavioral variable. Usually, the influencing variables consist of environmental characteristics and individual differences among people. For example, if we wished to study the things that would influence the tendency of students to speak out in a classroom, we could examine how such *environmental* variables as seating arrangements, room temperature, and acoustics would tend to make students speak more or less. We also know, however, that, in the same situation, some people will be very talkative while others will be silent. Therefore, we might also look at such *individual difference* variables as introversion or extraversion, physical health, age, social class, past education, and sex to help us account for differences in talkativeness.

In psychology, behavior is considered to be the result of other forces and is therefore labelled a *dependent variable*, because human behavior will *depend* on other variables. Variables that influence behavior, such as environmental and individual difference variables, are called *independent variables*. When psychologists attempt to investigate the influences on a given behavior, they first make a *hypoth-*

esis, or statement of the possible relationship between an independent variable and a dependent variable (behavior). For example, a plausible hypothesis might be, "People are more likely to speak when they are seated at seminar tables than when they are seated in auditorium seats."

Let us examine our hypothesis about seating arrangements and the likelihood of speaking. As you can probably guess, there are several serious problems with our hypothesis. Suppose that people actually *do* tend to speak more at seminar tables than in auditorium seats. How do we know that this effect wasn't due to the fact that fewer people can fit around seminar tables than can fit into an auditorium? Perhaps what we are really observing is a tendency for people to speak more in small groups than in large groups. Have we looked into the composition of the groups? Are there equal numbers of men and women, older and younger people, in each group?

Would you feel confident about the statement: "People seated at seminar tables in Cleveland talk more than people in auditoriums in Bolivia."? Here, we might be looking at cultural differences as well. In planning our research we have to be able to eliminate, or at least substantially reduce, the effects of unwanted variables and examine the effect of one independent variable on one dependent variable at a time. That is, we have to *control* for the possibility that other variables could have produced the same behavior. While it is fairly easy to invent hypotheses, it is very difficult to devise practical research methods and procedures that can control for the effects of all variables other than the one independent variable that concerns us.

Once researchers have established a reasonable experimental procedure and have carefully controlled the situation, they may find results that support their original hypothesis. Should they jump up and down and shout, "Eureka! Behold! Wowee!"? While it would be fun to do this, some serious questions still have to be asked.

One important question concerns the *reliability* of results. For example, can the procedure be repeated? Another question concerns the *validity* of the results. Does the procedure actually produce the results? Was the result greater than could be expected by chance alone? Still another question concerns the *generalizability* of results. Since experiments are often highly controlled, the results may become limited to very specific and somewhat artificial conditions. An experimental effect would be useless if it could only be obtained in one laboratory and not in others. More importantly, the experiment would be limited if it did not hold up in real-life situations. Researchers also ask whether their research findings are generalizable to different groups of people. For example, will the same results be found with people from other cultures?

As you can see, no single research study will ever conclusively establish a relationship among variables. Life is more complex than that. Scientists must constantly refine and retest their procedures and must vary conditions and subjects slightly to try to confirm the reliability, validity, and generalizability of their findings. Because of these problems, the task of firmly establishing findings in science is a constant, ongoing process.

Figure 1-6.   Child development researchers are often faced with the challenging problem of explaining the behavior of children in naturalistic settings far removed from the precision of the laboratory. (Hays/Monkmeyer Press Photo Service)

In this book we will mention many research examples that we feel have come from well-planned studies. As a student, however, you will find it useful to actively question whether the results obtained in any study will hold up under all circumstances, whether there are some uncontrolled variables, and whether there are possible sources of unreliability in the procedures used to obtain the results. Remember that research is designed by fallible human beings and that science progresses by carefully checking its own assumptions.

Research Strategies and Methodologies

The Experimental Method.   The experimental method is a very useful and highly precise method of scientific research. However, we shall see that experiments are not the only means for gathering scientific information. In the experimental method, the experimenter builds in controls by carefully selecting and arranging independent variables in a laboratory situation. For example, the effects of various environmental influences may be investigated by building apparatus that present stimuli to subjects in very precise ways. Instructions to subjects may be very carefully worded. Laboratories may be controlled for sound, lighting, and climate conditions. To investigate the effects of individual differences among people, subjects may be carefully selected and, in some cases, individual differences can be created by exposing subjects to such difference-producing processes as surgical procedures, drugs, learning experiences, and special motivating instructions. Laboratory experiments generally allow the greatest amount of procedural control because all subjects are exposed to the same procedures.

In order to investigate the effects of the independent variable on a dependent variable, the experimenter will randomly assign subjects to one or more treatment or control groups. For example, suppose that we wished to investigate whether children's vocabularies will increase as the result of nursery school attendance. We could obtain two comparison groups of children and, through one of a variety of sampling procedures, match the groups as closely as possible for such variables as age, sex, socioeconomic status, physical health, parental education, and any variables *other than* exposure to nursery school that might be related to vocabulary. By carefully matching our groups on all independent variables *except* the one that we were going to investigate, we could control for the effects of these variables.

We would give vocabulary tests to both groups of children and, if our sampling of the groups has been effective, we would probably not find any greater-than-chance differences between the two groups. Next we would assign one group to nursery school and call this group the *treatment group,* because it is being exposed to the independent variable. For comparison, the other group of children would stay at home and not attend nursery school; we would call this group the *control group.* Six months later we would give the children another vocabulary test. It is very likely that both groups of children would have increased vocabularies at the end of six months. If our hypothesis has been correct, however, the children in the nursery school group (our treatment group) will, on the average, show a larger increase in vocabulary than the control group children.

But then we may ask, "How much of an average difference would we consider to be a real and important difference?" To answer the question of whether the difference between the groups is a real difference and not just chance, researchers use one or more statistical tests to see if the average differences between the groups could possibly be attributed to chance effects. In general, we could start to rule out chance differences if:

1. the average score differences between the groups were large;
2. the sample sizes were large; and
3. the range of scores within each of the groups was small.

The results of statistical tests are always expressed in probabilistic terms. One such term is the *significance level,* which tells the probability that a result of a given size could have been obtained by chance alone. In research reports and journal articles a common way of reporting the significance level might be $p < .05$ or $p < .01$ or $p < .001$. A significance level of $p < .05$ means: *The probability that this result could be due to chance alone is less than 5 in 100.* For $p < .001$, the expression can be translated to: *The probability that this result could be due to chance alone is less than 1 in 100.* Another way to express the probability of results is to use the *confidence level,* which is simply the number 1 minus the significance level. Thus, $p < .05$ will correspond to a confidence level of .95, which translates to the statement: *We can be 95% confident that results of this size were not obtained by chance alone.* As the confidence level increases and the significance level decreases, we can be more assured that our results are not some random effect.

As with any method used in psychology, the laboratory experiment has some limitations. First, there are difficulties in obtaining representative samples of people. Second, there are difficulties in making the laboratory situation lifelike while, at the same time, controlling for unwanted variables. Finally, because human behavior is so complex, it is difficult to devise measurements and techniques that will meaningfully capture the rich variety of ongoing human experiences.

Correlational Methods.   While the experimental method permits careful and precise control of independent variables, there are many situations in which it may be inconvenient, unethical, or even impossible to conduct experiments. For example, suppose that we wanted to find out whether certain child-rearing practices could be associated with adult forms of schizophrenia. It would be unethical and inhuman to gather a treatment group of children and systematically drive them insane, then compare them to a control group of children reared under fairly wholesome conditions. We could, however, find adults who already are schizophrenic and attempt to see if there were any child-rearing practices that these patients encountered that were not experienced by non-schizophrenics. In this way we would be conducting a *correlational* study because we would be examining how one variable (the presence or absence of schizophrenia) "co-relates" to another variable (child-rearing practices).

Similarly, if we were studying the relationships among various abilities and skills, we would also be employing a correlational strategy. For example, let us imagine that we gave a vocabulary test and a space visualization test to five children, and their scores were as follows:

Child	Vocabulary Test Score	Space Visualization Score
Tommy	10	9
Jo Anne	7	8
Betsy	5	5
Peter	4	3
Jeffrey	2	1

In practice, we would use many more children than this. What, however, can we say about the relationship between vocabulary test scores and space visualization scores? It looks like there is a relationship between them because those who score high on one test also tend to obtain high scores on the other test. Conversely, low scorers on one test are also low scorers on the other test. We have just described a *correlation* (co-relation) between two tests and have noted that as scores on one test vary, so do scores on the other test.

Correlational strategies often provide convenient ways of gathering information. They can be non-interfering; that is, data can be gathered in such a way so as not to deliberately expose subjects to any harmful procedures or manipulations. By using sophisticated *multivariate statistical techniques,* researchers can examine how *many* intercorrelated variables will interact and they can statistically remove the effects of unwanted and interfering variables from each other. With modern multivariate computer programs it is now possible to examine the interrelationships among several hundred variables, while most experimental studies usually tend to examine the effects of no more than 5 independent variables on a single dependent variable.

With all of their advantages, correlational strategies have a serious drawback that can cause problems for us when we interpret correlational results. This problem concerns the fact that many people will tend to interpret a correlation between two variables as evidence that one variable *caused* the other variable. In reality, correlation does not necessarily imply causation. For example, we may find that there is a moderate positive correlation between scores on a reading test and scores on a space visualization test. It would be unwarranted to conclude that spatial abilities caused reading abilities or that reading abilities caused spatial abilities. It may be that both abilities are caused by a third, underlying ability. Perhaps the correlation between the two tests could be explained by the fact that both tests had rather elaborate printed instructions. Thus, a child with strong reading skills might do well on both tests. About the only finding we can be sure of is that we can predict that children who obtain high scores on one test will also obtain high scores on the other test and vice versa.

Cross-Sectional and Longitudinal Research Methods.
Since developmental psychologists are interested in differences in behavior at different ages and changes in behavior from one age to another, special techniques have been developed for observing age differences and behavior change over time. These techniques are called the *cross-sectional* and *longitudinal* methods.

In the *cross-sectional* method, several matched samples of subjects are chosen at each of several ages and each group is compared to the other groups on some variable. For example, if we were interested in vocabulary size at different ages, we could carefully pick five groups of children at ages 6 months, 12 months, 18 months, 24 months, and 30 months. To make sure that we were looking at the effects of age on vocabulary size, and not something else, we would make sure that all the children come from the same social class, are in good physical health, and had been raised in similar home environments. We would then use a technique to gather information on the children's vocabularies and would count the number of different words produced by each child. Finally, in analyzing our data, we would see an age trend appear in which the older children would use more words than the younger children.

The cross-sectional technique has many advantages. Researchers can save a great deal of time by comparing differing age groups and may be able to detect some important growth trends. There are some definite disadvantages and logical problems with the cross-sectional method, however. When researchers study differences in behavior from one age level to another, they are not really studying changes in the *same* children. Therefore, *individual patterns* of change cannot be followed. The researcher may also confuse *generational effects* with age effects (Buss, 1973, 1974; Riegel, 1972). For example, suppose we gave a questionnaire concerning sexual attitudes to a group of 15-year-olds, a group of 30-year-olds, a group of 45-year-olds, and a group of 60-year-olds. Suppose that we found that the younger groups had relatively liberal sexual attitudes and that the older groups displayed somewhat more conservative viewpoints. Could we legitimately say that as people grow older, their sexual attitudes become more conservative? Probably not. The 15-year-olds are not only 45 years younger than the 60-year-olds, but the society in which they were born and grew up may be very different from the way it was when the 60-year-olds were born. Societies and cultures change in many aspects over the years, and these changes may affect people in ways that produce generational changes. For example, adults who are now over 40 were born before the time when television became common in homes and before jet flights were known. Their children, however, have probably never known a time when these things did not exist.

Another research method which aims to detect growth trends is the *longitudinal method*. In this method, the *same* people are followed over a period of time and are re-observed at a number of age periods.

Longitudinal methods can provide a rich supply of data from real people as they go through their lives. Some serious problems are also found in the longitudinal approach, though. First, researchers must decide about what kinds of information they are going to gather at the very beginning of the study. These decisions will determine the character of the study for years to come, even though the researcher may later wish to change the study. New discoveries may cause an investigator to change techniques, but these changes would alter the possibility of comparisons with later findings. Second, the investigator may become dissatisfied with the research project and may wish to turn to other, more interesting projects if new research makes the study less relevant. Third, keeping track of the subjects and enlisting their continued cooperation over long time periods poses many problems. People move, marry, change names, and sometimes die in the course of a study. Often, the size of the original subject group will shrink to a small fraction of its original size. Finally, as in the cross-sectional method, changes due to historical and cultural changes may be confused with age-related growth changes. That is, as a person grows and changes, so does society, and the person may be strongly affected by societal changes.

Some methodologists have suggested combinations of cross-sectional and longitudinal designs that reduce some of the problems of each design alone (Buss,

1973; Glenn, 1977, Riegel, 1972). However, such combined designs still require huge amounts of time, effort, money, and subject cooperation to be carried out effectively.

Other Research Methods. While many obvious advantages result from cross-sectional and longitudinal experimental and correlational research, other useful methods are available. Among these techniques are:

1. *The clinical method.* The subjects may be clients in clinics or hospital patients. Diagnostic and treatment information may uncover abundant findings for further research. Most of Freud's original material for his theory of psychoanalysis came from clinical sources.

2. *Survey and interview methods.* If researchers want to know something about people, they sometimes ask them. People may distort their answers, however, to fit their own interpretations of how the survey or interview information will be used. To the extent that they may be unaware of some of their own behaviors or may not understand completely the meanings of questions asked of them, people cannot always give useful information. Finally, the samples of people chosen must be truly representative of the groups that the researcher wishes to describe. When properly designed and used, survey and interview techniques can provide a wide array of useful and relevant information from many people.

3. *Field observation and naturalistic information.* Experiments and surveys often create artificial constraints by placing people in situations in which they are forced to do or say things they would not ordinarily do or say. Psychologists have borrowed techniques from anthropologists and biologists which may provide somewhat more realistic views of actual behavior. If we wanted to know how families interact in public places like museums, parks, shopping centers, and city streets, it would be silly to place them in laboratory facsimiles of these situations. By questioning families, we might force them into giving us highly ideal, but not necessarily real, answers. It might be better to have observers watch families in public places in careful and non-interfering ways and then describe the kinds of behaviors that are observed. Such field observations may give us a record of real behavior in natural settings. We must be sure, however, that our observations are reliable and our descriptions are unbiased.

SUMMARY

In this chapter we have examined how notions of human development have evolved from ancient times until the present day. We have seen how theories and beliefs about human nature and child-rearing practices have been influenced by developments in philosophy, science and medicine, and by social, historical, and economic forces and ethical responsibilities.

We took a brief look at the underlying strategies of scientific methods in human development research. We noted how psychologists use each method and examined the strengths and weaknesses of each tactic. In the next chapter we will look at some major theories that have attempted to describe, explain, and predict the complex events and features of human development.

RECOMMENDED READINGS

Achenbach, T. M. *Research in Developmental Psychology: Concepts, Strategies, Methods.* New York: Free Press, 1978.

> This book discusses problems that developmental psychologists face as they attempt to investigate the complex issues of human development throughout the life span. The book shows how a large number of research techniques may be used to explore some current research problems.

Beekman, D. *The Mechanical Baby: A Popular History of the Theory and Practice of Childrearing.* New York: Meridian Books, 1977.

> A fascinating overview of beliefs about children from ancient times until the present day as reflected in the popular child-rearing books of each century.

White, R. R. *Lives in Progress* (3rd ed.). New York: Holt, Rinehart & Winston, 1974.

> An excellent example of a longitudinal research study. By following the lives of three people as they developed from their college years until they were older adults, this book explores the forces that change and maintain personality characteristics throughout the life span.

Four Pathways in the Search for Human Development Principles

THE ENTERPRISE OF THEORY CONSTRUCTION

How can we start our study of the rich and complex world of human behavior as it develops through a person's lifespan? Suppose that your professor asked you to write the following assignment as a term paper:

State, in as few statements as possible, general principles of human behavior that explain as much as possible about how people differ, why they do what they do, how they change and grow, and how they become both similar to other people and yet highly individual. Make sure that your statements are logically consistent and do not contradict one another. Show how your statements can describe not only how a person is acting right now but also how the person will act in the future. Make sure you can prove that your statements are accurate and correct under the widest range of circumstances with the widest range of people.

If you were to take on this assignment, you would be working on the intriguing process of theory construction. While the word "theory" often has an intimidating sound and may be dismissed by some people as too abstract to have relevance to real life, we will find that theories are neither sacred nor impractical. Let's see what a theory is.

Faced with a wide possibility of things and events to talk about, the theorists deliberately narrow their focus to a few variables they consider to be important. Of course, in doing this, they may draw heavily from their own experiences and knowledge and may not always be aware of other possibilities. They then try to make a few statements to cover as many facts as possible. We call this limiting of the number of statements *parsimony*. It is useful to be fairly parsimonious because, otherwise, we would be burdened by having to make a separate statement for each and every thing that we wished to describe or predict. Theorists try to arrange their statements logically in some systematic and consistent way. They may start with a few basic statements and then branch out into finer and more precise statements, in the same way that principles of geometry are organized by axioms, postulates, theorems, and corollaries. By systematically arranging their statements in a logical way, theorists will get a good outline of the area of knowledge they wish to cover.

Once arranged, the theoretical statements are ready to be tested. Hypotheses related to theoretical statements are challenged by experimental studies, surveys, and other research techniques discussed in Chapter 1. As evidence accumulates, the validity, or truth, of the theoretical statements is examined. Some of the statements may be confirmed, while other statements will have to be rejected. The theorist will then use the evidence to revise the theory. He might ask whether his statements are both necessary and sufficient to explain things. A series of other questions will be asked. "Can new statements be added?" "Must some statements be dropped?" "Is the whole approach sensible?" "Are there methods adequate enough to test the theory?" As theory construction progresses, theorists constantly rebuild the theory and refine their statements.

Suppose that, after a while, the theorist and others who have examined and tested the propositions generated by the theory come to realize that the theory is no longer useful. Has all been lost? Has time been wasted? Probably not. Theories are meant to be temporary devices, and they are *constructed,* or imagined, to make sense of a potentially confusing world of facts. One of the main purposes of theories can be called *heuristic.* By heuristic we mean *idea-generating,* because as we go through one theory, new ideas and new contradictions evolve which lead us closer to knowledge. These ideas may form the foundations of a new and better theory.

In the remainder of this chapter, we will introduce four theoretical approaches that have influenced our views of human development. We will focus on the main features of each theoretical approach in order to provide "maps" of the "territory" that we will explore in later chapters as we examine development at different ages and life stages.

BEHAVIORISM

Behaviorism has been one of the most influential forces in modern psychology. The term "behaviorism" and its underlying philosophy was first introduced by John B. Watson at Columbia University in 1912. Watson believed that psychology had placed too much emphasis on inner forces such as thoughts, feelings, and willpower as important determinants of behavior. While we can speak about the "mind," "consciousness," "images," "the will," "desire," and "purpose" in our everyday language, Watson believed that these terms were highly unscientific. For example, how could a person describe how his or her mind worked? Could the person answer such questions as: "How big is your mind?" "What color is it?" and "If I dropped your mind on the floor, at what point would it shatter?" Physical scientists, whom Watson deeply admired, do not have such conceptual problems. Chemists do not ask the compounds in their test tubes and laboratory flasks to reveal their feelings about being there or to talk about their plans for forming new compounds. Instead, chemists perform certain specific procedures on the chemicals and devise ways in which they can observe the behavior of the new compounds. Similarly, Watson believed that the only thing we can really observe is behavior, not the mind. In Watson's own words:

> The behaviorist asks: Why don't we make what we can *observe the real* field of psychology? Let us limit ourselves to things that can be observed and for- mulate laws concerning only those things. Now what can we observe? We can observe *behavior—what the organism does or says.* . . . The rule or measuring rod, which the behaviorist puts in front of him always, is: Can I describe this bit of behavior I see in terms of "stimulus and response?" By stimulus, we mean any object in the general environment or any change in the tissues them- selves. . . . By response we mean anything the animal does. . . .*

*J. B. Watson, *Behaviorism,* New York: W. W. Norton, 1930, p. 6. Reprinted with permission of the publisher.

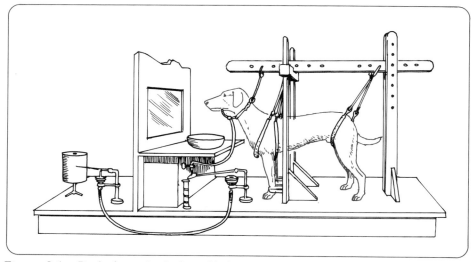

Figure 2-1.   Pavlov's method of establishing a conditioned reflex: In Pavlov's experiments, dogs were usually placed in an apparatus such as this. Food was presented to the dogs in a dish after they had heard a bell ring. To measure the strength of the conditioned salivary response, tubes were connected to the dogs' mouths to collect the saliva that flowed after each conditioning trial.

definition of behaviorism

To this day, Watson's statement has essentially defined the behaviorist's goal: To confine psychology to observable things and events such as environmental stimuli and behavioral responses; to reject internal explanations of behavior; and to favor explanations of behavior based on external forces.

How, then, could *stimulus-response* or S-R psychology proceed? Basically, S-R psychology proceeds by presenting stimuli (objects in the environment) to animals and humans and then seeing how these subjects behave. Watson, however, went beyond this simple level to investigate ways in which stimuli and responses could be re-associated in a variety of novel ways. Two major discoveries—Pavlov's discovery of classical conditioning (*Conditioned Reflexes,* Pavlov, 1927) and Edward Thorndike's studies of trial-and-error learning—provided important practical and theoretical tools for Watson's behavioristic approach. Both discoveries were concerned with the learning of fairly complex behavior and used objective and rather mechanical procedures. Also, although based on animal research, both discoveries could be easily extended to human behavior. The emphasis on learning and conditioning characteristic of behaviorism has provided important tools for studying human behavior.

Classical Conditioning

Ivan Petrovich Pavlov (1849–1936) was a Russian physiologist who won the Nobel Prize for medicine in 1904 for his studies of digestive processes. Pavlov's research subjects were dogs, whose digestive tracts were stimulated with meat for observation of their digestive responses. Among these responses were salivation in the mouth, increased stomach acidity, and peristalsis or muscle movements of the esophagus and stomach. Since all dogs naturally salivated when meat was placed in their mouths, Pavlov called these response processes *unconditioned reflexes,* consisting of an *unconditioned stimulus* or UCS (meat) and an *unconditioned response* or UCR (salivation). The term "unconditioned" means that the behavior was unlearned. Pavlov noticed, however, that an unexpected thing happened— the dogs produced salivary responses in which they drooled at the sight of food. In his Nobel Prize address in 1904, Pavlov reported his excitement: "At first sight, the psychical aspect of the salivary glands appears even more incontrovertible than the physiological. When any object that attracts the attention of the dog from a distance produces salivary secretion, one has all the grounds for assuming that this is a psychical and not a physical phenomenon" (1904; 1966, pp. 52–53).

Pavlov discussed how he studied this new phenomenon under laboratory conditions. He would first pair a neutral stimulus, such as a bell or light, with the meat; after a number of pairings, or *trials,* the bell or light alone would elicit salivation. Since the bell did not originally elicit salivation but came to do so after being paired with the meat, it was called a *conditioned stimulus* or CS. The animal had learned to respond to the CS. Figure 2-2 summarizes this process.

Pavlov soon found that once the dog responded to the conditioned stimulus, the dog would not salivate to the bell indefinitely. In fact, if the meat was not presented occasionally, the animal would eventually stop responding. This process is called *extinction.* Pavlov also observed that the more the meat UCS was presented, the stronger the tendency to salivate to the bell became.

Pavlov and his students performed hundreds of experiments in classical conditioning, and in 1926 he reported several important new findings. *Stimulus generalization* was the finding that animals learn to respond not only to the original CS but also to stimuli *similar* to the original CS. For example, an animal will salivate to a conditioned stimulus of 400 vibrations per second, but it will also respond to a tone of 410 vibrations, although to a lesser degree. Generalization is useful because it means we do not have to be retrained for every new task. In fact, if the old tasks are similar to the new ones, we are fairly well-prepared. Pavlov realized that although generalization naturally occurs in conditioning, he could limit generalization by selectively presenting the animal with the UCS only when the CS was present and not when any other stimuli were present. This process of selectively presenting the UCS and extinction is called *stimulus discrimination* and can be used to explain why we can learn to make specific responses to specific stimuli.

Pavlov conducted most of his studies with animal subjects. He was vitally concerned, however, with human behavior and encouraged others to work with human subjects. As early as 1907, two experiments on gastric and salivary conditioning had been reported on young children (Brackbill & Thompson, 1967). Over the past 15 years, Lewis Lipsitt and his associates at Brown University have done many conditioning studies with infants and young children. In one study Lipsitt and Kaye (1964) studied 20 three- to four-day-old infants (10 in an experimental group and 10 in a control group). The infants in the experimental group were given 20

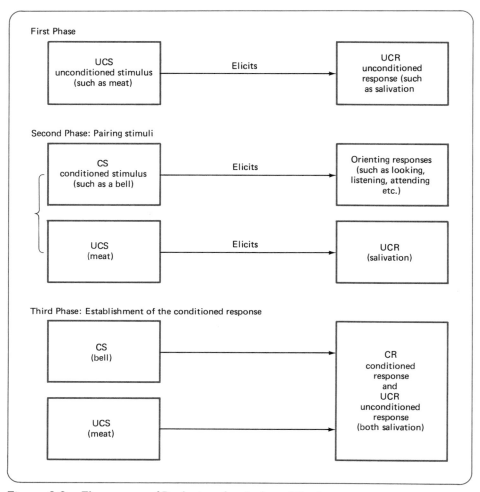

Figure 2-2.   The process of Pavlovian classical conditioning.

pairings of a tone conditioned stimulus (CS) and a pacifier nipple, which was the unconditioned stimulus (UCS). A nipple serves as an excellent unconditioned stimulus because newborn infants naturally start sucking at a nipple that is placed in their mouths within seconds after they are born. The infants in the control group received 25 unpaired presentations of the tone CS and nipple UCS. Although both groups displayed some increase in sucking to a tone, the experimental group produced considerably more sucking responses. When the sucking responses were extinguished by presenting the tone alone for up to 30 extinction trials, the experimental group again showed stronger evidence of being conditioned.

Findings of classical conditioning in newborn infants are important for several reasons. First, the findings suggest that some forms of learning can be achieved in the earliest days of life—long before infants' brains have matured. Second, conditioning techniques allow us to communicate with infants and investigate their ability to process sensory stimuli. That is, if we can condition an infant to a sound, a light, a touch, or a smell CS, then we can be certain that the baby can experience and process these stimuli.

Operant Conditioning

Burhus F. (Frederick) Skinner has conducted studies of operant conditioning over the past 40 years. In Skinner's studies, an animal, such as a rat, is placed in a special lever box (now called a "Skinner box"). Equipment is arranged in this box so that by pressing a lever the rat can release food into a feeding tray. The Skinner box is a kind of vending machine. A rat will at first wander around when hungry, but eventually it will press a lever and release some food. This response, in which the animal *operates* on some part of the environment, is called an *operant* response. Soon the rat will press the lever again and, consequently, will get food again. As the rat has more trials at this activity, it learns quickly to feed itself.

In this simple procedure, Skinner found that he had encountered another form of conditioning. This form of conditioning was quite unlike Pavlov's classical conditioning. Whereas Pavlov's conditioning generally worked on involuntary, elicited responses in restrained animals, Skinner's operant conditioning worked on voluntary responses made by freely moving subjects. The subject had made the response

Figure 2-3. B. F. Skinner, b. 1904. (Photo by the Bettmann Archive)

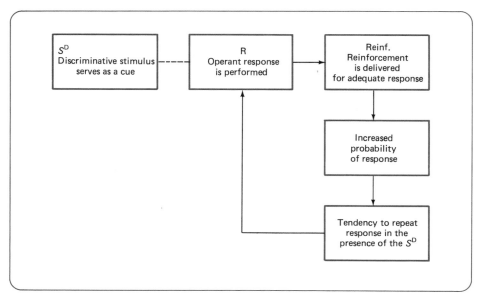

Figure 2-4.   The process of operant conditioning.

first, on its own and was *then* rewarded. In Pavlov's classical conditioning, reinforcement (*UCS*) is delivered *before* the response is made, while in operant conditioning reinforcement is delivered afterwards. Let us look at the operant conditioning procedure in a more formal way. Figure 2-4 presents a simple diagram of the operant conditioning process. A response, or operant, is first produced and then followed by reinforcement. As the response is reinforced more, it will be more likely to occur. As in classical conditioning, however, withdrawal of the reinforcement will produce extinction. Notice the symbol S^D in Figure 2-4. An S^D or *discriminative stimulus* serves as a cue for the animal that: "If a response is made at this time, you will be rewarded." If the S^D is absent, there will be no reinforcement. Many things can serve as discriminative stimuli, including lights, sounds, words, and many other stimuli.

In recent years, operant conditioning techniques have been used in a wide variety of ways. Some interesting studies of infants have attempted to determine ways in which infant behaviors can be specifically modified (Lipsitt, Kaye, & Bosack, 1966; Millar, 1972; Papousek, 1967; Siqueland, 1968; Siqueland & Lipsitt, 1966; Siqueland & DeLucia, 1969; Watson, 1969). In one study of three- six- and nine-month-old infants (Ramey & Ourth, 1971), researchers placed each infant in a crib and recorded the infant's vocalizations to establish a baseline of each child's normal amount of vocal activity. Following the establishment of a baseline, a six-minute conditioning period was undertaken. Each vocalization was reinforced by: (a) a light touch to the infant's abdomen, (b) a smile, and (c) repeating "That's a good baby."

The findings of the study indicate that if the reinforcement occurred with no delay, the infants' vocalizations increased significantly above the baseline. No significant increases were found in the amount of vocalization when there were delays in reinforcement of even a few seconds, which implies that immediate reinforcement may be necessary for learning in infants and that slight delays are to be avoided.

In another study, reinforcements of vocalizations were used in therapy for infants who had failed to thrive because of insufficient opportunities for social and emotional exchanges with parents. Through operant conditioning techniques, investigators attempted to increase vocalization and thus increase social responses. This therapy worked, because researchers found a significant increase in the infants' vocalization as a result of their interactions (Ramey, Heiger, & Klisz, 1972).

We have talked so far about simple operant conditioning in which simple responses such as lever pressing are followed with reinforcements such as food. But what about teaching children complex behaviors, such as swimming? We could possibly fling a child into the water and then reinforce any successful swimming movements with survival. Such a morbid maneuver would be inefficient, improbable, and highly unethical. A much nicer and more efficient technique is known as *shaping.*

In *shaping,* we would arrange a program of reinforcement for responses that come closer and closer to our final goal (in this case, swimming). At first we might reward a child with pleasant talk as we walk toward a beach or swimming pool. Then, while holding the child's hand, we would wade into the water and praise the child for walking into the shallow water. We would then shift our program slightly so that the child will be reinforced for walking into increasingly deeper water. Then supporting the child in the water, we would reinforce him or her whenever the child attempts to float. Later, we would reinforce arm movements, then leg movements, and then coordinated arm and leg movements, until we had reached our final goal of swimming. With this gradual method of reinforcing the child for successive approximations to a goal, we could efficiently condition the child to perform some rather complex behaviors.

Let's be realistic, however. It's nice to say that we can reinforce responses and increase the probability that these responses will be performed, but how can we explain how behavior continues without any obvious reinforcements? Two principles will help us out of this bind.

The first principle, that of *secondary reinforcement* (Skinner, 1969), states that stimuli which have been paired with basic (or primary) reinforcers can themselves become reinforcers through conditioning. For example, money can be a secondary reinforcer. An experimenter could pair money with a reward of candy. After a while, money would be associated with the candy and could serve as a reinforcer itself. The reward of money could then maintain behavior just as effectively as the direct reward of candy which was the original primary reinforcement.

A second principle which helps us to explain why behavior can be maintained for long periods without immediate reinforcement is the principle of *partial reinforcement* or *schedules of reinforcement.* We tend to think that reinforcement means providing a reward every time desired behavior occurs—for example, when a teacher says, "Good," for every correct answer. Reinforcement that is given each time is called *continuous* reinforcement. But in very few situations in a child's life is it possible to give continuous reinforcement. Therefore, a program of delayed or *partial reinforcement* is realistic. Theorists and researchers have investigated the effects of varying the timing and number of reinforcements. Thus, in experiments and in training programs, systems of reinforcement called *schedules of reinforcement* are employed.

These schedules may be classified as *interval schedules* in which a child might be rewarded for performing at least one response within a given time period, or *ratio schedules* in which a child might be reinforced for producing a given number of responses. These schedules may be further subdivided into *fixed schedules* in which a reinforcement is given for a constant number of responses or for performing within a constant time period. Alternately, the time intervals or number of responses may be varied around some average amount in order to produce *variable schedules*. We can then have schedules such as fixed interval, fixed ratio, variable interval, and variable ratio schedules of reinforcement.

In general, it is difficult to extinguish behavior that has been learned under scheduled reinforcement conditions because, unlike continuous reinforcement, the person does not expect to be reinforced immediately and, therefore, will continue to produce responses long after reinforcement has been withdrawn.

Latent Learning, Incidental Learning, and Observational Learning

Let us imagine three situations:

1. Suppose that Billy, a well-fed boy, watched his mother put some groceries away in the family freezer. The next day when he was hungry, Billy went to the freezer and, in no time at all, found ice cream that his mother had placed in an out-of-the -way place in the freezer.

2. Joey saw a western movie on television and at school recess the next day he and his classmates decided to play "sheriff and robbers." During this play he used some of the same words and gestures used by a character in the movie he saw the evening before. Learning had taken place at that time but neither Joey nor anyone else had deliberately planned it.

3. Four-year-old Betsy was playing in the sandbox at nursery school and was busy making sand castles, mud pies, and many other things that caught her fancy as she played contentedly. Her friend Karen was also absorbed in her own play and paid little attention to Betsy. At one point, however, Karen needed another shovel and quickly grabbed Betsy's. At that point, Betsy stood up to her full height of 40 inches and shouted, "Karen! You're annoying me! If you don't stop being obnoxious I'm going to belt you one!" Karen sulked, but in a few minutes came over to Betsy and said, "I'm sorry. Let's be friends. We'll cooperate." Betsy then gave Karen her shovel. It is very unlikely that anyone ever sat down with Betsy and directly reinforced or shaped her outburst. How did she learn to do what she did?

Each of these cases illustrates some learning processes that are quite different from classical and operant conditioning. First, there were no immediate reinforcements. Second, the actual learning took place in one context, basically by watching, but the final *performance* of the learned behavior took place in another context when rewards were present.

The three examples illustrate cognitive learning. The first example refers to *latent learning,* a situation in which learning is accomplished without direct reinforcement and is not performed immediately, but is performed later when needs arise. The second example illustrates *incidental learning* in which things not directly attended to are nevertheless absorbed in the learning process. The third type of learning has been called *observational learning, imitation, vicarious learning,* or *modelling.* In observational learning the child learns by observing the activities of peers or adults. The term refers to learning from other people who serve as models and therefore is a kind of symbolic imitation (Bandura & Walters, 1963; Bandura, 1969, 1971; Stevenson, 1970; Walters & Willows, 1968).

A well-known study by Bandura, Ross, and Ross (1963) illustrates the effect of models on learning. In this study, one-half of a group of nursery school children was allowed to observe aggressive behavior, and the other half observed nonaggressive behavior. Adult models in the study used a large inflated "Bobo" doll, a mallet, and a Tinker Toy set. A nonaggressive model spent time assembling the Tinker Toys and ignored the doll and mallet. Another model, however, turned from the Tinker Toys to the "Bobo" doll and began vigorously punching it. Using hostile language, the aggressive model kicked the big doll and pounded it with the mallet.

After observing the adult models, the children were taken to another room where they found toys that would not encourage aggressive play—crayons and cars. But they were also exposed to a "Bobo" doll and a mallet. As one might expect, the children who had observed the aggression now behaved similarly by attacking the doll. During this aggressive behavior the children, too, used hostile language as they pounded the doll. Bandura and his associates made the observation that learning by imitation is more efficient than learning by operant conditioning because operant conditioning requires the performance of an appropriate response before reinforcement. On the other hand, the use of models can bring about desired or undesired behavior immediately. They asserted that imitative learning is a short-cut to the development of desired behavior, without the necessity of providing successive reinforcements.

Many other studies on observational learning have been carried out since this investigation and various practical applications of the idea have been suggested. Several studies have indicated that children who make quick and impulsive responses after observing models and listening to their instructions do not score as highly or learn as well as more reflective children (Kagan, 1965). This finding suggests the possibility that if impulsive behavior can be altered, learning can be improved. To test this idea, a researcher undertook to alter the behavior of impulsive children by using sixth-grade children as behavior models for impulsive third-grade children. The older children provided examples of both impulsive and reflective behavior as they performed a visual discrimination task. The results indicated that boys and girls who observed a reflective model reduced their impulsive approaches to the tasks. It was also found that these children made fewer errors (Debus, 1970). Both theoretical and experimental information seems to support the importance of models for children. Using models to channel behavior is being developed with varied research and teaching strategies.

Latent, incidental, and observational learning challenge traditional behavioristic approaches. While the conditions that created the behaviors themselves and the final performances can be objectively observed, the actual learning can be best described as the formation of internal cognitive schemes, or plans, in which the person has an idea or image of the concept. Such learning occurs at a much more complex psychological level than the learning of specific responses to specific stimuli.

PSYCHOANALYSIS

The Freudian Approach

Basic Assumptions of Freudian Psychoanalysis.   To the average person, the words *psychology* and *psychologist* are often confused with *psychoanal-*

Figure 2-5. Sigmund Freud, 1856–1939. (Photo by the Bettmann Archive)

ysis and *psychoanalyst.* Most people are familiar with terms like *unconscious motives, defensiveness, blocking, repression,* and other terms which originated in psychoanalysis. Sigmund Freud (1856–1939), the founder of psychoanalysis, was a Viennese physician who was originally a neurologist. As his career developed, Freud treated many patients who were diagnosed as hysterics. Hysteria is a disorder in which patients often present symptoms that imitate physical disorders, and yet these patients have no actual physical damage. For example, a hysterical man may suddenly develop blindness, but a neurological or opthalmologic examination would reveal no physical damage to his visual system. In 1885, Freud went to Paris for a year to study with two physicians, Pierre Janet and Jean Charcot, who were treating hysterics with hypnotic suggestion. Upon his return to Vienna, he was joined by another physician, Joseph Breuer, in an active hypnosis practice.

Although Freud and Breuer at first employed hypnotic suggestion on their patients, they later departed from these techniques and started to ask people to recall memories while in hypnotic trances. While in the trance state, people often revealed sexual and aggressive fantasies that they would not talk about in their ordinary waking state. Many of these fantasies were clearly taboo topics by the social standard of the times.

As Freud became immersed in the thoughts and feelings expressed by his patients, he looked for the sources that seemed to underlie certain of their anxieties. He began to find evidence that there is more than one level of awareness or thought and that a patient's expressed ideas were often an indirect reflection of some deeper levels of thinking. In an effort to locate and analyze what might be occurring at this deeper level, Freud asked his patients to use *free-association,* or to talk randomly about whatever came to mind. This was an attempt to reach beyond a surface consciousness and explore what Freud immortalized as the world of the *unconscious* (Freud, 1914).

Once Freud gained access to this world of apparently unconscious preoccupations, he was able not only to help patients with specific underlying problems but was also able to construct a theory of the basic structures of human consciousness. The theory had some familiar elements and also some new ones. Like other biologically oriented theorists, Freud believed in the significance of instinctual drives (Bolles, 1967; Cofer & Appley, 1964). Instinctual drives arise at some place in the body, and human behavior results from an effort to reduce the stimulation aroused by the drive. Thus, gratification of drives becomes an important concept in psychoanalytic theory.

To help us understand Freud's theory and his explanation of how unconscious sexual and aggressive motives exert an influence on people's lives, we will introduce a few major assumptions of psychoanalysis:

1. *Psychic determinism.* Freud was a strong believer in the principle of *determinism,* the notion that there are no accidents in the universe and that for every effect there is at least one cause. For Freud, nothing in mental life was truly accidental—not dreams, not symptoms of disorders, and not even "accidents" of everyday life, such as slips of the tongue or forgetfulness.

2. *All behavior is motivated.* Freud felt that all behavior works to satisfy certain basic needs.

3. *All needs and motives are essentially instinctual.* Freud felt that all motives were derived essentially from two sets of instincts: *Eros,* or the life instincts associated with bodily pleasure and sexual activity, and *Thanatos,* a death principle in which the aim is to reduce objects to inert and non-living states. The instincts, which energize the person and direct behavior, were called *psychic energy* or libido.

4. *Instincts are asocial and thus society attempts to control them.* If human nature consists mainly of sexual and aggressive drives, why don't we see people constantly fighting, making love, or masturbating? Why are people as calm as they usually are? Like many other thinkers, Freud felt that the natural state of humanity was a lustful, energetic, animal existence. In order for society to survive, however, he felt that people must surrender some of their natural tendencies to live under social rules. In his book *Civilization and its Discontents,* Freud (1930; 1961) discussed how societies control the basic instincts of individuals through social institutions, rules, and repression. Many forbidden but basic urges were, then, repressed and hidden in the unconscious.

5. *The instinctual drives can be transformed.* "But," you may ask, "if drives are unconscious and repressed, why be concerned about them? Isn't out-of-sight, out-of-mind?" Freud believed that the instincts or psychic energy followed the laws of energy conservation; that is, instincts could be neither created nor completely destroyed. They could, however, be changed to other forms. Thus, a forbidden wish, a blocked drive, or a tabooed action could all reappear in other forms such as dreams, accidents, symptoms of disorders, lifelong personality patterns, or artworks. For the psychoanalyst, life is not always what it appears to be on the surface and many meanings may be hidden from conscious view.

Personality Structure.   Given these basic assumptions of Freud, how can we describe a person? Freud believed that humans exist on three levels: an animal level, a logical and rational level, and a moral level. Freud (1923) called the animal level the *id.* The id represents the mind of the child which is present at birth. The operation of the id is very simple as it knows only one rule—the *pleasure principle* which, simply stated, says "Seek pleasure and avoid pain." The id seeks pleasure without regard to time, place, or institution and thus, is a very basic and uncivilized structure.

A second structure in the personality is the *ego,* which grows out of the id and comes to constrain and limit the basic drives in accordance with environmental reality. The ego thus deals largely with the *reality principle* and helps the individual reach goals and desires without bringing on trouble from the external world. Freud saw reality adjustments as essentially the ability to delay gratification, to plan ahead, and to substitute desired objects. The ego also controls the ideas from within the id that may be allowed to enter into consciousness.

The third structure of the personality is the *superego,* which develops from the ego and helps the individual deal with moral issues. The superego can be called a

Figure 2-6. As the child's superego develops, the child becomes increasingly aware of behaviors and roles that will be rewarded by society and those that will be punished. As children play, they explore the roles presented to them by significant adults.

conscience and is developed from close association with parents, teachers, siblings, and others significant in the child's life. The superego represents other people's values as much as the person's own values.

As we might guess, the three structures may work in opposition. For example, a person might see an expensive watch in a store. The id would say, "I must have it. Now! I want it so badly, I'll steal it!" The ego would say, "You can't have it now. Later! Plan ahead and save for it. Pick something else that you can afford." The superego, always a bit prudish, would say, "You'd better not steal it. What would your mother and father say? Do good people do that? You'll be punished for it! What if everyone stole?" Fortunately, these three structures are usually in balance. The ego, since it deals with reality, is given the responsibility for mediating between the impulsive id, the strict superego, and the realistic situation itself. The ego may not always cope realistically, but may construct unconscious defense mechanisms. Some common defense mechanisms are illustrated in Box 2-1.

Psychosexual Development.   In Freudian theory, development takes place in a series of *psychosexual stages*. The term *psychosexual* refers to any bodily pleasure. In each stage, children discover erogenous zones, or body areas that

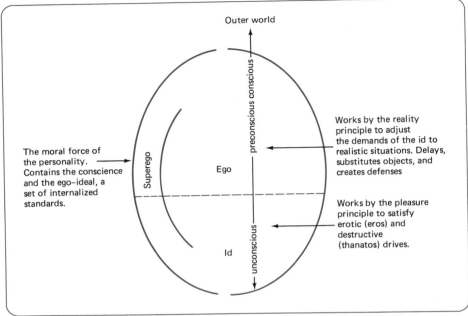

Figure 2-7. Freud's conceptualization of personality structure. (Adapted from S. Freud. *New Introductory Lectures on Psychoanalysis.* 1933; New York: Norton, 1965, p. 78.)

produce pleasure when stimulated. It is consistent with Freud's main assumptions that although children instinctively enjoy stimulating various erogenous zones, they will be frustrated by parents and others in their attempts to produce unlimited pleasure.

Freud felt that moderate amounts of frustration were necessary in order for children to develop the ego characteristics of delaying gratification and substitution. He also believed, however, that severe frustration would produce a *fixation,* or a desire for the missed stimulation, in later life. Fixations may be expressed in actual behaviors (as in the case of a baby weaned too early who, as an adult, sucks on pencils and fingers when tense), or they may be expressed in distant and symbolic ways. While most fixations occur as the result of severe frustration, Freud felt that a person could also become fixated by being overindulged. That is, a child may be so satisfied with unlimited stimulation in a certain psychosexual stage that the child remains at this stage and builds a set of permanent habits related to the stimulating activity.

In the first psychosexual stage, lasting from birth to about one year, the child derives great pleasure from activities connected with the mouth. In this *oral stage,* the child actively explores with the mouth and sucks and bites not only for food but for its own pleasurable activity as well. According to psychoanalytic theory, the child will be weaned at some time during this first stage. While most children will be ready for weaning in their first year, each child is biologically different and has

Box   2-1
Some Common Ego Defense Mechanisms

Basic Defenses

Denial

Definition: Refusal to deal with aspects of a stressful situation.
Example: Johnny walks into the room scratched, bloody, and with a torn shirt and announces, "I *wasn't* fighting."

Displacement

Definition: A defense in which a feeling, often of anger, is transferred from its original threatening source to a safer, less powerful person or object.
Example: Hillary's mother shouted at her. Hillary sulked and then went into the next room where she teased Beth, her younger sister.

Projection

Definition: The tendency to see a disliked or guilt- and shame-producing aspect of oneself in other people.
Example: As Betsy rode into the dark tunnel, she clutched her rag doll and told her mother, "Raggy's scared. I have to hug her."

Undoing

Definition: An unacceptable act that was already carried out is "undone" by later performing its opposite.
Example: One morning, Steve called his father "doody-head." That afternoon, he walked up to his father and, unannounced, kissed and hugged him.

Introjection

Definition: The internalization of other people's values in order to reduce threat.
Example: When Suzy was taking some cookies from the pantry, she thought she heard a little voice inside her say, "You shouldn't be doing this."

Regression

Definition: Under stress, a person may fall back on a tactic that was useful in reducing stress at an earlier life stage.
Example: When her parents brought her new baby brother home from the hospital, three-year-old Jennifer began to suck her thumb, demand to be picked up and cuddled frequently, and lost her toilet training.

Repression

Definition: Motivated forgetting of unpleasant material.
Example: Bill's mother told him to make sure to remember to mow the lawn that afternoon. Somehow, as his friends were playing ball next door, Bill forgot about lawnmowing.

Identification

Definition: In order to be protected against anxiety, a person may pattern his or her behavior after the behavior of a threatening person.
Example: Martin was hurt by being called "a little coward" by his insensitive camp counselor. Later that week, Martin was leading some other boys in a camp game, and he was able to get the other boys to follow his orders by calling them "little cowards."

Reaction Formation

Definition: Consciously performing the opposite of something that is desired on an unconscious level.
Example: Six-year-old Jim becomes very righteous and says, "Somebody should do something about those bad boys who shoot off firecrackers!"

More Advanced Defenses
Intellectualization and Isolation

Definition: De-emotionalizing a threatening situation by handling it as a cool, intellectual exercise.
Example: As Robert and Susan returned from the movies, Robert parked his car in a dark spot in a local "Lover's Lane." He looked up at the moon, said, "It's a beautiful moon," and then inched closer to Susan. Trembling a bit, Susan said, "Yes. Did you watch the astronauts on TV last week? Do you think that we will go beyond our galaxy in the next 30 years? . . . "

Rationalization

Definition: Presenting an excuse or justification for something about which the person feels guilt or shame.
Example: Kate accidentally dribbled mustard on her new blouse and felt foolish. She then told her friends, "I just wanted to see if anyone was paying attention around here."

highly individual needs for oral stimulation. For the child who is weaned too early or too late, fixations of this stage may lead to such oral personality traits as: reducing tension by overeating, drinking, smoking, nailbiting; becoming clinging and overly dependent on others in the same way that a baby clings to its mother; and becoming gullible—ready to "swallow anything" communicated by another person.

The second stage of psychosexual development is the *anal stage,* which occurs between about one and three years of age. In this stage there is a shift in emphasis from the oral region to the anal region. This shift in zone dominance occurs universally, because it is biologically based and results from maturational processes. During the first or *anal expulsive* part of this stage, children derive a great deal of pleasure from toilet-related activities, especially those involved with expelling feces. For example, many parents find that their children are fascinated with their own bowel movements. Many children have surprised their parents by suddenly becoming quiet after a fairly noisy day. The parent may have thought, "Thank goodness," and left the child's room for a well-deserved rest. When returning later to the room, the beaming child greets the parent with a truly amazing piece of artwork—a wall mural done in fingerpainted feces! Children will also enjoy playing with water, clay, and other potentially messy activities. Because they reflect the major interests of this stage, words associated with elimination become important vocabulary words.

While a child might obviously enjoy these activities, parents, for many reasons, do not enjoy them and will attempt to toilet train their children. Unfortunately, a child cannot really be toilet trained until the anal sphincter muscles, which regulate the passage of bowel movements from intestines to the anus, are sufficiently developed. Some children are ready for toilet training as early as one year, but other children may not be ready until several years later. For the severely trained *or* undertrained child, such anal expulsive fixations as these may appear: a tendency to be sloppy and messy; a desire to break rules, schedules, and disobey orders. Some children, however, are so severely trained that they become fixated in the opposite direction: they may become overly neat, overscheduled, and rigidly bound to authority, orders, and rules.

In the second part of the anal stage, called the *anal retentive stage,* children enjoy the new power of their sphincter muscles and hold back, or retain, feces. Struggles can occur between parents and children over bowel movements. For the child fixated at this phase, such traits as hoarding, holding back, stubbornness, and saving become important.

The *phallic stage,* occurring between about three and seven years of age, is the stage in which the genital region becomes the source of libidinal pleasure. During this stage children become interested in the anatomical differences between the sexes. Seeing a parent or sibling undressed, the child will commonly ask such questions as: "Why do boys [and daddies] have penises?" "How come [mommies and] girls don't have penises?" Little girls may experiment in urinating standing up like a boy. Masturbation is also very common and normal in this stage, and boys and girls will experience pleasure with genital play.

During the phallic stage children are capable of extreme jealousy. There may be jealousy for the love that parents have for each other, or there may be sibling rivalry—competition and jealousy between brothers and sisters. For boys such jealousy, according to Freud, leads to the *Oedipus complex,* in which the boy is attracted to his mother and sees his father as a rival. In Freud's view, the boy has fantasies and fears of castration and mutilation. Unable to actually be a rival with an adult, he will *identify* (take on the characteristics of) with the father. In girls, the similar process is called the *Electra complex.* According to Freudian theory, the girl equates her lack of a penis with inferiority. Such *penis envy* leads the girl to be attracted toward her father and have a sense of rivalry with her mother. Through conflict, the girl eventually identifies with her mother. Many critics, who assert that the theory of penis envy is highly inadequate to explain identification in girls, point to more convincing social, rather than biological, explanations (Horney, 1967).

At the end of the phallic stage, the child is supposed to identify with the parent of the same sex and to have formed less intense attachments to the opposite sex parent. In families in which it would be difficult to adequately identify with the parents, Freudian theory predicts that the child will later experience difficulty in sex-role identity and in relationships with authority figures such as supervisors, teachers, and social institutions.

The *latency stage* develops in the elementary school years (ages 7–12). Freud saw the latency stage as one of stability and as a time when social and cultural skills and understandings were acquired. This increase in skills strengthens the child's superego. Rebelliousness, if it occurs in the latter part of this stage, is viewed as part of the working through of the earlier Oedipal complex.

The *genital stage,* which is the last stage, occurs in adolescence. The individual again returns to sexual interest, but this interest is now focused on persons outside the family. For many adolescents the onset of puberty is highly traumatic. The adolescent asks, "What can I do with this new body? Am I attractive and popular enough? What are the 'facts of life,' anyhow?" Frdud believed that an adolescent's choice of a person of the opposite sex is often related to the Oedipus complex; thus, parental characteristics are preferred. In this stage, the child moves into adulthood and becomes less egocentric—pleasure is sought not only for the self but for others. Hopefully, adolescents integrate the teachings of the family, their own personal needs, and the demands of the culture into a personally satisfying life-style (see Table 2-1).

Many other psychoanalysts have objected to Freud's strong emphasis on sexual and aggressive factors in development and have suggested other motivational systems. Another criticism of Freud's theory is that psychoanalysis was applicable to life in European and American society at the turn of the century, but not to other cultures and other historical periods. Although there have been many revisions of psychoanalytic theory, one major revision which we will discuss has been provided by Erik Erikson.

Erikson's Psychosocial Theory

Erik Erikson's developmental theory has many features of Freudian psycho-analysis, but it also has some major differences. Erikson (1950, 1968) prefers to speak of *psychosocial stages* rather than psychosexual stages, because he believes that the major tasks of development involve the formation of a self in a social context. While the first five of Erikson's stages correspond closely to Freud's psychosexual stages, Erikson introduced three stages of adulthood that were not mentioned in Freud's theory. Thus, Erikson's theory covers a longer span of life than

Table 2-1

FREUDIAN PSYCHOSEXUAL STAGES

Psychosexual Stage	Oral	Anal	Phallic	Latency	Genital
Approximate Age	birth to one year and beyond	1½ to 3 years	3 through 5 or 6 years	7 through 12 years	12 through remainder of life
Erogenous Zone	mouth	anus	penis or clitoris	none	penis, clitoris, and vagina
Typical Activities	a. sucking b. biting	*first phase* a. feces interest b. feces play c. feces expulsion *second phase* a. feces retention	a. interest in sex differences b. masturbation c. jealousy d. imaginative play	a. peer group play b. skill learning	a. interest in opposite sex b. masturbation c. sexual experimentation d. attempts at adult roles
Fixations	a. overeating b. overdrinking c. smoking d. overdependency e. passivity	*first phase* a. messiness b. rigidity c. overscheduling d. overneatness *second phase* a. stubbornness b. hoarding c. negativism	a. sexual identity problems b. Oedipus complex (male) c. Electra complex (female) d. guilt e. preference for much older sex partners	none	none; the resolution of this stage is considered to be maturity

Freud's theory and, in its focus on psychosocial development, places stronger emphasis on environmental and interpersonal influences.

Erikson's theory can be called a crisis theory, as each stage presents the person with a new growth crisis. Success in meeting the crisis will lead to greater adult strengths, but failure in meeting the crisis will result in behavior similar to Freudian fixations. Erikson believes in an *epigenetic principle* through which successes and failures in each stage pave the way for, or influence, developments in the following stages.

In the first of Erikson's eight stages, children encounter the crisis of *Trust* vs. *Mistrust.* In such experiences as feeding, watching mothers come and go, waiting for food and diapering, children form basic notions of trust in other people. Some children, who may feel or actually experience deprivation, will form lasting patterns of mistrust of others. This stage corresponds to Freud's oral stage but goes far beyond the fact of whether the child gets oral stimulation. Instead, Erikson considers oral activities as one part of a broader pattern of social development.

The second stage, called *Autonomy* vs. *Shame and Doubt,* corresponds to Freud's anal stage. During this stage children experience struggles between their own wills and those of their parents. Children in this stage are highly concerned with doing things by themselves, even if they are inefficient and awkward. The age of two, for example, has been called the "terrible twos" because of children's stubborn insistence and negativism at this time. The "nos," "can'ts," and "won'ts" of children in this stage are attempts to assert their autonomy and build a sense of self. Many children pit their wills against their parents in the "holding back and letting go" activities of this stage, such as toilet training, and they may suffer badly. From failures in toilet training, self-feeding, and dressing, the child may experience shame. (Unfortunately, many children have been told: "Shame on you. You're dirty and smelly. I can't stand the way you are!") They may also develop deep doubts about whether they can ever get things done corrdctly.

The third stage, lasting from the ages of 3 to 6 years, is called the stage of *Initiative* vs. *Guilt* and corresponds to Freud's phallic stage. In this stage children take the initiative to start many things. They move actively, invent games involving conquests, and become more imaginative. With their increased activities (which can get them into trouble) and expanding imaginations, children may experience a sense of guilt. As in Freud's Oedipus complex, for example, the child may take the initiative for wanting to possess his mother and overpower his father. He may also, however, imagine and experience guilt for his incestuous fantasies.

An example of early guilt can be seen in the case of 3-year-old Betsy. One morning Betsy heard a fire siren in the street and became noticeably frightened. Her father saw this and said, "Why are you scared? The firemen are going to help people." This statement had no calming effect on Betsy at all. In fact, she looked even more frightened. "Oh, no," she said. "They're policemen, and they want to put me in jail." She was asked, "Why should they want to put you in jail?" Betsy looked down pensively and said, "'Cause I said a bad word this morning." Neither her father nor her mother remembered any such incident, but Betsy's guilt was apparent. "That's O.K., Betsy," her father said, "we all have mean ideas sometimes, and we all say bad words. You won't be punished. Do you know that sometimes policemen say bad words?"

Successful resolution of the crises of this stage leads to a sense of initiative. Belittling of the child's efforts, however, combined with the child's active imagination can lead to lasting guilt.

4ᵗʰ The fourth stage, *Industry* vs. *Inferiority,* occurs between about 6 to 12 years of age. This stage corresponds to Freud's latency stage and is the stage in which we will find most elementary schoolchildren. During this period, children are industrious. They work hard in the school and playground. They try to acquire a sense of mastery in everything they do. For example, children may memorize elaborate rhymes, practice highly skilled movements in jump-rope, and spend weeks practicing batting or attempting to shoot baskets. A ten-year-old "no hands" bicycle daredevil is strong proof of the need for mastery at this age.

Children can also experience a sense of inadequacy and inferiority. School exercises are graded, hobby projects may fall apart, and some children will be chosen last when the time arrives for choosing teams. Successes in this stage lead to a sense that, "I can do these things (and future things) well," while failures may lead to feelings that, "I can't (and won't be able to) learn to do things right."

5ᵗʰ The fifth stage, *Identity* vs. *Role Diffusion,* presents the adolescent with such questions as: "Who am I?" "Who was I?" and "Where am I going?" As in the Freudian genital stage, much concern revolves around some issues of sexual maturity. The stage covers much more than that, however. In essence, the adolescent must form a stable sense of self-identity or else experience the self as a series of scattered, disconnected, and inconsistent poses and roles. Finding a consistent sense of identity is never easy, and adolescents attempt to find that sense in many diverse activities. For some, the task involves escapes into and adventures in radically different lifestyles than they had led before. Others may drop out or experience a "moratorium phase," in which they can hopefully reassess their lives and formulate new plans and goals. Still others may not resolve their identity searches and may flounder aimlessly for a while.

6ᵗʰ The sixth stage, *Intimacy* vs. *Isolation,* has no counterpart in Freudian theory. This stage covers the young adult years between 20 and the early 30s. In this stage young adults experiment with intimate relations with others. The questions posed by the crises of this stage are, "How can I share my ideas and my body with someone else? Am I too selfish? Can I form lasting relationships?" If they are prepared by successes in earlier stages and have gained some positive experiences, young adults will develop a sense of intimacy. It is also possible, however, that failures at this stage will leave a person isolated and lonely, preferring to avoid the risks of interpersonal encounters by becoming insulated, cool, and aloof.

In the seventh stage, which occurs between the 30s through the late 50s, the person is faced with the crisis of *Generativity* vs. *Stagnation.* In Erikson's words, "generativity . . . concerns the establishment of the next generation" (Erikson, 1959, p. 97). People are concerned with the tasks of parenthood and also the full growth, or generation, of their careers. At this stage, however, the person is also faced with the prospect of stagnation—staying put, going nowhere, a continually boring existence. Since the person may see his or her lifespan half-finished, the fear of becoming stagnant may lead to radical shifts in career and family plans.

In the last stage, occurring from the 60s onward, the person experiences the crisis of *Integrity* vs. *Despair*. For many, old age is a time to review the past seven stages, to see an integrated life theme, and to bring the various events of the life together. Where younger people have had to make deals, accommodations, and compromises, older people have the integrity to stand by their own convictions. Failing health, limited social opportunities, economic hardships, and the prospect of death, however, plunge many people into despair as they feel there is little time to start again.

Unlike Freud, Erikson was highly concerned with the role of society in aiding a person's progress through each stage. In Erikson's words (1950, p. 277):

> . . . we suggest that, to understand either childhood or society, we must expand our scope to include the study of the way in which societies lighten the inescapable conflicts of childhood with a promise of some security, identity, and integrity. In thus reinforcing the values by which the ego exists, societies create the only condition under which human growth is possible.

Thus, for Erikson, growth is the result of the interaction of both individual, biological development, and social forces.

THE COGNITIVE DEVELOPMENTAL VIEW

"Cognitive," as defined by Webster's dictionary (1963, p. 161) means "the act or process of knowing, including both awareness and judgment." For the cognitive psychologist, the important topics and processes to be investigated are: language, thought, memory, symbols, problem-solving techniques, and creativity. At birth an infant's cognitive processes are not fully organized or developed. The newborn's behavior will depend to a great extent on reflex actions. Even though we now know that infants can react to many more sensory stimuli than we thought they could (Bower, 1977), they may attribute little meaning to the stimuli. Only through a gradual process of cognitive development can the child become capable of performing complex mental processes. For most cognitive development theories, development proceeds through a number of stages in which children gain increasing mastery and understanding of the world through expanding abilities in thought, language, and symbolization.

Jean Piaget's Theory of Cognitive Development

General Principles of Piaget's Theory.   The primary moving force and the most comprehensive view among cognitive developmental theories come from the

Table 2-2
ERIKSON'S PSYCHOSOCIAL STAGES OF DEVELOPMENT

Stage	Age	Freudian Counterpart	Successful Resolution	Unsuccessful Resolution
Trust vs. Basic Mistrust	birth to one year	Oral stage	Trust, optimism, trust in self	Mistrust, pessimism, easily frustrated, nostalgic
Autonomy vs. Shame and Doubt	1 to 3 years	Anal stage	Independent, self-assertive, flexible	Doubtful, ashamed, rigid, overcautious, overcontrolled
Initiative vs. Guilt	3 to 5 years	Phallic stage	Inventive, dynamic, ambitious, risk-taking	Inhibited, jealous, sexually afraid and blunted, guilty
Industry vs. Inferiority	6 to 11 years	Latency stage	Competent, hard-working, likes learning and achieving	Ineffective, wastes time, avoids competition
Identity vs. Identity Diffusion	12 through early 20s	Genital stage	Confident, has sense of self and future time perspective, sex roles defined	Sees self as phony, inconsistent set of loose roles, poor sexual identity, unsure of values and own future
Intimacy vs. Isolation	Young adulthood	. . . .	Candid and open, shares self with others, tactful	Cool, isolated and remote, experiments sexually but with little commitment
Generativity vs. Stagnation	Middle adulthood	. . . .	Productive, fosters the growth of the next generation	Unproductive, stagnating, old before one's time
Integrity vs. Despair	Later adulthood	. . . .	Understanding of life cycle, wisdom, principled ethics	Disgust with life, wish to "do it over again," fear of death, sees life as meaningless

Sources: Bischof (1970), Erikson (1959, 1963), Wessman and Ricks (1966).

work of Jean Piaget, the famous Swiss psychologist. Much of Piaget's early education was in the field of biology, but he soon developed an interest in philosophy and psychology and has integrated these disciplines with biology. He has undertaken to organize human behavior according to a biological framework. Piaget worked in several psychological laboratories at the University of Zurich and later went to the Paris laboratory of the pioneering experimental psychologists Alfred Binet and Theophile Simon. From them Piaget learned the approach used in the Binet tests of intelligence. For example, he became concerned with standardizing tasks at different age levels. More than Binet, however, Piaget was interested in the reasons *why* children are unable to correctly solve problems at one age and then able to correctly solve them at later ages.

Figure 2-8. Jean Piaget, b. 1896. (Photo by the Bettmann Archive)

While in Paris, Piaget also had an opportunity to learn about Freudian psycho-analysis, and his subsequent interest in observing individuals may be partly due to this influence. In any case, Piaget worked during the following years at the University of Geneva and at the Institute de Jean-Jacques Rousseau, at the same time studying his own children through extensive observation. This work led to the belief that the goal of laboratory investigations should be to substantiate ideas obtained in logical processes and that symbolic logic is a more important investigative technique than formal experimental methodology (Maier, 1969).

Much of Piaget's work in human development has been concerned with investigations of intelligence and thought and with the search forⁿconcepts that explain both how behavior is organized and adapted. Organization and adaptation are the basic functions for human beings. Simply put, *organization* refers to the integration of information and experience into related systems, and *adaptation* refers to ways of dealing effectively with the environment. Two important concepts of adaptation are *assimilation* and *accommodation.* Assimilation is the process by which, in interaction with the environment, new experiences are fit into existing understandings and capacities. New experiences may be impossible to fit into existing concepts. If this is so, then the child must modify, or *accommodate,* his own personal responses to fit the new experience. Two other concepts fundamental to the child's cognitive development are *schemes* and *equilibrium.* A *scheme* is a concept or a cognitive structure that changes during development. *Equilibrium* can be thought of as the balance between assimilation and accommodation—how much the child does of each in reference to the other. We will further develop Piaget's complex formulations in Chapter 5.

As most other biologically-oriented thinkers, Piaget thinks that behavior derives from forces originating within the individual and from interactions of the person with the environment. The essential interaction is a process which Piaget calls *cognitive structuring*. Because of his emphasis on these processes, Piaget has been frequently labeled either an "interactionist" or a "structuralist" (Piaget, 1954, 1970; Piaget & Inhelder, 1948; Inhelder & Sinclair, 1969).

On the basis of his observations, Piaget constructed a comprehensive sequence of stages and phases to explain the relationships that apply among the many facets of his theory.

Piaget's Views of Developmental Stages.   For Piaget and other proponents of cognitive developmental theory, cognitive processes and the development of thought are not so much the results of reinforcements from the environment or the quantity of things learned, but come from qualitative changes in the child's capacity for response. Piaget sees a sequence of developmental stages that characterize intellectual growth, with each stage being different in character (see Table 2-3).

The first stage of development in Piaget's theory is the *sensorimotor stage*, lasting from birth to about two years. Intelligence in this stage ". . .rests mainly on

Figure 2-9.   According to Piaget's theory of cognitive development, play provides an opportunity for children to develop schemes concerning objects and problem-solving strategies. As these children play, they not only entertain themselves but also develop a large number of cognitive skills. (Photo by Diana Blanchard)

Table 2-3
PIAGET'S STAGES OF COGNITIVE DEVELOPMENT

Stage	Approximate Age	Characteristic Behaviors
Sensorimotor	birth to about 18 months	The child progresses from simple reflexes to simple habits and then to more complex behaviors involving coordination of perception and movement, invention of means-end concepts, and a concept of object permanence.
Preoperational	2 years to 7 years	The child develops language, imagery, and imaginative play. Many perceptual and motor skills develop. Thought and language, however, are generally confined to present, concrete events. Thinking is egocentric, irreversible, and lacks the concept of conservation.
Concrete Operational	7 years to 12 years	The child can perform simple logical tasks involving conservation, reversibility, and ordering. Concepts of time become more realistic. Thought, however, is limited to concrete, tangible features of the environment.
Formal Operational	12 years through adulthood	The person can deal with logical problems that contain abstractions. Hypothetical, "as-if" or propositional problems can be solved. Mathematical and scientific problems can be solved in symbolic forms.

actions, on movements and perceptions without language . . . " (Piaget, 1962). For example, if a child pulls a carpet close in order to reach a toy, this would constitute a *schema* of action. The child is concerned with movements and the contact of nearby objects: "Thus, starting with the use of reflexes and the first acquired association, the child succeeds within a few months in constructing a system of schemas capable of unlimited combinations . . . " (Piaget, 1954, p. 357).

The *preoperational stage* lasts from about 2 to about 7 years of age. The child begins to use symbols, engages in imaginative play, and develops the ability to differentiate between words and things that are not present.

Although children are often very bright and highly talkative in the preoperational stage, we can be fooled into thinking that they know more than they actually know. Their thought processes are very primitive and they usually focus on only one limited aspect of a situation at a time. For example, suppose that we present a child with three water beakers: two identical, long, thin beakers and a third beaker that is wider and shorter than the other two. We fill the two thin beakers with water until the height of water is the same in both. We then ask the child to tell us if there is the same amount of water in each beaker. Usually a child will tell us that the amount of water is the same in both beakers. Next, we will pour the contents of one of the beakers into the shorter but wider beaker and then ask the child to compare the amount of water that was poured to the amount in the remaining beaker. We ask the child, "Do I have the same amount of water in this glass as in this glass? Do I have more or do I have less?" Most preoperational children will say that the amount of water has changed and that we have either more or less than we had before. They will rarely answer that the amount of water is the same, because they tend to focus on either the height or the area of the beaker but not on the combination of height and area which would give the correct judgment of volume. During this stage such logical contradictions are quite common, and the child's thought lacks many of the features of logic seen in older children and adults. The preoperational child will have difficulty organizing things into logical classes or sequences and will not be able to understand that things may change in shape and still have the same weight, volume, or mass as before.

The *concrete operational stage* lasts from about age 7 to age 12. During this stage the child can perform many logical operations. For example, in our water beaker problem (more formally called a *conservation* of liquid problem), most eight-year-olds will state that the amount of water remains the same when poured from beaker to beaker. When asked, "Why is this so?," they would give such explanations as: "It's just the same water but you poured it into a different jar"; "You can't fool me, silly! That glass is big and skinny and this one's short and fat, but there's the same room inside"; or "I could pour the water back in the first jar and show you that nothing has changed." The concrete operational child can perform conservation problems like the one above with many different objects and tasks. This means that he or she understands that characteristics such as length, weight, number, and volume can remain the same in spite of minor changes in appearance. The child can place events and things in order and usually has a clear understanding of part-whole relationships.

Although children display a considerable amount of logical thought in the concrete operational stage, their thought is limited to problems that are concrete, in which things can be immediately perceived, touched, or tasted. For example, children can give a mathematical proof for the problem, "Show me why five apples and three apples make eight apples," because they can visualize apples and can actually count them for us. If we ask a child to show why $5x + 3x = 8x$, however, we might see the child become very confused by this abstraction.

In the *formal operational stage,* which is reached between 12 and 14 years of age, abstract ideas and symbolic thought become important characteristics of reasoning processes. At this stage people can use hypothetical thinking and, therefore, can extend thoughts beyond the present situation. For example, an adolescent could ponder such questions as: "What if snow were black? How would it affect our weather patterns?" A young child would toss this hypothetical question aside with a comment such as, "Snow isn't black. I've seen it and it's white." For the younger child something is either concretely there or it is not; there are no hypothetical "what-if's" prior to the formal operational stage.

Advanced reasoning abilities lead to advances in moral judgments and social relationships. Adolescents become more attentive to values and are concerned, often self-consciously, about themselves in relation to others (Rubin & Schneider, 1973). Their developing concerns about life and life goals are important steps toward mature, adult thought processes.

Piaget's ideas about cognitive development have provided a rich basis for innovative explorations in cognitive development. Unlike the behaviorists, Piagetians view the child as a person who is not simply acted upon by the environment, but who actively approaches his or her surroundings with an inborn capacity and drive to understand. Piagetians maintain that when children explore their world, they are actively participating in their own development.

Much work remains to be carried out in Piaget's theory. For example, Piaget asserts that the order of stages of cognitive development varies relatively little. Each stage must precede the following stages in a sequence that does not vary from child to child or from culture to culture. Stages cannot be skipped. Piagetian theory also suggests that while we can help a child's growth through a given stage, we cannot radically accelerate the child's long-term growth by massive teaching and training exercises unless the child is ready for training. As we examine developmental issues at different life stages, we will see repeated attempts by researchers to support, modify, or refute these and other Piagetian concepts.

BIOLOGICAL AND ETHOLOGICAL APPROACHES TO DEVELOPMENT

Human beings are members of the animal kingdom and can be studied as biological organisms. Of course, many human behaviors and functions such as language, speech, thought, and tool usage have few, if any, parallels in other species. There are, however, many aspects of human behavior that can be profitably viewed from the standpoint of the biologist. In this section we will discuss *maturation* and *ethological* research to see what these biological topics can tell us about human development.

Maturation

When we discussed behaviorism, psychoanalysis, and cognitive development theories, we emphasized the idea that processes of learning and concept formation develop from interactions of the person with the environment. It is very important to realize, however, that in any developmental process, the environment alone does not create behavior; the person also brings something into the environmental situation. Among the things that people bring into situations are certain biological growth potentials that unfold in a process of maturation. According to Munn (1974, p. 89), *maturation* can be defined as "growth resulting from interaction between genes and internal environmental conditions which characterize the species, thus setting it off from the outcomes of exercise, or the use of structures already present.'' In other words, maturational processes are built-in and do not develop out of ordinary learning processes. For example, at birth many of the infant's body systems do not function very efficiently. Infants have difficulty in breathing because the respiratory centers in their brains are not yet able to send regular nerve impulses to the lungs so that breathing will be regular and strong. We cannot train an infant to breathe more regularly, but as time passes, the infant's nervous and respiratory systems will *mature* until breathing becomes smooth and effortless.

Other examples of maturation can be found in motor, or muscle, development. For instance, a very young infant's leg muscles usually cannot support the infant's body. As the months pass, though, their bodies develop rapidly and with little or no practice their legs become skilled at walking and crawling. In the case of motor development, the maturation process is governed by a person's own unique *schedule of maturation*. We are not sure why individuals have different rates of maturation, but it is undoubtedly due to some hereditary and biological influences.

Maturation prepares children for many behaviors, but learning and environmental factors are still important for their final development. For example, Hubel and Weisel (1970) found that newborn kittens had networks of cells or "feature detectors" in the visual cortex of the brain that were specialized for very sophisticated visual pattern detection. It looked like the kittens' eyes and brains had the basic "equipment" for vision at birth. Hubel and Weisel then attempted to see how well these visual pattern detectors would function if the kittens were deprived of the opportunities to see light and visual patterns. Several kittens were raised in the dark, and it was found that the feature detectors of these light-deprived animals failed to mature further, so that when brought into the light the kittens displayed a number of visual deficiencies. Therefore, while maturation may permit some skills to develop in the first place, environmental stimulation will often be necessary to bring them to their full development.

Maturational effects also set an upper limit on what can be learned at any given age. Parents may attempt to toilet train a child; however, unless the child's anal sphincter muscles have matured to the point where voluntary control is possible, such training efforts will be useless. In fact, we might reverse the concept and see children whose anal sphincters have not yet matured as toilet training their parents to come running to tend to the child's needs!

Basic Concepts of Ethology

One striking fact about infant behavior is that many behavior systems are so well formed that it would be difficult to imagine that babies actually learned these behaviors. For example, at around 2 or 3 months of age, most babies smile. Around 8 months of age, most infants display strong attachments to their parents and other caregivers. By one year, most infants understand at least several words. How can we explain these nearly universal behaviors?

It seems clear that, in spite of the continuing controversy over precisely how learning takes place, not all behavior is learned. Because the concept of unlearned behavior is very difficult to explain, many theorists have bypassed this issue. Other researchers who favor biological explanations of behavior have attempted to explore relatively inborn or *instinctive* behaviors in a theoretical approach known as *ethology*.

Although there is no precise definition of the term, *ethology* can be roughly defined as *the study of animal behaviors in natural settings, especially with respect to instinctive or species-specific behaviors.* By "species-specific," ethologists mean behaviors that are shown by all or most members of the species under the same conditions. Many ethologists think of themselves as biologists rather than psychologists and tend to draw parallels between some general biological questions and some behavioral questions. For example, as the biologist asks about embryological development, the ethologist asks about the "embryology" of behavior and, in doing so, can see how certain behaviors develop in an orderly progression in many species. Biologists since Darwin have asked how physical structures have helped various species to survive; similarly, ethologists question how species-specific behaviors have enabled a given species to survive. Biologists have traditionally been interested in exploring differences and similarities among species, and ethologists have searched for parallels and contrasts in the behavior patterns of various species in order to discover more general principles of behavior (Blurton-Jones, 1972).

We will now review some principles used by ethologists in their studies of both humans and animals. So far, much ethological research has focused on animal behavior, but many ethologists are clearly concerned with human development (Blurton-Jones, 1972; Lorenz, 1977).

Instinct.   The term *instinct* was very popular at the turn of the century and received a great deal of attention in the writings of William McDougall (1908, 1919). When behaviorists began to place strong emphasis on learning, however, interest in instinctual processes declined sharply. Instincts have several important characteristics. They are inborn patterns of behavior that are found in each member of a given species. They are triggered by specific patterns of stimuli, and animals do not, as a rule, have to learn to respond to these stimuli. In the evolution of the species, instinctual behavior helped the species to survive under some environmental conditions.

One of the most active ethological theorists and researchers is Konrad Lorenz, who won the Nobel Prize for his discoveries in ethology (Lorenz, 1935, 1937, 1977). In his research with birds, Lorenz maintained that the birds' responses to many objects in their environment were dependent on inborn abilities that were necessary for the survival of the birds. Newly-hatched wild geese, for example, must follow their mothers in order to obtain food and water. They can only survive with the mothers' protection. Lorenz was able to demonstrate how the young geese were innately able to follow, avoid enemies, attach themselves to, and signal their mothers.

Figure 2-10.   Ethologists have made us aware that many species form strong social bonds through an imprinting process. Is this also true of human children? (Bazhnsen / Monkmeyer Press Photo Service)

Not all instinctive behavior is completely inborn. Learning also has some effect on instinctual processes. Niko Tinbergen (1951), who shared the Nobel Prize with Lorenz, studied jackdaws (birds similar to crows) and found that these birds could learn both attraction and antagonism to other birds. For example, a female in a flock of birds may have an inferior status and therefore be attacked by the other birds. If she mates with one of the aggressive males in the flock, her status actually improves, and the other birds will reduce their attacks upon her. Although fighting behaviors and status systems in lower animals are often determined by biological factors, it seems that some learning and modification of these instinctive behaviors can occur—even in an animal as simple as a jackdaw!

Some researchers prefer to avoid the term *instinctive* because they feel that the term has become a receptacle for all kinds of unexplored complex behavior patterns. Some prefer to use the term *fixed action pattern* instead, because most instinctual behaviors are fairly rigid, because an entire pattern of behaviors is usually involved and not just a simple response, and because the animal responds to pre-determined patterns of stimuli.

Releasers and Sign Stimuli.   One of the most important features of ethological theory is the concept of *releaser stimuli.* This term refers to the fact that a stimulus can bring about a reaction by triggering innate response tendencies. Stimuli that can induce such behaviors are called *sign stimuli* or *releasers*. Animals are fairly selective in responding to releaser stimuli, and this responsiveness is itself genetically programmed. For example, without prior learning, a newborn kangaroo can blindly find the way to its mother's pouch by using touch and smell stimuli that release its attaching behavior. One of the authors accidentally released a fighting behavior in a pet cat as he was tying a balloon for one of his children. Unfortunately, the balloon slipped out of his hands and went hissing and bobbing wildly across the room. To the cat, this probably signalled another hissing animal, so she chased and pounced at the balloon in order to take on the challenge. As crazy as this behavior may appear, ordinarily attacking or running away from something that hisses would probably help the cat's survival. In this case, however, a fairly rigid pattern was released..

Critical Periods and Imprinting.   Ethological theory becomes linked with developmental processes through its insistence that appropriate releaser stimuli are required by an animal or person at a certain *critical age,* or sensitive period, in development. The concept of critical age is not exclusive with ethologists, but ethologists are distinctive in their view that specific kinds of releaser stimuli must be present at a critical point in time after birth. If, at a specific point in the organism's development, a significant object is not found in the perceptual field, other objects are substituted, or else the behavior does not occur. For example, when a mother goose is not present at the critical time, her goslings will follow other moving objects such as a human being or even a mechanical goose decoy. Once this behavior occurs, or is released, it cannot be altered by the subsequent appearance of the significant object (such as the mother goose). The goslings will continue to follow the object of their first attachment. This *imprinting* of the behavior at a critical period is described as a biologically inherited influence on which survival depends. In the wild, as explained earlier, the goslings must follow their mother in order to obtain food. The innate force impelling them toward the "following" behavior can be easily altered during the critical period but becomes increasingly more difficult to change after this period. In addition, it comes into being only as a result of the presence of releaser stimuli.

Imprinting might be said to involve learning, because it could be argued that the goslings *learn* to follow the mother or some releasing object. Eckhard Hess (1970) points out that the ethologist considers imprinting to be the integration of both learned and unlearned behavior. Learned behavior contributes to flexibility and allows the animal to adapt to various environmental conditions. On the other hand, inborn factors ensure that responses will first take place automatically without the necessity of learning. Therefore, inborn factors can also contribute to survival.

Reservoir of Behavior.   Another ethological concept is that of the *reservoir of behavior.* This concept states that if releaser stimuli are not present in the animal's environment then energy builds up and may be discharged into unrelated or inappropriate activities. Therefore, if instinctive behavior is blocked, a displacement activity results. Many psychologists, however, are quite skeptical about the value of the reservoir of behavior concept.

Ethological Views of the Process of Development

Some explanations of basic development processes by instinct theorists and ethologists seem to be related to other theoretical systems, but ethologists place much more emphasis on developmental patterns of behavior that are essentially unlearned. Ethologists claim that other developmentalists are actually admitting the existence of innate mechanisms and other ethological ideas when they take the position that some origins of behavior are not shaped entirely by experience. That is, if certain behaviors *unfold* in maturational stages, such behaviors could be considered to be dependent upon innate mechanisms. Hess asserted that Piaget's idea of the schema is a "sequence of action that does not vary" and thus is very similar to the ethologist's explanation of a fixed action pattern (Hess, 1970). As we discussed previously, Piaget included learning in his theory and maintained that a child's development does not occur by chance learnings, but results from an orderly and innately established sequence. This denial of random, or chance, development is central to both points of view. Hess insisted that the smiling of newborn infants is both an ethological fixed action pattern and a Piagetian schema—virtually the same. When a human face triggers smiling in an infant, the face is considered a *releaser stimulus,* according to an ethologist. The ethologist suggests that the smiling of the infant contributes to its survival, as it brings about a closer emotional relationship with the mother.

Ethological principles are valuable for showing that behavior results from biological foundations and adaptive functions in addition to learned responses. Ethology places importance on understanding human development in relation to biological factors, so that developmental experiences will not be provided in such a way that fulfillment of innate needs is denied. Ethologists consider the early childhood period to be crucial and believe that damage from deprivation of appropriate experience during these years is irreparable. In their view of critical stages, releaser stimuli must be present for the normal course of cognitive growth to take place. The implication is that ordinary development will not take place unless certain stimuli and experiences are present to release the behavior—perhaps even to allow further development of abilities that must be learned. Thus, an ethological view might suggest that the "Head Start" preschool educational programs for five-year-olds were a failure because these children had already passed a critical learning period, beyond which their learning abilities could not be released sufficiently. Learning theorists and others argue, to the contrary, that the main causes of failure were the environmental experiences in the children's backgrounds.

SUMMARY

In this chapter we examined development from four different perspectives. Behaviorism viewed human development as the result of learning experiences that come about through encounters between the growing person and the environment. Psychoanalysis tended to focus on how social forces and biologically based instinctual needs interact to form the human personality and motivational systems in both their conscious and unconscious aspects. Cognitive development theories focused on the development of thought, perception, and intelligence through the interplay of the tendencies of accommodation and assimilation, which force the child to actively construct concepts of objects, time, space, causality, and problem-solving skills. Ethology examined human development from an evolutionary perspective and attempted to show how many human behaviors, especially those that can be considered innate, might have aided the survival of human beings through thousands of years of evolution.

RECOMMENDED READINGS

Cowan, P. A. *Piaget with Feeling: Cognitive, Social, and Emotional Dimensions.* New York: Holt, Rinehart & Winston, 1978.

> An excellent summary of Piaget's work and its implications for a broad range of psychological issues. A good place to start before digging into Piaget's highly difficult writings.

Erikson, E. H. *Childhood and Society.* 2d ed. New York: Norton, 1963. *Identity: Youth and Crisis.* New York: Norton, 1968.

> These two books contain a series of essays written by Erikson from the 1940s through the 1960s. Together, they present the main concepts of his theory in a brilliantly clear form.

Freud, S. *A General Introduction to Psychoanalysis.* New York: Washington Square Press, 1952 (originally published in 1924). *New Introductory Lectures on Psychoanalysis.* New York: Norton, 1933.

> A complete overview of psychoanalysis in Freud's own words.

Manning, A. *An Introduction to Animal Behavior.* Reading, Mass.: Addison-Wesley, 1967.

> An excellent survey of ethology packed into a brief, understandable book.

Skinner, B. F. *About Behaviorism.* New York: Knopf, 1974.

> In this book Skinner discusses the underlying philosophy of modern behaviorism and compares his approach to other schools of thought.

Thomas, R. M. *Comparing Theories of Child Development.* Belmont, Ca.: Wadsworth, 1979.

> For a highly readable overview of over 25 theories of child development, this book is a must!

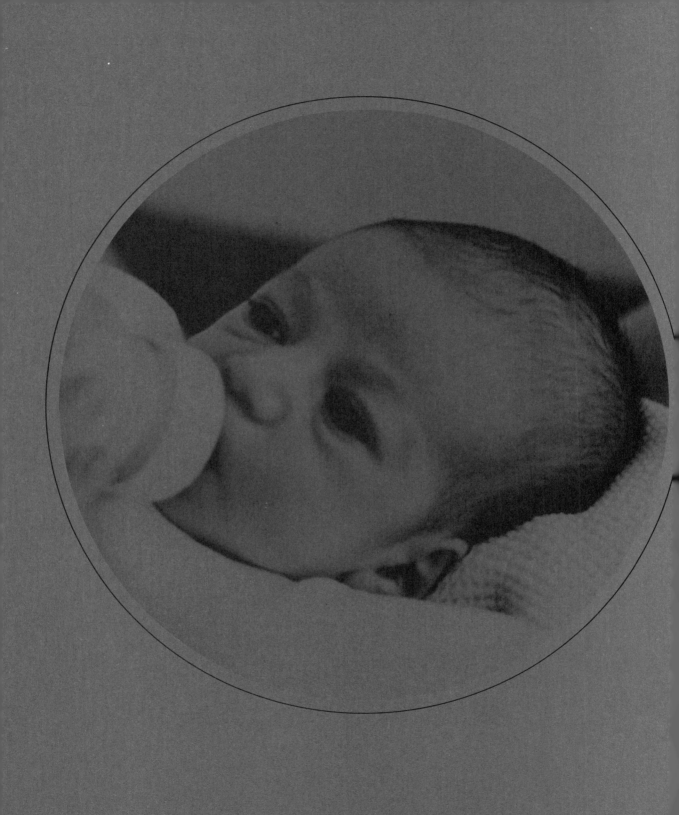

PRENATAL DEVELOPMENT AND EARLY INFANCY

3

How Life Begins

How does life begin? How do hereditary factors influence a person's later behavior? Can a mother's health during pregnancy have long-lasting effects on her children? What are the physical and behavioral characteristics of embryos and fetuses?

In this chapter we shall study the prenatal period which starts at conception and ends approximately nine months later in childbirth. We will look at some research in human heredity, embryology, fetal biology, and childbirth in order to understand how the prenatal period lays the foundations for later life.

PRINCIPLES OF INHERITANCE

A new individual begins when two sex cells or *gametes* —the father's sperm cell and the mother's ovum, or egg cell—are joined at conception. After conception,

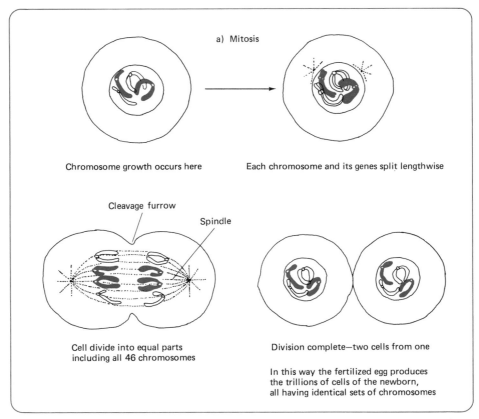

Figure 3-1. Mitosis (above) and meiosis (next page): schematic representation of the difference between the two processes. Mitosis results in two identical daughter cells, meiosis in sperm or ova having half the original number of chromosomes. (From R. Rugh and L. B. Shettles, *From conception to birth.* New York: Harper & Row, 1971. By permission of the estate of Dr. Roberts Rugh.)

the first step of growth, known as *mitosis,* begins. Mitosis is the process in which the fertilized ovum, or *zygote,* divides into two cells, which each divide into two other cells; the process continues for thousands of other divisions (see Figure 3-1). In mitosis, some cells will eventually become specialized body parts and body systems such as the gastrointestinal tract, the nervous system, the endocrine system, and the circulatory system.

The gametes (the sperm and ovum) themselves contain the material that will give the individual his or her biological heritage. The gametes are different from all other cells in the body and are created through a special reduction-division process called *meiosis.* Unlike the usual form of cell division called mitosis, in meiosis the germ cells split in half so that the resulting gametes have only one-half of the necessary elements for a complete cell (see Figure 3-1). When the two gametes (one male and one female) unite, the resulting *zygote* then contains a complete set of cellular material and reproduction will be accomplished.

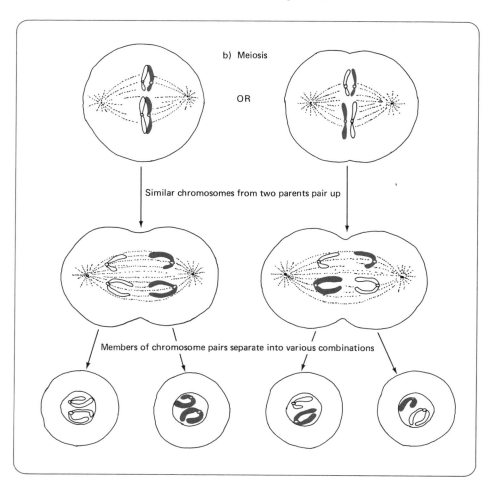

b) Meiosis

OR

Similar chromosomes from two parents pair up

Members of chromosome pairs separate into various combinations

The new individual will be different from all other human beings because he or she has inherited an entirely unique combination of characteristics that were contained in the gametes from both parents. These characteristics are determined by the *chromosomes* of the gametes (see Figure 3-2). Each gamete has 23 chromosomes. At conception, the new individual gets 46 chromosomes since one set comes from each parent. Chromosomes are threadlike structures that are found not only in the gametes but also in every cell of the body (Krone & Wolf, 1972).

Each chromosome contains thousands (perhaps 48,000) of minute bits of biochemical material called *genes,* which are located in certain positions along the

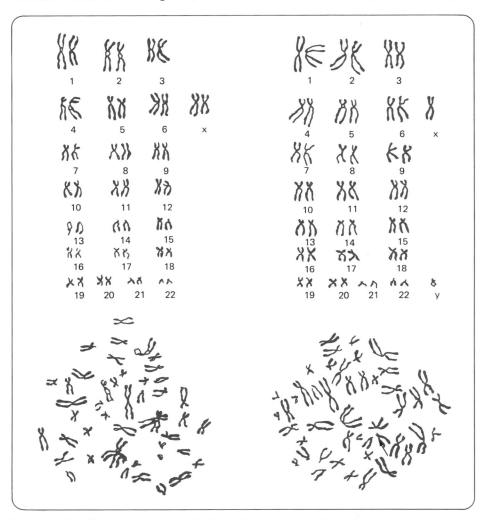

Figure 3-2.   Chromosomes: on the left, chromosomes of the human female; on the right, chromosomes of the human male. (From R. Rugh and L. B. Shettles, *From conception to birth.* New York: Harper & Row, 1971. By permission of the estate of Dr. Roberts Rugh.)

chromosome. Each gene carries certain characteristics of the new individual, such as the person's eye color, hair color, hair texture, height, and sex. A gene is considered to be a fundamental biological unit, and in the development of a human being many genes will contribute to the formation of any single organ or any single physical characteristic (Hunt, 1966; Scheinfeld, 1971, 1972; Stahl, 1964; Thiessen & Rodgers, 1967).

Although a person may possess a gene for a certain characteristic, the gene's influence may not be expressed. For example, a person who has both a gene for blue eyes and a gene for brown eyes, may have brown eyes. Geneticists have distinguished between the terms *genotype* and *phenotype*. A phenotype refers to the outward appearance of an individual in such things as height, hair, eye color, and skin pigmentation. A genotype refers to the underlying genetic makeup of the individual. A person may have the genes and, therefore, the genotype for both black hair and blond hair. However, because of certain laws of heredity and certain environmental influences that we shall discuss, the person will have black hair. Therefore, we would say that the person is *phenotypically* black-haired. The distinction between genotypes and phenotypes is not easily made, because each individual's genetic pattern is likely to be affected by environmental influences from the moment of conception and, therefore, the effects of a genotype might not ever be fully expressed.

We will now look at some basic principles or laws that are used to explain how biological characteristics are transmitted from one generation to another. Although the science of genetics is basically a twentieth-century development, its roots go back to the nineteenth century and are due primarily to the work of an Austrian monk named Gregor Mendel.

Mendelian Principles of Inheritance

Gregor Johann Mendel (1822–1884) is the man whose experiments on the inheritance of plant characterisitcs laid the foundation for modern genetics. Mendel grew two varieties of peas (tall peas and dwarf peas) in his monastery garden and experimented by crossbreeding the peas to produce varying combinations of tall and short peas in each generation of peas. In 1865 Mendel reported his discoveries to a scientific society. Although he published several articles on his work and these articles were stored in libraries throughout the world, Mendel's work remained generally unknown in his lifetime. The importance of his work was recognized in 1900 by Tschermak in Austria, de Vries in Holland, and Correns in Germany (Serra, 1965); but it was not until well into the twentieth century that Mendel became known as a great scientist and the founder of genetics.

As a result of Mendel's original work, some general principles of heredity have been derived that can help us understand human development. A basic principle of heredity is that each person has two paired genes, called *alleles,* that influence every physical characteristic. One allele of each gene pair comes from the father's sperm cell and the other comes from the mother's ovum. The two alleles for a specific characteristic may be alike. For example, both alleles for hair color may contain the genetic code for black hair, and geneticists call such similar pairs *homo-*

zygous. When one allele is different from the other, the pair is called *heterozygous.* When the two alleles are dissimilar, one of them is likely to be *dominant* over the other. The other allele, which will remain unexpressed, is then called *recessive.* An example of dominance can be seen in the following situation: If the gene for black hair is dominant and one allele or gene in the pair is for black hair and the other gene is for blond hair, the child will be heterozygous for hair color and will appear to have black hair. Although the blond gene may not appear in one generation, it is possible to pass it on to the other generations. If, for example, the heterozygous black-haired person married another heterozygous black-haired person, there would be a 25 percent chance that the recessive trait would be expressed in a child with blond hair. When a pair of genes of a heterozygous black-haired person separates to form a sperm cell or an egg cell, the gamete may carry the gene for either black or blond hair. Therefore, even though one or both of the parents may appear to have black hair, the gametes could still be carrying genes for blond hair.

Another principle of heredity is called *random assortment,* which means that

Figure 3-3.   The number of possible genetic combinations is so large that it is unlikely that any two people will ever have exactly the same pattern of genes. One exception, however, is identical twins, who have identical chromosomes and genes. (Photo by Mary M. Duncan)

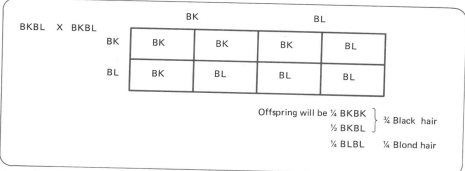

Figure 3-4. Probability of inheritance of hair color from parents heterozygous for black and blond hair. In this example, black hair is considered to be dominant and blond hair recessive.

genes for different traits such as hair or eye color operate separately (unless they are located near each other on the same chromosome). The determination of traits is thus an independent process, and a person who has black hair will not necessarily also have dark eyes. The person may have blue or hazel or brown eyes (see Figure 3-4).

Variations in Inheritance

Geneticists have observed that there is an enormous number of possible genetic combinations. So many, in fact, that every person (except identical twins) is biologically different from any other past, present, or future person in the universe! This is because each sperm and egg cell is likely to carry different combinations of genes. Furthermore, during meiosis, just before the cells divide, the chromosomes line up in pairs and either or both of the genes of a pair cross over to the opposite chromosome. In this "crossing-over" process there is an additional shuffle of genes as they become part of a sperm or egg cell.

Because of all of the random possibilities, each child will have a unique mixture of genes. We have all heard someone say, "She's got her father's eyes, her mother's nose, her grandmother's hands." But have you ever wondered how unlikely it would be for a child to have *all* of the characteristics of *only* one parent? Figure 3-5 shows some of the possible facial features that have been known to be genetic.

The Determination of Sex

A child's sex, like any other characteristic, is determined by a chance assortment of chromosomes (see Figure 3-6). In the case of sex, however, it is the father's

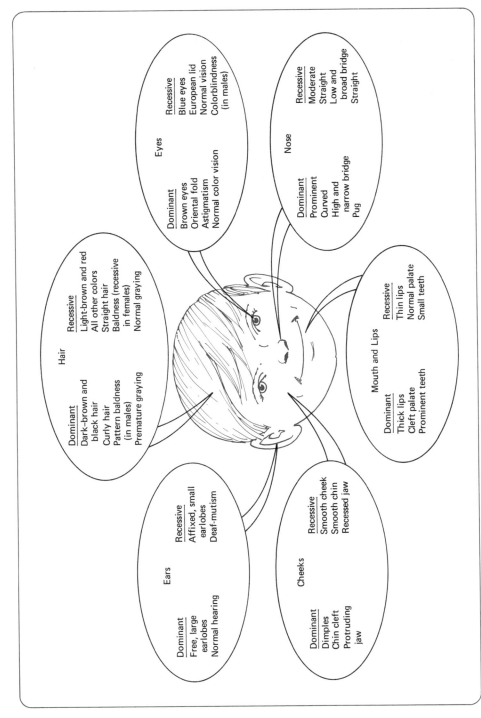

Figure 3-5. Dominant and recessive facial characteristics.

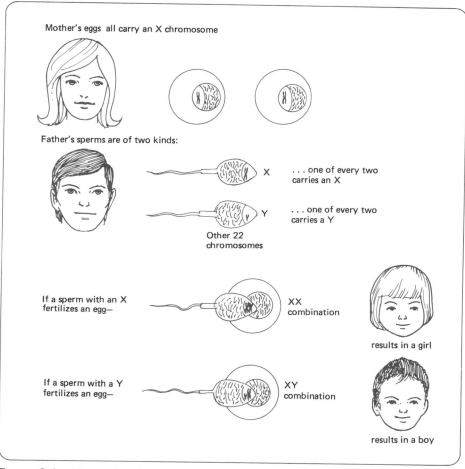

Mother's eggs all carry an X chromosome

Father's sperms are of two kinds:

X   . . . one of every two carries an X

Y   . . . one of every two carries a Y

Other 22 chromosomes

If a sperm with an X fertilizes an egg—   XX combination   results in a girl

If a sperm with a Y fertilizes an egg—   XY combination   results in a boy

Figure 3-6.   How a baby's sex is determined. (After Avram Scheinfeld, *Heredity in humans*. Philadelphia: Lippincott, 1972. By permission of the author.)

chromosomes that will determine whether a child will be a girl or a boy. Of the 23 chromosome pairs, one pair is responsible for sex characteristics. Each gamete has a specific pair of chromosomes known as the sex chromosomes. In men the pair is called an XY pair, and in women the pair is called the XX chromosome pair.

During meiosis, when the male gamete divides and produces two sperm cells, one of the cells receives an X chromosome from the pair and one of the sperms receives the Y chromosome. Therefore, half of the sperm carry X chromosomes and the other half carry Y chromosomes. When the female germ cell splits to form two ova, each one contains an X chromosome. If an ovum is fertilized by a sperm carrying a Y chromosome, the resulting XY pair will produce a boy. If an X-bearing chromosome fertilizes the egg, the resulting XX pair will produce a girl. Therefore, the sperm cell determines the sex of the child, since the egg cell contains only X chromosomes.

Heredity and Problems of Development

Many hereditary factors are easily visible in a child's outward appearance. There are other physical characteristics that are not so obvious, such as metabolic rate, blood type, immunity and resistance to disease, susceptibility to heat and cold, and the structure and functioning of body organs. All physical characteristics, however, are likely to be modified somewhat by environmental influences.

Many diseases and handicaps are now known to result from genetic influences. Genetic influences can cause defects in such areas as vision and hearing, the circulatory system, and the central nervous system. Because of these defects and others which can affect behavior, some researchers believe that certain forms of mental disorder might also be inherited (Mendlewicz, Fliess, & Fieve, 1972).

One example of a genetic disease that causes mental retardation is *phenylketonuria* or PKU. PKU results from the lack of an enzyme needed to process *phenylalanine,* a substance found in milk products. When the enzyme is missing, an acid called phenylpyruvic acid rises to poisonous levels and causes brain damage. If an infant is found to have inherited PKU, he or she can be placed on a diet which is low in phenylalanine and the damage of PKU can be prevented. Fortu-

Figure 3-7.   There are numerous family resemblances among the members of this multigenerational family. Notice, however, that there are also important differences among these close relatives. (Photo by Mary M. Duncan)

Table 3-1
SOME COMMON BIRTH DEFECTS IN THE U.S.A.

Birth Defect	Annual Incidence*	Prevalence†	Cause	Detection	Treatment
Down's Syndrome	3,500	30,000	chromosomal abnormality	chromosome analysis, amniocentesis	corrective surgery, physical training, and schooling
Low birth-weight prematurity	50,000	unknown	hereditary and/or environmental: poor prenatal care	prenatal monitoring, inspection at birth	intensive care of new-born, high nutritional diet
Muscular dystrophy	unknown	200,000	hereditary, often recessive	apparent at onset	physical therapy
Cleft lip and palate	4,300	71,000	hereditary and environmental	visual inspection at birth	corrective surgery
Cystic fibrosis	2,000	10,000	hereditary, recessive	sweat and blood tests	treat respiratory and digestive complications
Sickle cell anemia	1,200	16,000	hereditary, incomplete dominance, occurs mainly in Black people	blood test	medication, transfusions
Phenylketonuria (PKU)	310	3,100	hereditary, recessive	blood test	special diet
Spina bifida and/or hydrocephalus (water on the brain)	6,200	53,000	hereditary and environmental	prenatal X ray, maternal blood test, ultrasound	corrective surgery, physical training, schooling
Diabetes mellitus	unknown (late appearing)	90,000	hereditary and/or environmental	appears in childhood or later, urine tests	oral medication, diet, insulin injections
Hemophilia	1,200	12,400	hereditary, sex-linked recessive	blood test	medication, transfusions

Adapted from The March of Dimes, *Birth Defects: The Tragedy and the Hope.* White Plains, New York: The National Foundation of the March of Dimes, 1978. Reprinted with the permission of the March of Dimes.
*The number of new cases diagnosed within a specific time period (1978 data).
† Total number of living people less than 20 years of age who are diagnosed as having the disorder.

77

nately, the disease is rare and we now have several effective methods of detecting PKU at birth (Formentin, Mack & Hockey, 1972).

The list of genetic defects in humans is such a long one that many physicians believe that, since most infectious diseases can now be treated or prevented, genetic diseases will become the major health problem in modern society. At present we can counsel people about the possibility of genetic defects, but we cannot yet replace or alter defective genes (Friedmann & Roblin, 1972). *Table 3-1* lists and describes some common genetic diseases.

Some genetic defects are called *sex-linked defects* because they appear in only one sex, and the genes for these disorders are carried on the X chromosomes. Two examples of such defects are color blindness and hemophilia, an inability to form adequate blood clots when injured. These two diseases are caused by recessive genes contained in the X chromosomes; Y chromosomes cannot carry these genes. Because of this, there are disorders that may be carried on a mother's chromosomes but only expressed in boys. If a defective X chromosome is paired with a Y chromosome which is normal, the result will be a boy with color-blindness or hemophilia. If a defective X chromosome is paired with a normal X chromosome, the resulting girl will not develop hemophilia or color blindness, but she will be a *carrier* of a defective gene and may pass this gene along to her male descendents. Hemophilia has plagued the royal families of Europe for several centuries. Some European princes were hemophiliacs, and some queens and princesses were known carriers of hemophilia genes.

Another genetic problem, which affects about one in twelve pregnancies, is related to the inheritance of the genes for a blood factor known as the *Rh* or *rhesus* factor (since it was originally found in Rhesus monkeys). Most people in the population have *Rh positive* (*Rh +*) blood, but about 15 percent of the population has *Rh negative* (*Rh −*) blood (see Figure 3-8). No difficulties will arise if a mother has Rh+ blood regardless of the father's blood type, because Rh+ is a dominant characteristic. If both parents' Rh factors are positive *or* both are negative, there will be no harmful effects. If the father has Rh+ blood and the mother has Rh− blood, however, there may be a problem of blood incompatibility because the fetus will have some of its blood cells destroyed by antibodies from the mother's Rh− blood factor. The resulting disease is called *erythroblastosis fetalis,* and it can cause serious anemia and resulting brain damage.

It is possible to give blood tests to the parents during or before pregnancy so that they can be alerted to any blood incompatibility. During pregnancy, it is possible to obtain a sample of amniotic fluid through the technique of *amniocentesis* in order to detect if the child has erythroblastosis. Delivery may be induced if the child has erythroblastosis, and the newborn child can be given a blood transfusion which will prevent the harmful effects of the disease. Since the mother with Rh− blood does not usually build up a high enough level of blood-destroying antibodies in her first pregnancy to harm her firstborn child, she may be injected with a drug called *Rhogam* around the time of her first delivery which will reduce the possibilities of blood incompatibilities in later pregnancies.

Sometimes defects are the result of entire chromosomes that are defective. One

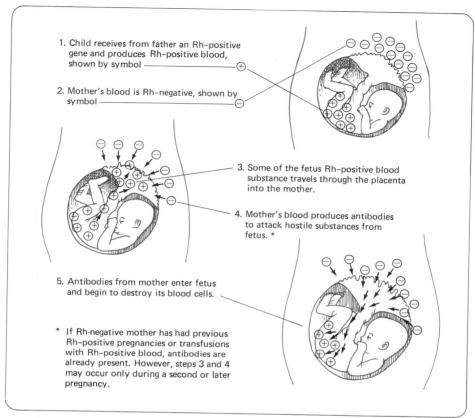

1. Child receives from father an Rh-positive gene and produces Rh-positive blood, shown by symbol ⊕

2. Mother's blood is Rh-negative, shown by symbol ⊖

3. Some of the fetus Rh-positive blood substance travels through the placenta into the mother.

4. Mother's blood produces antibodies to attack hostile substances from fetus. *

5. Antibodies from mother enter fetus and begin to destroy its blood cells.

* If Rh-negative mother has had previous Rh-positive pregnancies or transfusions with Rh-positive blood, antibodies are already present. However, steps 3 and 4 may occur only during a second or later pregnancy.

Figure 3-8. How an Rh-diseased baby is produced. (From Avram Scheinfeld, *Heredity in humans*. Philadelphia: Lippincott, 1972. By permission of the author.)

kind of chromosomal defect is *trisomy,* in which there are 47 instead of 46 chromosomes. In one type of trisomy, a 47th chromosome is formed when the 21st chromosome pair fails to separate during meiosis. The child obtains two chromosomes from the mother and one chromosome from the father for the 21st chromosome location. This is known as *Down's Syndrome* (formerly referred to as *Mongolism*), in which the afflicted child suffers mental retardation, has an abnormal white blood cell count, and an abnormal eye-fold pattern.

Another form of trisomy is one in which a man may have an extra Y chromosome (Ferrier, Ferrier & Kelley, 1970; McClearn, 1971). It was previously thought that men with the XYY pattern, who are taller than the average man and who also have rather high rates of criminal arrest records, were biologically predisposed to hyperaggressive behavior (Hook & Kim, 1971; Harrison & Tennent, 1972). New research, however, has shown that XYY men typically have lower than average intelligence test scores. It is possible that their poor social judgment might get them into more trouble with the law. Most of these men, if they are criminals, do not commit crimes of violence, but commit crimes against property such as theft and burglary (Witkin, Goodenough & Hirschorn, 1977). Many do not commit any crimes at all. It should not be overlooked that many physical difficulties may make it more difficult for a person to cope with society's demands in an effective way. The case of XYY research shows that the effects of genetic and chromosomal defects may be quite indirect.

HOW A LIFE BEGINS

Fertilization and Initial Development

Fertilization takes place in the Fallopian tubes. Out of millions of sperm cells, only one passes through the clear substance that covers the ovum and its membrane. The surviving sperm can enter at any point on the ovum's surface. After the head of the sperm enters, the tail is lost and only a cell nucleus with 23 chromosomes remains.*

As the sperm enters the ovum, the protoplasm within the ovum begins to move and nuclear material (a pronucleus) with 23 chromosomes migrates to the center to meet the pronucleus and the 23 chromosomes of the sperm. The fertilized ovum, the *zygote,* now has 46 chromosomes and will soon begin the process of division called mitosis (Thompson & Wilde, 1973).

Division of the newly fertilized cell, or zygote, takes place in about 36 hours, and after that the rate of cell division increases rapidly. This process causes the completely fertilized cell to gradually pinch together in the middle and then divide into two separate cells. These cells then become separate entities and are held together in a cluster (Ville, 1966).

Sometimes the two cells that result from the first division of the zygote separate entirely and, instead of remaining in a single cluster, they may begin to form two separate zygotes. Identical twins develop in this way, and their heredity is exactly the same. The production of identical twins is unusual and the cause of such development is mysterious, because ordinarily twins come from two separate eggs that have been fertilized by two separate sperm. This more usual type of twins is called *fraternal* or *dizygotic* twins, and they are no more alike in hereditary characteristics than any other pair of brothers or sisters.

In the normal course of events, further cell division takes place. By the fourth day the cells have continued to divide until they have formed a *morula,* a roundish mass that looks somewhat like a mulberry (see Figure 3-9). Around the fourth day the morula migrates from the Fallopian tubes toward the uterus. At first the cells

---

*This and the following description of events during the prenatal period of development is based in part on the valuable work of Roberts Rugh and Landrum B. Shettles, *From Conception to Birth* (New York: Harper & Row, 1971).

are nourished by the yolk of the ovum, but when this disappears new nutrients must be supplied by the mother. Once it arrives in the uterus, the hollow sphere of cells is called the *blastula.* Some of the blastula's cells will become the embryo itself while other cells will become part of the *placenta,* a network of blood vessels and tissue that will exchange nutrients and wastes between mother and fetus.

By the ninth day the blastula becomes embedded in the wall of the uterus, and a mass of cells called the *blastoderm* forms on one side. This blastoderm has two layers: an outer layer called the *ectoderm,* which will become the brain, the spinal cord, the sense organs, and the skin; and an inner layer called the *endoderm,* which will become the lining of the digestive tract. Later, a middle layer called the *mesoderm* develops, which eventually will become the skeletal and muscular systems, as well as some internal organs.

Soon the blastula becomes the embryo. During the embryonic period, from the second through the seventh week after conception, the embryo starts to form the various body organs.

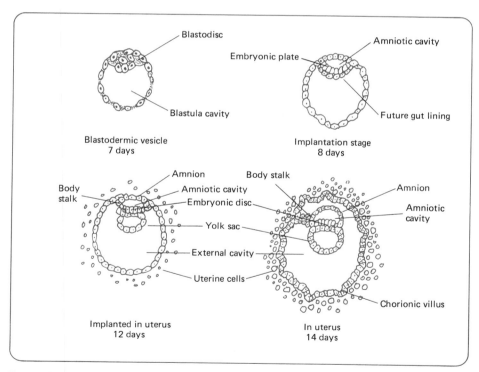

Figure 3-9.   The first two weeks of embryonic development. (From R. Rugh and L. B. Shettles, *From conception to birth.* New York: Harper & Row, 1971. By permission of the estate of Dr. Roberts Rugh.)

Structures and Processes Essential for Development

By the tenth day the embryo is firmly attached to the wall of the uterus. The blood vessels of the uterus are filled with an unusual amount of blood, and the glands in the uterine lining become highly active. As small blood vessels rupture, the uterine tissues secrete a substance called *glycogen,* which is converted into glucose and serves as a nutrient for the growing embryo.

Cells around the blastula form several protective membranes: an outer membrane called the *chorion,* which aids in carrying out exchanges of food and waste products between the embryo and the mother; and the *amnion,* which encloses the amniotic fluid that provides a protective cushion around the embryo.

The *placenta* began to form when the embryo buried itself in the uterine wall. The embryo is connected to the placenta by an *umbilical cord,* a pipeline to the mother which contains two arteries and one vein to carry nutrients and waste products between the mother and the developing child. In addition, the placenta has a role in hormonal functioning and is believed to contribute to the process of labor and birth. At this point, the mechanisms for nourishing the embryo have been established.

THE PROCESSES OF EMBRYONIC AND FETAL DEVELOPMENT AND CHILDBIRTH

So far we have dealt with the events that occur during conception and in the two weeks immediately after conception. We have seen that the ovum is transformed from a zygote to a morula, then to a blastula and, finally, it becomes an embryo embedded in the uterine wall. We shall now look further into the process of embryonic development.

The Growth of the Embryo

The embryonic period is brief, but the essential development of the body organs begins in this period. At the beginning of the embryonic period (at about 18 to 21 days), a neural groove is formed, from which the brain, the spinal cord, and the nerves will eventually develop. At about 22 days, the muscular system also forms, and the nerve and muscle cells then form the heart (see Figure 3-10). Thus, in a little over one month's time, a progression occurs from the joining of the sperm and ovum to the formation of an embryo with several million cells (Eichorn, 1970).

Fetal Development

At the end of the first month, the embryo is about one-fifth of an inch long. By the end of the seventh week after conception, or the fifth week of the embryonic period, the *fetus* is formed. The nervous system has branched out to all parts of

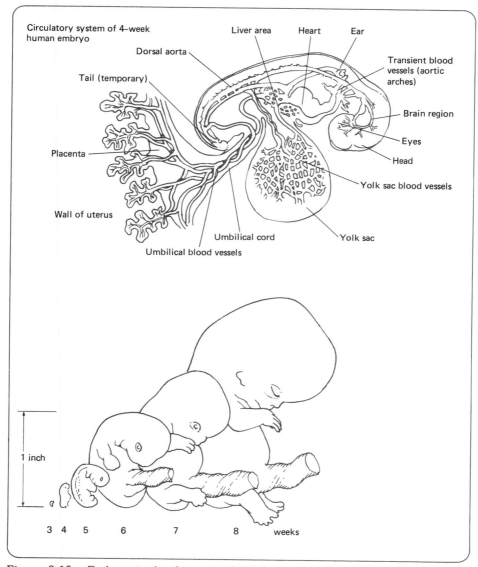

Figure 3-10.　Embryonic development, third through eighth weeks. (From R. Rugh and L. B. Shettles, *From conception to birth*. New York: Harper & Row, 1971. By permission of the estate of Dr. Roberts Rugh.)

the body. The outline of eyes, ears, and nose can be easily seen, and the beginnings of the arms and legs become visible.

At the end of the second month many more changes have taken place. The length of the fetus has increased to about 1½ inches from head to buttocks; it weighs about 1/13 ounce; its limbs, including hands and feet are formed; and it has enough muscular development to make some reflex movements possible. In the second month, since all the organ systems have been started, the individual has achieved a degree of completeness that marks the fetal stage. The fetus appears to be clearly human in appearance, although the head area is so large that it makes up about half the length of the fetus.

By the end of the first three months, or trimester, of pregnancy, the following physical milestones have been reached: the fetus is about 3 inches long; the brain has grown until the main divisions of the brain at that time are much the same as they will be at birth; the head can turn; and if the fetus is touched, it will feel sensations on the forehead, skin, and other parts of the body. The fetus has also started some sucking movements and other movements that will be important in breathing. Thus, by the end of three months, the fetus has developed its major body systems and is nearing completion as an individual, although it still cannot survive outside of the mother's body.

In the next three months, rapid development continues and the bones begin to form. The first bone to form is the breastbone. As the bones form, they soon contain enough calcium for X-rays to reveal a skeleton consisting of 222 bones. Because of the rapid rate of bone growth, mothers need more than the ordinary amounts of calcium. By the end of the sixth month, the fetus is between 10 and 12 inches long and weighs about 1½ pounds.

The last three months is important because the sexual development of the fetus is completed in this stage. In the first three months, the sex of the fetus is difficult to determine, but during the last three months, the differences are quite visible. By this time the testes in the male have descended into the scrotum (Jost, 1970).

In the eighth month the fetus weighs between 4 and 5 pounds and has developed a fat layer that covers the body. The fetus is between 19 and 20 inches long. It is usually resting in an upside-down position in the uterus, and this seems to be the best position for delivery (see Figure 3-11). The fetus' body movements may have contributed to its arrival in this position. But since the head is also the heaviest part of the fetus' body, the head-down position may be due to gravity. In general, the fetus' movements are limited because of its increased size. Its growth rate also slows down in the last few weeks before birth, and there are changes in the placenta. By 40 weeks, the fetus is ready to be born, and a new phase of development begins.

Birth and Perinatal Events

The Birth Process.   The birth process can be divided into three periods: *labor, delivery,* and *afterbirth.* The first period is the *labor* stage, in which muscle contractions of the uterus move the fetus along the birth canal. The second period is known as *delivery,* in which the fetus passes through the birth canal and emerges as a newborn infant. The third phase is one in which the placenta and membranes are expelled from the birth canal as an *afterbirth.*

In the nine months of pregnancy, the tissues of the mother's cervix have helped to keep the fetus within the uterus. When it is time for birth, the cervix is stretched by labor contractions while simultaneously relaxed by hormones secreted by the

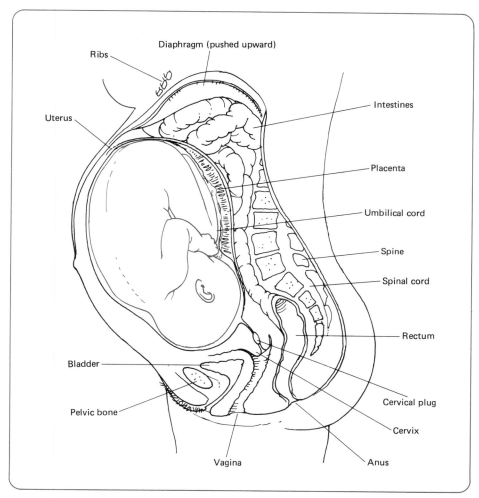

Figure 3-11. Position of the fetus about one month before birth. (From R. Rugh and L. B. Shettles, *From conception to birth.* New York: Harper & Row, 1971. By permission of the estate of Dr. Roberts Rugh.)

ovaries. The vagina secretes glycogen that turns to glucose and lactic acid, which seems to have antibacterial properties that protect the mother and infant. In the beginning of labor, birth contractions are minimal and may last from 15 to 20 seconds. At first the contractions are about 10 to 15 minutes apart but, a short time later, they occur in 3 to 5 minute intervals, become stronger, and last for longer periods of time. The entire process of labor usually lasts from 7 to 12 hours. For firstborn children, the process may last from 16 to 18 hours (Jolly, 1972).

The second stage, *delivery,* lasts from 30 minutes to 2 hours and begins when the infant's head passes through the cervix. At this time, it is usual for the amniotic

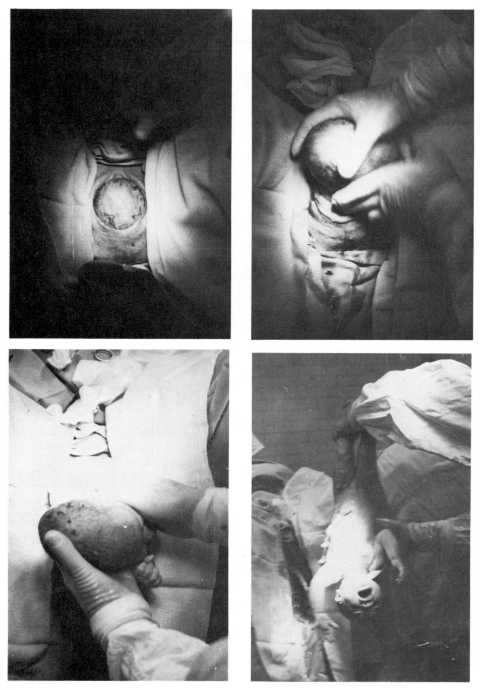

Figure 3-12.   The birth process. (Photographs by Dr. Landrum B. Shettles)

sac to rupture and allow the amniotic fluid to drain away from the fetus (sometimes called the "breaking of the waters"). Contractions of the uterus come about 2 to 3 minutes apart and last for about one minute. As the head emerges, however, the contractions become almost continuous. Once the infant's head is through the birth canal, the body passes through easily. Immediately upon birth, the infant is cleaned and given to the mother—a moment that is one of the most remarkable and significant human experiences.

After the child is born, the placenta separates from the uterus and is expelled by contractions of the uterus and abdominal muscles. The *afterbirth* contractions of the uterine muscles also aid in closing many blood vessels and reduce hemorrhaging.

The Newborn.   The newborn infant, or *neonate,* now must begin life as a separate person. At the moment of birth, the infant's lungs are filled with some mucous and amniotic fluid and must be cleared. Soon a concentration of carbon dioxide builds up in the infant's bloodstream, and this increase causes the muscles controlling the rib cage and diaphragm to contract and fill the lungs with air. The infant also has to exhale, and most babies usually cry when they first exhale. The first cries are good indicators that the lungs are functioning properly. Their breathing rate is rapid at first, and the newborn usually breathes about 45 times per minute. Gradually, however, the breathing rate decreases to about 18 to 25 times per minute.

The infant's circulatory system must undergo rapid change, because at birth blood is directed to the lungs for oxygenation for the first time. The infant's heart increases its workload, too, partly because of increased body activity, to a rate of 125 to 130 beats per minute.

Before birth the infant's kidneys develop the capacity to function, but they are not activated because the fetus' wastes are taken care of by the placenta and are eventually eliminated by the mother's kidneys. Since there is an inadequate amount of kidney functioning shortly after birth, infants are usually not given water for the first 6 to 8 hours. They experience a small amount of dehydration, but after this initial period they are often given a 5 percent solution of sugar water.

Control of body temperature is carried out by a center in the brain, but in the newborn the center does not function efficiently and the baby's body heat is inadequate. Body temperature is also affected by food intake, but since the infant's temperature regulation center, circulatory system, and digestive tract are not completely functioning, the baby has to rely on its layer of body fat for both energy and insulation. The body temperature of the newborn can be expected to drop about 2 to 5 degrees immediately after birth while the infant body makes necessary adjustments. Within a few hours, however, the temperature rises to its normal level.

In the first two days after birth, the mother's breasts secrete a pre-milk substance called *colostrum* until milk becomes available on the fourth day. The mother's milk contains milk fat, protein, and lactose and is usually a nearly complete diet for the infant. If the mother decides not to breastfeed the infant, bottle formulas that imitate the composition of mother's milk are given to the baby. Thus, normal infants are

Box   3-1
The Apgar Scale: Rating the Health of a Newborn Infant*

Dr. Virginia Apgar developed a rating system for evaluating the health of newborn infants. The Apgar scale is used throughout the world and is usually given twice: at one minute after the baby is born and then again at five minutes after birth. An Apgar score of 10 indicates that the infant is in excellent health; a score of 7 to 9 indicates good health; a score of 4 to 6 is considered fair. A score of 0 to 3 is extremely poor and, if living, the child will need intensive emergency care.

The Apgar scoring system is presented below. Each infant is rated on each of the five categories and can receive a score between zero and ten.

Apgar Scoring Chart

Sign	0 points	1 point	2 points
Heart rate	None detectable	Slow ($<$ 100)	Over 100
Respiratory effort	Absent	Slow; irregular	Good; crying
Muscle tone	Flaccid (limp)	Some flexion of arms and legs	Active motion
Reflex irritability	No response	Cry and grimace	Strong cry
Color	Blue, pale	Body pink; arms and legs blue	Completely pink

*Adapted from Apgar, V., "A proposal for a new method of evaluation of the newborn infant," *Current Research in Anesthesia and Analgesia*, 1953, *32*, 260–267; and Apgar, V., and James, L. S., "Further observations on the newborn scoring system," *American Journal of Diseases of Children*, 1962, *104*, 419–428.

introduced into a new existence in which their bodies must function adequately for their own life support.

Unfortunately, for some infants and their mothers, pregnancy and childbirth may have abnormalities and difficulties. Let's look at some of the causes of problems in the embryonic and fetal periods and also explore some methods available for preventing such difficulties. In considering these hazards to development, we will return to our discussion of fetal development and trace the effects of environmental influences that make their way to the fetus even though it is protected, to some degree, by the mother's body.

INFLUENCES ON FETAL DEVELOPMENT

There are more hazards to the infant's health in the first three months of pregnancy than at any other time because the embryo that develops during this period is easily affected by harmful influences. Interruptions or delays in development in the first three months can have very serious effects later on. Therefore, the effects of disease, drugs, or accidents are considered to be particularly serious at this time. If the mother contracts a disease such as *rubella,* or German measles, during the first three months, it is likely that there will be some harmful effects. This disease is often considered to be serious enough to form the basis for a therapeutic abortion.

Maternal Age

People often do not consider the mother's age at pregnancy to be a risk to fetal development. Definite decisions about the ideal age to become a parent have to

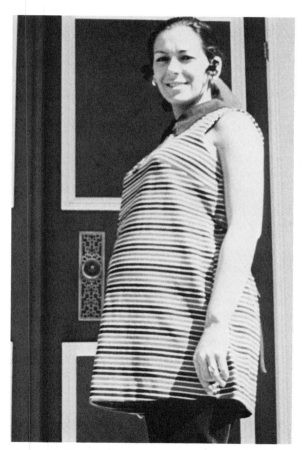

Figure 3-13. Modern research on prenatal influences on later development will enable this future mother to maximize the chances that her infant will enjoy a healthy infancy and childhood.

be made cautiously, but current research indicates that women in their twenties seem to be at the best age for childbearing. Many younger and older women bear children, of course, but the chances of disorders for both mother and child are greater in very early and very late pregnancies (Rugh & Shettles, 1971). The probability of miscarriages, delivery difficulties, fetal defects, and pregnancy complications occur more often outside the age span of 18 to 38, especially among women in adolescence and in their forties. Down's syndrome, discussed earlier, seems to occur much more frequently in the infants of older mothers.

Maternal Nutrition

An old saying cautions mothers to eat "for two" during pregnancy. Modern nutritionists have, however, questioned the wisdom of this saying. The average woman needs about 2300 calories each day when not pregnant and, since many women are actually less active during pregnancy, a reduction in caloric intake may be desirable for some women. If the amount of food consumed becomes excessive, the resulting overweight condition may be dangerous both to the mother's health and to the delivery of her baby. The developing child needs nutrients, and an estimate of about 2600 calories per day is a normal average intake during pregnancy. Although this relatively small increase in food is not radically different from a woman's usual diet, care must be taken to ensure that the mother and fetus will obtain adequate amounts of protein, vitamins, and minerals rather than empty calories from fattening but non-nutritive food.

An adequate diet during pregnancy is necessary because nutritional deficiencies can prolong labor, delay maternal recovery, and increase the likelihood of miscarriages, stillbirths, and prematurity. Illnesses in newborns are also more frequent if the mother has been malnourished during her pregnancy. To prevent malnourishment, pregnancy diets are often enriched with added vitamins and minerals.

Adjusting the diet may be very tricky because the nausea that some women experience during pregnancy may interfere with adequate food intake. In addition, some women develop cravings for specific foods and this may result in overindulgence. The reasons for unusual desires for certain foods are unclear, but the desires are thought to stem from dietary deficiencies. Satisfying the craving may be unwise because too much food can create hazards but, on the other hand, too little food can reduce the birth weight of the infant.

An infant's weight at birth is generally considered to be normal if it falls between 6 and 8 pounds. In order to reach this average, pregnant women should ordinarily gain between 15 to 20 pounds, but definite weight recommendations should be tailored to the woman's own specific nutritional needs by her physician.

Research on human pregnancies must be done with a great deal of caution. Investigations obviously cannot experiment with diets that are deliberately deficient. Animal research studies on the effects of dietary deficiencies show, however, that both the mother and fetus can be affected (Slob, Snow, & de Natris-Mathot, 1973).

Hormonal Effects

An interesting research problem in human development concerns the effects of hormones on the developing body. Hormones from the mother and the fetus are most likely to interact in prenatal development, and because these powerful substances have a significant effect on the developing fetus, we should pay attention to them. One of the observed effects of maternal hormones on fetuses is the enlargement of the mammary glands in both boy and girl fetuses when *prolactin,* a hormone that stimulates the mother's own breasts, is present in the fetal bloodstream. Most of the endocrine glands in the fetus begin to function during the second three months, and it is likely that the fetal pituitary gland begins to function in the fourth or fifth month. Hormones from the pituitary gland stimulate the thyroid gland to secrete a substance called *thyroxin,* which is necessary for brain development and the production of proteins needed for the nervous system.

Sex hormones are usually secreted by the ovaries and testes, but they may also be released from the placenta and the adrenal glands. Generally, male sex hormones, or *androgens,* are produced in the testes and female sex hormones, or *estrogens,* are produced in the ovaries and placenta. Another hormone group, the *progestins,* which are required for proper conditions in pregnancy, are produced in the ovaries and the placenta (Andersen, 1966; Russell & Warburton, 1973). The functions of these hormones are complex and, as mentioned, separation of hormones into those produced by the mother and those produced by the fetus has not been clearly established.

During the second three months of pregnancy, the sexual organs of the fetus begin to develop as the end result of the hormonal activity of the endocrine glands. In the female fetus the two Fallopian tubes merge to form a uterus, accompanied by the formation of a cervical canal and a vagina. At first, the external sexual organs look similar in both male and female fetuses, but later the original sexual structures differentiate into a penis in the male and a clitoris in the female fetus.

In some cases, chromosomal and hormonal conditions will affect sexual development. For example, in a disorder known as *Turner's syndrome,* there is only a single X chromosome. The person with Turner's syndrome develops ovaries, but they are deficient in sex hormones. These people look like very short, sexually immature women (Poenaru, Stanesco, Poenaru, & Stoian, 1970). Other deviations from typical sexual development come from genetic causes and result in lack of hormones or inadequate amounts of hormones. Fortunately, these conditions are fairly infrequent.

Other substances can create far-reaching damage to the fetus, as we shall see in the next section.

Drug Effects on the Developing Fetus

Today many researchers have been particularly interested in finding out how various chemical compounds can be passed from the mother's body to the fetus.

Although the bloodstream of the embryo and the mother are actually separated, the placenta's membranes allow some very small particles to pass into each of the bloodstreams. Blood cells are too large to pass through the placental membranes, but these membranes will permit oxygen and nutrients to go from mother to fetus, and they will allow wastes and carbon dioxide to pass from the fetus into the mother's bloodstream. Because people use large amounts of all kinds of drugs today and because we are exposed to an increasing number of manufactured chemical compounds, it is important to know how drugs can affect the fetus.

Recent studies have shown that the placenta does not provide as complete a barrier to drugs taken by the mother as was formerly believed. One incident in the 1960s which spurred a number of drug research projects was associated with the use of *thalidomide*, a tranquilizing drug that produced many birth defects in the children of mothers who used the drug.

Table   3-2
THE EFFECTS OF DRUGS TAKEN DURING PREGNANCY ON THE HEALTH OF THE FETUS*

Drug	Effect on Fetus and Newborn
Adrenaline	Rapid, irregular heartbeat
Androgens (male hormones)	Masculinization of fetus
Anaesthetics	Depression of fetal activity, asphyxia
Antihistamines	Miscarriage or malformations
Aspirin	Neonatal bleeding, abnormal heart
Barbiturates	Depressed breathing, drowsy fetus affected as long as 6 days
Blood pressure depressants	Respiratory problems, death
Demerol	Brain damage (?)
Estrogens (female hormones)	Malformations, hyperactivity of fetal adrenal glands
Heroin and morphine	Convulsions, tremor (shaking), neonatal death
Insulin shock	Fetal loss
Lead	Anemia, hemorrhaging, miscarriage
LSD	Possible chromosomal abnormalities (?)
Phenothiazines (thorazine, compazine, stelazine, etc.)	Hyperbilirubinemia (?)
Progestins (used in birth control pills)	Masculinization of females
Smoking (nicotine)	Stunting, accelerated heartbeat, premature birth, organ congestion, fits and convulsions
Sodium seconal (a barbiturate)	Electrical depression of brain waves
Tranquilizers	Retarded depression

*Adapted from Rugh, R., and Shettles, L. G. *From Conception to Birth*. New York: Harper and Row, 1971. By permission of the estate of Dr. Robert Rugh.

Drugs that can harm a fetus are considered by many physicians to be a much greater threat to the fetus' health than infectious diseases. Because the use of both addictive and psychoactive drugs has increased in recent years, many research projects have focused on the use of these drugs. Harmful effects can come from the mother's use of alcohol, amphetamines, sedatives, tranquilizers, painkillers, and antibiotics. Some investigators also believe that cigarette smoking by the mother may be harmful to the fetus (Rugh & Shettles, 1971). Table 3-2 lists some of the drugs that are known or suspected to cause fetal damage. It is clear that drugs can have powerful effects on the developing embryo and fetus. It is wise to limit the use of drugs during pregnancy to those drugs which have been prescribed or approved by a physician.

Radiation Hazards

Radiation damage is a hazard to the developing fetus and, therefore, the effects of X-rays, fluoroscopic examinations, or radioactive elements cause concern. Low-level radiation from a dental X-ray and simple X-rays of body areas are not believed to be harmful, but intense or prolonged exposure to radiation may result in damage to the fetus' central nervous system. There are conflicting views considering safe radiation dosage levels. Some animal studies show that even small degrees of exposure can produce brain damage (Nash, 1973), and some investigators feel that even exposure to naturally occurring radiation can be hazardous.

The Effects of Disease

It is important to know whether certain diseases that the mother may contract can produce damage in the fetus (see Table 3-3). Although the placenta provides a barrier that prevents many infections from reaching the fetus, a number of infections and diseases can be transmitted through it. One such disease is *tuberculosis,* a disease caused by bacteria that affect the respiratory system but spread to other parts of the body as well. Another example is *toxoplasmosis,* a disease caused by a one-celled parasite found in mammals, birds, and human beings. This disease may have only a slight effect on the mother's lungs, but it may have serious effects on the fetus, including encephalitis, hydrocephaly (enlargement of the skull), hepatitis, and damage to the brain and heart.

Other diseases which are considered to be less serious children's diseases, such as chicken pox, measles, mumps, and scarlet fever, can infect and have harmful effects on the fetus. Epidemic diseases caused by viruses, such as some types of influenza, can also be hazardous. Most bacteria are too large to pass through the placental barrier (viruses are small enough to pass through), but their toxins or poisonous by-products may pass from the mother's bloodstream through the placenta to the fetus.

On the positive side, immunity to many diseases can be passed through the

Table   3-3
SOME MATERNAL INFECTIONS AFFECTING THE FETUS OR NEWBORN

Maternal Disease	Effects on Fetus or Newborn	Prevention
Acute bacterial infection	Prematurity	Early treatment
Tuberculosis	Congenital tuberculosis	Separation from mother
Specific Viral Infections		
Rubella (German measles)	Malformation	(see text)
Influenza (flu)	Malformations (?)	Immunization during epidemic (?)
Poliomyelitis (polio)	Polio	Maternal immunization
Chickenpox	Chickenpox	Isolate asymptomatic infant from mother
Mumps	Not established	Isolate asymptomatic infant from mother
Measles	Stillbirth; miscarriage	Maternal immunization
Nonspecific Viral Infections		
Upper respiratory infections	None	None
Severe viral infections	Prematurity (?)	None
Spirochetal Infections		
Syphilis	Congenital syphilis	Prenatal bloodtests and treatment

Sources for this table were: Rugh, R., & Shettles, L. B. *From Conception to Birth.* New York: Harper and Row, 1971, and *Proceedings of the White House Conference on Mental Retardation,* U. S. Government Printing Office, Washington D.C., 1963.

placenta because many antibodies are small enough to pass through. Some immunity to measles, mumps, polio, smallpox, and various respiratory illnesses may be acquired in this way. This passive immunity can sometimes last for six months after birth and may also provide some protection against pneumonia, scarlet fever, typhoid, and some streptococcal and staphylococcal toxins. Because many diseases can now be prevented, infectious diseases are less of a problem today than they were in earlier times.

The relatively mild effects of *rubella,* or German measles, on the mother can have a disastrous effect on the fetus. For example, infection of the mother during the first month of development might cause blindness, deafness, and multiple handicaps in the fetus. A vaccine is now available that can protect a person from rubella for up to three years. Since a live virus is used in the vaccine, it cannot be given during pregnancy for fear of damage to the fetus, but it can be given up to two months before conception. Pediatricians recommend that all children be vaccinated early, because this procedure will help to prevent women who have not yet been inoculated from contracting the disease from infected children.

Chronic diseases in the mother are also a problem. For example, diabetes, which results in an insufficient amount of insulin and abnormally high levels of blood sugar, may cause a 50 percent probability of abnormalities in the fetus. Modern medical care can, however, reduce the harmful effects of this disease as well as certain others.

The Problem of Premature Birth

Some infants are born prematurely, before the usual nine months of pregnancy. If the infant weighs less than 5½ pounds and has arrived well before the expected delivery date, the infant is often considered to be premature. The normal full-term pregnancy lasts for 266 days after conception. A fetus has a chance of survival after 7 months, but even at this time there are many hazards to the infant's life.

Several problems of prematurity are evident. The premature infant has great difficulty in breathing, regulating body temperature, and digesting food. The premature infant's brain may not have reached the level where it could control these functions (Bawkin & Bawkin, 1972). Considerable assistance can be given to the premature infant by providing sufficient oxygen, warmth in an incubator, and frequent food in small amounts.

By eight months, the probability of survival in premature infants increases to about 70 percent, although temperature control is still a problem and oxygen may have to be provided also. Food intake is less of a problem, but the infant is more likely to lose weight after birth than the normal-term infant. In part, this is because the digestive system cannot function adequately since the stomach, liver, and pancreas are still too immature.

Premature infants have a larger number of disorders than do full-term infants, with central nervous system disorders that affect muscle control among the most common problems (Lubshenko, Horner, Reed, Hix, Metcalf, Cohig, Elliot, & Bourg, 1967). It has been shown that a majority of the children in such studies have abnormal electroencephalogram (EEG, or brain wave) patterns which resemble the patterns usually found in convulsive disorders. The largest amount of EEG abnormality was found in children who suffered some degree of intellectual retardation; these difficulties may be the result of oxygen deprivation (anoxia) at birth or soon after. Inadequate oxygen supplies may result in the destruction of brain cells and may cause permanent brain damage. Several studies of premature infants indicated that an unusually high rate of myopia (nearsightedness) and strabismus (crossed eyes) was found in these children.

Among premature children there seems to be a high incidence of respiratory problems and infections following birth. Those infants who are born earliest seem to have the greatest number of infections. Investigators (Lubshenko, et al., 1969) found that when premature children reached school age, they showed a higher

Table   3-4
HIGH-RISK INFANTS

Family History
Presence of mutant genes
Central nervous system disorders
Low socioeconomic group

Previous defective sibling
Parents are close blood relatives
Intrafamilial emotional disorder

Medical History of Mother
Diabetes
Hypertension (high blood pressure)
Exposure to radiation

Heart or kidney diseases
Thyroid disease

Previous Obstetrical History of Mother
Toxemia
Miscarriage immediately preceding
  pregnancy
Size of infants

Large number of children prior to present
  child
Prolonged infertility

Present Pregnancy
Maternal age less than 18
  or greater than 38
Multiple births
Medications
Radiations

Maternal rubella in first three months of
  pregnancy
Diabetes
Toxemia
Fetal-maternal blood group incompatibility
Anaesthesia

Labor and Delivery
Absence of prenatal care
Prematurity
Postmaturity-dysmaturity

Precipitated, prolonged, or complicated
  delivery
Low Apgar score in first 5 minutes

Placental
Massive infarction of placenta
Placentitus

Neonatal
Single umbilical artery
Jaundice
Abnormal head size
Dehydration
Failure to regain birth weight by 10 days

Infection
Hypoxia (lack of oxygen)
Convulsions
Low birth weight
Survival following brain injury

Adapted from *Proceedings of the White House Conference on Mental Retardation*, U. S. Government Printing Office, Washington, D. C., 1963.

than average incidence of school problems and lower than average scores on intelligence tests. Even among those children who scored in the normal range of intelligence, there were frequent difficulties in mastering reading skills and numerical concepts. Because of such observations, a number of other researchers have concluded that premature birth may lead to a higher incidence of all kinds of problems when compared to full-term birth (Fitzhardinge, 1972). Other researchers believe that premature children may need more special learning and remediation opportunities than full-term children and that special programs might be arranged for such children and their parents (Scarr-Salapatek & Williams, 1973).

It should be clear that many different kinds of influences can damage the developing embryo and fetus. We have discussed problems that can arise because of genetic combinations, diseases, drug usage, and birth complications. We are just beginning to understand the roles of these *teratogenic* (literally, monster-producing) factors. Fortunately, most children develop normally, and there are some natural safeguards which protect children from potential hazards. Among these safeguards are the amniotic sac, the placental barrier, natural immunities passed on from the mother, and a natural tolerance for a moderate degree of oxygen deprivation at birth. Because of these protections and many more, most infants are born within the normal range of physical health and can start life in the world with adequate biological capability. Table 3-4 describes some of the factors that contribute to high birth defects in newborn infants. More research needs to be done on prenatal influences.

SUMMARY

In this chapter we have focused our attention on the large number of events that occur during the nine months preceding birth. We examined the role of heredity and have seen how the genes and chromosomes can influence a wide variety of both normal and abnormal traits. We then looked at the events of embryonic and fetal development and saw how the basic features of the human body are rapidly and accurately formed during the first few months of life. We looked at birth and delivery processes, and we discussed normal and abnormal births. Because the prenatal period, especially the first three months of pregnancy, is so critical for later development, we ended our examination of prenatal development with a discussion of hazards to normal development. In the next chapter we will turn to the typical behaviors and abilities of young infants.

RECOMMENDED READINGS

MacFarlane, A. *The Psychology of Childbirth*. Cambridge: Harvard University Press, 1977.

This book examines the delivery process and the social and emotional interactions between parents and newborns that take place during the first few days after birth.

Nilsson, L. *A Child is Born: The Drama of Life Before Birth*. New York: Delacorte, 1968.

This book was intended for future parents and contains some remarkably beautiful photographs of embryonic and fetal development.

Rugh, R., and Shettles, L. B. *From Conception to Birth: The Drama of LIfe's Beginnings.* New York: Harper & Row, 1971.

This book contains an extremely well-written and exciting text, as well as numerous diagrams, tables, and photographs. A modern classic on prenatal development.

Scheinfeld, A. *Heredity in Humans.* 2nd ed. Philadelphia: Lippincott, 1972.

This book is intended for the intelligent lay reader and provides a clear account of human genetics and genetic abnormalities.

4

Growth and Development in Infancy

In this chapter we shall consider the capabilities of infants, their physical growth, and the development of their skills. We shall pay special attention to their inborn characteristics for adaptation, and we shall examine how these characteristics are modified by experience.

THE CAPABILITIES OF INFANTS

What are the capabilities of infants? In order to provide appropriate opportunities for an infant's development, we need to know what these are. As we have indicated, Piaget emphasizes the importance of reflexes in the newborn infant and sees reflexes as the foundations for developing behavior. But what are the other skills that infants can use in interacting with their surroundings? What, for example, are the limits of their abilities in seeing, hearing, smelling, touching, and recognizing the positions of their own bodies? In answering these questions, we will examine some research that has been concerned with the sensory and perceptual capabilities of infants. We need to know about the ways in which infants are studied. We shall see what has already been found out and, more importantly, what we still do not know.

In addition to looking at research on sensory abilities, we will look at the overall development of the motor skills involved in reaching, sitting, crawling, and walking.

Infants' Reflex Behaviors—Adaptation and Maturation

Many of the newborn's early responses to the environment are reflexes. Most of these help the baby to survive, and among them the *sucking reflex* and the *rooting reflex* (turning the head and grasping things with the lips when touched on the cheek) are especially necessary in feeding. The *startle reflex* resulting from a loud noise, the *grasp reflex* of holding to a person's finger, the *withdrawal reflex* of moving away from pain or discomfort, and the *pupillary reflex* in which the pupil of the eye dilates in dim light and constricts to guard the eyes against too much light, may all be highly important in the infant's survival (Bijou & Baer, 1965; Curtis, Jacobson, & Marcus, 1972).

The sucking reflex is partly inborn, but it also is likely to be modified by the infant's learning experiences. Sucking is more than just an automatic, simple reflex, because infants will not suck under all conditions. If their stomachs are full and they become sleepy, they will refuse to respond to opportunities to nurse. On the other hand, if they are hungry they are likely to be alert and responsive to the opportunity to suck when it becomes available.

Although it looks simple, sucking is really a very complex activity. It is necessary for infants to coordinate the muscle movements of sucking, breathing, and swallowing. Swallowing is prompted by the amount of liquid in the infant's mouth, but it must take place between inhaling and exhaling. The intake of liquids must be adjusted to amounts that can comfortably be swallowed at the same time that adjustments are made for breathing. The complex nature of this activity has been investigated by researchers who have used X rays and other procedures to gain knowledge of this remarkable capability of the newborn infant.

Some insight into how infant sucking behaviors change with new conditions can be gained from a study which investigated how different temperature and body positions affected sucking. The infants in the study were bottle-fed, normal children ranging from 3 to 5 days old. Sucking pressure was measured in various test situations in which the infants were either lying down in horizontal positions or were supported at angles. Their cribs were open at the top, and were equipped with heating elements placed under the mattresses so that their crib temperatures could be raised up to 90°F. Sucking pressures were measured with pressure gauges connected by tubing to nipples. As the nipples remained in the infants' mouths for one minute, the peak of sucking pressure could be recorded. Results of the study showed that temperature, the infants' ages, and the time of the feeding period were all important factors in determining sucking pressure. During morning feedings, for example, sucking pressure was higher than during afternoon feedings; older infants demonstrated greater sucking pressures than younger infants; and crib temperatures higher than that of the room (80°F) caused the infants' sucking pressures to decrease. The investigator found no significant correlation, however, between sucking pressures and infants' body positions, sex, weight, or activity levels (Elder, 1970).

A study of infants' hand and thumb sucking by Kravitz and Boehm (1971) showed that hand sucking occurred in all the normal infants in their study. The infants were observed from the minute they were born, and 60 percent of them sucked their hands within the first hour of life. This early sucking of normal infants contrasts with the delayed sucking times of abnormal infants. Therefore, thumb and finger sucking may be signs of normal, healthy maturation of a baby's nervous system.

Another easily observed infant reflex is the *Moro reflex,* which occurs if the baby's head is allowed to fall backward or if the baby is exposed to other sudden movements. In the Moro reflex, the baby's arms spread out and then are quickly brought together across the chest in what is called a "grasp gesture." The reflex disappears after a few months, possibly because the brain's center of control is shifting from the brain stem to the more advanced cerebral cortex (the outer layer of the brain) that controls conscious processes such as perception, thought, and memory. As the cortex gains control, the more primitive brain stem loses control over this reflex. If, however, the Moro reflex happens to be present for longer than a few months, some nervous system disorder might be suspected. This explanation of the Moro reflex is still controversial, and the phenomenon has to be explored further (Kessen, Haith, & Salapatek, 1970).

The *Babinski reflex* is another well-known reflex in infancy. If the bottom of an infant's foot is stroked gently, or even touched, the toes spread outward. This reflex, like the Moro reflex, disappears at some time before six months. If an adult's or an older child's foot is tickled (go ahead—try it!), the toes will curl inward rather than outward, so that persistence of the Babinski reflex might also indicate neurological disorder.

Altogether, a rather large number of other reflexes can be demonstrated in the infant. Most of them disappear in time, but some continue and become important tools for later environmental interactions. One important reflex that continues is the ability to focus the eyes which is, of course, an essential in visual and perceptual development. Reflex behavior is often quite complicated and highly coordinated and shows us that the newborn child already has some elementary forms of organized behavior.

Position Senses and Body Orientation.
Infants can perceive their own body positions, or *orientation*, and they prefer to be in certain positions when they are held or when they are sleeping. A further sign of their ability to sense directions can be seen in their dislike of being held upside-down. Infants also show an awareness of pressure and seem to feel more secure when they are closely wrapped in a blanket and are held firmly and closely. This kind of sensitivity to positions helps them later in balancing their bodies and walking, since coordination of their muscles with the balance equipment, or *vestibular organs* of the inner ear, is necessary before walking can be achieved. In order to enjoy such coordination, the infant must first have a sense of its own orientation in space.

It should be noted that slight rhythmic changes of the newborn and young infant's position in space are soothing, and throughout the world rocking is used to calm crying children (Pederson & Ter Vrugt, 1973). Many disturbed children and adults rock themselves, perhaps to provide themselves with a primitive kind of tranquilizer. Premature infants, who usually are not handled as much as other newborn infants, may be handicapped in their development by a lack of vestibular stimulation and may therefore have difficulty in balancing themselves.

The Orienting Reflex and Habituation.
Infants do not just receive stimulation from the outside world. They also pay selective attention to some stimuli and tend to ignore others. They become alert to novel stimuli and get bored by repeating and monotonous stimuli.

Pavlov first discovered the *orienting reflex*, or the "What is it?" response, when he observed that dogs would react to novel stimuli by stiffening their ears and looking alert. Researchers have continued to study this reflex in many species (Kessen, Haith, & Salapatek, 1970; Madsen, 1973).

The orienting reflex is defined as an overall response to stimuli through any type of sensory experience. One study of this kind was performed by Brotsky and Kagan (1971). They presented novel sights and sounds to infants of four, eight, and thirteen months of age and observed how the infants' heart rates changed in response to these stimuli. The first stimulus of a series that was used at four months of age was an outline of a male face. Later, at eight months of age, the infants were placed in high chairs behind an enclosure. The visual stimuli used formerly were again presented but now were followed by a tape recording of a male voice reciting nonsense syllables in a monotone. (Other auditory and visual stimuli were also

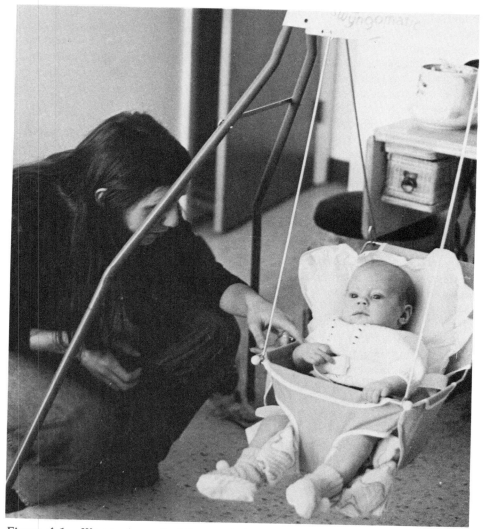

Figure 4-1.   We now know that the vestibular stimulation provided by this swing and by other rocking activities not only is highly enjoyable but also is important for developing sensory and motor skills. (Photo by Mary M. Duncan)

used). At thirteen months of age, three-dimensional figures were shown to the infants. Some infants were shown a male doll, some were shown a doll with parts arranged asymmetrically, and some were shown a free-form stimulus that had the same general area, color, and texture as the other stimuli. The auditory stimuli were also repeated at the thirteen-month age level. The orientation response was determined by the degree of cardiac deceleration (slowing down of the heart rate). It was found that the orienting reflex and cardiac deceleration were significantly related: as infants reacted to novel stimuli, their heart rates became slower. Brotsky and Kagan's study, as well as others, suggest that orienting responses are independent to some degree from simple memory functioning. It appears that infants do not automatically give orienting responses to all stimuli but, rather, to those stimuli that are new and interesting.

As we have seen, babies pay a lot of attention to new and complex objects. We might ask, however, "How do they know whether something is novel or whether it is old, familiar, and ordinary?"

Habituation, or becoming familiar with an object, has been studied for a number of years, and research studies have indicated that infants can remember what they have seen over a period of time (Fagan, 1971; Friedman, Nagy, & Carpenter, 1970; Graham, Clifton, & Hatton, 1968; Lewis, Goldberg & Campbell, 1969; Messer, Kagan, & McCall, 1970; McCall & Melson, 1970). Generally, investigators familiarize infants with a stimulus by continuously or repeatedly presenting it to the infants. They study habituation by analyzing the length of time the infants look at an object (visual fixation) and noting changes in the infants' heartbeat rate. Research has shown that infants' visual fixation times and heart rates change at the first appearance of a stimulus, but after repeated exposures these responses are lessened as infants become habituated and bored (Miller, 1972; Greenberg, O'Donnell, & Crawford, 1973; McCall, Hogarty, Hamilton, & Vincent, 1973).

Studies of habituation have led to the conclusion that infants must have at least some capacity for memory because after awhile old objects no longer bring about responses, but new ones will. Thus, some newborn infants are able to store visual information in their brains and use it to see differences in objects or environmental changes (Baer & Wright, 1974; Friedman, 1972).

Further support for this idea comes from a study of infants who became accustomed to mobiles that they had seen in their homes each day over several weeks. These infants were then taken to a laboratory where they were shown another mobile. The study showed that the infants looked longer at the laboratory mobile when it was moderately different from the ones they had seen at home (Super, Kagan, Morrison, Haith, & Weiffenbach, 1972). If the laboratory mobile differed from the home mobile only a little *or* a great deal, however, it attracted less attention from the infants. So babies, like adults, prefer a little novelty—a little "spice" in their lives. But when the experience differs tremendously from what they are familiar with or when it is too similar, they are not so interested.

Orientation and habituation thus include visual fixation, quieting, and often a slowing of the heart rate. If the object is only minimally different from earlier ones, a brief orientation will occur accompanied by a slowing heart rate. Moderate differences cause the infant to look longer, and heart rate increase may then occur. If the object is too different, infants are unlikely to show interest in it.

The Ability of Infants to See and Perceive

The visual abilities of infants have been studied in recent years by a number of investigators. These studies indicate that newborn infants can easily discriminate

Figure 4-2. Stimuli used in the study of pattern vision in young infants. (Adapted from R. L. Fantz. Pattern vision in young infants. *The Psychological Record*, 1958, 8, 43–47. Reprinted by permission of the publisher.)

between light and dark and apparently can perceive colors. Very young infants can follow moving lights with their eyes, and therefore have some eye-muscle coordination. Their eye movements are not smooth, however, and their first following actions are very jerky and inefficient. In vision, it is very important to have coordinated eye movement patterns. One such coordinated movement pattern is called *convergence,* in which the eyes rotate inward toward the nose when viewing near objects and out toward the sides of the head when viewing distant objects. By using converging movements, the infant can focus the two eyes so that one image of an object is carried to the brain. At birth, efficiency in focusing is quite limited and babies may look a bit cross-eyed, but after about two months there is very efficient convergence.

Another focusing strategy, *visual accommodation,* or adjustment of the eye lens curvature in such a way that light properly reaches the light-sensitive area called the retina, is also inefficient in the newborn infant. By the age of three or four months, however, accommodation is achieved. Neonates can, however, focus objects up to about 8 inches away—the usual distance between mother and infant during nursing. A number of investigators now consider infants to have relatively well-developed visual abilities, and new research is revealing additional information (Bower, 1973, 1974; Kessen, Haith, & Salapatek, 1970).

Researchers have recently found that infants pay more attention to things around them than anyone had previously believed was possible. One of the ways to test an infant's ability to pay attention to objects is by measuring the amount of time that he or she spends in looking at various designs. Robert Fantz showed infants (one to fourteen weeks of age) four pairs of patterns that were displayed over their heads as they lay in their cribs (see Figure 4-2). Fantz found that a majority of the infants preferred to look at complex and novel patterns, like checkerboard patterns, longer than at ordinary patterns such as squares. Most infants showed more interest in a bull's eye pattern than in a pattern of stripes. This finding about infants' abilities interested many other research workers and spurred many research projects. In a later study, Fantz found that infants paid attention to certain stimuli in the following order (see Figure 4-3): They paid attention most to a normal human face; next most to a scrambled face pattern; and least to a blank oval (Fantz, 1973). Some investigators think these findings indicate that babies have a way of understanding the significance or meaning of objects. Others think that the findings indicate only that babies have an innate preference for complexity (Forgus, 1971). Whatever the interpretation, young infants are clearly interested in their surroundings, and many parents now provide their infants with mobiles, bright decorations, and other interesting things to look at.

Following the early work by Fantz, most infant researchers now believe that infants prefer to look at complex patterns and need to experience a certain amount of novelty. This information suggests that they can understand more than we had thought. In fact, it has raised the question whether we might be losing an opportunity in the education of infants. At the very least, we can make their lives more interesting by providing them with interesting things to look at.

Eye and Hand Movements. Vision is also important in guiding an infant's movements because infants will look at objects and then try to reach out and grasp

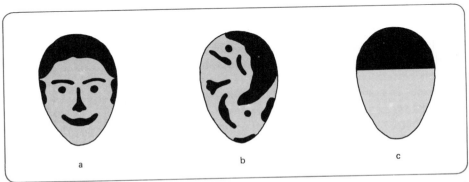

Figure 4-3. Face patterns used by Fantz. Infants' attention to faces was tested with these three face patterns. (From R. L. Fantz. The origin of form perception. *Scientific American,* May, 1961, 204, 71–72. Copyright © by Scientific American, Inc.)

them. The ability to grasp is something that newborn infants can do easily. If you place your finger in an infant's hand, it will be grasped tightly. Infants can also follow moving objects with their eyes and look at bright lights. Therefore, the basic abilities for grasping an object are present at birth, but the young infant is not yet able to integrate these talents into a smooth pattern (White, 1971). Integration of eye and hand movements first occurs when an infant looks at its own hand as the hand moves. Babies of two to four months do this often and it is a spectacular discovery! When eye-hand, or visual-motor, coordination develops from this attention to the hand, observed objects can be grasped. This coordination is generally achieved at five or six months of age (Yendovitskaya, Zinchenko, & Ruzskaya, 1971).

Although infants can reach for and grasp an object by the age of six months, this behavior is not completely efficient. At this young age babies still tend to lack sufficient visual and manual touch sensitivity to give them adequate coordination and independent muscle actions for fine movements.

Other Sensory and Motor Abilities

Although there is some basis for thinking that vision is the most important sense, other forms of sensory experience are also highly important.

Auditory Sensations and Perceptions.   A newborn's ability to hear can be easily demonstrated, because a loud noise will cause a baby to react by jerking arms and legs and tensing the body. In fact, when infants hear a loud noise, they will interrupt most other activities. If they are nursing, they will stop; if they are busy looking at an object or a bright light, they will quickly turn their heads toward the sound. In addition to such movements, other body changes occur in response to sounds. Among these are changes in heart rate. If a sound continues, infants may become habituated to it, and their response to the stimulus will decrease or stop. A new sound, however, will again cause the babies to return to their earlier response pattern. It should be noted that the loudness of a sound seems to play an important role in infants' response, and any generalizations about responses should take loudness into account (Bower, 1974; Brackbill, 1975).

Although experimental results do not all agree, it seems that newborn infants can distinguish among sounds on the basis of pitch as well as loudness and timing. There is also evidence that infant responses to sounds indicate a basic capacity for self-protection, and that their specific attentiveness demonstrates a capacity for selective and organized response to auditory stimulation (Stratton & Connolly, 1973; Kearsley, 1973).

As we know, infants are soothed by rhythmic rocking and also respond to sound rhythms. Laboratory studies have now provided evidence that newborns have the ability to differentiate among fine variations in sound and can be affected in various ways by them. For example, the pediatric psychologist Lee Salk (1962) hypothesized that a mother's heartbeat will accustom the fetus to rhythms and that the newborn's response to rhythm could be explained in terms of imprinting in the uterus. To test this hypothesis, Salk played a recording of a human heartbeat to neonates during the first few days after they were born. The newborns who were exposed to these sounds cried less and increased in weight. Other investigators, however, assert that although rhythmic sounds can reduce crying, heartbeat sounds are no more beneficial than other sounds. For example, the effect of heartbeat sounds, a lullaby, and the sounds of a metronome seem to differ little (Brackbill, Adams, Crowell, & Gray, 1966).

Is crying contagious? Hospital nursery attendants have often noticed that when one infant begins to cry, many others will also cry. From an early study (Blanton, 1917) until the present day, some investigators have thought that the crying of infants in response to the cries of other infants is only a reaction to a loud noise and that no significance other than that of a reaction should be claimed for the crying response.

On the other hand, a few researchers have claimed that the imitation of crying is a genuine social response to other infants. In one study of infants who ranged in age from sixty-six to seventy-two hours old, the tape-recorded cry of a five-day-old girl prior to her mid-morning feeding was used as a stimulus. In the experimental group, a tape player was mounted in the infants' cribs so that the experimenters could gather data on the heart rate, respiration, and activity levels of the infants as the crying sounds were played. On the basis of the results gathered, the investigator concluded that vocal properties of the stimulus (sound of crying) did, indeed, affect the other infants (Simner, 1971). This information does not indicate conclusively, however, that the response to the crying is a social response rather than a reaction to noise.

Infants apparently can, even in the first few months of life, discriminate among the speech sounds they hear. For example, some discrimination ability has been shown to exist in the perception of consonants (Moffitt, 1971; Morse, 1972; Trehub & Rabinovitch, 1972), and by the age of four months, infants can distinguish between vowel sounds (Trehub, 1973).

Infants hear sounds and they can also respond vocally to those sounds that they hear. A relationship between auditory stimuli and vocalization was investigated by stimulating seven-month-old infants with high-fidelity tape recordings of vowel sounds that were spoken in either high- or low-pitched voices. The stimuli consisted of recordings of a woman's voice that repeated vowels (a as in "ask," a as in "calm," e as in "beet," ou as in "flow," and u as in "look"). The sounds were stopped at intervals so that the infant could have a chance to respond to them. The experiment was carried out in the infant's home, and each infant was placed in a playpen with a microphone close by. A tape recorder presented the stimulus sounds while another tape recorder recorded the infant's vocalization. The investigators concluded that the sounds affected the vocalization of the infants because the infants reduced their own vocalizations and listened to the voice sounds as they were presented (Webster, Steinhardt, & Senter, 1972).

Sounds can differ along three dimensions: pitch, loudness, and *timbre* (the mixture of tones to produce a unique sound quality). An infant's response to various dimensions of auditory stimuli is difficult to determine because most laboratory studies use pure electronic tones. The natural sounds of everyday life, however, are often too complex to be submitted to controlled study. Nevertheless, such real stimuli as the squeak of a rubber toy, the crumpling of paper, and various sound makers have been tried. As to the dimension of pitch, it has been reported that low-frequency tones tend to affect infant responses more than high-frequency tones (Bims, Blank, Bridger, & Escalona, 1965). With respect to loudness, the evidence generally suggests that infants are likely to respond to stimuli of about 60 decibels (about the level of normal conversation) of intensity, and their movements seem to increase with rising sound intensity (Kessen, Haith, & Salapatek, 1970).

Many investigators conclude that the infant's arousal level, or degree of responsiveness, is an important consideration when studying responses to sound stimuli because infants are sleeping much of the time. At present, definitive conclusions based on the available information about responsiveness to sounds in different stages of arousal are not possible.

Taste and Olfactory Perception.   While some investigators have stated that newborns have no sense of taste, infants only a few weeks old have been observed to make facial grimaces when given bitter-tasting fruit juice and have been seen to smack their lips when tasting sugar. In one study taste responses of forty-eight boy and forty-eight girl infants (aged one to three days) were investigated with water solutions of two kinds of sugar: glucose and sucrose. Different concentrations of sugar were fed through an apparatus which permitted the experimenters to record the number of sucking responses and the amount of fluid that each infant consumed. Testing sessions took place midway between regular feedings. The presentation of the substances was varied, and their order seemed to be important. For example, when sugar was given before water, the infant's sucking increased according to the concentration of sugar in solution. But when sugar was given after the water was given, the same pattern was not found.

The study indicated that newborn infants can discriminate between flavors and that they definitely prefer sucrose over glucose. This is also true of adults. (Adults perceive sucrose to be sweeter than glucose, and sucrose is the sugar that is used as a sweetener.) The investigators (Engen, Lipsitt, & Peck, 1974) saw their findings as supporting the view that some taste preferences are inborn. Since the order in which the substances were given was important, perhaps taste preferences can be easily influenced by experience. At present, however, there is little evidence to suggest that infants will reject foods on the basis of taste alone.

It is known that infants respond to odors since their body movements often show that they try to avoid certain kinds of smells. For example, the strong odor of ammonia will cause infants to turn away (Engen & Lipsitt, 1965). Although a number of research workers have studied variations of heart rate in the presence of a disliked olfactory stimulus (Lipsitt & Jacklin, 1971), several other ways of investigating infants' responses to olfactory stimuli have been devised. For example, one experimenter placed infants in a "stabilometer" (an arrangement of a crib or bassinet which registered body activity) and observed that different patterns of body movement resulted from olfactory stimuli (Rovee, 1972). Other investigators observed breathing rates as infants reacted to various smells (oil of anise [a licorice smell], tincture of asafetida, oil of lavender, and tincture of valerian [the smell of rancid butter]). It was found that the infants responded to three of the four odors by the time they were only 72 hours old. Arousal level made a difference, because the infants responded to the odors more when they were in deep sleep than when they were more awake (Self, Horowitz, & Paden, 1972). The study also found, as other investigators have reported, that the infants showed large individual differences in responses.

Sensitivity to Touch, Cold, Heat, and Pain.   The perception of tactile stimuli in newborn infants has been satisfactorily established, but some questions about touch still remain to be answered. In a study of the heart rate response to tactile, auditory, and vestibular (movement) stimulation before and after a feeding and while sleeping and while quietly awake, certain factors were found to affect responses to touch. The study indicated that the heart rate response was associated with arousal state and feeding conditions in response to all three types of stimuli (Pomerleau-Malcuit & Clifton, 1973). The experimenters found that the heart rate *increased* in sleeping infants when: (1) their faces were touched with a soft brush (tactile stimulus); (2) they were moved (vestibular stimulus); and (3) special apparatus made a sound (auditory stimulus). The heart rate of awake subjects *slowed down* when they were stimulated before feeding and *increased* in response to stimuli after feeding. Other investigators generally agree that internal conditions cause differences in infants' response (Rewey, 1973), but our knowledge of the exact kinds of responses that can be associated with these variations is not complete.

Let us examine other forms of skin sensitivity. Many of us have had to comfort babies who had wet their diapers or were cold or were pricked with pins. As we know, babies' skins are very sensitive to many kinds of touch. Infants respond to temperature changes, although it takes time for them to respond efficiently. Normally their bodies cope with cold by increasing the metabolic rate in order to create more heat. The metabolic rate can be increased by shivering or by rapid movements, but shivering is actually the most efficient way. Not all investigators agree that newborns can shiver. When they are cold, the babies' bodies require more fuel and if intake of food is not possible, their bodies use stored fat for energy. Within a few minutes after birth, infants' bodies respond to cool environments by constricting the blood vessels and producing body heat. In two or three hours after birth, the metabolic response improves. This occurs even though the infants receive little or no food in the first one or two days of life. Because the insulating layer of fat under their skin is thin, infants have a greater ability to conduct temperature through the skin than do older children. Since infants' skin temperatures are higher than the temperatures of their surroundings, body heat is easily lost. An infant's heat loss is about four times greater than that of an adult until thermal stability is gradually achieved (Eichorn, 1970). This is why babies usually feel very warm to adults and why they can easily become chilled or overheated.

In terms of coping with heat, infants are relatively unable to lower their body temperatures. This may be due to the fact that when they are too warm, they become restless. Thus, they may actually increase their body temperatures. While it seems that on exposure to heat the rerouting of blood toward the skin for cooling may be possible in infants, their sweating is limited and inefficient; therefore, from the standpoint of an overall consideration, their resistance to heat is not very successful.

Pain perception is present in the first few days after birth. Early experimenters used pinpricks on the foot as tests, but it is doubtful that this kind of research would be carried out today. Nearly two decades ago mild electric shocks were applied to infants' feet, and it was found that girls seemed to be more sensitive to pain than boys (Lipsitt & Levy, 1959). As Maccoby and Jacklin (1974) point out, sensitivity-to-pain thresholds and tolerances for pain are really quite different issues, and the research has not been definitive in this case.

To summarize, infants at birth, or shortly thereafter, are sensitive to touch, temperature, and pain. There is evidence that these forms of response are innate and depend little on learning.

THE PHYSICAL GROWTH OF INFANTS

Directions of Growth

We can view the physical and, to some extent, the mental growth of children as following a few general growth trends called *growth gradients*. Through experimentation and observation, several concepts of growth have been developed. One of the growth gradients is the *cephalo-caudal* (head-to-tail) *gradient* in which growth proceeds from the head downwards. For example, head turning and eye movements develop first, followed by hand and arm activity, and then crawling. When standing and beginning to walk, young children balance themselves by holding onto objects because their legs cannot yet be depended upon (an indication of prior development of hand and arm activity). If we watch infants and toddlers as they try to climb over objects, we sometimes see them topple and fall headfirst, because while their heads, arms, and upper torsos are well-developed, their legs and lower bodies are less mature.

Another growth gradient is called the *proximo-distal gradient,* which means that growth proceeds from the center of the body to the outer limbs. Development of arm movements, for example, proceeds from the shoulder to the elbow to the wrist and then to the hand. The development of larger movements close to the trunk precede the finer movements of the wrist and hand, and the same sequence also is true for the lower limbs.

Still another growth gradient can be called the *gross-specific gradient,* because large body movements precede fine and coordinated movements. As very young infants reach for a nursing bottle, they may respond with gross, whole-body movements such as tensing their trunks, kicking their legs, and waving their arms. They use few of the specific or precise movements that could lead toward grasping the bottle. Specific reaching responses come after maturation has reached the wrist, the hand, and the fingers; only then can movements toward the bottle be direct and specific. This kind of interaction with the environment, of course, is dependent upon the brain, and the development of the brain is central to motor skills and environmental interaction.

During the developmental years the central nervous system, consisting of the brain and the spinal cord, changes at a rate that is faster than that of any other organ system. Its development in relation to motor functions is especially rapid until the infant is about six months old, but after this time the rate decreases.

At birth an infant's brain weighs about three-fourths of a pound. But by the end of infancy, the brain has grown to a weight of two and one-half pounds and has gained about 75 percent of its final adult weight. Tissue changes that have occurred make the brain of a two-year-old very similar to that of an adult.

Normal Expectations of Growth

Expectations about physical growth are expressed in terms of *norms* and *averages.* Using data from the many children who have been studied, physical growth and developmental behavior can be summarized in terms of *averages,* or what most children attain at a particular age (Meredith, 1970, 1973). For example, most infants will follow a moving object with their eyes. Their following movements may extend from a state of "no attention" to a state of "careful attention" through the entire path of an object's movement. But an infant's attention will usually be somewhere in between these two extremes. Of course, in a research sample few, if any, infants will exactly fit an average. By definition, half of all children will be above average and half will be below average. The average is a rough summary and reflects the common characteristics of all infants in a sample. *Norms* refer to growth levels and behavior attainments that are *expected* to occur by a certain age or that are attained by most children of a certain age.

The usual way of determining whether a child is growing normally (according to norms) is to compare the child's progress at different points in time to the average growth of a large number of children who are similar in age. An individual child's growth curve can be plotted in order to show how the child's growth compares to the average child of the same age.

Although individual infants or young children deviate from the average on some traits, they do not necessarily have a problem. Most normative tables give a "normal range" in which a child may be somewhat above or below average but still be considered normal. In fact, a norm is a statistical term and is not to be interpreted as an ideal that all children should attain.

Individual differences are clearly present at birth. Variations of weight usually range from 5½ to 9½ pounds for full-term infants, with the average birth weight being about 7½ pounds. Heredity, maternal diet, and possible infection or other problems have all determined the infant's weight at birth.

Shortly after birth infants begin a very rapid growth rate that continues through-out the first year. The average change in the first year for both height and weight is about 33 percent, but after that the rate increases gradually and then levels off in a steady trend at the end of infancy (or the second year of life). During the entire infancy period, the infant grows from about 20 inches to about 34 inches in length, and from a birth weight of about 7 pounds to about 28 pounds.

From the many complex techniques devised for measuring and tabulating growth data, we have valuable information on growth trends in tissue, bones, and brain size, as well as information about the water, fat, and protein composition of the infant's body (Owen & Brozek, 1966). This kind of information is useful in planning health care for whole populations, as well as for individual children. We know, for example, that maturation and rate of growth seem to be related to body type or build. A large, heavy child tends to grow at a more rapid rate than a slender child. The larger child, however, is likely to reach his or her maximum size at an earlier age than the slender child who is likely to continue growing for a longer time.

During the period of infancy, the body proportions and growth rates of boys and girls are similar, but this does not mean that differences in body composition do not exist. Girls have more subcutaneous (under the skin) fat than boys have. They also have less muscle and less water and, as time passes, a girl's growth rate is more rapid and stable than a boy's. In both sexes the head grows more slowly than the trunk, arms, and legs as the body's overall proportions become more like the adult form. Some evidence suggests that we can predict adult height from the height of infants at two years of age (Bayley, 1946).

Various factors determine the growth rate, the final body size, and the propor-tions of the infant's body. Genetic factors are largely responsible for growth in infancy, but as the months pass, the environment plays an increasingly important role as it affects potential changes in size and shape through diet, diseases, or acci-dents. Internally, hormones begin to have an important effect on growth. For example, thyroxin from the thyroid gland and the growth hormone from the ante-rior part of the pituitary gland are essential for normal growth and development. Later, in adolescence, the pituitary hormones stimulate the ovaries to produce estrogens and the testes to produce androgens. These hormonal factors in growth, in addition to the influence of the genes and nutrition already mentioned, have varying effects according to an individual's physical characteristics. Because of the different combinations of these factors, highly individualistic patterns of growth result.

Dental Development

In infant growth, parents often see the first appearance of teeth as an important milestone. The teeth begin to form in the fetus at about the sixth week. By birth all twenty of the so-called "baby" teeth, as well as the first permanent teeth, are begin-ning to develop, although none are visible except in rare instances. The first teeth

Figure 4-4.   For this infant, the appearance of the first teeth will provide new opportunities for tasting and exploring new foods. In addition, these teeth will allow the infant to become more competent in self-feeding.

are called *deciduous teeth,* or temporary teeth, and they will eventually fall out and provide paths for the larger permanent teeth which appear later.

The lower front teeth are the first to erupt, usually when the infant is about six to seven months old, but sometimes they appear as late as twelve months (Graber, 1966). At about fifteen months the first molars erupt, and by the end of the infancy period about 10 percent of children will have all twenty deciduous teeth. Realistically, by the age of three years, most children will have all of their first teeth.

Skeletal Changes

The change of body proportions in infancy takes place partly as the result of the growth of the skeleton, particularly the long bones. Many bones in the newborn infant are really soft, or cartilagenous, tissue, which hardens with age, maturation, and intake of minerals (mainly calcium). Although the beginnings of ossification (conversion of soft tissue to bone) takes place before birth, this process continues throughout the developmental years.

As might be expected, the process of ossification varies according to individuals and according to sex. Girls' bones grow more rapidly than do those of boys. Both inherited tendencies and environmental influences are important in skeletal growth and, as in other aspects of growth, disease and nutritional deficiencies may delay ossification and bone growth. A notable example is the disease *rickets,* which is caused by a lack of vitamin D that delays calcification of long bones and causes them to bend under as the child's weight increases. The process of ossification begins at the centers of the bones and then spreads outward. Therefore, as bones ossify they also become wider. The order of change in the bones, though not the rate of change, is the same for everyone.

One way to determine skeletal age and the progress of growth is through X-ray photographs of the bones. While any part of the skeleton can be used for determination of skeletal growth, the bones of the hand are most frequently used, because they are easily accessible and the rest of the body need not be exposed to radiation. In one kind of assessment the X ray is compared with standard X-ray plates of normal bone growth at successive chronological age levels in other children. The standard X-ray plate that matches the individual child's X ray provides an estimate of the child's "skeletal age." A skeletal maturity level is valuable as a scale of development because every individual eventually reaches the same level of bone growth. Skeletal age, therefore, is generally considered a dependable indication of physical development (Tanner, 1970).

Motor Development

The infant's activity is important for muscle growth and neural coordination, as rolling over, crawling, reaching, grasping, and manipulation provide a foundation for further development. The accomplishments of sitting up, crawling, standing, and walking usually develop in a sequence. Most infants can sit up with some help by three or four months and can sit alone by six or seven months. They can move forward on their stomachs a month or so later. At about ten months their hands and knees are strong enough to support their weight, and new forms of locomotion are then possible.

When average infants are about a year old, they can pull themselves to their feet and walk around furniture while holding onto it. By fourteen months they can stand alone, and by fifteen months can walk alone. Some children walk as early as ten months by moving through the sequences rapidly or by omitting a stage, while others may not walk until they are almost two years old. It should be noted that precocious motor development has not been shown to be necessarily related to superior intelligence, to sex, or to social class differences.

How necessary is the child's own activity in helping the maturation of the muscular and nervous systems? This question has been a source of interest for some time. Early investigators wondered about the effects of the cradle board on the motor development of American Indian children. Hopi Indian infants were kept tied in cradle boards, or backpacks, most of the time in early life. It was found, however, that they showed no delay in walking (Dennis, 1941). Recently, some orthopedic defects have been noted in these children, however, and the practice is now questioned.

A child's individual rate of motor development does not seem to be a significant

Figure 4-5.   Although most infants can walk with support at around one year, there is a wide range of ages at which children take their first steps. In any event, all children seem to go through the same stages as they develop walking skills. (Photo by Mary M. Duncan)

factor in the final accomplishment, and there is little reason for attaching any great value to rapid acquisition of motor skills. Some children who develop walking rather late may turn out to be excellent athletes, while other more precocious children do not necessarily develop better. A parent's insistence that a child learn to crawl or walk early is really of little value and may, indeed, cause unnecessary anxiety. Nor is it necessary to teach a child to walk. A child will learn to walk without adult help. As in any area of child development, normal development depends upon an adequate environment, and children need to have the opportunity to explore the environment according to their age and level of development.

SIGNIFICANCE OF INDIVIDUAL DIFFERENCES IN GROWTH AND DEVELOPMENT

As discussed in Chapter 3, genetic differences account for many of the differences in growth and development patterns in infancy, but as the child develops, environmental influences become important contributors to individual differences. Considering the unique experiences with parents and other family members that

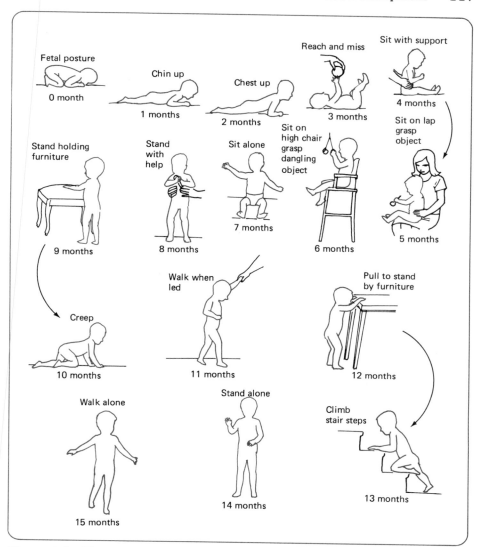

Figure 4-6.   The sequence of a child's motor development.

each infant has, it is easy to see that each child is a product of many influences and that the concept of the "average infant" has very little meaning. Despite this, the efforts of many researchers depend upon norms and control groups of "average" children. Some compromise is possible if ranges are used, for trends are valuable in helping us to predict the sequences of development. For example, we know that crawling usually comes before walking. It is important, however, that we do not force children into a mold and that we allow them to develop according to their own unique schedules of maturation.

Innate Factors in Individual Differences

As children grow, individual differences become apparent in their responses to the environment. Some infants are sensitive to noise shortly after birth and are easily awakened at the sound of a door or a barking dog, while others are not disturbed at all; some can tolerate feedings spaced at long intervals, while others demand to be fed frequently.

After a few months some infants are alert and interested in such things as a mobile hung above their crib; others make an effort to follow the activities of a pet dog; and still others spend much time sleeping and eating and show little interest in events or people. Some theorists have taken the position that, since activity and willingness to explore new situations lead to new experiences within the environment, the active and energetic infant is likely to progress more rapidly in developing new response patterns than will the more placid child. These variations in activity may influence developmental trends that will become apparent later.

Individual differences in activity are related to individual differences in body processes and genetically determined biochemical functions. For example, variations in circulatory system efficiency may cause particular sensitivity to temperature changes or ranges; and physiological conditions as well as body size and weight may influence feeding time demands. Thus, some individual characteristics result from developmental trends that were underway prior to birth. The efficient functioning of organ systems provides the basis for the infant's responses to the environment and, in turn, influences the learning experiences of the young child.

By the end of the infancy period and the second birthday, children walk, begin to communicate with words, and store images of the world that provide a basis for new learning and response patterns. Since children are now easily seen as people with individual likes and dislikes, parents are obliged to recognize these characteristics—they must accommodate to some degree these new little people who have taken important roles in the dramas of their own lives.

SUMMARY

We have seen that although many people assume that newborn infants are totally helpless creatures who cannot see, hear, taste, smell, or move, this is simply not true. Numerous research examples indicate that the perceptual and sensory systems of neonates are much more sophisticated than we might have imagined. We have seen that newborns have a wide variety of motor abilities available. Within the first year the growth of motor skills is both remarkably rapid and remarkably predictable. Although the development of sensory and motor systems is quite orderly, healthy infants can display highly individual patterns of development in these areas. Therefore, although the notion of the "average" child provides a useful summary of *milestones* of development, we must not overlook the fact that deviations from average patterns can still be healthy.

RECOMMENDED READINGS

Caplan, F. *The First Twelve Months of Life.* Princeton, N.J.: Edcom Systems, 1973. (Also available as Grosset & Dunlap and Bantam paperbacks.)

This highly popular book clearly explains current research on infancy to the intelligent reader. It is organized in a month-by-month fashion and contains numerous illustrations and tables describing the typical behaviors that can be found at each month of development.

Lewin, R. (Ed.) *Child Alive!* Garden City, N.Y.: Anchor Press/Doubleday, 1975.

This book contains an exciting selection of the work of British developmental psychologists who are exploring social behavior, play, language, cognition, sex differences, and physical development during infancy.

3

INFANCY AND TODDLERHOOD

5

Early Cognitive Development and the Beginnings of Language

From the very moment of birth, human infants are equipped with potentials that enable them to be distinctively human and yet quite different from infants of any other species. Among the characteristics that seem to be particularly specialized in humans are the enormous amounts of flexibility in language and thought, the ability to make and use tools, and the ability to form a wide variety of social organizations. Although recent studies by both psychologists and zoologists have revealed some crude forms of these behaviors in other primate species such as chimpanzees and gorillas, only in humans are these characteristics so well-developed and so consistently used. We shall explore the speech and language of infants and examine how various theoretical explanations have been used to account for language development. As language involves the communication of thoughts and ideas, toward the end of the chapter we will discuss the beginnings of cognitive development.

While the origins of language lie in infancy, in early childhood there is also substantial progress. Following our chronological approach, we will divide the discussion of language and mental development into chapters that deal with infancy and early childhood. In this chapter, we will deal specifically with the language and thought of infants.

THE FOUNDATIONS OF LANGUAGE

Do the first sounds made by infants have any relationship to adult speech? In trying to answer this question investigators are seeking information about the ways that infants make sounds and how their use of these sounds comes to form language. Researchers are also trying to understand the ways in which infants respond to the speech and language of others. Let us examine some current viewpoints and studies on the early vocalizations of infants.

Early Vocalization

Within seconds after birth infants will start to cry. They are well-equipped for crying and, in its first stage, crying is a pure reflex activity. A baby's first cries are diffuse and unspecialized and come whenever the baby is uncomfortable. Later, however, crying becomes more specific and infants develop unique cries for hunger and pain (Eisenson, Auer, & Irwin, 1963). Before long, infants make other sounds that express not only discomfort but pleasure, comfort, and joy as well.

Infants can make both vowel and consonant sounds soon after they are born. The newborn infant can produce such vowel sounds as *e* (as in *pet*), *a* (as in *fat*), *u* (as in *but*), and *i* (as in *hit*). Within a few days after birth, the consonants *h, k,* and *w* may be produced. In the first few weeks of life infants use more vowels than consonants, but with further maturation consonants begin to predominate. Studies by psycholinguists such as David McNeill (1971) and Charles Osgood (1953) indicate that within their first year of life, infants all over the world normally produce the sounds used in all of the 3,000 or more known human languages. Infants only a few months old can make all of the basic sounds for such diverse languages as English, Chinese, Hindi, Russian, Swahili, and Hebrew. Furthermore, some sophisticated studies have shown that infants can discriminate among vowels and consonants within the first few weeks of life (Trehub, 1973, 1976).

When we go beyond the production of simple sound units and look at the production of more complex speech sounds, we find a progression from *cooing* (low, soft sounds) to *babbling* (continuous meaningless vocalization, often of one syllable) to the use of actual words. Cooing and babbling are not precise terms and, although linguists use them, they are fairly difficult to define. Cooing usually appears during the second month of life and differs from crying because it does not indicate distress and represents the ability to make sounds by using the tongue for modulation.

When infants are about six months old, their cooing turns to babbling and they use both vowels and consonants in combinations like *ma, da,* or *di.* Babbling is found in all cultures. Even the children of deaf parents babble incessantly at this age. The infants' vocalizations are now very expressive, reflecting their wishes, moods, and emotions (La Barbera, Izard, Vietze, & Parisi, 1976). By about ten months of age, most infant vocalizations are mixed with "sound-play," such as gurgling and other mouth activities. Although most of the sounds are made purely for pleasure, they will become useful in later speech activities. Also, playing with sounds is an enjoyable activity in itself, and the ability to produce and listen to their own sounds gives infants a tremendous sense of their own competence. In effect, it says, "Hey! Look what I can do." At this age they also try to imitate the sounds or words that have been repeated to them, although imitations are only occasional and are rarely exact imitations of adult speech. Nevertheless, a beginning is achieved in forming correct responses to words—perhaps such specific and familiar words as *bottle* or the name of the family's pet dog or cat.

In English and in most European languages, combinations of sounds develop from a consonant followed by a vowel (as in *ma*). These combinations become small units of meaning as well as units of sound. Although we are beginning to see emerging patterns of speech and language in infants, we still do not fully understand why one stage of language and speech development precedes another stage. To help us deal with these issues, we shall review some theoretical approaches to the development of language.

Some linguists have suggested that babbling is a developmental stage that most infants pass through on their way toward true speech. But since most adult speech has little in common with babbling, why do infants babble? We can reasonably argue that in language acquisition, babbling is a stage similar to crawling before walking. That is, both babbling and crawling are activities that lead to more complex, skilled behaviors. From this point of view, babbling can be considered to be a stage in a maturational sequence that infants reach before developing further. Neither babbling nor crawling, however, seem to be absolutely necessary for later functioning. There have been children who walked perfectly but had very little crawling experience and, similarly, there have been children who spoke well despite having little opportunity to babble. The babbling stage may provide the infant with some exercise in producing and listening to his or her own speech sounds, but strong evidence that this stage is necessary for later language stages is lacking.

There may be other uses for early vocalizations, though. A study by Cameron, Livson, and Bayley (1967) indicated that infants who vocalized frequently also tended to achieve higher scores on intelligence tests given later in life than those children who vocalized little. Another study reported that infants who displayed a great deal of vocalization at six months tended to have larger vocabularies when they were two and three years old than infants who showed less vocalization (Moore, 1967). These results suggest that extent of vocalization may provide a basis for predicting vocabulary size and may help predict performance on intelligence tests that depend on verbal measures. The extent of vocalization also seems to be related to syntax development and greater verbal fluency.

Progress in early vocalization is also thought by some investigators and theorists to be related to cognitive development. Language and thought are highly related, but as we shall see when discussing Piaget's theory later in this chapter, the connection is fairly complex.

In summary, speech, in the sense of using sounds, begins at birth and progressively becomes more complex in the first year. While most children will be speaking between eighteen and twenty-four months (Kaplan & Kaplan, 1971), a few children (about 1 percent) do not speak until they are as old as four years (Lenneberg, 1971). "Mama" or "dada" are often the infant's first recognizable words. When producing these words, the infant continues earlier patterns by repeating simple sounds. Speech sounds are not only patterns of vibrations; they become meaningful symbols that refer to some "thing" or "action" and thus become part of the infant's widening experience.

The Beginnings of Recognizable Speech

Now that we have looked at the child's ability to vocalize, or produce sound units, let us look at the production of the child's first meaningful words and sentences. Linguists have divided speech into units called *phonemes* and *morphemes*. *Phonemes* are the basic sound units necessary for speech (for example, syllables) and *morphemes* are the smallest units of meaning (for example, *un*). While we can teach a parrot or mynah bird to produce phonemes, it is unlikely that we can teach the bird morphemes. One of the amazing characteristics of human language lies in the fact that while a few words have morphemes that are imitations of the actual sounds of phonemes of the objects that produced them *(squash, splash, thump),* the morphemes of most words are fairly arbitrary. For example, an English-speaking child can talk about a *dog,* a Latin American child can talk about a *perro,* and a French child can talk about a *chien* and mean the same thing. It is difficult to see any direct connection between the sound, or phonetic, structure and the meanings of most words. In Chapter 8, we will have more to say about the development of language, especially language structure.

The First Words

Anthropologists who have studied child-rearing practices in different cultures tell us that there are considerable differences in the environments in which infants are raised. Across all cultures, however, one aspect of language is universal: the age at which recognizable language begins. When infants are between ten and eighteen months old, they are likely to at least understand speech, and most will

Table 5-1
SEMANTIC CATEGORIES OF EARLY GENERAL NOMINAL WORDS BY FUNCTIONAL GROUP AND ACQUISITION ORDER

	Group (Percent)		
	Referential	Expressive	Total
First ten words:			
Animals	23	50	34
Food	25	18	23
Toys	16	14	15
Vehicles	11	5	9
Household items	7	9	7
Clothing, personal	9	—	6
People	7	5	6
Miscellaneous	2	—	1
Total	100%	100%	100%
After 40 words:			
Animals	10	18	13
Food	28	32	30
Toys	—	4	2
Vehicles	4	4	4
Household items	8	16	11
Clothing, personal	13	18	15
People	—	4	2
Body parts	28	—	17
Miscellaneous	8	2	6
Total	100%	100%	100%

From K. Nelson, "Structure and strategy in learning to talk." *Monographs of the Society for Research in Child Development.* Copyright 1973 by the Society for Research in Child Development, Inc. Serial No. 149, p. 30. Reprinted with the permission of the Society for Research in Child Development.

build up vocabularies of considerable size. The argument that there is a maturational sequence of developmental stages that depends largely on biological factors cannot be easily dismissed. Arguments in favor of this viewpoint should not forget, however, that a child's vocabulary development always depends upon a cultural setting for full growth.

Some recent research by Katherine Nelson (1973) provides insight into the infant's early vocabulary. Eighteen ten- to fifteen-month-old middle-class children served as her research subjects. In the first six months of the study Nelson gathered information on vocabulary and on mother-child interactions in the home. During the second part of her study, she obtained information about the amounts and kinds of imitation, language comprehension, and verbalization shown by each child in various activities.

Even at this early age there were large individual differences in the kinds of things the infants spoke about. Some of the children used words that referred mainly to actions, people, and feelings. Nelson called these infants the *expressive group*. Other children named many things but had few people-related and feeling-related words; Nelson called this latter group the *referential group*.

When Nelson grouped the children's first words into the categories shown in Table 5-1, she found that animal names were most likely to be the first words produced. This was true in spite of the fact that very few of the children in the study actually had pets. The words usually referred to animal toys and pictures or to other people's pets. Even in urban settings animals held the children's interest and dominated their first vocabularies. Food words were next in importance; and after the first fifty words were learned, the emphasis changed so that food words predominated over animal words.

Another finding from Nelson's study reveals more about children's early interests and interactions by indicating what they *did not* learn. All of the infants wore diapers and, of course, were familiar with being diapered; yet no word for "diaper" appeared in the children's language. Words for pants, overalls, jackets, sweaters, and pajamas were also lacking in their vocabularies. No words for large furniture, such as tables, sofas, televisions, and refrigerators, were represented, although these objects were all present in the children's homes. Apparently, the presence and direct experience of objects does not guarantee that these words will appear in early language.

Many of the children's first words referred to actions and to things they could act upon such as toys, socks, and shoes. Some words were characterized by sound and movement. Thus, the children were not only attracted to things that moved but also to things within their own control such as wind-up toys, clocks, and animals.

These findings agree with the emphasis of Piaget and others on the importance of active participation in forming the child's concepts of the world. Although children are influenced by parents and others in their selection of words, the present evidence indicates that the child's own selection of words is significant. Children are not just passive receivers of other people's words; they seem to be quite capable of selecting from a wide array of possible words.

An infant's first words are usually unclear to others and become recognizable only after they have been used for a time. Some linguists maintain that after the first ten words are learned, true speech is underway. For the children in Nelson's study, the first ten words appeared at an average age of about fifteen months. The average age for attaining a 50-word vocabulary is about nineteen months, and the usual rate of gaining new words is about 11 words per month. By twenty-four months, the end of infancy, the child has an average vocabulary of about 190 words. These figures apply to single words. The next significant step, that of using words in combination, depends on further progress in cognitive development and related maturation of the nervous system.

Early Word Combinations and Sentences

The actual beginning of phrase usage is difficult to determine since an infant's first sentences may often be expressed in a single word. Linguists call such language *holophrastic speech,* meaning that the infant may use a single word to express a *whole* idea. For example, in saying "cat," the infant may mean "I find this animal very interesting," or "Hi there, cat," or "I'm afraid of the cat!" Holophrastic speech such as this signifies that infants are limited in language development, but that their thoughts often extend far beyond what they can say.

Such limited speech is often used in emotional situations (Bullowa, Jones, & Bever, 1971) where the one-word sentences serve as an efficient way to express feelings quickly. "Cat" could also mean "I'm afraid" and therefore serves the purpose of both a label and an emotional expression. Some researchers believe that holophrastic speech is the beginning of true language (Brown, 1968; Brown & Bellugi, 1966). Holophrastic speech may also be used to help the infant direct his or her own actions. For example, an infant might say "Go" and then leave the room.

As language develops, the infant's language structure becomes more complex, and at about twenty months of age, the child begins to combine words in orderly ways. Among the first patterns of word combinations that we can see is a pattern called *telegraphic speech* (Brown & Fraser, 1971) because the child leaves out articles, auxiliary verbs, and inflections in the same way that an adult might compose a telegram. Like the receivers of telegrams, parents are often very skilled in expanding these condensed messages into meaningful statements. Witness, for example, this dialogue between Johnny and his father:

"Hi, Daddy."*
"Hi, Johnny. Did Mommy buy this truck?"

---

*From D. S. Palermo, "Language acquisition," in H. W. Reese and L. P. Lipsitt, eds., *Experimental Child Psychology* (New York: Academic Press, 1970). By permission.

"This truck."

"Can you make it go fast?"

"Go fast. Hat off. Shirt off. Pants off. That blue."

"Yes, my pants are blue."

"Sweater on. Chair."

"Where's the kitty?"

"Kitty allgone. Here is. See Mummy. There Mummy."

"Yes, here comes Mommy."

"Here Mummy."

"I'll go out and help her carry in the groceries."

"Groceries. Bye bye. Two bag. Chicken. That red. Here kitty. Bag fall. Close it."

"I can't close the box, so we'll have pizza for dinner."

"John dinner."

"We'll make your dinner now."

"Baby dinner."

"Yes, we'll make dinner for the baby, too."

"Pick glove."

"I'll pick up my glove. Say, how did your knees get so dirty?"

"Knee dirty. See knee."

"Let's wash you off before dinner."

"Wash off."

"Where's the washcloth?"

"Washcloth. Here is. Two cloth. Dirty. Dirty allgone."

It should be noted that Johnny's words were expressed in an orderly arrangement. Such word arrangements obey certain rules of *syntax,* or *grammar.* Many researchers have attempted to discover the syntactical rules that children use in their early sentences but the answers to this puzzle have not been completely found. There are several reasons for this. One reason concerns the possibility that children may have far greater language competence than we can observe from their spoken performances (Chomsky, 1968). For example, as adults we know that we often comprehend more words when we read than we would ordinarily use in speaking. Another major problem concerns the fact that it is very difficult to gather adequate samples of language performance from infants and very young children. As a result, most researchers have studied only very small samples of children and even then large individual differences among children have been seen.

One promising approach toward finding the rules used by children in their first sentences can be seen in the work of Roger Brown (1973) and his colleagues. According to Brown, about 75 percent of early sentences fall into the following patterns:

1. Nominative: Naming things, such as "That dolly."
2. Recurrence: Statements about repetition, such as "More milk."
3. Expressions of disappearance or non-existence: such as "Allgone doggy."
4. Possessive: Statements such as "Mommy cup."
5. Locative: References to places, such as "Cat chair." (The cat is on the chair).
6. Agent-action patterns: A person does something, such as "Mommy sit."
7. Action-object patterns: Something happens to something, such as "Throw toy."
8. Agent-object patterns: A person and a thing, omitting the action, such as "Mommy spoon" which might mean "Mommy uses a spoon" or "Mommy, give me the spoon."

Brown observed a few other, much rarer, patterns in the first sentences of children, such as experiencer-state relations ("I hear"), indirect object statements ("Give Daddy"), commands ("Walk Mommy"), and statements referring to the uses of things ("Soap clean").

There are some things that we can be sure of in children's first sentences. One is that the sentences are not random collections of words but, instead, follow some kind of rules. Another is that these rules are not always the rules of adult language. Finally, there seem to be individual differences in the kinds of rules that children use.

In Table 5-2 we have presented some of the milestones of language that occur in the first two years. As with any averages, the ages at which these language abilities occur are to be taken as approximations. Some children will develop earlier and some will develop later than these average figures indicate.

DIFFERING VIEWS OF LANGUAGE ACQUISITION

Several theories have attempted to explain how children acquire language. As we shall see, while each theory has some research support, none can completely explain all of the complexities of language acquisition. We will look first at the work of the behaviorists, who emphasize the role of the environment in the child's acquisition of language and then at the views of the transformational linguists, who emphasize universal biologically-determined factors in language development.

Table 5-2
MILESTONES OF LANGUAGE DEVELOPMENT IN THE FIRST TWO YEARS

Approximate Age of Occurence	Sound, Language, and Speech Production		Sound, Language, and Speech Reception	
	Nonsocial	Social	Nonsocial	Social
Birth to 1 month	Crying	Crying?	Responds to sounds and locates the sound source	Distinguishes between human voices and other sounds
1–2 months	Can vocalize and produce non-crying vowel sounds such as *ah, eh, oo*		Will stop crying when a novel sound such as a bell occurs	Responds to voices with greater attention
2–3 months	Produces several different vocalizations; laughs	Laughs?		Smiles and vocalizes when spoken to; can discriminate among emotional qualities of adult speech.
3–4 months	Cooing; produces several vowel syllables	Laughs and shows other signs of pleasure when spoken to		Perceives syllables
4–5 months	Coos and chuckles; babbles and plays with syllables such as *ba, da, ka.*	May start to imitate sounds		
5–6 months	Increased sound play	Imitates inflections; babbles to gain attention		Attends to differences in intonation and rhythm in adult speech; watches mouths as people talk; turns head to speaker and may recognize own name
6–7 months	Babbles things like *ma, mu, da, di, ba* repeatedly; produces consonants like *f, v, s, sh, z, sz, m, n*	"Talks" to people		Responds to emotions in others' voices
7–8 months	"Singing" tones;	Repeats two syllables		Will mimic mouth

Age			
	may name an object by imitating its sound; for example: "bow-wow" for dog	and imitates speech sounds; may say "dada" or "mama" but not to a specific person	movements; can recognize familiar words
8–9 months	Combines syllables	Signals emotions; imitates sounds like coughs, tongue clicks, and hisses	Listens to conversations; may carry out simple commands
9–10 months		Starts to vocalize in speech-like gibberish; may say "mama" or "dada" to a specific person	
10–11 months		Waves "bye-bye" and may say it; more likely to say "mama" or "dada" to the correct person	Can clearly distinguish between phonemes in speech
11–12 months		Says at least one word meaningfully, usually a noun	
12–18 months		Imitates animal sounds in games with parents; uses words meaningfully; imitates some words; mixes meaningful words with jargon	Starts to respond to commands like "no" and "Don't do that!"
18–24 months		Names objects; has a vocabulary that may range from about 20 words at 18 months to about 200 words or more at 24 months; will combine two or more words into simple "telegraphic" phrases	Can point to pictures, objects, and body parts on request; answers questions; can follow several directions in order

Source: This table combines information on early speech and language from a number of sources. The most valuable were Caplan (1971), Illingworth (1975), Kaplan and Kaplan (1971), Lenneberg (1966), and McCarthy (1946).

These are average ages that should be treated as approximations. There are large individual differences in the rates at which children develop language. Therefore, small-to-moderate differences between these averages and any individual child's speech and language development should not be interpreted as indications of precocious or retarded development.

Behaviorism and Language Learning

As discussed in Chapter 2, behaviorism is based on evidence from experiments in human and animal learning. Behaviorism stresses the importance of both people and events in the environment as providers of reinforcements that shape the child's language. The behaviorists have focused on three types of learning which may be useful in explaining some aspects of language.

One important form of learning is the *classical conditioning* discovered by Ivan Pavlov. When we think of stimuli we tend to think of lights, sounds, smells, and touches. However, words are also stimuli and can become conditioned stimuli. Let's suppose that one-year-old Billy touched a hot water faucet and withdrew his hand in pain. The faucet can be considered to be an unconditioned stimulus; it elicits such unconditioned responses as pain, hand withdrawal, and probably some memory or internal representation of the experience. Suppose that just as Billy was going to reach for the faucet, his mother shouted "Hot!" It was too late, however, and Billy touched the faucet before his mother could stop him. His mother's word "hot" can serve as a conditioned stimulus and, when paired with the hot faucet, can later elicit some of the components of the original unconditioned response. Then, when Billy hears "hot," he may withdraw his hand or recall the original pain or some other related unpleasant experience. In this way, learning theory may explain the acquisition of word meaning.

Operant conditioning, studied extensively by B. F. Skinner, is another powerful influence on behavior. As an example of the use of operant conditioning in explaining a child's speech productions, imagine the following scenario. A little girl named Suzy was happily babbling away in her playpen. Among her favorite babbles was the string of phonemes "ma-ma-ma." Suzy's mother entered the room, walked over to the playpen, and thought, "She's calling me." She smiled and cheerfully picked Suzy up, saying, "You want to talk to me!" Suzy may not have had the slightest idea of what "mama" meant, but she certainly knew and enjoyed her mother's reinforcing smiles and warm interactions with her. We could predict that the next time her mother approached her, Suzy would be more likely to say "mama" again and, most probably, her mother would also reinforce her speech. We can predict also that not everyone will reinforce Suzy's "mama" utterances and that she will therefore become more selective in her use of "mama." During World War II, when one of the authors was a baby, his father was in the Navy. For him, a Navy uniform was a cue for eliciting "Daddy," and he often embarrassed his mother by running up to sailors, shouting "Daddy," and hugging them. Needless to say, this activity was soon extinguished, and he became more discriminating in his use of the word "Daddy."

Another basic form of learning which has been used in explanations of language learning is imitation. In imitation (or observational learning), there are two participants: a *model* and an *observer*. The model produces a word response and is often rewarded for it. The observer, who has watched and listened to the model, tends to follow suit and produces a replica of the model's response. Although we cannot ask an infant who has not yet acquired language, it is quite probable that the infant may expect the same reward that the model received.

It would seem that learning through imitation might be an important source of human vocabulary expansion. At present, however, we have only a few studies that support this idea because obtaining this kind of information is difficult. Furthermore, defining when a child is imitating is difficult in practice. Should a speech sound be considered imitation if it only remotely resembles a model's speech? Most, if not all, infant imitations of adult speech are only crude approximations and, therefore, investigations of imitation in early language development are limited.

When infants begin to use words at around one year of age, direct attempts to bring about imitation are generally unsuccessful. Nelson (1973) reported that she found a low level of imitation at this age, noting that less than three percent of her recorded infant vocalizations were imitations. At approximately twenty months, when mothers said words to children as they looked at pictures together, there was a high correlation between the child's vocabulary size and the amount of imitation that the child displayed. This correlation suggests that vocabulary size may facilitate imitation but not vice-versa.

The same study also indicated that when imitation occurred, object names (names for the pictured objects shown to the children in the experiment) were not imitated more often than function words (words that fulfill only a grammatical function). Thus, if imitation is purposefully used as a teaching method, it appears that names of objects are no more effective than other words. Nelson concluded that imitation is likely if the child already knows the word and that whether or not the word is used appropriately in association with an object matters little to the child. Similarly, Bloom, Hood, and Lightbown (1974) recorded the speech of six infants and found that when the infants imitated words and phrases, they usually did so with things they had already become familiar with through nonverbal means such as looking, touching, and listening. Therefore, imitation may not be very useful for learning the names of new things but may be highly useful for learning the labels of things that the infant already knows. Bloom and her colleagues also observed that when children imitated sentences, they rarely imitated sentences that were either much simpler or much more complex than those they had spontaneously produced by themselves. Thus, in this case, imitation seemed to strengthen the language skills that the children were already acquiring on their own.

Transformational Linguistics and Language Development

Noam Chomsky, a linguist from the Massachusetts Institute of Technology, and his followers at various universities throughout the world have explored an approach to language development that differs considerably from learning theories. Chomsky has raised several points about language that strongly challenge learning theory viewpoints. One point is that no normal, native speaker of any language on earth puts together words purely at random (other than for fun). For example, we might say "The boy ran home" or "Was it the boy who ran home?" It would be highly unlikely for anyone to say "Ran boy the home." In fact, children everywhere use and understand some of the basic principles of grammar and syntax required by their native languages without being taught. It would be difficult to imagine that

an infant or a very young child would ever be directly reinforced for learning grammar and syntax principles. In addition, most children have very little opportunity to
watch models use all of the possible syntactical constructions of their language.

Chomsky also points out that most of the sentences we produce are fairly original. That is, we usually have never produced the sentences before, and we probably will never say them again in exactly the same ways. Remarkably, other people
usually do understand our sentences. How can we explain these observations in
learning terms? The answer is that we really cannot explain sentence originality in
learning terms because learning theories explain how we are likely to *repeat* a
response *after* some initial exposure to a learning situation.

Children make characteristic errors with irregular nouns and verbs that adults
are unlikely to make. For example, we might say to a two-year-old: "One dog, two
dogs," "One sheep, two _____." The young child will usually answer "sheeps"
although adults would say "sheep." This mistake is not a sign of the child's ignorance. In fact, it shows that the child has learned the rule for pluralization that,
unfortunately, doesn't fit this particular irregular case (Berko, 1958). Since the child
hasn't heard adults use the word "sheeps" and probably will not be reinforced for
saying the word, how can we explain this observation in learning terms?

Children and adults can transform sentences with different *surface structures*
such as the following into sentences with the same *deep structures* or underlying
meanings:

The girl ate the cake. (A simple declarative sentence)

The cake was eaten by the girl. (Passive)

Did the girl eat the cake? (Question)

Was the cake eaten by the girl? (Passive question)

Wasn't the cake eaten by the girl? (Passive negative question)

Chomsky (1968) and other *transformational linguists* suggest that the reasons
why children and adults have such remarkable linguistic competencies may be due
to a biologically-determined *Language Acquisition Device,* or LAD. While Chomsky thinks that imitation and reinforcement have some influence on the development of vocabulary, the child's capacity to use language is believed to be primarily
innate.

The notion that an inborn disposition to language exists and that it is species
specific for the human species has been highly controversial. Chomsky, nevertheless, believes that human beings are born with aptitudes to acquire the phonemic,
syntactic, and semantic bases for language. Other researchers have also explored
the possibility that there are some universal characteristics of language. Some early
studies of human phonetic abilities seemed to show universal patterns in which
certain sounds are acquired at increasing ages (Irwin, 1947a, 1947b, 1947c, 1948).

INFLUENCES ON LANGUAGE ACQUISITION

Language is influenced by biological, cognitive, and social factors (Ervin-Tripp, 1976). By *biological factors* we mean that the maturation of the nervous system and the systems for speech and hearing will necessarily aid, as well as limit, the infant's language capabilities. By *cognitive factors* we mean that the infant must first know about and understand things and events in order to talk about them. That is, a child has probably spent a considerable amount of time playing with, looking at, and getting familiar with the properties of objects before actually asking for or producing the words for them. By *social factors* we mean that the infant learns the meaning of things in the presence of other people. Language is developed in social settings. Through language children can express feelings, request actions and things, state opinions, and ask questions of other people. In the following sections we shall explore some of these influences on speech and language in greater detail.

Biological Factors

Because language and speech are such natural characteristics of human behavior, we often forget that the mechanisms behind speech and language are quite complex. In order to receive spoken language, we must be able to detect small variations in the pitch, loudness, and timing of sounds.

Over 30 years ago, researchers Jack Bernard and Lester Sontag (1947) placed loudspeakers on the abdomens of women who were in their last months of pregnancy. It was found that when tones were presented through the loudspeakers, the fetal heart rates would increase for a short time after stimulation and then return to their normal rates after the tones were turned off. As mentioned in Chapter 4, several studies have indicated that very young infants not only respond to sounds but can also discriminate among vowels and consonants (Eimas et al., 1971; Trehub, 1972). Some recent studies also indicate that neonates as young as one day old can synchronize their body movements to their mothers' speech (Condon, 1975). It appears, therefore, that as far as hearing language goes, infants are fairly well-equipped at, or shortly after, birth.

But what about the mechanisms for connecting sounds and ideas and for producing words? It seems that infants are not so well-equipped in this respect. The areas of the brain that are important in speech and language are not very well developed at birth. In fact, the language areas in the frontal and temporal lobes of the brain are among the slowest parts of the brain to mature (Carmichael, 1964). In addition, speech production requires highly complex coordination of breathing, movements of the lip, tongue, and mouth, and positioning of the vocal cords. Although infants can cry at birth, it takes a considerable amount of time before the structures that are necessary for complex speech sounds have matured.

Language involves the exchange of symbols. To talk about something, we have to remember words, phrases, and ideas from the past, and we also have to plan what we are going to say. Until the brain structures involved in memory and planning have matured, the child's communication abilities will be limited.

While we have talked so far about the biological limitations on language, it is very important to realize that language appears in all children at roughly the same times. Certain sequences of language development seem to be universal. For example, infants produce vowel sounds before consonants, and nearly everywhere cooing and babbling precede the production of words. Even congenitally deaf infants go through a babbling stage, although they may never have heard the sounds of their own voices (Lenneberg, 1964). It seems that language functions are an important product of human evolution and that these functions are moderately well-established in early life.

Cognitive Factors

Suppose that you were asked to speak about some topic such as "The things that you like about your friends," or "Your opinions about your education," or "Whether it's going to rain tomorrow." As you discussed these topics, a number of cognitive processes would be taking place.

Most probably, you would be relying on memory functions in order to talk about things that are not immediately present. You would use imagery so that you could picture things in your mind as you talked about them. In doing this you might also have to rely on your concepts of time and space in order to get the order and location of topics correct. Hopefully, since stories usually have a beginning, a middle, and an end, you probably would create an overall plan with which to put the parts of your discussion together. Because you're going to tell this story to other people, you would have to assess your audience in order to adjust your communication to their needs, their interests, and their language capabilities.

Unless you were under a great deal of stress or had suffered from a brain injury, you probably would find this task fairly easy to do. For an infant, however, many of these cognitive functions have not been fully developed. In order to talk about something, you have to know something about it. In order to talk to people, you have to know something about them. In order to ask, "What is that?", you have to know something about "that" in the first place (Bloom, 1978; McNamara, 1972).

Later in this chapter, when we discuss Piaget's discoveries on the sensorimotor stage of infancy, we shall see how infants develop the underlying cognitive skills necessary for language. We will see that infants actively develop schemes involving the representation and recognition of objects, notions of time and space, and the recognition of other people.

Social Factors

Human beings not only have the most complex language patterns of any species, they also form the most complex social organizations. Through language we can ask questions; we can order people to do things for us; we can tell them our feelings and try to understand theirs; and we can perform social rituals such as greetings and farewells (Ervin-Tripp, 1976). Through joking, singing, and storytelling we can entertain ourselves and other people. Language allows us to know about people, places, and things that go far beyond our present time and place. It is highly unlikely that any species other than the human species has the ability to concern itself with the future.

Because we are in constant contact with other people, it is not surprising that language development should be affected by social forces. Let us look at the social environments in which language is acquired from other people.

Experience with Social Stimulation. As language is a major aspect of social interaction, we can expect to find that vocalization and early speech are both influenced by the amount and quality of stimulation that infants receive from the important people in their lives. Infants whose mothers talk to them a great deal tend to vocalize more than children whose mothers talk very little (Barrett-Goldfarb & Whitehurst, 1973). Talkative mothers influence not only the sheer amount of vocalization that their babies will produce but also the variety of sounds that their infants produce (Dodd, 1972).

Life in an institution such as an orphanage or hospital makes a difference in early speech patterns. Institutionalized infants who have had limited opportunities to interact with other people do not vocalize as much as do infants who were raised in their own homes (Yarrow, Rubenstein, & Pedersen, 1975; Langmeier & Matejcek, 1975). Researchers have found that the amount of vocalization in institutionalized infants increases when attendants, nurses, and other caregivers respond to the infants' vocalizations by smiling, making sounds, and by touching them (Rheingold, Gewirtz, & Ross, 1959). Individual differences among children also play a role in this process. While increased stimulation and rewarding reinforcements increase the amount of babbling in some infants (Schwartz, Rosenberg, & Brackbill, 1970), other infants do not seem to need as much external stimulation and will vocalize frequently and for long periods of time without it. Other infants, however, seem to require a great deal of stimulation. In any event, vocalizations and social responses do not seem to increase as rapidly in institution-reared children as they do in home-raised children because the caregivers are assigned to many infants and are usually not in attendance as often as are parents in the home.

Linguistic Experience in the Home. Since many children begin to use language at home, researchers have tried to gain some information about the child's experiences there. Friedlander, Jacobs, Davis, and Wetstone (1972) explored the language environments of two one-year-old children. A girl, Tena Jones, and a boy, Mark Smith, and their families were studied intensively. Voice-activated tape recorders were placed in the children's homes and were set to turn on for a five-minute period every twenty minutes. The total sample of recordings covered approximately three hours of verbalization in each family. The data gathered from these recordings were analyzed for both the quantity (how much the child heard) and the quality (how effective was the exposure) of verbalizations heard by each child.

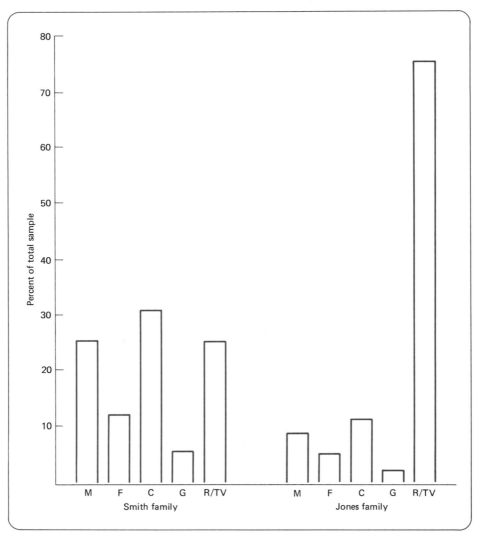

Figure 5-1.   Systematic sample analysis of the duration of all language sources tape-recorded in the home environment for two twelve-month-old infants. M = mother; F = father; C = child; G = guests; R/TV = radio/television. (From B. Z. Friedlander, A. C. Jacobs, B. B. Davis, and H. S. Wetstone. Time-sampling analysis of infants' natural language environments in the home. *Child Development*, 1972, **43**, 733. Copyright 1972 by the Society for Research in Child Development, Inc. By permission.)

In the analysis of their data, the investigators counted and recorded the amount of verbalization and conversation from the mother (M), the father (F), the child (C), guests (G), and from sources such as radio and television (R/TV). The language experiences of Mark and Tena according to source are shown in Figure 5-1. In Mark's home 25 percent of his total language experience came from radio and television. The remaining 75 percent came from his mother, his father, and the family's guests. Tena's experiences, however, were the reverse of Mark's. About 75 percent of her language experience came from radio and television, and only about 25 percent was from her family and other people.

Analysis of the data from the two families indicated that the relative speaking times of the members were similar. Most of the conversations with the infants came from their mothers. Fathers had very few exchanges with their children, a finding supported by other studies (Rebelsky & Hanks, 1971). At the time of the study the fathers were graduate students and, although their exchanges with their children were very limited, they actually may have spent more time at home during their children's waking hours than other more regularly employed fathers.

Some other non-obvious differences in the families were discovered. For example, Tena's father spoke only Spanish to her even though he was a native speaker of standard American English. His overall contributions to Tena's language experiences were small (less than 5 percent of the total), yet Tena had a basic understanding of Spanish when she was one year old. In a follow-up study six months later, it was found that Tena could carry out a series of instructions in Spanish and could actually construct simple Spanish sentences. The investigators considered the child's acquisition of her second language to be remarkable in view of her limited experience with it.

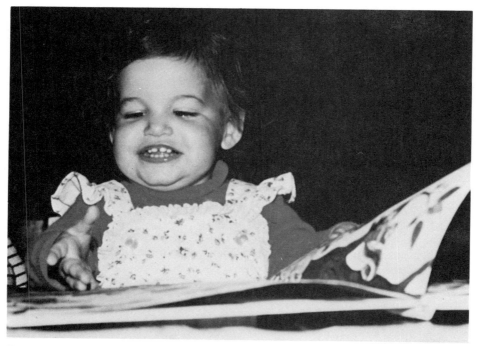

Figure 5-2.   Research in language development during infancy has alerted us to the fact that a wide variety of social, biological, and cognitive factors contribute to language development. Close, warm contacts between parents and children and increased exposure to many language sources may play important roles in forming children's language abilities.

Studies such as the one we have just mentioned provide a new direction for infancy researchers. Many studies have paid attention to communications between mothers and infants in activities such as feeding, bathing, and playing. This study went further, to explore the much larger *receptive language environment.* Hopefully, future studies will also attend to language sources such as television and radio and conversations going on around the infant, so that we may assess the impact of whole environments on the infant's language development.

We have now examined the development of language in infants and young children and have seen that language is influenced by the interplay of innate biological tendencies, cognitive, and social factors. We will discuss language development in older children in later chapters, but since language development is accompanied by advances in cognitive development, we shall now turn to consideration of the mental development of the infant.

COGNITIVE DEVELOPMENT IN INFANCY: PIAGET'S RESEARCH

In recent years an increasing number of psychologists have turned to the work of Jean Piaget on infant intelligence. Piaget was originally trained as a biologist, and throughout his career he has been interested in how organisms adapt to their environments. One such adaptation is intelligence. For Piaget, the concept of stages of intellectual development is based on the notion of biological development and evolution which underlies much of his thinking.

As we had mentioned in Chapter 2, Piaget sees children as going through a series of stages whose order never varies. The order of developmental stages is a critical aspect of Piaget's theory. Although he believes children may arrive at each stage at slightly different times, they always go through the stages in the same order. Another important aspect of Piaget's theory is that in each stage children actually create a series of active "experiments" on their environments and, as a result of these experiments, they construct new views of the world for themselves (Piaget, 1952; 1954; 1970). It may be difficult for adults to understand that children's thinking is different from adult thinking not only in the *amounts* of information that children possess, but more importantly in the *ways* that they know things. Piaget believes that infants are not only influenced *by* the environment, but infants also *influence* the environment and construct personal views of it.

The Development of Intelligence

As an overview, let us recall that in Piagetian theory the growth of intelligence is divided into four major periods or stages. The first, the *sensorimotor stage,* occurs in infancy and covers most of the first two years of life. During this first period, the child's capacity in symbol usage, language, imagery, and concept formation is limited. The major theme of this period is action, and actions such as sucking, grasping, crawling, and walking lay the foundations for increasingly more complex behaviors.

In the next three stages we begin to see *conceptual intelligence.* This kind of intelligence is apparent in the last part of the infancy period. Conceptual intelligence includes three stages. In the second stage, the *preoperational stage,* which lasts from the end of the sensorimotor period until about seven years of age, children begin to use language and symbols. Their behavior increases in complexity. In this stage there is a great increase in imaginative play. In the third stage, the *concrete operational stage,* which lasts from about seven to eleven years of age, children begin to understand cause-and-effect relationships and are able to understand concepts involving time, quantity, weight, volume, and matter. The final stage of intellectual development, the *formal operational stage,* is reached around the twelfth year. This stage is marked by the ability to perceive and deal effectively with high-level abstractions and symbolic thought. In this chapter we will focus on the sensorimotor stage.

The Sensorimotor Period of Development

Piaget divided the sensorimotor stage into six substages. The first four substages are usually completed in the first year, and the last two are reached in the second year. As is true of most age-related behaviors, the age spans of the following stages are approximate.

Stage 1: Use of Reflexes.   This stage, which occurs between birth and one month of age, is one in which the infant uses many inborn reflexes. The reflexes provide the earliest behaviors that the infant has for dealing with the environment. These reflexes soon become modified by experience.

One common reflex that Piaget (1952) and others have studied extensively is sucking. At first a newborn infant may automatically and reflexively start sucking movements whenever a nipple is touched to the infant's mouth. In this sense, the sucking can be considered an act of assimilation because the infant is responding to the situation with a scheme that has already been developed. But some problems soon arise that force the infant to modify this simple reflex. For example, the infant's mother may change her position so that the nipple will not make direct contact with the infant's mouth. Also, the infant has to coordinate sucking, breathing, and swallowing movements. Because of these challenges, the infant will have to accommodate to the new situation by moving the head to meet the nipple or by slowing breathing in order to adjust to sucking. Soon new schemes will be developed and the infant may combine these schemes with still other schemes.

In this first stage infants will actively practice their new schemes and will attempt to assimilate other activities into sucking. For example, infants will try to suck at things other than nipples—thumbs, toys, and clothing. Through these activities the infant may also develop some basic schemes.

Stage 2: Development of Simple Habits and Primary Circular Reactions.

The second stage of the sensorimotor period takes place between one and four months and is characterized by the formation of simple habit patterns. Piaget uses the term *primary circular reactions* to describe a characteristic behavior of this stage. The term refers to a situation in which a behavior that was originally random and purposeless produces some accidental result that becomes pleasing to the child and is then repeated. For example, a baby's random arm movements may activate a mobile that is hanging over the crib. The infant may smile and then try to repeat the act, possibly succeeding after several attempts. After many such repetitions, the activity can be said to be a "habit." Piaget denies that these habits can truly be called intelligence, but compared to the reflexes in Stage 1 they are not automatic and have a "greater range in space and time."

In the second substage, new behaviors are integrated with a number of actions, such as sucking, seeing, and grasping and holding objects. Infants proceed from simple grasping and holding of objects, in which nothing much is done to the objects, to a new phase in which they can coordinate seeing an object, grasping it, and placing it in their mouths. The circular reactions of this second stage grow out of reflex movements. By the second month the movements become systematized so that the infants are capable of gradual accommodation and assimilation.

Piaget's series of observations of his own children provided examples of the kind of data that he used in the development of his theory (Piaget, 1952). Here are some characteristic Stage 2 behaviors that Piaget observed in his son Laurent:

> . . . At 0;1(8) [0 years, 1 month, 8th day] Laurent's arm is stretched out and almost immobile while his hand opens, half closes and then opens again, etc. When the palm of his hand strikes the covers, he grasps them, lets them go in unceasing oscillating motion. It is difficult to describe these vague movements, but it is also difficult not to see in them grasping, or even empty grasping analogous to the phenomena described in connection with sucking, vision, etc. But there does not yet exist, in such behavior patterns, either true accommodation to the object or even any continuity. (p. 90)

> . . . Beginning at 0;1(22), on the other hand, there seems to be more continuity in the grasping movements. Thus at 0;1(22), Laurent holds in his hand four and a half minutes an unfolded handkerchief which he grasped by chance (his arm is occasionally immobile and occasionally in slow movement). (p. 91)

> . . . At 0;3(8) after the experiment with the rattle . . . he loses it on the right side (but he has let it go with his left hand while he was shaking it from side to side). Laurent then looks four or five times in succession at the empty left hand. He even shakes his hand very markedly, at a certain moment, as though this shaking would start the sound of the rattle! Regardless of this last point, in any case he marks with his glance the position of his hand. (p. 113)

According to Piaget, these behaviors are the beginnings of essential coordination of schemata. From this stage of development onward, infants *reach out* and

grasp a variety of objects that are distant but are still in sight. In other words, infa
are no longer under the control of simple, automatic reflexes. They are beginn.
to become freed from having to respond in a rigid way to just any stimulus tl
presents itself to them. Before we think, however, that infants' actions are nc
completely free, we find that an important element of behavior is still missing in th
stage—planning or *intention*. Although infants can grasp an object and appear to
be looking at it, we cannot be sure that such behaviors are conscious, planned, and
purposeful. The beginning of intention does not occur until the next stage.

Stage 3: Secondary Circular Reactions. In the third stage, occurring
between four and eight months, infants intentionally branch out toward their now
ever-widening worlds. In this stage their repetitive or circular reactions are called
secondary circular reactions. These reactions are different from the previous primary circular reactions because they deal mainly with objects in the environment,
while the earlier reactions dealt mainly with the infant's own body. Many favorite
activities in this stage involve repetitive actions. Babies at this stage love toys that
rattle and shake, bounce up and down, or sway back and forth. At first, they look
surprised when a favorite toy sways, bounces, or swings. At some point, however,
they will accidentally strike the toy and soon notice that they can personally initiate
a whole range of actions in the toy. These discoveries are explored further by each
infant, and soon they become very busy initiating actions and looking for their
repetitions.

One game that infants play at this stage involves throwing rattles and toys out
of a crib or playpen. Usually a parent will pick up the toy and find that as soon as
the toy is returned, the child will toss the toy out of the crib again. These cycles of
discarding and retrieving can be repeated many times. While the patience of many
parents becomes frayed at this point, the child is actually making some very important and serious discoveries.

Before this third stage is reached, infants respond to objects that are placed
directly in front of them, but they spend very little time moving their bodies to
actively search for objects. Is this because they do not have the muscle strength or
coordination to turn around? Actually, this is not the case. It seems that infants
don't believe that objects still exist when they are out of view. Given this notion,
why *should* the child look for things? For adults the notion that things will completely cease to exist when out of sight is inconceivable. If you were asked to shut
your eyes and try to picture some pleasant thing that you are going to do tomorrow,
it is likely that you would come up with a fairly vivid image. Infants, however, do
not have the images we enjoy as adults. To them, the world is a series of disconnected scenes that are about as sensible as a badly spliced film.

To return to our rattle-tossing baby—at first, the baby's surprise at the rattle's
return seems to say, "How in the world did this reappear? Wasn't it gone?" Later
experiments in rattle-tossing seem to say, "Let's see if this thing can come back
even if I don't see it right away." Eventually, the baby's experiments become
attempts to confirm to his or her own satisfaction the notion of *object permanence*—the idea that "out of sight" is not "out of mind." At this point, infants
begin to be capable of forming memories of the missing objects.

Infants in this stage still rely upon chance opportunities for interaction with the environment. They still depend upon accidental discoveries of interesting stimuli and upon luck in obtaining objects that they want. Thus, the assimilation characteristic of Stage 3 is a further elaboration of the previous stage. In Stage 2 objects existed for sucking, looking at, listening to, touching, and grasping; but in this stage the more active child sees things as existing for shaking, swinging, and rubbing.

Stage 4: Coordination of Secondary Schemes and Their Application to New Situations. This stage lasts from around eight months to about twelve months. During this time infants tend to construct new schemata around previously acquired schemata and start to use them in new situations. They often "intend" to do things, and in doing so they create crude plans that have both ends in sight and the means to achieve these ends.

Figure 5-3. By the fourth stage of the sensorimotor period, infants can combine several schemes and then use them in new situations. This infant is using schemes involving exploring, lifting, and classifying, as well as elementary concepts of objects and space. (Photo by Joseph Karpen)

Consider an eleven-month-old baby who was playing with some blocks. After becoming bored with the blocks and putting them aside, she crawled toward her toy box. Once there, she pushed up the lid and reached inside for a small rubber ball. As she did this, however, a rag doll slipped down and covered the ball. She then pushed her rag doll aside and reached again for the ball. In this example we can see that the child seemed to be using a deliberate plan. The plan involved a combination of the schemes for crawling, searching, pushing, and reaching as a means toward the end of getting another toy. It is also important to realize that some mental representation of the ball must have been present because she was able to keep the notion of the ball in mind while pushing aside the rag doll.

In this stage babies also make considerable progress in understanding objects. The need for an object to be directly visible becomes less important in their goal-seeking behaviors. There will still be some difficulty in dealing with objects, however. The following example is a variation of the ''shell game'' played by magicians and shows some typical behaviors of the Stage 4 infant.

A baby watches while a toy car is put under a bowl; the baby can easily retrieve the car. If two bowls are used, however, one yellow and the other green, then the baby will have a problem. First, let's put the toy under the yellow bowl and allow him to get it. Then, while he is watching us, we will put the toy under the yellow bowl, take it out, and show it to him. Then, we will put the toy under the green bowl while the baby is watching. At this point, we might ask, ''What will the infant do?'' The answer is, ''Look for the toy under the yellow bowl!'' In this situation the infant would repeat a behavior that was successful in obtaining the toy previously. In the new situation the baby was unable to search for the object in the place where it was put later. Piaget called this searching in the wrong place the typical reaction of Stage 4. Although children in this stage are making progress in understanding the permanence of objects, they have some remaining deficiencies in understanding such problems.

Stage 5: Tertiary Circular Reactions and the Discovery of New Means Through Active Experimentation.

The fifth stage occurs between twelve and eighteen months and has been called the *tertiary circular reaction stage.* Piaget sees this stage as a creative series of experiments in which infants seek novelty for its own sake, trying new ways of doing things. They truly adapt themselves to unfamiliar situations and invent new behaviors through vigorous experimentation. These new adaptations occur not only because earlier schemata have become established but because new ones are becoming established as well. This kind of behavior leads not only to *functioning intelligence,* according to Piaget, but to the beginnings of *concrete thought.*

In an observation of his son Laurent at ten months, Piaget illustrated the change from the fourth to fifth stage. One way of describing this change would be in terms of a transition from secondary to tertiary circular reactions. Piaget described how a previous repetition of a secondary circular reaction that was pleasurable (letting go of a piece of bread from his hand) became a tertiary reaction when Laurent shifted his attention from the repeated act itself (letting go) to the consequence of the act (the bread falling to the floor). Piaget showed that Laurent could then react to that consequence by picking up the fallen bread.

The following example gives some of the flavor of this stage:

Leanne, a twelve-month-old, was walking across her front lawn. With each of her shaky, toddling steps, she felt the texture of the grass under her feet, and she smiled a big, broad smile that displayed all six of her teeth. At one point she paused and got down on her hands and knees to look backward through her legs. Seeing her mother, she giggled and then turned around and repeated this action several times.

After a minute or so, she picked herself up and ambled over to a small pine tree. As she reached out and touched its prickly needles, she pulled back, vocalized, and stared at the branches. Then she grabbed a low branch that had no needles and started to shake the branch back and forth while chanting in a singsong babbling way.

In this stage an infant such as Leanne will come upon something interesting and will then grab and play with the object for its own sake. In these playful acts, children are also increasing their knowledge about objects and about time and space relations.

Infants often discover new results of behaviors by chance. Experiments in finding novelty, therefore, are always begun by repetition. In their searches infants vary and escalate their movements. Thus, new means of doing things are discovered through experimentation. Piaget concluded that this behavior is accompanied by the infants' structuring of the environment into objects that have permanence and into spatial patterns that are consistent.

Stage 6: Invention of New Means Through Mental Combinations.

The last stage of the sensorimotor period occurs between eighteen and twenty-four months. In this stage, infants begin to represent objects through mental images. Thus, they can now internally represent objects that are no longer present. Picturing things in their heads can lead to problem-solving attempts where possible solutions can be pictured and tried out mentally before any final action toward solution is taken.

In this stage, when children wish to find a toy and have not already achieved behavior patterns that would help them solve the problem, they mentally invent new ones. In doing this, their behavior becomes more advanced. In solving problems, they can move beyond simple trial-and-error attempts in which they have to touch things toward planned, intentional explorations. The important accomplishments of this stage, therefore, are representation and invention. This stage can be seen as a connection between the sensorimotor stage and later complex behaviors involving language and symbols. The sixth stage is only the beginning, a transition period, toward this kind of behavior (Piaget [1930] 1960, [1947] 1972, 1954; Piaget & Inhelder [1948] 1967).

With the end of the sixth substage of the sensorimotor period, the child enters the preoperational stage, which we shall discuss in a later chapter. Let us pause a moment and reconsider what we have seen. In fact, we have seen a revolution. While we don't usually imagine revolutionaries in cribs or playpens, the baby is truly a revolutionary. Our peaceful revolutionary has gone through a mental revolution in which his or her whole mental world has been reorganized through struggles between assimilation and accommodation. With the help of benevolent caretakers, the child has emerged from being a helpless animal to being a bright, exploring human being.

Too often we think of separate categories of behavior without bothering to put them together into one whole human being. Table 5-3 attempts to integrate some of the growth trends in perception and motor behavior seen in the last chapter with some of the cognitive and language development patterns discussed in the present chapter. It shows that some general principles appear to play a role in abilities that seem quite different at first glance.

Challenges to Piaget's Sensorimotor Stage Theory

Piaget's work has inspired and stimulated a huge number of research projects on the capabilities of infants. A good psychological theory should provide an overall map of the subject to be covered and should also suggest directions for new research. As increasing numbers of researchers explore the boundaries of a theory, they often find that parts of the theory are invalid or need revision. Piaget's theory is no exception, because several new findings on infancy indicate that infants may be able to perform certain kinds of tasks at much earlier ages than Piaget's sensorimotor stage theory would suggest.

One example of remarkably early development can be seen in the discoveries of Colwyn Trevarthen and his colleagues (1975). In their studies of infants who were between the ages of one day and six months, Trevarthen's team found that infants as young as one week old could follow moving objects with their eyes for short distances and could simultaneously attempt to reach for the objects. According to Piagetian theory, reaching and looking behaviors such as these are supposed to appear at their earliest in the second substage (primary circular reactions, 1–4 months) and more typically appear in the third substage (secondary circular reactions, 4–8 months).

A similar set of challenges to Piaget's theory has been provided by Thomas Bower and his colleagues at Harvard University and the University of Edinburgh. In a series of ingenious experiments, Bower (1977) has shown that infants are much better developed when it comes to perceiving movement patterns, making depth judgments, and expecting events to occur than Piaget's infancy observations would suggest.

For a number of years, I. Uzgiris and J. McVicker Hunt at the University of Illinois have been developing a series of scales that would be useful in assessing cognitive development in infancy. In general, their research has been strongly

Table 5-3
THE SENSORY-MOTOR INTELLIGENCE SERIES AS MANIFESTED BY HUMAN INFANTS

Stage	Age (mos.)	Tactile/ Kinesthetic	Visual/Body	Visual/Facial	Example Visual/Gestural	Vocal	Auditory
1 Reflex	0–1	Roots; sucks	Moro reflex; startle reflex*	Reflex smile	—	Reflexive vocalization (crying)	—
2 Primary circular reaction	1–4	Repetitive finger-sucking; repetitive hand-hand clasping		Smile in response to human face	—	Repetitive self-vocalization (cooing)	—
3 Secondary circular reaction	4–8	Repeatedly strikes object; repeatedly rubs object on substrate; repeatedly pushes-pulls object	Repeatedly wiggles body to shake object and watches; kicks legs in response to smiling adult*	Facial expressions of emotion (noncircular); laughing; crying; smile used in circular reaction with smiling adult	Repeatedly swings object and watches	Emotional (noncircular) vocalizations: laughing, crying; back-and-forth vocalizing "games"; repeatedly vocalizes to another in order to obtain a like response (babbling)	Repeatedly shakes, strikes or rubs noise-making object
4 Coordination of secondary behaviors; their application to new situations	8–12	Pushes adult's hand to make him resume previous activity	Rises on tiptoes and raises arms to be picked up*	Looks, smiles at adult to obtain social contact	Removes one object in order to obtain another; reaches up to adult's face to obtain social contact	Begins to combine sounds (babbling); attempts to imitate new sounds and words (echolalia); vocalizes to adult to obtain social contact	Pushes adult's hand toward bell so he will ring it

150

5 Tertiary circular reaction, and the discovery of new means by active experimentation	12–18	Gravity/space: postures the body to accommodate to gravity-space relationships: catches a ball; pushes box under object that is out of reach Trial & error approach-avoidance play*	Plays "keep-away"*	Trial & error face-making in mirror;* facial expressions used to obtain a goal—looks at adult then at desired object	Gravity/space: water play (watches drips, submersion); piles objects; tosses object in air and catches it; puts one object into another Object/object Uses one object (stick) to obtain another (toy); feeds mother;* reaches hand toward desired object that is out of reach and looks at adult*	First words, Vocalizations, including single words used to obtain desired end: vocalizes to adult and reaches toward chair (adult places child in chair)	Object-banging to attain desired end. e.g., bangs on high chair tray to be put down* Trial & error rhymical and musical combinations*
6 Invention of new means through mental combinations	18+	Mentally figures out body-force and body-space relationships; mentally figures out tactics for "keep-away"*		Mentally figures out desired facial expressions often to attain a goal (as in lying)	Gravity/space: anticipates gravity-space relationships; mentally figures out new object-object relationships	Babbling ceases: 2-word utterances often to attain a goal	Mentally figures out rhythmical musical combinations*

Source: From S. Chevalier-Skolnikoff, "The ontogeny of primate intelligence and its implications for communication." *Annals of the New York Academy of Sciences*, 1976, 280, 173–211. Reprinted with permission of the New York Academy of Sciences and Dr. Chevalier-Skolnikoff.
*Chevalier-Skolnikoff, personal observations.

guided by Piaget's theory. In 1975 they published a report on six subscales: an object permanence scale, a development of means and ends scale, a vocal and a gestural expression scale, a scale to measure "operational causality," a spatial relations scale, and a scale to measure the development of schemes related to objects (Uzgiris & Hunt, 1975). It was found that each of their scales corresponded to Piagetian stages, so that at each Piagetian stage infants tended to obtain higher scores on each of Uzgiris and Hunt's scales. These researchers, however, found that infants could vocalize and gesture at earlier stages than Piaget's observations had indicated.

In further statistical analysis of their scales, Uzgiris and Hunt found that their six scales were moderately correlated with each other, so that high performance on one scale generally predicted high performance on the other scales. On the other hand, the correlations among the scales were not so large as to rule out the possibility that development in each area might be relatively independent of development in other areas. Since Piaget's theory states that the same or similar underlying mechanisms are necessary for the performance of a number of behaviors at the same stage, findings such as these tend to weaken Piaget's position.

In all, Piaget has provided researchers who are interested in infant development with a remarkable set of concepts for exploring infancy. As more evidence accumulates, we will be able to see how well his theory can predict and describe infant development. As studies such as those that we have mentioned give us new findings, we may have to revise and replace some of the concepts of Piaget's larger theory.

One of Piaget's most important concepts is his insistence that the child is not only passively acted upon but initiates and undertakes action which, in turn, influences the environment. Hence, children play an important role in setting their own personal goals and directions.

SUMMARY

In this chapter we have discussed two important aspects of infancy: the development of language and the development of intelligence. Language development follows a highly predictable sequence that seems to be nearly universal. Behavioristic approaches to language development view language development as a learning process that is similar, if not identical, to learning processes found in the development of other skills. Transformational linguistic theories see the development of language skills as being due primarily to innate, biological structures that have evolved for the purposes of handling the complexities of language. Biological, cognitive, and social factors all influence language acquisition.

In explaining the development of intelligence during infancy and toddlerhood, Piaget observes that infants in the sensorimotor stage develop from reflexive, biological beings to children who begin to think, to imagine, to remember, and to plan ahead. The findings of some researchers have challenged and some have confirmed Piaget's research on infancy.

RECOMMENDED READINGS

Dale, P. S. *Language Development: Structure and Function.* New York: Holt, Rinehart, & Winston, 1976.

> This book provides a highly readable summary of theories and research on language development during infancy and early childhood.

Piaget, J. *The Origins of Intelligence in Children.* New York: Norton, 1952.

> This book is the definitive book on Piaget's sensorimotor substages. It contains many delightful examples drawn from observations of Piaget's own children.

White, B. L. *The First Three Years of Life.* Englewood Cliffs, N.J.: Prentice-Hall, 1975.

> In this book White describes his original research on cognitive, motor, and emotional development during the first three years and gives a number of interesting suggestions on ways of fostering competence in infants and young children. While different from Piaget's stage sequence, White's seven-phase developmental sequence strongly complements Piaget's work.

6

Social Development in Infancy

In the preceding chapter, we paid particular attention to how infants interact with mainly non-living objects. In this chapter we shall look at how infants deal with even more significant stimuli—other people. Infants begin their lives highly dependent upon the care and concern of others. Although some animals are capable of independent survival at birth, human infants are not. In fact, the human infant has the longest period of dependence of any member of the animal kingdom, and this period lasts for almost twenty years in many parts of the world. During this time, the long association between parents and children has a profound effect on the child's development. Accordingly, from the very beginning of life, the infant's social interaction experiences lay a foundation not only for those relationships in the child's own family, but also for the patterns of social behavior that will take place outside of the home.

SOCIAL INTERACTION IN INFANCY

The Infant's Interaction Abilities

We might first ask ourselves whether infants come into the world ready for social interaction. Some current research has provided strong evidence that even very young infants can and do perform highly complex social behaviors.

If we think of some of the essential characteristics of social interaction, one characteristic that stands out is *coordination*. That is, when we interact with others, we tend to coordinate our actions with theirs. For example, when talking to someone else we would take turns in speaking and listening. We might giggle and smile or cry and frown together. As the person we are talking to moves toward us, we might move toward him or her. We may also move away, however, if the person is getting too close for comfort. In our interaction we would also be giving others feedback about how we feel or think about their behavior. In any case, we would be coordinating our actions with theirs. Infants also coordinate many of their actions with those of their caregivers and seem to be well on their way toward significant social interactions.

In England, William Condon (1975) and his associates have been analyzing films and videotapes of infants who were sometimes only twelve hours old. Analyses of these films indicate that infants tend to move their bodies in almost perfect synchronization with their mothers' voice inflections, as though they were sharing in the give-and-take of conversations. Although voices are certainly important, non-verbal communication may be even more important than voice communication for infants.

Genevieve Carpenter and her colleagues at the Boston University Medical School (Carpenter, 1975) have found that infants as young as two weeks of age can distinguish between their mothers' faces and the faces of strangers. In her studies of both black and white infants, each infant looked through a special viewer that allowed the infant to see either the mother's face or three-dimensional mannequin faces. Interestingly, the infants spent the *least* amount of time looking at their mothers' faces and spent most of their time looking at the strangers' faces. By two weeks of age, the infants had already become used to their mothers' faces and were spending more time exploring the more novel artificial faces. In further studies, however, Carpenter found that when infants were shown their mothers' faces or actual (not mannequin) strangers' faces, they spent more time looking at the mother's face. Perhaps the actual faces were threatening, and so they avoided looking at them. In any case, these studies demonstrate that infants are equipped to discriminate among some of the facial patterns that will play an important role in their later social interactions.

As Carpenter's studies have indicated, babies can recognize faces. How sophisticated are they in doing this? What do they actually see? In 1977, Andrew Meltzoff and Keith Moore of the University of Washington reported an astounding discovery: that infants who were between two and three weeks old could accurately imitate such adult facial expressions as sticking out the tongue, opening the mouth in surprise, and jutting out the lips! Furthermore, the infants were able to imitate finger movements. What makes these results so surprising is not only the fact that such young infants could imitate adults but more importantly, that they could imitate expressions and gestures even though they had never seen their own faces!

We have seen that infants actively look at their parent's faces and move to their parent's voices. When they start to vocalize at around three months of age, they also start to talk *to* their parents. In several studies conducted at the New York State Psychiatric Institute, Daniel Stern and his colleagues examined videotape recordings of mother-and-infant pairs (Stern, 1977; Stern, Jaffe, Beebe, and Bennett, 1975). They discovered not one but two significant communication patterns in the recordings. One pattern appeared when the infants were fairly relaxed: the infants and their mothers seemed to be taking turns, so that when the mother talked the infant would listen and when the infant vocalized the mother would listen. Under high arousal conditions, however, another pattern emerged. This pattern could be called *coaction,* or *chorusing,* because when the mother and infant were active and playing both would tend to vocalize together or remain silent at the same time. Stern (1977) thought this latter pattern a possible indicator of mutuality between the mother and child because in many emotionally close situations, people laugh together, cry together, simultaneously look at each other, and make similar gestures and body movements. In this way, people deliberately (and sometimes unconsciously) exchange gestures and signals that maintain the social interaction.

Discoveries such as those we have just reviewed point out the fact that even in early infancy, social skills and social interactions can be highly complex. As in any other area, individual differences among infants play important roles in their social behavior. One such difference is temperament—a term that can be roughly defined as a person's characteristic mode or style of emotional behavior.

Temperament and Infant Behavior in Social Interaction

Tendencies such as activity level, irritability, and passivity have been called *temperament traits* by many researchers (Thomas and Chess, 1977). Some infants are very active shortly after birth. They wave their arms and legs, twist their bodies,

Box 6-1
Interaction Patterns Between Infants and Their Mothers

Michael Lewis and Susan Lee-Painter studied the interaction patterns of 55 twelve-week-old infants and their mothers. Each mother-infant pair was observed for a total of 720 ten-second intervals. During each interval, the presence or absence of three acts—vocalizing, touching, and smiling—was recorded.

The *figure below* summarizes the patterns of interactions among infants and mothers. The numbers next to each arrow represent the average number of ten-second periods in which an act was performed. The most frequent acts were vocalizations and, on the average, infants vocalized about twenty-nine times to their mothers while the mothers spoke about twenty-four times to their infants. By looking at the figure, we can see the probabilities of certain interaction patterns. For example, the most likely pattern is:

infant's vocalization→mother's vocalization

However, we might also see the pattern:

infant's vocalization→mother's touch→

infant's smile→mother's vocalization→ infant's vocalization

and other more complicated patterns.

In any event, infants appear to be clearly interacting with adults in orderly and predictable ways.

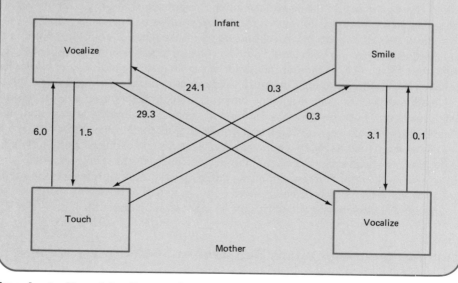

From Lewis, M. and Lee-Painter, S. An interactional approach to the mother-infant dyad. In M. Lewis and L. Rosenblum, eds. *The Effect of the Infant on its Caregiver.* New York: Wiley, 1974, p. 43. Reprinted with permission of the publisher.

and respond very vigorously to many stimuli. They may also show excessive responses to stress. For example, if they are wet or hungry, they may cry loudly and continually, showing such signs of stress as red faces and bodies. The physiological changes in these infants are similar to the emotional reactions of adults who are experiencing stress. Their heart rates increase, their body temperatures rise, they may vomit or move their bowels, and they may develop skin rashes and hives. Other infants in the same situation, however, will be generally placid and contented and will show very few signs of irritability.

Since the 1950s, a research team consisting of Herbert Birch, Alexander Thomas, Stella Chess, and Samuel Korn has been studying individual differences in the temperament patterns of infants, children, and adolescents. An intensive longitudinal study of 141 middle-class, 95 working-class, 68 premature, and 52 retarded infants was started when the infants were two or three months old. At this time, the research team questioned the parents about each infant's behavior and rated the infants on nine categories of behavior. The nine categories were: (1) *activity* level; (2) *rhythmicity,* how predictable or recurring the infant's behavior was; (3) *approach or withdrawal* to new stimuli such as foods, toys, or people; (4) *adaptability,* or how the child adapted to new situations; (5) *threshold of responsiveness,* the amount of stimulation needed to evoke a response from the child; (6) *intensity of reaction;* (7) *general quality of mood,* such as joyful, friendly, depressed, or crying; (8) *distractibility;* and (9) *attention span* and persistence at tasks.

The infants displayed a wide variety of responses on the nine variables, but three separate general temperament patterns were detected in the infants. Some infants could be classified as *easy* infants. These children had regular eating, sleeping, and toilet habits. They warmly approached people, were typically cheerful, and adapted easily to new situations. The "easy" children were clearly easy to handle. Other children, however, could be classified as *difficult.* The difficult children often showed intense responses, displayed negative moods, and withdrew from people. These children generally adapted poorly to new situations and had irregular feeding and eating habits. A third group of children could be classified as *slow to warm up,* because they would usually enter new situations with some uneasiness and were slow to adapt to changes of all sorts. These children would eventually adapt, however, when given the chance.

Thomas and Chess (1977) noted that about 40 percent of the middle-class infants could be classified as *easy,* about 10 percent as *difficult,* and about 15 percent as *slow to warm up.* About 35 percent of the infants had highly individual patterns that could not be neatly fitted into any of these three temperament patterns.

As the infants grew older, the researchers gathered a wide variety of data from psychological tests, school records, behavior observations, and interviews with each of the children. The children were observed when they were three, six, nine, and sixteen to seventeen years of age. The researchers found that the children's temperament patterns remained moderately stable in some of the nine categories from year to year. Some temperament variables, however, were quite unstable and inconsistent over time. Thus, while there was some continuity from one age to another, temperament patterns were by no means completely fixed.

Infant temperament patterns were shown to be related to later behavior problems. About 70 percent of the *difficult* children had behavior problems, but only 18 percent of the *easy* children displayed problem behaviors. At first glance, we might be led to believe that the difficult child is predestined for trouble and that the easy child is blessed with good fortune. This, however, is not the case. The important factor in determining if a child with a certain temperament pattern would develop a psychological disorder was whether the child's parents could or would cope with the child's style of behavior.

Thomas and Chess pointed out that some parents of difficult children were confused, angry, and depressed about their children's behaviors. In turn, they acted negatively to their children. Other parents tended to see their difficult children as vigorous, spunky, and challenging. These parents often had positive, energetic encounters with their children and, although often exhausted, enjoyed their children. Easy children were often delightful children who elicited smiles and warm, positive responses from their parents. Some parents found their easy children so easy to cope with that they often ignored them for the more difficult children in their families. In some ways, these children may have been deprived because they were so undemanding. It seems, therefore, that behavior problems are likely to occur when a child's behavior patterns conflict with his or her parent's temperaments. It also appears that each child can flourish in his or her own way when parents respect the temperamental individuality of their children and do not use a rigid style of coping with their children's behavior.

In a similar way Schaeffer and Emerson (1965) followed babies over their first eighteen months of life and found they could detect some temperament differences among the infants. One group of infants were called "cuddlers" because, in most situations, the infants enjoyed close physical contact with people. Another group of infants were classified as "non-cuddlers" because they avoided being held closely, disliked being hugged, and tended to avoid any activity that limited their physical freedom. The cuddler vs. non-cuddler distinction is similar to Birch, Thomas, and Chess' *easy* vs. *difficult* child distinction.

CONCEPTS OF ATTACHMENT IN SOCIAL DEVELOPMENT

Infants, especially in the second six months of life, form strong emotional attachments both to people and to things. Research workers from several theoretical backgrounds have attempted to define *attachment* and have tried to explain why and how infants form attachments. Some believe that when an infant directs attention and actions toward a specific person, he or she will establish a significant emotional relationship with that person. As a result, the infant will become emotionally dependent on the person as well as being dependent on the person for life-support care. Others think that dependency for physical needs is not an important variable in attachment behavior because all infants are naturally dependent.

It is easy to see why dependency and attachment are often confused for each other. The basis for this confusion lies in the fact that many theorists see an infant as having emotional relationships with people who are important in their daily care

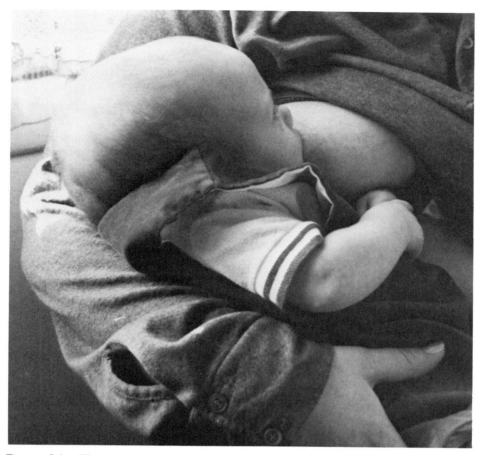

Figure 6-1.   There is no doubt that close relationships during infancy can have powerful effects on social development. However, we still need to know more about the
many aspects of parent–infant interaction that lead to later social development. (Photo
by Mary M. Duncan)

(Ainsworth, 1972; Combs, Richards, and Richards, 1976). This dilemma is mentioned since later discussions will show that not all experts think attachment applies
only to mother-infant pairs. Some researchers, in fact, see little difference between
the importance of mothers and fathers in emotional relationships since infants can
obviously have important interactions with both. Relationships with mothers and
fathers may provide different *kinds* of experiences for an infant, however. A father
may engage in more rough-and-tumble play than a mother would while a mother
might engage in more verbal exchanges and more touching and soothing than a
father would (Lamb, 1977).

    In the following sections, we will look for explanations of attachment in terms
of some of the theories of development discussed in Chapter 2. Most of the studies
that we will review concern mother-infant interactions, and very few of them will

talk about father-infant interactions. Unfortunately, mothers have been more convenient subjects for researchers to study and, as a result, we have very little information on the behavior of fathers.

We shall first discuss how the ethological approach may be used to explain attachment. Since ethological theories emphasize the role of imprinting and releaser stimuli in early development, we will examine whether a mother can serve as a releaser stimulus and whether her infant can become imprinted to follow (to seek or to be close to) her. We will then look at psychoanalytic explanations of attachment in which theorists believe that the mother becomes a love object to whom psychic energy is directed. In the cognitive developmental framework and in some of Piaget's ideas, we will see how concepts of object permanence might be applied to attachment. Finally, we will look at some behavioristic views of attachment that focus on early social learning. A number of social learning researchers emphasize dependency as well as reinforcement in their explanations of attachment.

Theoretical Explanations of Attachment

As mentioned in Chapter 2, ethologists view many behaviors as basically innate and species-specific, or instinctual in origin. We know that many animal species display very complex parenting behaviors and that the infants of many species are instinctively prepared to follow, to touch, to call, and to hide behind their mothers. We also know that, within a certain critical time period in early childhood, many animals become attached to parents in a primitive form of learning called imprinting (Hess, 1970) and that from such imprinting they will form strong social bonds.

Ethologists consider attachment to include behaviors that take the infant close to a specific person and behaviors that restore close proximity to the person if a separation should occur (Bowlby, 1969, 1973). It can be said that the imprinting principle in which young animals bond themselves to parents or parent substitutes, might apply not only to less advanced species such as birds, but also to other, more advanced species. Drawing from ethological theory, attachment in human infants may be an instinct-based set of behaviors somewhat like the process of imprinting in other species. For some ethologists, attachment is a *fixed-action pattern;* that is, a pattern which originates within the infant and depends only on environmental stimuli such as the mother to serve as a releaser stimulus for the underlying behavior.

In explaining the origins of attachment, ethological principles could be applied to two social growth periods. The first period would be a general imprinting period in which the infant may be imprinted to respond to any or all human beings. For example, a young infant's first smiles are usually fairly unselective. During the second period, in the second six months of life, however, imprinting might become more specific and would involve a person such as the mother or other caregiver. In this latter period, infants may discriminate between people who are in the family and those who are strangers by smiling more at relatives and by fretting and crying when exposed to strangers.

A number of people who have adopted an ethological viewpoint believe that attachment behavior in animals, and possibly in humans, has an important survival function. Through the infants' attachment behavior, mothers will be more likely to protect their offspring when they are close. Two conditions, *separation* and *threat*, may force an infant to stay close to its mother. But in order to maintain closeness and to perform following responses, the infant needs to be aware of the mother's location and presence through sight, sound, and touch cues. Therefore, threats and fear can be eliminated or reduced by close contact.

Attachment behavior in infants, whether animal or human, seems to involve two kinds of response patterns: (1) *signalling responses* and (2) *executive responses* (Maccoby and Masters, 1970). The signalling response pattern includes behavior in which an infant's distress is made known to the mother by crying or calling. The executive response is a more direct clinging or following response that the infant uses to come closer to the mother. In both animal and human infants, distress signals stimulate the mother's actions and get her to attend to her infant. When this occurs, the closeness of the mother usually brings the infant's behavior back to a state of calmness (Tracy, Lamb, and Ainsworth, 1976).

How can infants carry out such elaborate signalling functions and be able to know when their mothers are near or far away? According to ethologists, the capacities for signalling and judging closeness are inborn. They have attempted to show that accurate discrimination among stimuli is possible even in young infants. Research has shown, for example, that infants are especially likely to respond to stimuli that come from other human beings. Of these stimuli, the most significant ones are the sounds of the human voice, the pattern of the human face, and the tactile stimuli of the caretaker's hands and body. These stimuli could be considered to be releaser stimuli because they evoke such instinctive responses as sucking. In summary, the ethological explanation of attachment maintains that attachment behavior is basically an instinctive and biological characteristic of the human species.

Psychoanalytic explanations of mother-infant interaction also emphasize instincts. Although attachment is a relatively recent concept not used in classical Freudian psychoanalytic theory, the importance of emotional relationships between mothers and infants is emphasized in both Freud's earlier works and in later revisions of psychoanalysis (Mahler, Pine, and Bergmann, 1975). When mothers are perceived as sources of pleasure and comfort by infants, they become *love objects* (Freud, 1959). Psychoanalytic theory holds that while an infant's ability to discriminate among people is at first diffuse, psychic energy, or *libido,* soon becomes specific and is directed toward the mother. In this sense, the relationship can be described as attachment (Spitz, 1965).

According to psychoanalytic theory, if a separation occurs during the period of the infant's strong attachment to the mother, a yearning for the former pleasurable state may take place. Thus, such abrupt changes as separation will lead to a *fixation* of development and may become the basis for serious mental disorders.

In order to use principles from Piaget's cognitive development theory to explain the concept of attachment, it is necessary to recall certain elements in the theory. As with the two theories just discussed, it is apparent that here, too, the infant's own perceptual, motor, and cognitive abilities are important in explaining interacions with the environment. Although the cognitive developmentalists do not emphasize instincts, they do consider maturation and the emergence of physical capacities to be important. Cognitive theory also relies on the significant influence of surrounding stimuli but does not use the ethological idea of releaser stimuli. Most proponents of Piaget's ideas would not rely strongly on the psychoanalytic idea of libidinal urges.

The cognitive-developmental approach centers on development of thought, perception, and imagery. In explaining the concept of attachment, attention is given to infants' abilities to know things in their surroundings. For example, in order to be near a specific person, perceptual discrimination abilities would have to reach a point of development in which infants can readily distinguish between their mothers and all other people. This idea would be quite compatible with the ethological and psychoanalytic theories. In addition, the cognitive developmental position emphasizes the importance of the ability to understand object permanence. It assumes that infants are able to store the perceived characteristics of their mothers as a memory image and thus can understand that she still exists even though she is not present.

We shall now turn to ways in which conditioning and social learning principles have been applied to attachment. None of the learning theories deal directly with the concept of attachment, so we can only try to assess the value of certain principles in each that would explain the idea of a strong bond of the infant for the mother.

As we have seen in Chapter 2, reinforcement is an essential element in operant conditioning. One can use this principle to explain attachment by maintaining that an infant's seeking behavior toward the mother is reinforced by her and thus attachment becomes a learned habit.

Classical conditioning could also be used in explanations of attachment. The sight of the mother may become paired with the stimuli of feeding, touching, and comforting. Therefore, the sight of the mother can become pleasant through conditioning. After four to eight months, the sight of the mother can serve as a reinforcement for the child's seeking behaviors.

Unlike others, behaviorists emphasize the possibility that a great many of an infant's social actions can be learned and modified through reinforcement. Some behaviorists see the infant's behavior as resulting mainly from rewards in the environment rather than from any inner factors on the infant's part. Other behaviorists, however, emphasize inborn as well as environmental factors.

Let us look more closely now at social learning explanations of attachment. Some social learning views hold that attachment and dependency are based upon the fulfillment of the infant's needs and the nurturant, or caregiving, behavior of the mother. Robert Sears and his co-workers (1965) see dependency as an *action system* in which the mother's nurturant behavior consists of rewarding events. The infant's dependency on the mother comes from the mother's stimulation and reinforcement of the infant's behavior. The mother shapes the child's responses into a "stable pattern of dependent behavior" in which the infant learns to ask for the mother's behavior. The essential function of the mother, according to this view, is to give positive reinforcement to the infant and to avoid negative reinforcement

(Bijou and Baer, 1965). In general, social learning theorists explain attachment as resulting from the mother's reinforcement of the infant's behavior.

These various theoretical orientations attempt to account for dependency or attachment. A complete integration is not yet possible, although the theories do tend to complement each other.

Anxiety in Social Interaction Related to Attachment

We can see a marked change in the behavior of many infants at approximately eight months of age. At this time, some infants begin to become noticeably afraid of strangers. This reaction has been called *stranger anxiety*. Even very friendly babies who previously smiled at nearly everyone will start to howl, cry, and shy away from strangers. Many parents become worried and think that some terrible change has come over their lovable baby. They may ask: "Is this anxiety in reality a 'normal' developmental one that can be expected? Or is it, instead, the result of some particular traumatic experience?" Slightly later, a similar form of anxiety appears when the infant is separated from the mother. Some infants become very upset at separation. Again, we could ask whether *separation anxiety* is maturational, in the sense that the behavior normally emerges with growth. Or, again, we could ask if this behavior is a result of past learning. Theorists and researchers differ in their explanations of the origins of anxiety in young infants and debate whether or not there are really two different forms of anxiety and even whether or not such basic anxiety exists at all (Lewis, 1972). We shall make a distinction between stranger anxiety and separation anxiety.

Stranger Anxiety.   Some theorists do not think that it is necessary to make a sharp distinction between stranger anxiety and separation anxiety. Those who take an ethological position on attachment do not necessarily have to distinguish between the two. Since infants are imprinted with an image of their mothers, anxiety results when strangers are present and when mothers are absent. Since imprinting is fairly selective, persons other than the mothers are not accepted. Strangers, or even familiar persons, cannot be mother substitutes. In this sense, ethologists see separation as the origin of both forms of anxiety.

The psychoanalytic view stresses separation as a source of anxiety and, therefore, the presence of strangers signifies separation to the child. Thus, it is claimed that an infant's reaction to a stranger is not caused by any direct fear of the stranger, but rather by the possibility that the stranger threatens a separation between the child and the mother (Spitz, 1965).

The psychoanalytic explanation of stranger anxiety is similar to the cognitive developmental explanation. Piaget explains that by six or eight months an infant has developed a schema, or concept, of the mother. This would include elements of pleasure and comforting experiences. Thus, it could be argued that when a stranger appears, the new image of the stranger will conflict with the existing schema of the mother. It has been demonstrated that six-month-old infants already have the ability to differentiate between the mother and people who look similar to

Figure 6-2. Most infants become wary of strangers toward the latter part of the first year. This little girl is displaying a reaction that is found throughout the world. (Photo by Mary M. Duncan)

the mother (Kagan, 1972). Furthermore, we know that an infant often requires some time to discover the unfamiliar characteristics of the stranger before beginning to cry. Some researchers suggest that during these delays, the infant is trying to deal with the discrepancy between the new object (stranger) and the familiar object (mother) and that crying results because the infant cannot deal with the discrepancy.

Still another approach to stranger anxiety is related to learning or reinforcement theory. The suggestion is that the infants have been conditioned to the presence of their mothers. A mother's presence is associated with food and comforting activities, and the mother is the center of the infant's environment. Her disappearance, whether she is replaced by a stranger or is absent with no one to take her place, will result in distress because the rewards that were expected are not present. Anxiety, therefore, appears because of the increased ability of the infant to store images of past experiences and because the infant understands the significance of the mother's absence.

We might ask: "Can frequent contact with strangers reduce wariness and anxiety about strangers?" "Can an infant get used to being with strangers?" To try to answer these questions, investigators have studied infants in the first year of life, because during this time they begin to distinguish between familiar and unfamiliar people. In one study, a male and a female experimenter went into homes and made observations of infants' reactions to strange adults and unfamiliar objects

(Bronson, 1972). Data were gathered when the infants were three, six, and nine months old. Each time, the infants were exposed to a near approach of a stranger and to unfamiliar objects such as a mobile, bracelets, and a box that made sounds or beeps. In the first weeks of life, some mild signs of distress were observed when the infants were in the presence of a stranger. There was definite concern at four months and continuing wariness during the latter half of the first year. The findings did not support the idea that exposure to a wide variety of persons would reduce anxiety about strangers. Similarly, other researchers report that neither day-care nor home-rearing experiences altered the responses of infants to strangers (Brookhart and Hock, 1976).

Some researchers question the concept of stranger anxiety entirely. Rheingold and Eckerman (1973) assert that although they were strangers to hundreds of infants, they rarely saw an infant show stranger anxiety. They also studied a special sample of twenty-four infants (twelve boys and twelve girls) at the ages of eight, ten, and twelve months. They arranged four testing situations in which the role of the stranger was varied in the presence of the infant and mother. In the last test, the stranger briefly held the infant. The researchers reported that the infants not only did not show a fear of strangers, but they also made overtures to the strangers. Although they were only a short distance away from a stranger, the infants played with toys, left the mother's side, smiled, and vocalized.

Rheingold and Eckerman's comments about stranger anxiety have been recently debated by Alan Sroufe (1977). Sroufe believes that Rheingold and Eckerman may be quite correct in stating that infants may display positive approaches to strangers under some conditions, but he also thinks we should not forget that many studies have shown that infants who are older than seven or eight months show a great deal of wariness toward strangers. Sroufe cited many research studies that suggested that stranger anxiety is not a simple all-or-none phenomenon but may or may not appear depending on the situation the baby is in. For example, when strangers are far away, when a parent is close by, or when the child is in a familiar setting, stranger anxiety is reduced. If infants are suddenly exposed to strangers while in strange settings or while separated from their mothers, however, the amount of stranger anxiety shown by infants will be quite strong.

Separation Anxiety.   Separation anxiety can be seen when a baby cries and shows signs of distress after the mother has left its presence for even a short while. Some psychologists see separation anxiety as a serious threat to the infant's psychological well-being. In his book *Separation: Anxiety and Anger,* the British psychoanalyst John Bowlby (1973) described infants who, when they were placed in nursery schools or children's homes, became attached to one attendant in particular and showed distress when she left them. Bowlby saw separation anxiety as follows: whenever children are separated from their mothers they show distress, and if they are put in a strange place with strange people, the distress is likely to significantly damage and delay social development.

According to Bowlby, a characteristic sequence of behaviors can be seen in separation anxiety. At first, the infant *protests* vigorously and tries to follow or calls out and cries for help and attention. Next, the child seems to sink into a state of *despair,* but is still preoccupied with the mother's return. Finally, the child seems to become *detached* from the mother and loses interest in her. If the period of separation is fairly short and the infant is reunited with the mother, the attachment will be renewed. The infant's behavior may still be changed, however. In many instances, signs of anxiety are shown by the infant's increased desire to stay close to the mother. The separation sequence is interpreted as follows: the infant's protest indicates separation anxiety; despair indicates the infant's grief; and detachment or disinterest indicates the infant is trying to defend itself against further distress. For Bowlby, the main source of anxiety has always been perceived as the separation of the child from loved figures. Not all theorists and investigators agree with this point of view, however.

Theoretical views and research on separation anxiety lead to some conclusions as well as some conflicts. Separation anxiety appears in the latter part of the first year; a number of researchers and theorists agree on that. There is little evidence to make a clear distinction between separation anxiety and stranger anxiety. An infant who cries in the presence of a stranger may not be afraid of the stranger, but fearful about possible separation from the mother. Presently, we cannot say that stranger anxiety and separation anxiety are two different and distinct categories of behavior or that anxiety is an inherited temperament or trait. We can say, however, that anxiety about unfamiliar people and objects is observed in some infants and that separation from the mother causes distress in some infants.

Are There Healthy Separation Experiences?

That separation may produce fear and anxiety in infants and that such fear experiences may form the basis for later personal and social problems is clearly disturbing. A certain amount of separation of the infant and the mother, however, also seems to be necessary for healthy social development. As we would be likely to think that children who fail to form attachments to others are seriously disturbed, we would also consider the idea that children who fail to form a certain amount of separation, individuality, and detachment from their parents are possibly disturbed.

In many studies of animals, infants have been observed to first bond themselves to adults and display following, calling, and contacting behaviors. Once attachment bonds are moderately secure, animal infants usually start to use their mothers as a security base and to take progressively longer excursions away from their mothers. As they do this, they tend to increase their knowledge of their environments and, at the same time, develop a sense of their own competence.

In a series of studies of how infants and young children separate from their mothers, Rheingold and Eckerman (1970) observed forty-eight children who were between ten months and five years of age. The studies were conducted in natural home-like settings in which mothers sat in a laboratory room or an outdoor garden. The infants and young children were free to move away from their mothers and, as they did, the researchers were able to record the distances that the children had separated from their mothers. It was found that as the children became older, they were more likely to wander further and further away from their mothers. For example, one-year-olds traveled an average distance of about 7 meters from their mothers, two-year-olds averaged about 15 meters, while four-year-olds averaged about 21 meters.

Rheingold and Eckerman observed that ten-month-olds would often crawl away from their mothers with very little, if any, distress. These infants were also more likely to wander off to places that had toys than to places that had no toys. Some infants would even go off to places that had no toys at all. Interestingly, infants would often wander off, play with a toy, wander back to their mothers, and then go back to the toys again as if they were making sure that their mothers were still in their original places.

It appears that there is a natural sequence of detachment in which children travel progressively further from their parents and, in doing so, build up a sense of their own competence and uniqueness. Parents also seem to follow a natural progression in which they allow their children greater freedom and distance as the children grow older.

Figure 6-3. Toys and other familiar objects may play an important role in reducing stranger and separation anxiety. For many toddlers, favorite stuffed animals, blankets, pacifiers, and bottles serve to comfort the child in stressful situations. (Photo by Diana Blanchard)

INSTITUTIONALIZED INFANTS AND SOCIAL DEPRIVATION

Early Studies on the Effects of Institutionalization

What is the effect on infants when they are not raised by their parents but, instead, grow up in institutions? If infants are placed in group care after attachments to their mothers have been formed, what will be the effects of continuing separation? Will infants in group settings show attachment behavior and seek relationships with one nurse or care-giver? Can the behavior of infants in an institution be altered by providing more than routine care by one person? Does the behavior of infants alter the behavior of the care-givers toward them?

Our exploration of various ways of finding answers to these questions takes us back to England during World War II. At that time, in order to escape the German bombings of English cities, many infants and young children were taken to the countryside and cared for in groups. Reports of their experiences were made by Dorothy Burlingham and Anna Freud (1942) and Dorothy Burlingham (1944). These reports influenced the thinking of a number of people about the effects of separating infants from their families, and they have influenced policies on the provision of substitute care in institutions. First, Burlingham and Freud emphasized that it was difficult to supply the emotional needs of such infants because of their

Figure 6-4. Anna Freud (b. 1895). (Photo by the Bettmann Archive)

prior attachments to one person, usually the mother. Second, a number of the infants became attached to the new care-givers in abnormal ways. For example, some of them had fits of rage and crying when their care-givers paid attention to other children. These behaviors suggested to Freud and Burlingham that the children needed opportunities for an emotional relationship with one person and that their needs were not completely filled in the foster care setting. They made the observation that the children could actually withstand the terror of air raids and bombings much better than they could endure the isolation from their parents.

Why did these children become so possessive toward their care-givers and why did they become so upset at their absence? Had the infants been subjected to too many mother substitutes?

In the mid-1940s Rene Spitz observed infants who were raised in institutions. Attendants diapered, fed, and clothed the infants but rarely interacted with them in any affectionate way. Spitz described a pattern that he called "hospitalism," in which some of the infants became apathetic, unsmiling, and withdrawn. These infants often displayed strange postures and movements, retarded mental development, and often lost interest in people. In some children, the pattern became so pronounced that the infants lost their appetites and became susceptible to a number of infectious diseases (Spitz, 1946).

As other researchers started to observe similar patterns in institutionalized and homeless children, a strong movement to explore the effects of deprivation experiences on infants and young children was well underway by the late 1940s. In 1948, John Bowlby was commissioned by the United Nations World Health Organization to prepare a report on the effects of early deprivation. In a very influential book, *Maternal Care and Mental Health,* he reviewed a number of studies conducted by himself and many other researchers and concluded that in order for a child to develop fully, the child must have a continuous and warm, affectionate bond to a mother or mother substitute during the first few years of life (Bowlby, 1951). He believed that if such bonds are broken, or never formed at all, then such short-term effects on the infant as distress and an increased need to cling to the mother and such long-term effects as adult depression, suicide proneness, antisocial behavior, and mental retardation would occur.

At the University of Wisconsin, Harry Harlow has been conducting numerous experiments on the formation and disruption of social bonds in infant rhesus monkeys since 1950 (Harlow, 1971). In his studies, monkeys have been exposed to nearly every kind of social deprivation experience imaginable. Some have been isolated from parents; some have been isolated from peers as well as parents; some have been raised on wire and cloth mother substitutes; and some have been totally isolated from all social contact for as long as a year. In many of his studies, Harlow has observed effects similar to those found by Spitz and Bowlby. For example, isolated infant monkeys often displayed bizarre rocking motions and self-aggression patterns similar to those seen in seriously disturbed children. They often displayed extreme emotional behavior. They were easily frightened and could not easily find comfort or security. They often displayed emotional withdrawal, and some of them were so withdrawn that they seemed to be emotionally burned out. In terms of social and sexual behaviors, these monkeys were unskilled in playing with other monkeys and, as adults, displayed a number of abnormal sexual and parenting behaviors.

The early reports of Freud, Spitz, Bowlby, and Harlow raised a large amount of interest and concern for the humane care of infants, especially institutionalized infants. These reports raised a number of serious questions. Can children be damaged by the kind of parent-child separation experienced in day-care and nursery school experiences? Will children be harmed psychologically by the absence of working mothers? Can brief separations between parents and infants have long-term effects? What are the effects of adoption and foster care on children?

Today, nobody would deny that children can be affected by separations. Neither would anyone deny that severe separation experiences may be associated with future disturbances. Fortunately, however, we now have some evidence that early researchers may have overstated the effects of separation. Let us look at some of the more recent findings and reinterpretations of pioneering research projects (Clarke and Clarke, 1976; Rutter, 1972).

A Further Look at Deprivation and Separation Studies

One of the problems that we can reexamine is the problem of maternal deprivation. Although Bowlby, himself, did not focus exclusively on mother-child relationships, many researchers were led to use the term *maternal deprivation* to refer to the effects of early childhood deprivations. The term also led many to believe that only a mother could satisfy an infant's social needs. According to Michael Rutter, in *Maternal Deprivation: Reassessed* (1972), there is nothing magic about the mother. Rutter points out that although infants are usually exposed most to their mothers, some may develop even stronger attachments to their fathers, siblings, or other family members. It is very important for a child to have a strong attachment to at least one other person, but this person does not have to be the infant's mother. Therefore, it might be possible to think of a healthy, but nontraditional, situation in which an infant's mother was away for a considerable amount of time during the day but the child, nevertheless, had a healthy attachment to a father, grandparent, older brother or sister, or housekeeper.

Under what conditions are children and parents separated? It seems that the children who are most affected by separations are those who have been separated when their families were undergoing financial crises or when death, divorce, mental or physical illness, or imprisonment placed the family in a crisis situation. On the other hand, children from relatively happy families may not be particularly damaged by brief separations (Rutter, 1972).

Another important question to be asked is, "What exactly is deprivation?" Although we have assumed that *social deprivation* caused these problems, it may very well be that many of the devastating effects seen by researchers have been due to other kinds of deprivation. For example, many of the children whom Spitz and Bowlby observed were raised in dull, toyless environments that were often only slightly better than kennels. We know that *sensory and perceptual deprivation* can have strong effects on cognitive and emotional development in infant animals. Undoubtedly, these kinds of deprivation can also affect human infants. In addition, many studies of deprivation probably observed children who were either malnourished at the time or whose mothers may have been malnourished during pregnancy. The effects of malnourishment must be investigated further.

Recently, some researchers have turned the question of maternal deprivation around by asking whether mothers could be affected by deprivation as well as infants. In one study conducted in a maternity hospital, pediatricians Marshall Klaus and H. John Kennel (1972, 1975) studied two groups of mothers and their infants. One group of fourteen mothers were allowed to interact with their newborn infants for about five hours a day for the first three days after the infants were born. As a control group, another fourteen mothers interacted with their babies in a way that is typical in many hospitals: seeing the infant at the moment of birth; seeing the infant again a few hours after birth; and then feeding the infant for about a half hour every four hours. When the infants were one month old, they and their mothers returned to the hospital for physical examinations, interviews, and staff observations of mother-infant interaction. In this situation, the experimental group mothers, who had more contact with their children, tended to be more likely to touch, comfort, and look at their infants than did the control group mothers. At follow-up sessions one and two years later, these mothers still displayed more interaction with their children than did the control group mothers. It may be that not only does the child need to form an attachment to a special person but that a mother (or other care-giver) might have to form an attachment to the infant. It seems that the sooner this is achieved, the better.

Another study concerned itself with a comparison of three groups of mothers and their infants. One group consisted of mothers and their full-term infants. Another group consisted of mothers and their premature infants. In the second group, the mothers were allowed full contact with their infants, who were in incubators. A third group consisted of premature infants and their mothers. The mothers in this group were only permitted to look at their infants, who were lying in incubators. Observations of the infants and mothers were made for two years after the infants left the hospital (Liefer, Leiderman, Barnett, and Williams, 1972). In comparing the groups, the researchers found that the mothers of the full-term babies smiled at their infants more and held them more closely. The three groups of mothers spent about equal amounts of time, however, on more distant interactions such as looking at or talking to their infants. In a follow-up, it was found that those mothers who were not allowed to touch their infants had high rates of marital separation and divorce, and two mothers in this group had relinquished custody of their children. This study, as in the Klaus and Kennel studies, shows that it is important to see attachment as a two-way process in which parents and infants become mutually attached to each other. These studies also point to the possibility that very early experiences in parenting may have long-term effects for both the parent and the child.

Early writings on separation experiences in early childhood and infancy hinted at the irreversible effects of deprivation. Fortunately, we now have some evidence that some of the harmful effects can be at least partially reversed (Clarke and Clarke, 1976). In some of his later research, Harlow and his colleagues attempted to rehabilitate rhesus monkeys that were exposed to severe social deprivation during the first six months of life (Harlow, 1971). Although they were withdrawn and socially aloof at first, after six months of exposure to normally-raised younger "therapist" monkeys, the deprived monkeys displayed normal social behaviors.

Jerome Kagan (1973) conducted a study of infants who were raised in San Marcos, a small village in Guatemala. In this village, it was customary to keep infants on the dirt floors of small, hot, dark huts without toys and without much parental care during most of the infant's day. In comparison to American infants in the first two years of life, these infants were very poorly developed. Their language development was considerably behind that of American infants. These children were also usually apathetic. For example, they smiled very little and were disinterested in both people and things. Kagan wondered if this lag in development would continue into later childhood.

In San Marcos, however, it is also customary to allow children to play out-of-doors as soon as they are able to walk. Therefore, from the time that these infants were about sixteen months old, they started to lead fairly active lives. When they were between four and twelve, the children were given several series of psychological tests. In comparison to urban Guatemalan children and to American children, many of the early deficits in the San Marcos children seemed to have disappeared. For example, on tests of memory and perceptual skills, the children performed at levels that were only slightly lower than American and other Guatemalan children. This example illustrates that some early losses due to severe deprivation may be compensated for with later care.

Although they are not as severe as original reports had indicated, the effects of early social deprivation on children and infants can be seen. Unfortuately, many children have to spend part of their lives in institutions. While a few institutions seem to avoid some of the problems that we have mentioned (Tizard and Tizard, 1971), many institutionalized children do suffer long-term consequences.

The Question of Day-Care and Communal Childcare

In the United States and Canada, the use of day-care centers for infants of working mothers has rapidly increased over the past few years. Several factors have influenced this trend. With divorce and marital separation on the increase, many mothers have to work in order to support their children. Some intact families also need at least two incomes in order to meet their expenses. With increased opportunities in employment and education, many women are now combining education and career development with child-rearing. The traditional family structure is also changing. Grandparents and in-laws are often no longer nearby or available for babysitting.

Some people see early day-care as an opportunity for high-quality care for potentially neglected children. A mother's career development and the fact that she can become financially independent may stop the vicious cycle of perpetual poverty, unemployment, and lack of education that many poor families have experienced for generations. Because of the possible benefits for families, charitable organizations and government agencies have invested in day-care centers, especially in lower income areas.

By its very nature, day-care involves separation between parents and children for at least several hours per day. Can such separation experiences have harmful effects on young children? Will these children suffer severe and long-lasting separation anxiety? One study that sheds some light on this issue has been provided by Sally Provence, Audrey Naylor, and June Patterson (1977), who are affiliated with Yale University's Children's House, an inner-city day-care center.

Although children at the center are likely to experience some separation anxiety, the amount of anxiety can be greatly reduced by using several techniques. Parents were encouraged to have their children bring toys, dolls, and blankets from home that can serve as reassuring bridges between the home and the day-care center. Photographs of the parents were placed in the children's lockers and cubbyholes, and the children were encouraged to look at these pictures during the day. Sometimes, the children would speak to their parents on the telephone— again providing an important continuity between the home and the day-care center. Very importantly, the staff was trained to talk to the children about their separation feelings. These authors also stressed that good day-care centers are not simply babysitting centers. Instead, these centers can have active programs for teaching personal and social skills, language skills, and cognitive skills. Furthermore, these programs can be evaluated and their impact measured.

While large-scale day-care is a relatively new American experience, several countries such as Israel and the Soviet Union have had organized communal child-rearing programs for over fifty years.

In Israel, for example, many children in the various *kibbutz,* or commune settlements, are with their parents during only a small portion of the day. They spend the rest of the day with trained child workers and with other children. Child-rearing methods of the *kibbutzim* in Israel have attracted attention in this country. Judgments about the results should be cautiously made, however, because situations vary. In a study of mother-child relationships that compared development in the United States and Israel, several investigators reported few significant differences.

An important factor, it seems, is that in both the U.S. and in Israel, infants are with their own mothers for at least the first six months of life. Other observers assert that in Israel teachers make a strong effort to provide emotional security for children in the groups (Devereux, Shouval, Bronfenbrenner, Rodgers, Kav-venaki, Kiely, and Karson, 1974). Many researchers also see a continuity between the family and the kibbutz child-care centers (Gerwitz and Gerwitz, 1969). Some observers point out that the continued presence of the family in the children's lives helps to make the kibbutz like one large nuclear family. Still others maintain that since kibbutz families come together for several hours each day in a relaxed setting without intervening responsibilities, their emotional satisfaction is actually increased (Brossard and Decarie, 1972). Other investigators note some differences in behavior of kibbutz children from their American counterparts. For example, kibbutz children spoke less often, smiled less often, and showed objects to strangers less often than did their American counterparts (Maccoby and Feldman, 1972).

Variations in parents' child-rearing practices and the individual differences among children make comparisons of settings difficult. However, the wide variety of potentially positive ways of raising children should encourage us to search for the benefits as well as the possible dangers of alternate styles of caring for children.

SUMMARY

In this chapter, we have seen how the infant is an active participant in ongoing social interactions. Not only do parents influence infants, but infants also exert a great deal of influence on their parents' behaviors. An infant's highly individual temperament pattern may shape the kinds of interactions that occur between the infant and his or her parents. We looked at the formation of attachment bonds and explored some of the theoretical explanations for such attachment-related behaviors as stranger and separation anxieties. Finally, we turned our attention to institutionalization and maternal deprivation, which limit attachment, and discussed how, why, and under what conditions these situations would be healthy or harmful.

RECOMMENDED READINGS

Klaus, M., & Kennel, H. J. *Maternal-Infant Bonding.* St. Louis: C. V. Mosby, 1976.
Unlike most researchers who have examined how infants form social bonds toward parents, these researchers explore how parents become attached to infants in the first few days and hours after birth.

Lewis, M., & Rosenblum, R., eds. *The Effect of the Infant on Its Caregiver.* New York: Wiley, 1974.
The contributors to this volume concern themselves with the active role of the infant in the parent-infant social system.

Richards, M. P. M., ed. *The Integration of the Child into a Social World.* London: Cambridge University Press, 1974.
This multi-authored book focuses on the complex network of family and cultural systems that the infant enters at birth and then explores how the infant builds attachments and learns to become a member of the social system.

Rutter, M. *Maternal Deprivation Reassessed.* Baltimore: Penguin, 1972.
This book critically examines the maternal deprivation research that followed in the wake of Spitz and Bowlby's studies and concludes that the overall notion of *maternal deprivation* is too broad to be useful. Instead, Rutter demonstrates that many variables underly deprivation experiences and that precise definitions of each variable will be necessary.

4

EARLY CHILDHOOD

7

Intellectual and Cognitive Development in Early Childhood

When describing ourselves and others we may call some people "intelligent" and "bright" and refer to others as "unintelligent" and "dull." What do we actually mean by "intelligence?" Psychologists who have studied intelligence have tended to favor definitions that include such concepts as the ability to perform complex tasks, the ability to solve problems, and the ability to draw logical conclusions. For practical purposes, intelligence tests have been used to evaluate individual differences among children. We may look at intelligence as a relative concept. We could ask, for example, how the intelligence test performance of one child compares to the performances of other children of the same age. We could also compare the child's performance to those of children who are somewhat older or younger. That is, we might ask whether a ten-year-old performs at a higher or lower level than other ten-year-olds and whether the child's performance is similar to, or different from, that of an average twelve-year-old.

In this chapter, we will view the concept of intelligence from two perspectives. First, we will examine intelligence from a *psychometric* perspective in which we will explore the history, the nature, and the uses of standardized intelligence tests. Then we will look at intelligence from a *Piagetian* perspective and see how some of Piaget's theories and research can be used to explain the cognitive development and intellectual performance of children in the *preoperational* stage, between the ages of two and seven.

We will see that there has been a considerable amount of controversy about the nature of intelligence and the uses for which intelligence tests are commonly employed. Many psychologists have explored relationships among linguistic and problem-solving abilities and have debated the issue of whether intelligence tests should rely heavily on language. Piaget feels that while thought is often reflected in a person's language, a person may have much more knowledge than can be expressed in words. American intelligence tests, however, have included many verbal items which ask children to define words and to choose between verbal concepts. These tests often give elaborate verbal instructions to children taking the tests.

Inclusion of test items that require the naming of objects reflects a purpose in American tests to measure what appears to be a learned ability rather than an innate, or inborn, ability. It is because of this continuing emphasis on verbal abilities that many psychologists think intelligence tests fail to measure any innate ability but, instead, measure what the child has already learned from his or her culture.

In spite of the strong emphasis on *acquired intelligence* in current tests and the consequent rejection of these tests by some psychologists and educators, intelligence tests are widely used throughout American society. Among the largest test consumers are schools, colleges, and industrial and military organizations. Many teachers and guidance counselors rely heavily on tests and see them, at the very least, as predictors of school grades and occupational success. Other educators, however, see very little value in the test results and maintain that the tests are limited by a child's motivation, his or her cultural background, and the level of emotional stress at the time the child is taking the test. As a result, there have been many controversies about the use of test scores and the placement of intelligence tests scores on children's permanent school records.

THE NATURE OF INTELLIGENCE

Modern concepts of intelligence and the definition of the word *intelligence* are closely related to the methods used to test and measure intelligence. We often think of an intelligent person as one who has a wide range of abilities, who can cope with new situations, and who can remember learned information. From the beginning, intelligence tests have contained a wide variety of tasks.

For some researchers and theorists, intelligence is a general ability that gives an overall view of how well a person will perform many kinds of intellectual tasks. Others, however, see many different kinds of intelligence. As a result, some intelligence tests have included tasks as widely different as matching different colored blocks and knowledge of vocabulary words. Because different tests may appear, at least at first glance, to be measuring somewhat different abilities, some psychologists have defined intelligence by adopting a bit of circular reasoning: "Intelligence is what intelligence tests measure."

The Beginning of Mental Testing

The use of tests for demonstrating abilities is very old. As long as 3000 years ago, persons in China who wanted civil service positions were examined in music, archery, handling horses, writing, arithmetic, and knowledge of ceremonies (Dubois, 1970). During the Middle Ages in Europe, candidates for academic

Figure 7-1.   Alfred Binet, 1857–1911. (Photo by the Bettmann Archive)

degrees were given examinations. Substantial progress in devising comprehensive tests of intellectual ability is a twentieth-century accomplishment, however.

The first practical intelligence test was devised by Alfred Binet, a pioneering French experimental psychologist. The Paris school system asked Binet to devise a way to judge whether some children were mentally retarded and, if so, whether they should be placed in special schools or in ordinary classrooms. Binet had conducted many experiments on thought and perception and had been experimenting with tests in his laboratory at the Sorbonne in Paris. In 1903 he had published a study of his two daughters, Armande and Marguerite, in which he used different kinds of tests to reveal personality differences between the girls (Peterson, 1926, 1969). A few years later, he became interested in children who did not learn as easily in school as did their classmates.

As a result of this work, Binet and his collaborator, Theophile Simon, published a thirty-item *intelligence scale* in 1905. Their scale assembled a wide range of tasks that Binet and Simon thought would reveal a child's abilities. Many of the test items had been used before in tests developed by other researchers. For example, Binet and Simon borrowed an item that required a child to compare the length of two lines. The new and ingenious part of Binet and Simon's scale involved the gathering of the test items into an intelligence test with progressive levels of difficulty. Binet knew that as children grew older, they could solve increasingly more difficult problems and, in 1908, he developed the notion of *mental age* (or *MA*) to describe a child's performance in terms of the average ages at which children could solve certain problems. For example, if a child can solve all of the test problems that average ten-year-olds can solve, then the child's mental age, or MA, is at least ten years.

The 1908 version of the test had a collection of varied items. One item contained a picture of a large number of objects from which the child would have to search for a specific object, such as a window or a broom. Binet obtained MA scores by determining the number of tasks that children completed at each age level. The average performance scores that his original sample group obtained on this collection of tasks provided the standard for defining that mental age. A number of items from Binet's original 1905 test are still in use today, such as identifying parts of the body, repeating a series of numbers, and defining vocabulary words.

At about this time, the German psychologist Wilhelm Stern suggested that a very useful score could be derived from a relationship between a child's mental age (MA) and the child's chronological age (CA), or age since the child was born. The score was called the *intelligence quotient,* or IQ, and is defined by the formula:

$$IQ = \frac{\text{Mental Age}}{\text{Chronological Age}} \times 100$$

Suppose that a ten-year-old child performs like the average six-year-old on an intelligence test. We would see the child as somewhat dull, as his IQ would be:

$$IQ = \frac{MA}{CA} \times 100 = \frac{6 \text{ years}}{10 \text{ years}} \times 100 = 60$$

A very bright ten-year-old who performs like an average fifteen-year-old would obtain an IQ of:

$$IQ = \frac{MA}{CA} \times 100 = \frac{15}{10} \times 100 = 150$$

Another ten-year-old might perform like an average ten-year-old and would obtain an IQ of exactly 100, which is the average IQ score. The concept of the IQ score was quickly adopted and has almost become a synonym for intelligence. Binet's scale was translated into several languages and was soon brought to America where it was modified further.

THE MEASUREMENT OF INTELLIGENCE

If we think of intelligence as varying from one person to another, we might wonder whether we ourselves have more or less. How can we find out? To evaluate the mental capabilities of people, we need an objective measurement tech- As intelligence is often defined as the *ability* to use what has been learned, we could say that intelligence is an ability to use things that were already mastered in the past and to *reason* in such a way that new problems are solved. Piaget sees intelligence as important in children's adaptation to their environment and as a capability that becomes most complex in the formal operational stage of adolescence. Unlike Piaget, many American researchers have not been as concerned with how a child's intelligence changes in terms of types of mental operations that can be performed at different stages as they have been in testing to study overall differences in the amounts of intelligence that people demonstrate on tests. Thus, much of the research in the first half of this century emphasizes ways to use measurement techniques rather than theoretical issues. This trend seems to be changing, however, as an increasing amount of research is being undertaken to investigate theoretical issues concerning the formation of abilities.

Determining the IQ

In the measurement of intelligence, the Stanford-Binet scale has been the most influential instrument. In America, there were several translations of Binet's test. Among them, the modification by Lewis M. Terman and his co-workers at Stanford University in 1916 became the most widely accepted test and the prototype for many modern intelligence tests. As a result, many intelligence tests are similar to each other and to the Binet test in their inclusion of verbal and performance items. Many tests use items that are similar to the Binet's choices for the four-year-level mental age. Among these items are the naming of common objects, remembering names, discrimination among forms, defining words on a vocabulary list, and showing an ability in memorization by repeating a sentence.

In administering the Stanford-Binet to a child, an examiner's first goal is to gain the child's confidence and to make the test a pleasant experience. The examiner begins with easy items or tests that are below the child's estimated ability. When the child passes all of the tests up to a certain mental age level, that level is called the child's *basal age.* Then the examiner proceeds to give harder and more advanced tests until the child reaches a *ceiling age* and fails all of the items at the next higher mental age level. The tests passed are then added to the child's basal age to obtain a score called the mental age. The next step is to divide the mental age by the child's chronological age. Tables of ages in months, provided in the Binet Manual, reduce the arithmetic involved. Some adjustments have been made in the tables, however, and slight variations from one's own arithmetic will be found. After obtaining a child's IQ, the score can be compared with scores obtained by other children in the population.

The Distribution of IQs

The distribution of IQs among the children tested in one of the earlier revisions of the Stanford-Binet is shown in Figure 7-2. The IQs fall into a pattern correspond-

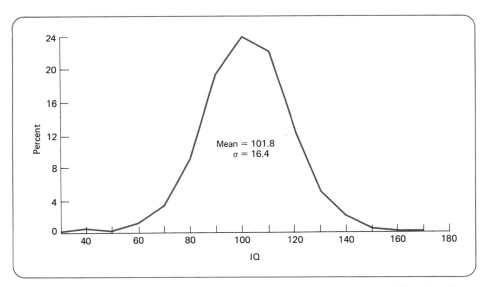

Figure 7-2.   The distribution of IQs of the subjects on which the 1937 Stanford–Binet was standardized. The authors of the test and manual point out that approximately 46% of the subjects used in the standardization group attained IQs between 90 and 110. This group, they believe, should be considered a standard for "average ability." This range makes up the largest single grouping. (From L.M. Ternan and M.A. Merrill. *Stanford–Binet intelligence scale, manual for the third revision, form L-M* [1972 norms, 1973]. Boston: Houghton Mifflin. By permission of the publisher.)

ing closely to a statistical distribution called the *normal curve*. This distribution is found when many naturally-occurring characteristics, such as height and weight are measured. In a normal curve, most scores fall fairly close to the *mean,* or average score. Further away from the mean score, there are fewer and fewer cases of each score. For example, the mean height of American men is about 5'10'', and the majority of men will have heights close to 5'10''. As we go further away from 5'10'', we will find fewer men. While some adults are 7 feet tall and some are 4 feet tall, the odds of finding such people at random will be extremely small. Similarly, most of the children's IQs surround the center at an IQ of 100—about an equal number fall above and below the midpoint (or, as shown in Figure 7-2, to the left and right of the center). In this *standardization group* about 46% of the individuals obtained IQs between 90 and 110, and the authors used the group as a standard for *average* mental ability.

A classification of IQs according to the interpretation of Terman and Merrill is shown in Table 7-1. Their classification of IQ ranges from "very superior" for the highest scores to "mentally defective" for the lowest. In Table 7-1 it can be seen that children having a superior IQ of 120–129 are in the upper 8.2% of the population. This categorical arrangement of IQ reflects the interest in practical applica-

Table 7-1
DISTRIBUTION OF THE 1937 STANDARDIZATION GROUP

IQ	Percent	Classification
160–169	0.03	
150–159	0.2	Very superior
140–149	1.1	
130–139	3.1	
120–129	8.2	Superior
110–119	18.1	High average
100–109	23.5	
90–99	23.0	Normal or average
80–89	14.5	Low average
70–79	5.6	Borderline defective
60–69	2.0	
50–59	0.4	
40–49	0.2	Mentally defective
30–39	0.03	

Source: L. M. Terman and M. A. Merrill, *Stanford-Binet intelligence scale, manual for the third revision, form L-M,* 1960. By permission. Houghton Mifflin Company, Boston.

tion of the measurement of intelligence. The foundation of this application stems from Binet's assumption that the performance of a sample of children at a certain chronological age level on specific tasks, will establish a mental age against which other children can be compared.

Some Varieties of Intelligence Tests

The Stanford-Binet.   The most widely used intelligence test for young children today, as we have just discussed, is the Stanford-Binet Scale. The Stanford-Binet test is not without its critics, however. In the Stanford-Binet, children are given many different tasks, but they receive only one IQ score for their performance on the whole test. Thus, the scoring of the Binet test treats intelligence as if it were a single factor. Many researchers felt that if intelligence was composed of somewhat independent factors, then separate scores should be provided for performance on different kinds of tasks. The Stanford-Binet items involve many motor and perceptual skills at the early mental age levels and become increasingly more verbal at higher mental age levels. This leads to two problems. One problem lies in the possibility that the test may be measuring different things at different ages. Another problem is the fact that the test may place children who are not proficient in English at a definite disadvantage. Among this group of children would be deaf children and children from homes in which English is not the primary spoken language, as well as children from places where English dialects other than Standard American English are spoken.

The WISC-R.   At New York University Medical Center at Bellevue Hospital, David Wechsler designed a series of tests which were meant to be improvements on the Stanford-Binet. Wechsler felt it was not possible to equate intelligence with any single ability, but considered that intelligence may be an overall organization of several related abilities. He first developed an intelligence test for adults called the Wechsler Adult Intelligence Scale (*WAIS*) but soon extended his work with the development of a children's test called the WISC (Wechsler Intelligence Scale for Children, Wechsler, 1949), which in its newest revision is called the WISC-R (Wechsler, 1974).

Wechsler divided his test into two basic scales. The *Verbal Scale* contains six subscales—General Information, General Comprehension, Arithmetic, Similarities of Meaning, Vocabulary, and Digit Span (a memory test). The *Performance Scale* also contains six subscales—Picture Completion, Picture Arrangement, Block Design, Object Assembly, Coding, and Mazes (See Table 7-2). An examiner could obtain one IQ estimate for the highly language-oriented tests of the Verbal Scale and a separate IQ estimate for the relatively nonverbal Performance Scale. This is especially useful in testing language-disadvantaged children, who might do poorly on the Verbal Scale but may do very well on the Performance Scale. Similarly, some children with perceptual and motor handicaps may do well on the Verbal Scale but relatively worse on the Performance Scale. By providing separate scores for each of the subscales, an examiner can detect patterns of deficits and strengths in abilities that might help to provide important diagnostic clues. Because each child takes every subtest, the test measures the same things at each age. A total IQ score can be derived from a weighted combination of the Verbal and Performance scale scores to give an overall picture of intellectual functioning.

Although differences are apparent between the Stanford-Binet and the Wechsler Scale, the results of testing are quite similar, partly because of a similarity in test items. For example, both the Stanford-Binet and the WISC-R rely on the results of a vocabulary test as a contribution to the total score on which an IQ is based. Wechsler concludes that an IQ from the WISC-R is "fairly close" to the Stanford-Binet IQ and that of other well-standardized tests.

The WPPSI.   Wechsler (1967) also developed the *Wechsler Preschool and Primary Scale of Intelligence* (WPPSI) for use with children between the ages of four through six. The WPPSI is similar in form and content to the 1947 WISC, and it has found wide use in nursery schools, children's clinics, kindergartens, and day-care centers. According to Wechsler, children can solve many kinds of problems in the preschool age span. He believes that the intellectual abilities of preschoolers can be determined if appropriate tests are used. The WPPSI is like the WISC in that it is also divided into Verbal and Performance scales.

Wechsler believes that intelligence cannot be measured in the early years in exactly the same way as at later ages because a number of intellectual functions have not fully emerged. For example, vocabulary tests cannot be used until the child has a good command of language. Verbal ability measures are part of most intelligence tests used in the later years of childhood, however. Wechsler maintains that the same abilities should be studied at an early age that one studies at a later age, if we wish to understand the process of growth of intelligence. He uses this view as an argument to support the similarity of the WPPSI and the WISC; most of the WPPSI subtests could be considered easier versions or close parallels to WISC subtests.

One important variation between the WISC and the WPPSI is the "Animal House" test, designed to interest young children. The test is like the Coding Test of the WISC-R, because in both tests children have to pair signs and symbols. In the WISC Coding Test, children are asked to write a symbol next to a number. Since young children cannot handle pencils well, in the Animal House test the child is asked to associate a color with a picture of an animal, by placing an appropriately colored cylinder of wood in a hole under a picture of each animal. A key is provided so that the child will know which color is to be associated with each picture.

Wechsler believes that it is important to study the intellectual ability of children from four to six because at these ages intellectual ability is well-defined and complex. Many seem to agree with him, as the WPPSI and the WISC are both widely used.

Table 7-2
A DESCRIPTION OF THE WISC-R TESTS

Subtest	Description of a Typical Task	Functions Tested	Influencing Factors
Verbal Scale			
Information	"What is a play?"	Long-term memory; association and organization of experience	Cultural environment, interests
Comprehension	"Why do we wash clothes?"	Reasoning with abstraction; organization of knowledge; concept formation	Cultural opportunities; response to reality situations
Arithmetic	"How many inches are there in ½ foot?"	Retention of arithmetic processes; attention span	Opportunity to acquire the fundamental arithmetic processes
Vocabulary	"What does 'mammal' mean?"	Language development; concept formation	Cultural opportunities
Digit Span	Repeat digits forward and backward	Immediate recall; auditory imagery; visual imagery (at times)	Attention span
Similarities	"In what way is a bicycle like a car?"	Analysis of relationships; verbal concept formation	Cultural opportunities

Performance Scale

Picture Arrangement	Arrangement of related pictures to form a cartoon-like story	Visual perception of relationships; synthesis of nonverbal material	A minimum of cultural opportunities; visual acuity
Picture Completion	Name the important missing part in each of a series of pictures	Visual perception; visual imagery	Environmental experience; visual acuity (at times)
Object Assembly	A puzzle task in which the child takes a familiar pattern and puts it together to form a meaningful whole (duck, cow, toy)	Visual perception: synthesis, visual-motor integration	Rate and precision of motor activity
Block Design	Construction of designs with colored blocks	Perception of form; visual perception and analysis; visual-motor integration	Rate of motor activity; minimum of color vision
Coding	Pairing symbols with numbers according to a sample	Immediate recall; visual-motor integration; visual imagery	Rate of motor activity
Mazes	Finding a pathway through a paper maze pattern	Ability to plan ahead; freedom from distraction	Rate and precision of motor activity; anxiety

Source: Adapted from Freeman, F. S. *Theory and practice of psychological testing (3rd ed.),* pp. 249–250. New York: Holt, Rinehart, and Winston, 1962. Reprinted with the permission of the publisher and Dr. Freeman.

THE DETERMINANTS OF INTELLIGENCE

From the very beginning of the intelligence testing movement, questions arose as to whether differences in intelligence are mainly influenced by heredity and are inborn or whether they are mainly influenced by the environment and are, therefore, learned. Sir Francis Galton, one of the earliest psychologists and a cousin of Charles Darwin, was convinced that intelligence was mainly influenced by heredity and wrote a book called *Hereditary Genius* (Galton, 1892). Alfred Binet, however, was not at all convinced that intelligence was fixed by heredity and felt it was highly pessimistic to think that intelligence could not be changed through learning (Kamin, 1974). Lewis Terman, the developer of the Stanford-Binet test, had mixed feelings about the roles of heredity and environment. At times, Terman believed that the poor intelligence test performance shown by lower-class children might be due to their lack of opportunities to learn intellectual skills. At other times, however, Terman (1916, p. 116) stated that he believed that, except for extreme situations, environmental factors played a minimal role in determining intelligence.

The Role of Heredity and Environment

Heredity has an important role in the functioning of every living thing. There are strong relationships between body structures and behaviors, and there are important inherited "blueprints" for many biological characteristics that are passed on from the previous generation. But can biological characteristics help or hinder the development of intellectual ability? In the case of certain forms of mental retardation, genetic and chromosomal factors play definite roles in producing intellectual defects. But what role does heredity play in less extreme cases?

Several methods have been used to try to answer questions about the influence of heredity on intelligence. One well-known research technique that has been used over the years involves the use of comparison studies of family members who have a common hereditary relationship. For example, a researcher might compare the IQs of parents and their children, of brothers and sisters, or of twins. They predict that if intelligence is inherited, the greater the genetic similarity between two people, the greater will be the similarity in their IQs. Since identical twins have identical genes, a similarity in their IQs should lend support to a hereditary theory of intelligence. Several investigators have been particularly interested in comparing twins who grow up in different environments (Hunt, 1969; Bayley, 1970).

Nancy Bayley, at the University of California in Berkeley, developed scales for assessing infant intelligence and found that the scores of identical, or *monozygotic twins* (twins from the same fertilized egg), were more alike than were the scores of fraternal, or *dizygotic twins*. She also reported a study made of the twins' social responses, use of toys, activities, and emotions. Judges independently rated the infants' behavior on her Infant Behavior Record, and the results indicated that differences among fraternal twins were much greater than among identical twins.

Sharp exchanges have taken place between investigators and theoreticians on the issue of heredity versus environment. For example, Arthur Jensen (1969) asserted that current evidence such as that from twin and other family studies indicates that the basis for intelligence is primarily heredity. He explained his belief that programs to improve the mental ability of young children living in poverty cannot be highly successful because he thinks that low mental ability stems from genetic factors. Jensen's views have been controversial, since evidence is available that indicates that intelligence as shown by IQ test scores can be increased by learning and environmental influences.

As children grow, the diffuse response patterns found in infancy gradually give way to the specific and predictable responses of middle childhood. Children improve in their ability to solve problems as they get older (especially toward school age) and their intelligence test scores become better predictors of later behavior than they were at younger ages (Bayley, 1970; McCall, Hogarty, and Hurlburt, 1972; Stenhouse, 1974). In the earliest years, the mental growth rate is erratic, but in the latter part of the preschool years the child's mental ability becomes very similar to that found during the elementary school years. Bayley sees a significant change in intellectual growth taking place between fifteen months and three years of age. She calls this an *unfolding* based on innate factors as well as environmental influences. Each child, according to Bayley, has an individual pattern of change. Other research workers have also attached particular importance to the age of three.

Still, questions about the direct influence of heredity and environment on intelligence remain. Comparison of twins continues to interest psychologists because the chromosomes of identical twins are identical. Therefore, twins provide a rare opportunity to see individuals whose heredity patterns are identical. Such research usually assumes that if heredity is to be considered a primary factor in the development of intelligence in the preschool years, then monozygotic twins should show more similar intellectual development patterns than do dizygotic twins. Information is often sought about the progressive influence of environmental factors such as parental socioeconomic status and educational level, in the belief that if these factors are influential in mental development, then a close relationship to intelligence test scores ought to be found.

Patterns of Change in Mental Development

One false assumption that is often made about intelligence is that intelligence is rigidly fixed and unchangeable throughout the person's lifetime. In fact, researchers have discovered many patterns of IQ change in individuals.

Patterns of mental development are interesting because they not only provide a basis for predictions about individuals, but also help us understand the forces that direct a child's life. In one project in which longitudinal data were gathered at the Fels Institute in Yellow Springs, Ohio, investigators conceded that IQ tests are not fair to all people but maintained that IQ scores do reflect some kinds of mental competence and will serve as predictors of some kinds of academic and occupational success (McCall, Appelbaum, and Hogarty, 1973). In the view of these researchers, IQ is not stable after the age of six, as some assert. They insist that longitudinal studies such as the Harvard Growth Study, the Berkeley Guidance Study, the Fels Study, and the University of Chicago Study have reported significant changes over time in both groups of people and in individual persons (Dearborn and Rothney, 1941; Honzik, Macfarlane, and Allen, 1948; Sontag, Baker, and Nelson, 1958; Freeman and Flory, 1937; Bayley, 1940, 1949). In spite of the findings that IQ scores generally increase during a person's lifespan, it was found that a small number of individuals tended to have IQs that decreased.

This information on the decline of IQ has some similarity to the findings of an early study of disadvantaged children, since known as the study of "hollow folk" (Sherman and Key, 1932). Mandel Sherman of the University of Chicago and Cora Key of the Washington Child Research Center went to an isolated area in the Appalachian Mountains to collect data. The children in the study were descendants of early settlers who established homes in the valleys surrounded by the mountain ranges of the Appalachians. Through the years, these mountain people had continued to live in mud-plastered log houses. No roads led from the hollows to the outside world, and these isolated people tended to marry relatives. Because of the high rate of intermarriage, most of the people in a hollow had the same last names. Children in four of the hollows, as well as children in a nearby village, were given a number of intelligence tests, including the Stanford-Binet. At the time of the testing, the children ranged in age from six to sixteen years.

The results showed that the children had difficulty with tasks that depended upon verbal facility and speed. Tasks that required them to "comprehend and solve a simple problem involving foresight and planning" gave special difficulty. The results also showed that IQs decreased markedly as chronological ages increased, so that the older children were found to be in the retarded range on many of the tests. Sherman and Key concluded that "the expression of intelligence, as measured by standardized tests, depends in a large measure upon the opportunities to gather information and upon the requirements made upon the individual by his environment."

Referring to the problem of heredity, the investigators said, "Since the ancestry of the children of all of the hollows came from the same stock, claim cannot be made that some of these mountain people are 'degenerate'." Rather, Sherman and Key maintained that the increasing decline in IQ with age probably resulted from the environment's lack of demands upon the children. Yet, the study reveals some uncontrolled variables that make it hard to say that the decline in IQs was due only to environmental influences. How can one say that heredity might not also have been a factor, as the investigators reported marriage patterns that were quite different from marriages between nonrelatives? Consequently, separation of hereditary and environmental influences continues to be a source of disagreement.

Raising the Level of Mental Performance

Some children enter school with an ability to read, with an elementary knowledge of numbers, and with a large vocabulary. Such children are often eager to learn and have little difficulty adapting to school life. Other children, however, have limited vocabularies and limited abilities and tend to lag behind their classmates. They begin to feel discouraged, show lack of interest, and often give up on the tasks set by the school. What can be done to help these children?

In some studies, researchers have tried to determine whether certain teaching techniques could reverse the downward trend of school performance of children from ''disadvantaged'' and poverty-stricken homes. In one study of poor children by Klaus and Gray (1968), one group of children attended preschool sessions and a second group had, in addition, ''home visitors'' who provided activities similar to their preschool activities. A third group of children who did not attend the preschool sessions served as the control group.

Most of the parents of these children had only an eighth grade education, which limited their employment opportunities to unskilled or semiskilled occupations. In characterizing the home environments, Klaus and Gray described the homes as disorganized and generally lacking in opportunities for the children to explore

Figure 7-3. At present, we do not know all the variables that are responsible for intellectual development. However, it appears that the opportunity to practice a wide variety of culturally valued skills in a warm, supportive atmosphere may have a powerful effect on later intellectual functioning. (Sybil Shelton/Monkmeyer Press Photo Service)

objects. Parental help was minimal. In one-third of the homes, no father was present and in the others fathers had little influence.

An important feature of the teaching program was the ratio of adults to children in the school—about five teachers for the approximately twenty children in *each* experimental group. It was reported that the preschool program had a general beneficial effect as the children's intelligence test scores, obtained on both the Stanford-Binet and the WISC, exceeded the scores of the children in the control group. The beneficial effect of the program continued through the second year of regular public school.

In the mid-1960s, when Congress passed the Economic Opportunity Act, a national effort began to change the outlook for young children entering the educational system. In cities that did not have kindergarten programs for five-year-olds, children entered the new preschool program at that age. Where a kindergarten program was available, the children entered the new preschools at three and four years of age. This program gained national prominence as "Project Head Start" and attracted attention in many countries throughout the world. Thirteen regional research centers gathered national data in the largest research program for children ever conducted.

Findings on the Head Start program seem to indicate that while the preschool experience had immediate beneficial effects, the continuing effectiveness of the program was related to continuing environmental problems (*Head Start Data Analysis,* 1972; *Report of Two National Samples of Head Start Classes,* 1972). That is, because the children returned daily to poverty and continued to be poor, their chances for educational improvement decreased.

Other researchers have tried to develop techniques to help children learn by imitating adults and other children. One study of three- and four-year-old children from deprived backgrounds showed that providing models for the children to follow was an effective technique for teaching concepts (Jacobson and Greeson, 1972). In this study, initial testing results showed high increases in the children's IQs, but on tests given over a year later the children retained only about half of their original gain. Thus, for some time, the training was effective. The tendency for initial gains to decrease later is noteworthy because it shows the necessity of continuing efforts to help these children.

In a follow-through study of children who had been in Head Start programs, the effect of the early school training was examined after the children reached the second grade. The children had had different kinds of preschool training, as some Head Start classes used operant conditioning programs and others used a more conventional program. Unfortunately, the researchers found no lasting effects over the four years of the study (Miller and Dyer, 1975).

As we have pointed out, however, if children remain in disadvantaged environments, school programs may not be able to undo the effects of their surroundings. Still, such programs can prevent an even further downward trend. The problems of the disadvantaged child remain complex, and clear paths to alleviation of these problems are not in sight. Many see the need to improve the intellectual opportunites of poor children as a high-priority social goal.

Heredity vs. Environment: A Pseudoquestion?

For many researchers, the question of hereditary *versus* environmental influences may be an artifical question. Anne Anastasi (1958), a former President of the American Psychological Association and a prominent psychological testing expert, suggested that psychologists might ask a more useful question: "How do hereditary and environmental influences interact?"

Anastasi's question of interaction is useful for several reasons. For one thing, although genes may set the potential for a behavior to develop they often cannot exert their influence unless certain environmental factors are present. For example, some people have genes for light skin and will tan or sunburn fairly easily. Without sunlight or a tanning lamp in the environment, however, a person will not become sunburnt. Some people are tall and muscular and have inherited physcial traits that would be useful in basketball. Without proper training opportunities and motivating experiences, however, it is unlikely that the person will become a good basketball player. Similarly, if genes provide the potential for intelligence, their influence may be increased or decreased by environmental forces.

The term *environment* is very difficult to define. In fact, we have few tools for describing environments. As an example, try to describe the place in which you are now reading this book. What is important in this place? Where does the environment start and where does it end? For example, we could look at the environment of the embryo in the uterus, at the biochemical environment of the fetus, or at the environment of the delivery room at birth. We might find that all of these environments are important.

We must also remember that the psychological environment is not exactly the same as the physical environment. As Piaget and others believe, the child selects and constructs his or her own representation of the environment at different ages. Therefore, two people in the same room can actually experience very different environments.

Finally, hereditary and environmental influences may affect one another in highly complex ways. Hereditary influences may predispose people to take advantage of certain environmental opportunities. Similarly, environments may permit or inhibit the expression of certain genetic traits.

PIAGET'S VIEW OF COGNITIVE DEVELOPMENT IN EARLY CHILDHOOD

The Preoperational Period

Our focus in the remainder of this chapter will be on the *preoperational period* of childhood, which usually lasts from the age of two until about the age of seven. In the preoperational period, sensorimotor thought patterns change toward patterns in which there is increased capacity to use symbols and images of things in the environment. In the previous sensorimotor stage, children became capable of dealing with the properties of objects, but their thought patterns were still linked to objects that could be immediately seen, felt, or moved.

The early part of the preoperational stage, which is called the *intuitive* or *preconceptual period,* lasts from two to four years of age. Children develop the *symbolic function* which allows them to use words and pictures to represent objects that are not immediately present in the environment. For example, the child can now think of a cookie and ask for one when cookies are neither in sight nor available. The ability to engage in symbolic thought makes it possible for the child to deal with increasingly more complex thoughts and, therefore, to interact more effectively with the environment.

It is not easy to precisely define *mental symbols,* since we do not yet know much about how symbols are formed and how they are represented in the brain. Nevertheless, we can attempt to define symbols by describing them as images and representations of objects and events. Although we usually think of images as visual, we can also think of imagery in other senses: the smell of baking bread or the sounds of a good piece of music will trigger many images in several different senses at once.

During the early part of the preoperational period, language is one of the important symbolic functions. As we discussed in Chapter 5, the child at first uses holophrastic speech, in which single words are used to express whole sentences. By the time the child is four, however, holophrastic speech decreases, and the child's speech becomes fairly grammatical. Many four-year-olds seem to be aware that holophrastic speech is "baby talk," because in playing with dolls they often have their "babies" say one-word phrases.

As the ability to handle situations increases, the ability to form concepts also increases. Piaget believes that although a child's language may tell us about the child's thought processes, language is not the sole cause of thought. That is, thought is not simply "talking to ourselves." Thought precedes language, and children usually know a lot more than they can talk about. This view is supported by the fact that children who are born deaf and do not develop the typical patterns of spoken language nevertheless develop logical thought (Furth, 1971).

At about four years of age, children enter the second substage of the preoperational stage, called *intuitive thought.* In this substage, the child possesses prelogical "representational actions," which Piaget calls *intuitions.* These intuitions are rather primitive and do not yet become the logical operations characteristic of the next period, *concrete operations* (Piaget, 1967).

Limitations in the Development of Logical Thought

Johnny is four. His mother and father recently became very worried about his behavior and decided to bring him to a psychological clinic. They felt that Johnny was becoming troublesome, especially when carrying out requests to play cooperatively with his younger brother and to carry out errands. "After all," his mother said, "Johnny is a big, healthy boy. He's very smart. He knows all sorts of words that he picks up every day from us and from TV shows. He was a happy baby, and he's still a very happy, spunky kid. How come he doesn't listen to me anymore? How is it that I always have to pull Timmy and Johnny apart when they fight?"

"Johnny draws beautifully. You should see some of the drawings he made. He's very active and he's quite a little athlete. Last week, I saw him doing headstands in the living room. With all this, how come he doesn't remember to wipe his feet when he comes in from playing in the mud? I could tell him to wipe his feet a million times, but would he listen? No! I try to reason with him, and I say, 'Johnny, how would you like it if you had to clean up after me every day?' When my husband and I are talking at dinner, Johnny always interrupts us. When I say, 'Johnny, be quiet for a minute, I want to talk to Daddy,' he says, 'But I *have* to say something NOW!' He doesn't listen. He just isn't reasonable and I'm getting fed up! Did I do something wrong to turn him into such a little monster?"

Johnny's mother's complaints are not unusual, and Johnny is not a "problem child." In fact, Johnny is a rather typical four-year-old who is functioning like most healthy four-year-olds. Johnny's case points out to us that because many preoperational children are active, bright, and happy, they might impress us as being small adults. Certainly, they are no longer babies. Even with their increasingly large vocabularies and often surprising motor skills, however, they are far from being adults. Many aspects of their thinking will show that they are by no means using the same reasoning processes that adults use. Johnny is not "reasonable" in adult terms. His problems in cooperation and in carrying out errands and rules point to the differences in the thinking of preoperational-stage children and children who are in later stages of cognitive development.

In the preoperational stage, a child's thought is usually limited to very simple, rather one-dimensional thinking, in which the child focuses narrowly on one aspect of a task or situation. The preoperational child's thinking doesn't possess such complexities as: "what if," "on the other hand," "yes, but . . . ," and "let's look at it this way. . . ." Adults may use terms like this in talking to children, but the child does not necessarily understand them in the same way as adults do.

We will discuss five related aspects of preoperational thought: *egocentrism, difficulty in transformation, difficulty in reversibility, centration,* and *non-conservation.* We will also discuss experiments and observations that Piaget and his students have used to explore thought in the preoperational stage. Many of their experiments are remarkably easy to perform, and you are encouraged to try some of them with children you know. One word of caution, however. Children in the preoperational stage are often strongly convinced that their wrong answers are not at all incorrect. They will often say, "That's the way things are" and will be satisfied with their answers, which may strike us as rather bizarre. Do *not* be tempted to say, "You're wrong" or "I'll tell you the right answer," because the child will probably not be ready to understand the logical principles behind a correct answer. Furthermore, such failure experiences would probably reinforce a child's tendency to avoid you and any stressful experiences that you may introduce.

Egocentrism.   One characteristic of children in the preoperational stage is *egocentrism,* an inability to understand things from any viewpoint other than the child's own viewpoint. Johnny's mother's question, "How would you feel if you had to clean up after me all the time?" was probably not understood by him because, like many preoperational children, he could not easily understand things from someone else's viewpoint. Many people use *egocentrism* in the narrow sense of the term and interpret it to mean "self-centered," "selfish," or "inconsiderate." While this is partly true of children, Piaget's definition of egocentrism focuses on the thought processes of the child and not on motives of greed or uncooperativeness (Piaget, 1972, 1975).

Piaget points out that egocentrism limits a child's opportunity to learn things from other people and often leads to fights and conflicts with other children and adults. Such conflicts may, however, force the child to accommodate other viewpoints and therefore to gain in social learning.

As they play, young children will often play more in the presence of each other than *with* each other. A pair of two-year-olds may be chattering away in the same playroom and will occasionally hand (or more likely, grab) toys to one other. Their social interactions will consist of playful, imaginative, monologues and not true dialogues, however.

Egocentrism often leads the child to believe that everyone will have the same thoughts and feelings that he or she has. For example, a child may walk over and switch off a television news program that the parent is watching, because, "That's dumb stuff. Cartoons are better." A three-year-old boy became frustrated by one of us as he was being asked to answer some difficult questions. The boy shut his

Figure 7-4.   **Preoperational children are typically very egocentric. As their egocentrism declines, they become able to engage in cooperative play and highly elaborate games.**

eyes and then said "Go away!" When asked, "How come you're closing your eyes now? Are you angry at me?" the boy shouted loudly," 'Cause I'm invisible and you can't see me anymore!" To the egocentric child, it makes perfect sense to assume that if he cannot see other people, they also cannot see him!

A number of writers emphasize the importance of Piaget's views in regard to social interaction (Hunt, 1969; Flavell and Wohlwill, 1969; Furth, 1969, 1971; Mischel, 1971; Sigel, 1969; Taylor, 1971; Toulmin, 1971). Piaget attaches significance to children's social exchanges with others in the development of their capacity to deal with the environment effectively. Piaget stresses, however, that until children reach the end of the preoperational stage, they do not become aware of the necessity of reducing egocentrism in their play with others. In order to play a complex game like baseball or checkers it is extremely important to know what the roles of the other players are going to be. Without such a "social map," the game cannot be played. The preoperational child lacks such a map.

Some investigators question the approach of Piaget and Inhelder (1948/1967) in their demonstration of egocentrism (Borke, 1975; Hoy, 1974; Fishbein, Lewis, and Keiffer, 1972; Garner and Plant, 1972). In a well-known experiment by Piaget and Inhelder, children were required to imagine how a doll would view a mountain scene from several different perspectives. Young children can describe their own viewpoints well, but they find it difficult to describe "what the doll sees." Borke asserted that if an "age-appropriate" task were used, we would find that three- and four-year-olds *can* understand the perspective of another person.

Other studies also suggest that when appropriate instructions and tasks are given, children as young as two or three years show a good amount of skill in making inferences about another person's "looking-seeing" activity (Masangkay, McCluskey, McIntyre, Sims-Knight, Vaughn, and Flavell, 1974). The researchers see young children as particularly *object-oriented,* and thus they have difficulty in tasks that require an overall *view-orientation* as is required in Piaget's "mountain" task.

Piaget explained that because of their new experiences in social relations, by the end of the preoperational stage children learn new ideas by comparing their own thoughts with those of others. Egocentrism, according to Piaget, is not at a constant level in this age period, nor is it confined to this one period of development. Although the characteristic seems to decrease in the preoperational and concrete operational stages, there appears to be an increase in egocentrism in adolescence.

Difficulties in Transformation.   A second problem in the thought of the preoperational child is that of dealing with *transformations.* This difficulty arises from the fact that the child's thought is static, and the child is more able to deal with fixed, immovable things than with processes which involve change. Although children can perceive that the form of an object has changed, they cannot understand the sequence of steps that led to the change.

One of the reasons why children have difficulty understanding transformations is that they use a form of reasoning called *transductive reasoning* (Piaget, 1924,

1964, pp. 180–195). As adults, our logical thought takes the form of *deductive reasoning,* in which we proceed logically from the general to the particular, as in the following example:

a) All dogs are mammals.
b) This is a dog.
c) *Therefore,* this is a mammal.

We may also use *inductive reasoning,* in which we go from particular examples to more general rules. For example:

a) Billy has a bicycle.
b) Tommy does not have a bicycle.
c) *Therefore,* all children do not have bicycles.

A preoperational child rarely uses either of these forms of logic. In transductive reasoning the child's mind goes from particular example to particular example without concern for logic or generalizations. For example, a child tells us, "I have a toy, so it must be Christmas." Here the child uses two particular incidents—"I get toys at Christmas," and "Now I have a toy"—to draw an illogical conclusion by linking superficial features of the two statements into a more general statement. The child may not realize that causes come *before* their effects, so that it is possible for the child to think that by laughing, he or she will "cause" something funny to happen. Cause and effect and notions of sequence are often confused by young children. We might ask a child to tell us the positions that a pencil would take as it falls from an upright to a horizontal position. If we did this, we would find that most preoperational children cannot explain the transformations in positions from vertical to horizontal (Flavell, 1963; Elkind, 1969; Mischel, 1971; Wadsworth, 1971).

A very simple experiment will illustrate some other characteristics of preoperational thought. We will show two equally spaced rows of ten checkers each to some four-year-old children and say to each child, "This row of checkers will be mine, and this row of checkers is yours. Do you have more checkers or less checkers or the same number of checkers as me?" Most children would say that the two rows of checkers are equal. Then, as the child watches us, we will make one row of checkers longer than the other by spreading out the checkers. If we again ask the child whether he or she has more, less, or the same number of checkers as we have, most preoperational children will say that the rows have unequal amounts of checkers (Piaget, 1947/1966, 1965). If we ask them why this is so, they will usually answer, "Because there's more here." To make sure that we really know what the child means by "more," we could ask, "Does it just *look* like more or are there *really* more checkers?" The children will usually tell us that there *really* are more checkers.

This is puzzling in several ways. First, many four-year-olds can easily count up to and beyond ten. Why don't they count the checkers? Furthermore, since the children saw us spreading out the checkers in front of them, how could they believe that we had magically produced more checkers in one of the rows? In experiments such as this one, Piaget has shown that the preoperational child's thought has the important characteristics of *irreversibility* and *centration*.

Reversibility.   If you were asked: "How can a person go from your home to your next-door-neighbor's house?" and "How can you go from your next-door-neighbor's house to your house?" you would not think these were difficult questions. Nor would you be puzzled by the following question: "If I had five apples in a bag and then I put five more apples in the bag, and then I took five apples out of the bag, how many apples would be left in the bag?" Preoperational children find these problems difficult because their thinking lacks reversibility.

Similarly, in the checkers experiment, an older child or adult could reason that the two rows of checkers still had the same number of checkers. The *older* child could demonstrate that the rows were the same by pushing the spread-out row back to its original spacing. The child might say something like, "I'll push them back and then they will be the same."

Centration.   Another characteristic of preoperational thought is the fact that the child's attention is usually *centered* on a limited aspect of a situation, and the child rarely shifts his or her attention to other parts. In a sense they are fixed on one property and "fail to see the forest for the trees" by not *decentering,* or attending to the whole situation. In the checkers example, many children center only on the changed length of the row and ignore the fact that the actual number of checkers has not changed. An older child, according to Piaget, is able to decenter attention in problem-solving and perception. An older child might say: "Yes. It *looks* longer, *but* if you count them, there are ten checkers in your row and ten in mine."

The Child's Acquisition of Conservation

Conservation refers to the ability to understand that the actual *quantities* of things may remain the same, although their *qualitative appearance* may be changed. In order to be able to perform conservation tasks, the child must be able to decenter attention, to use reversibility, and to understand transformations. In the checkers example, we saw a task involving the *conservation of number,* in which children were faced with the question of whether the number of checkers was the same even though they were spaced differently. Piaget and his colleagues have found that the preoperational child cannot perform many kinds of conservation tasks. Figure 7-6 illustrates several kinds of conservation tasks that have been frequently used in research. In each task, the child can demonstrate that conservation has been acquired by using any one of three essential reasons for stating that the quantities are the same. These reasons are:

1. *Identity*—For example, "It's really the *same* amount. You didn't really change anything."

2. *Compensation*—For example, in the conservation of liquid problem, the child could say, "You put the water into a tall glass *but* it's *also* not as wide."

3. *Reversibility*—The child justifies answers by showing that the transformation can be reversed to reproduce the original product. For example, in the conservation of matter experiment, the child may justify his or her answer by saying, "I can take the piece of clay that looks like a hot dog and roll it *back* into a ball that will be *just like it was before.*"

Piaget maintains that different kinds of conservation are acquired in a sequence, because the solution of some conservation problems will require schemata needed in other problems. Conservation of number usually appears earliest, and most six-year-olds can handle number problems, but conservation of volume is usually the last to develop and is rarely seen in a child younger than ten.

Figure 7-5.   This boy is taking part in an experiment designed to test his ability to understand conservation of liquid quantities. There is the same amount of water in each of the containers, but most preoperational children are unable to find ways of proving that although the appearance of the liquids differs, the actual quantity of liquids is the same. (Mimi Forsyth/Monkmeyer Press Photo Service)

Research Related to Piaget's Theory of Preoperational Thought

A number of research investigators have supported Piaget's view of children's abilities to deal with conservation problems, but several questions about preoperational thought have prompted researchers to test, modify, and challenge some of his findings. Piaget's theory proposes a natural, unvarying order of stages, and he also believes that we cannot teach a concept to a child unless the child has reached the stage where understanding is possible. Some researchers have challenged this viewpoint by attempting to train children in certain concepts and, therefore, accelerate cognitive growth. One study by Gruen (1965) investigated the effect of training in conservation. The investigator trained five-year-old children to solve conservation of number problems. In his procedure, Gruen demonstrated to the children the "invariance of numerical values" (that the number of checkers remained the same despite perceptual cues to the contrary). Gruen's results said that "confronting the child repeatedly with the invariance of numerical values in the face of irrelevant perceptual changes" is *not* effective in bringing about conservation of number. Nevertheless, he qualified his conclusions by pointing out that *during* the period of his study a number of children did acquire the ability to conserve. This result might be expected in the course of any study lasting for a long time; some children could be expected to mature and perhaps reach the next stage of ability anyway. It may be, too, that one should not expect to *absolutely* establish such theoretical principles.

Other researchers studied the effect of training on children by attempting to teach the concepts of reversibility, addition, and subtraction to first graders. Although the addition and subtraction training was ineffective, *reversibility training* did affect conservation (Wallach, Wall, and Anderson, 1967). In an experiment with five- and six-year-old children, another investigator reported that training *was* effective in acquisition of the concept of conservation of matter. This positive finding, in relation to the negative findings just described, suggests that the nature of the experimental task and the demands made upon children may play significant roles in mastering conservation (Sheppard, 1974).

Although many studies have had mixed results in regard to the effectiveness of training in conservation tasks, research investigations seem to generally support Piaget's idea that long-lasting knowledge of conservation cannot be brought about by training. Perhaps it would be appropriate to say that research has tended to support the idea of the ineffectiveness of training in the acquisition of conservation. Also, the *kind* of training or experience seems to be important in achieving the ability to conserve.

Piaget's theory has a strong biological emphasis. Can we say that cognitive development stages are the same in different cultures? Alternately, can we say that cultural influences, such as the effect of learning experiences in school, could affect a child's ability to perform conservation tasks? With cultural influences in mind, one study compared rural children who had not been in school with those who had been in school, on various tests of conservation. No significant differences were

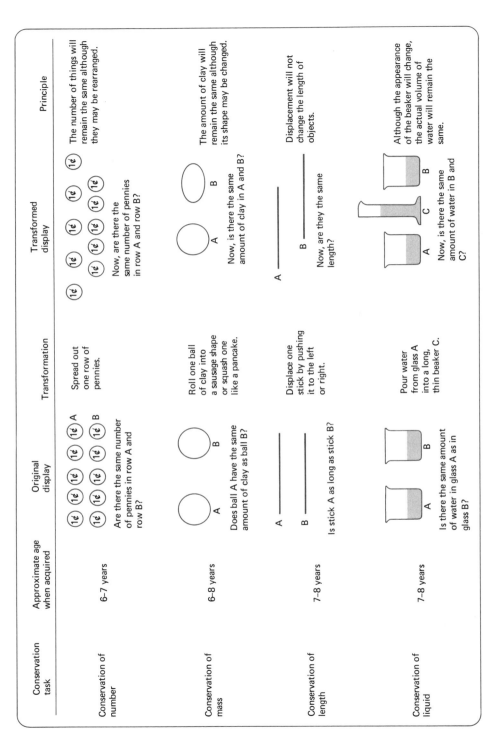

Figure 7-6. Conservation tasks.

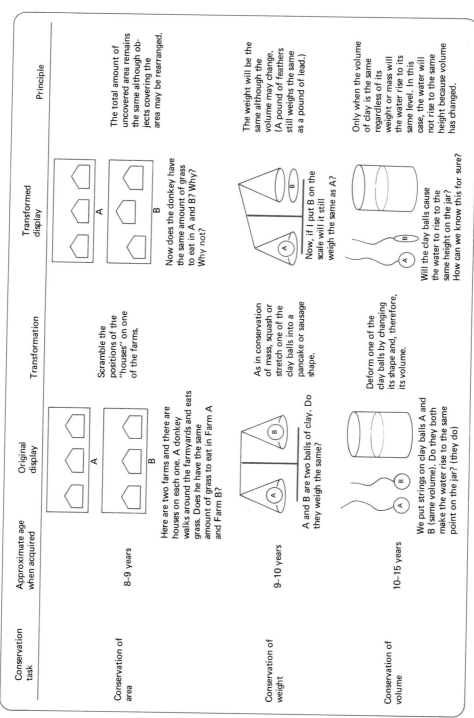

Figure 7-6. (continued)

207

encountered on several conservation tasks, but some mixed results were found (Mermelstein and Shulman, 1967). An investigator in another study tested lower-class children in the first three grades of school and asked them to perform conservation tasks of area, number, quantity, weight, and matter (Gaudia, 1972). Significant differences were found among Black children, American Indian children, and white children, in regard to the ages at which they acquired conservation concepts, although the latter two groups were similar. The findings led the investigator to conclude that some major differences in the rates of acquisition of conservation may exist between children of different ethnic and social class backgrounds.

Piaget's views about preoperational thought indicate that preoperational children are mentally advanced over sensorimotor children. Toward the end of the preoperational period, conservation ability begins to arise from the experiences most children have in interaction with the environment. These abilities emerge in all children at about the same age, in a sequence that does not vary. Children who do not have formal schooling seem to achieve the ability to conserve at about the same age as those who attend school. The gradually attained ability to conserve is not entirely due to learning. Research suggests that efforts to train children to conserve in the preoperational period have very few long-term effects on their ability to conserve. According to Piaget, conservation abilities do not develop until cognitive structures are established and this accomplishment comes about when the child has further assimilated and accommodated new objects and has formed new schemata.

In attaining the ability to conserve, children must be able to perceive reversibility, to decenter, and to cope with transformations. They must come to question their own thinking and reasoning in order to reduce egocentrism. Language is an important aid in the development of the capability for *representational thought,* or symbolic thinking. Language becomes closely associated with thought processes, and its acquisition helps to reduce egocentrism as the child becomes able to share ideas with other people. By the end of the preoperational period, around the age of six or seven, the child is much more able than earlier to exchange ideas with others.

Thus, the preoperational thought of the child is shown by an inability to reverse operations, to understand the significance of transformations, to decenter perceptions, and to go beyond egocentric responses. By the end of the period, the child has progressed closer to a capability for concrete operational thought—the next stage of mental development.

SUMMARY

In this chapter, we have examined intelligence in early childhood from a psychometric and a Piagetian perspective. We have seen that although intelligence tests have been used for many years, a number of questions about intelligence still remain to be answered. In an attempt to approach these questions, we discussed the techniques used for measuring intelligence and the roles that hereditary and environmental factors play in the development of intelligence.

In examining the development of intelligence from a Piagetian perspective, we looked at typical behaviors of children in the preoperational stage. We learned that their abilities to reason logically are limited by egocentrism, an inability to mentally reverse processes, centration on limited aspects of problems, and an inability to handle transformations. In the next chapter, we shall examine the development of language in early childhood.

RECOMMENDED READINGS

Kamin, L. *The Science and Politics of IQ.* Potomac, Md.: Erlbaum Associates, 1974. Loehlin, J. C., Lindzey, G., and Spuhler, J. N. *Race differences in intelligence.* San Francisco: Freeman, 1975.

> These two books should be read together because they provide scholarly, brilliant examinations of the roles of hereditary and genetic factors in intelligence. Kamin's book provides a strong case for considering IQ test scores to be the products of social forces, while the Loehlin book takes a strong biological stance.

Piaget, J. *The Language and Thought of the Child.* New York: Meridian Books, 1955 (orig. 1923).

———. *Judgment and Reasoning of the Child.* Patterson, N.J.: Littlefield Adams, 1967 (orig. 1924).

———. *The Child's Conception of the World.* Patterson, N.J.: Littlefield Adams, 1969 (orig. 1926).

———. *The Child's Conception of Physical Causality.* Patterson, N.J.: Littlefield Adams, 1972 (1927).

> These books were written early in Piaget's career and before his theory reached its present stage of formal development. However, these books provide a delightful view of the minds of preoperational children. Although written over fifty years ago in Switzerland, these books are still highly relevant today.

The Accomplishment of Language

IDEAS ABOUT LANGUAGE

In Chapter 5 we traced the course of infants' gradual recognition that human sounds are used in a symbolic system to communicate meaning. What is so special about our symbolic system? Is language exclusively a human ability or can animals develop language like ours? As we shall discover, answers to such questions depend on how we define language.

Animal Studies as a Key to Human Language

Animals appear to have language, since they can communicate meaning to each other and to us. When Rover the family dog runs to the front door and scratches, we recognize that this is a signal for us to open the door and let him out. He can communicate a basic need to us through a special signal.

Many authorities feel that language involves more than just communication. The gestural systems used by animals to communicate with each other, like that of the bees, may not meet other criteria for true language. At one level, there is no chance to develop *new* forms of expression and the gestures remain static and fixed. At another level the gestural systems used in animal communication do not have any flexibility to describe new objects or to be used in new situations (Russell & Russell, 1971). At still another level, animal gestures do not appear to represent a true language since they cannot express false statements or ideas with no concrete referent (Hockett, 1960). When these criteria are used to assess whether animals have language, it becomes clear that communicative gestures do not fit our definition. Although language involves communication, the ability to communicate is not the only criterion for true language.

In only exceptional instances have we been able to find language present in animals. In the monumental work of the Gardners (1969), a female chimpanzee named Washoe was taught to use the sign language for the deaf. Washoe was reared much like a human infant in the home of the psychologists. With considerable patient instruction Washoe developed a limited vocabulary of more than one hundred words. Both Brown (1970) and Russell and Russell (1971) carefully examined the manner in which Washoe used these words. They concluded that Washoe had in fact acquired a true language system. Washoe combined words, initially learned one at a time, to describe new objects. Washoe also used words in unique combinations and in a variety of different situations. When Washoe heard a dog barking outside, she combined the sign words "listen + dog."

Generally such special situations do little more than convince us that language is a very unusual human ability. It is language which permits us to have infinite freedom and flexibility in our behavior. Language is found in all human societies and is easily and rapidly acquired by children with only simple exposure to adult speakers. Most psychologists feel that biological factors, our unique genetic heritage, play an important role in the development of children's language. From Chapter 5, however, it should also be clear that any explanation of children's language must recognize the significant role of the child's experiences. Let us first look at the contributions of biology in understanding language.

The Brain and Language

Human beings have the left side of the brain typically set aside for language specific behaviors. In comparison to other species, only human beings have evidence of this bilateral asymmetry, in which there is dominance of one side of the brain over the other. Bilateral asymmetry is not only found for language functions but also is related to whether we prefer to use our left or right hand (McNeill, 1970).

Much of our information about the link between language development and the brain and central nervous system of the child has come from the work of neurologists. They have studied the effects of brain injuries, localized on the left side, on various language skills (see Figure 8-1). If Broca's area is damaged, then motor

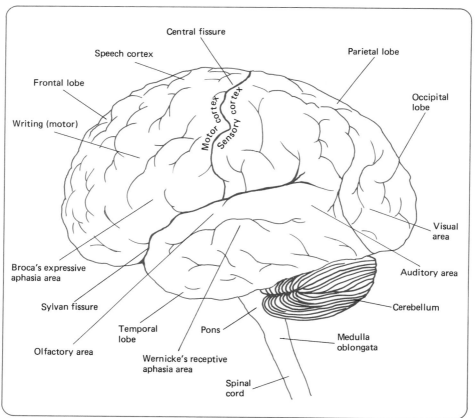

Figure 8-1.   Speech areas of the dominant hemisphere. (Based on B. A. Curtis, S. Jacobson, and E. M. Marcus, *An introduction to the neurosciences.* Philadelphia: Saunders, 1972, p. 525.)

aphasia occurs. Even though words may be formed in a person's mind, they cannot be expressed because there is an inability to remember the proper sequence of movements of the tongue and lips to make the appropriate sounds. If Wernicke's area is injured, receptive aphasia occurs. There is an inability to respond to and process auditory statements or commands. Individuals with this type of injury cannot follow a set of verbal instructions such as: "Put the pencil in the drawer and bring me a piece of paper."

According to Lenneberg (1969) our ability to overcome such damage to the left side of the brain decreases as we get older. There is minimal recovery from such damage in adolescents and adults. However, the ability to completely regain language skills lost through brain injury dramatically increases with younger and younger children. With infants and children up to three years of age it appears that the right side of the brain can take over language functions usually reserved for the left side. Such plasticity is not possible if language has already been specifically localized or *lateralized* in the brain, as in the case of adolescents and adults. Lateralization of the brain is a maturational process which sets limits, or establishes a critical period, for the development of language. Its presence prevents the further development of language in other parts of the brain (McNeill, 1970). Such information appears basic to our understanding the biological contribution to our development of language.

The Components of Language

In examining language, regardless of culture, linguists and psychologists have developed two fundamental ways of discussing language. All languages have both an inherent *structure* and an inherent *meaning* component. The structure of any language refers to the system of rules which govern native speakers' language constructions in three areas. Thus, one way of studying a language is to describe its basic rules in the areas of: (1) *phonology*—what individual speech sounds are permitted; (2) *morphology*—what combination of sounds is used to express meaning; (3) *syntax*—how meaning units, for example, words, are organized into understandable statements (Deese, 1971). While we can isolate these three structural aspects of language in research studies, we must recognize that the child makes no such distinctions. Furthermore, there is growing concern that children must first understand semantically what is said, prior to their developing a system of phonological, morphological, or syntactical rules (MacNamara, 1972). It seems that it is through the semantic, or meaning, component of language that children acquire their knowledge of the structural rules of language.

Phonemes are the basic sounds of any language. Children begin to distinguish acceptable sound combinations from those that are not acceptable (for example, English does not permit initial *nk* combinations). Such phonological rules are acquired as the child learns the meaning of words (Glucksberg & Danks, 1975). This fits well with the common observation that children, in the course of language development, comprehend far more than they can produce. Their ability to understand language is much more well developed than their ability to use the structural rules of phonology, morphology, and syntax in their language production.

Most attempts to describe the development of the child's phonology are based on analysis of how basic phonemes are produced by the speech organs. Two primary types of phoneme sounds can be produced in all languages. In one type, *vowels,* air from the lungs is allowed to flow freely through the mouth after passing over the vocal cords; for example, when we say the sound *oo.* The second type, *consonants,* occurs when we obstruct the flow of air from the lungs with the lips, teeth, or tongue; for example, as we say the initial or final *t* sound in *toot.*

Children's passive recognition of phonemes clearly surpasses by many months and years their ability to actively and accurately produce these sounds on their own. Often children use sound (letter) substitutions which are interpreted as "cute" mispronunciations. Glucksburg and Danks (1975) note the following exchange in a little girl named Ericka (pp. 125–126):

> "When Ericka was three she would pronounce her name 'Ewicka.' If someone repeated, 'Ewicka?', she would protest, 'No, Ewicka!' 'Is it Ericka, then?' 'Yes, you siwwy, Ewicka!'"

We usually do not perceive, however, that children can detect these differences in the speech of others. In a normative analysis of such children's errors, Templin (1957) discovered that for three-year-olds like Ericka, nearly half of their articulations involve errors of this general substitution type. Not until most children reach eight years of age are they able to demonstrate mastery of all the phonological rules of our language. The easiest sounds to master appear to be those which involve minimal movements of the speech organs—for example, the consonant sounds *p, m,* or *h.* Those that are more difficult are ones that involve more complex coordination of the vocal apparatus—for example, the sounds *r, l, ch,* and *z.* Most linguists feel that maturation underlies this sequence of articulation difficulty.

When children systematically begin to put phonemes together to express meaning, morphological development can be studied. A *morpheme* is the smallest unit of language which conveys meaning. While we usually consider words to be good examples of morphemes, it should be emphasized that not all morphemes are words. A child who expresses the past tense by adding the morpheme *ed* to a verb (e.g., "I walk*ed* to the store today") is using a morpheme. Similarly, meanings are conveyed by certain prefixes like *non* or *ex,* or suffixes such as *ly* or *ing,* all of which are morphemes but not words. At the foundation of children's use of morphemes is the attempt to communicate meaning by using a combination of phonemes to stand for an idea, thought, or symbol. Thus, even the child's one- and two-word utterances may be important points to examine to help unravel the complexities of morphological development in children.

It has been somewhat easier, however, for psychologists to study children's morphological rules once the child has moved beyond one- or two-word utterances and developed more complex language. Berko's (1958) study with children four to eight years old is often cited as an example of research on children's morphology. She was interested in children's ability to pluralize nouns, as well as their ability to use the past tense, possessives, and third person singular verbs. Let's look at the imaginative procedure she used to assess children's pluralization of nouns. All the children were presented with pictures of objects and a label or name describing the object. The label name was either a nonsense word or a real word. For example, in showing a child a small birdlike animal she said, "This is a wug. Now there is another one. There are two of them. There are two ___?___." Children's ability to pluralize this word could thus be assessed. In her study children were aware of plurals. They could easily pluralize nonsense labels with either the appropriate sound /s/ (used in such cases as books, facts, or cigarettes) or /z/ (for such words as guns, dogs, or "wugs"). There was considerable difficulty, however, in using a third pluralization rule which required the /əs/ sound, in such examples as houses, watches, or briefcases. Although most older children could use this pluralization rule correctly with a real word such as glass (glasses), less than 40% could do so with a nonsense word such as "gutch" (gutches). Children can use pluralization rules by four years of age; however, their rules are incomplete since they are missing the /əz/ category. It is not until nearly eight years of age that children successfully broaden their pluralization rules to include this third category (Palermo, 1978). Further evidence of this difficulty in children's use of the /əz/ plural form can be seen in Anisfeld and Tucker's (1967) study with five- and six-year-olds. The difficulties children have with this third pluralization rule /əz/, are *productive* ones, according to Palermo. Children have the conceptual understanding of what a plural is and the ability to recognize correct and incorrect pluralization from listening to the speech of others, but they do not produce the /əz/ rule as early or as easily as the other plural forms in their overt speech.

The final structural feature of language is syntax. *Syntactic rules* describe how morphemes can be combined into statements. Our ability to speak or write "proper" English and to use "good grammar" implies that we have learned some syntactic rules. From our English classes, we learn that there is a grammar which should be used to arrange words and phrases in proper sequence. Psychologists recognize that while we may have the basic *competence* to recognize grammatically correct sentences, we often violate these rules in our everyday *performance* of speaking or writing, much to the chagrin of our former English teachers. In listening to the lectures of college professors, we can find numerous performance errors, such as false starts, memory failures (e.g., forgetting if the subject of a sentence was singular or plural), and repetitions. These errors are all evidence for the distinction between performance and grammatical competence.

Chomsky's Theory of Transformational Grammar

In order to see how children acquire and use syntactic rules it is important for us to see that syntax and semantics, or meaning, are closely related. In the minds of some psychologists these two features are inseparable. Chomsky (1965), in fact, developed his Transformational Grammar to account for this relation. A description of a child's syntax, for Chomsky, is superficial because it describes only the *surface structure,* or overt relationships, in a sentence. Surface structure is much like the "tree diagrams" painstakingly drawn in English classes devoted to sentence diagramming. Chomsky feels that, in addition to surface structure, each sentence has a *deep structure* which is concerned with the meaning of the sentence or its semantic expression. Children use language because they want to communicate meaning or deep structure.

Analysis of syntax alone can result in many problems. Chomsky recognized that two sentences can have identical surface structures but different deep structures. Consider the following two contrasting sentences which have identical surface structures:

John is eager to please.
John is *easy* to please.

Conversely, there are many different surface structures which can be used to express the same semantic concept. Consider the following sentences which have identical deep structures:

A flying bird may be hit by an arrow.
An arrow might hit a bird as it flies.
With an arrow, a flying bird might be hit.

Such illustrations help identify the important link that exists between syntax (surface structure) and meaning (deep structure). Chomsky analyzed this necessary link between deep and surface structure. He provided a system of transformations that describes how speakers move from meaning to syntax. We all use transformational rules, but these are only identifiable by psychologists or linguists who study how we construct our language. Even though we do not realize that we are using a system of syntactic rules, the systematic manner in which we construct sentences every time we speak is ample evidence that such rules are being followed. Transformational rules allow us to construct passives or negatives in the same way as other speakers in our language. We do not move haphazardly from deep to surface structure but instead rely on these transformations, or rules.

We will look at these transformations for children and see how they compare to those of adults. First, however, it is necessary to examine how children acquire transformational rules. Specific transformational rules are acquired by children through: (1) exposure to the language of their parents and other speakers—listening to the surface structure, and (2) recognizing what those speakers mean semantically—deep structure (Cazden, 1972; McNeill, 1971b). One of Chomsky's most interesting ideas is that all children have an innate capability for acquiring transformation rules because of a *language acquisition device* (LAD). The LAD is present in all children and allows them to construct transformational rules from the language they hear around them. The LAD merely has to be exposed to language and it will begin to process the *corpus*, or body, of speech it receives so that the child will develop a system of transformations. The diagram below (see Figure 8-2) describes the way in which the LAD generates grammatical competence.

The LAD operates successfully for any language corpus to which a child is exposed (for example, French, German, English, Swahili). Slobin (1973) has wondered whether there are certain fundamental, or *universal*, features of all languages to which the LAD is likely to respond. Some of these universals of language may include noun phrases, verb phrases, and sentences. Slobin has also identified that all languages have some system of suffixes and prefixes. Suffixes seem to be attended to more readily by children than prefixes. Finding the universals common to languages throughout the world should help us develop more understanding of the inner workings of the LAD, how it operates on the language corpus, and what aspects of it are innate. Children may have sensitivity to specific types of linguistic universals and a more general set of skills which allows them to abstract transformations from the language environment. By studying linguistic universals it may be possible to learn more about the language development of children (Allen & Van Buren, 1971).

SYNTAX

Syntactic Development in Preschoolers

Another way to see that children's language involves transformations of the type identified by Chomsky (1965) is to examine the types of errors that are made in certain "target" syntactic constructions (Palermo, 1978). Analyses of these errors show that children often incorrectly infer the syntactic rules used by adults. These errors are highly systematic and predictable, made by all children.

One type of syntactic error, the misuse of the past tense, has been studied by Ervin (1964). Initially, children use irregular verb forms such as came, saw, went,

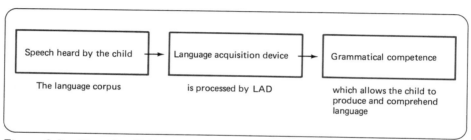

Figure 8-2. The role of LAD in children's language development.

Figure 8-3.   Children actively construct transformational rules from the language to which they have been exposed. (Hays/Monkmeyer Press Photo Service)

and broke. Later, they begin to use the *-ed* marker at the end of regular verbs such as walked, jumped, or carried. With the development of the *-ed* marker, however, children lose their formerly developed skills with irregular past tense forms. They regularize all verbs and express the past tense by adding *-ed* to all verbs. Thus, "came" becomes "comed," "ran" becomes "runned," and "taught" becomes "teached." These past tense forms are never used by adults and could not be due to modeling or direct imitation. These errors fit nicely with Chomsky's theory, indicating that the child is using syntactic rules to express meaning. The rules are constructed actively by the child and go through a series of revisions as indicated by the systematic errors identified. Gradually, the child's syntactic rules are modified so that they match those used by adults. The presence of systematic syntactic errors suggests that each child is a kind of miniature scientist, actively trying to construct a set of rules relating syntax and semantics by listening to the adult corpus of speech. Like most scientific theories, the child's early rules have to be modified to accommodate new information. These errors also reveal that adult teaching, direct imitation, or reinforcement do not account for the child's progressive mastery of syntactic rules.

Analyses of other syntactic structures also reveal that children make systematic, rule-governed errors before they acquire adult rules. Klima and Bellugi (1966) have identified three basic rules which children follow sequentially in expressing the negative. Initially children use any simple negative element, which they place either before or after a positive statement. "No" is the form most often used in children's statements: "No go" or "No hungry" or "Nap no" or "See doggie no." A more advanced developmental rule involves using a greater variety of negatives which are placed *within* the sentence. This can be seen in such statements as: "I not tired!" or "This no taste good" or "Why not Daddy go work?" The third rule developed by children allows the use of both a variety of negatives and the appropriate auxiliary verbs. Children's errors at this level involve errors of: (1) indefinite determiners and pronouns, such as "I didn't do something," and (2) indefinite negatives, such as "Nobody can't hear us" (Palermo, 1978).

Syntactic Development in School-Age Children

Children continue to show a variety of new forms of syntactic construction in their development from five to ten years of age. Triplett (1972), for example, has recognized the increasing use of infinitives and participles, and Carroll (1971) notes an increase in the correct use of both passives and auxiliary verbs such as *have*. A number of investigators have also been interested in more advanced comprehension of rather sophisticated syntactic forms.

In one study, Chomsky (1969) used a "clinical interview" method similar to that of Piaget to assess elementary school children's use of the *minimal distance principle*. The minimal distance principle states that: "The subject of a complement (a verb with *to*) is the noun phrase most immediately preceding it" (Dale, 1976, p. 132). For example, the rule applies in the following sentences:

Mother told Susie to leave.
Mother wanted Susie to leave.

Certain verbs, however, such as *ask* or *promise*, violate the minimal distance principle. For example, consider the following uses:

Mother asked Susie when to leave.
Mother promised Susie to leave.

Chomsky found that not until children were nearly eight years old could they deal with the exceptions to the minimal distance principle; that is, the verbs *ask* or *promise*. The trend among younger children was to apply the principle in all cases.

Following Chomsky's work, Kessel (1970) studied the minimal distance principle in kindergarten, first, second, third, and fifth graders. Figure 8-3 shows a typical comprehension task. After a sentence was read to the children, they had to identify which of two pictures described the sentence they had heard. The words used were

Figure 8-4. Two situational drawings from the Kessel experiment. Children were asked to choose the drawing that would match the sentence, "The boy asks the girl which shoe he should wear." (From F. S. Kessel, the role of syntax in children's comprehension from ages 6 to 12. *Monographs of the Society for Research in Child Development,* 35, 1970 [6, Serial No. 139]. Copyright 1970 by the Society for Research in Child Development. By permission.)

tell, which always follows the minimal distance principle, and *ask,* which only follows the principle when it conveys a "request or order." The statement "Mrs. Smith asked Mary to read" follows the principle; the subject of the infinitive phrase is the noun closest to it. An exception to the minimal distance rule occurs when *ask* is used as a question as in: "Mrs. Smith asked Mary what to read." Most eight-year-olds could make the appropriate distinctions between the pictures presented, while younger children had more difficulty. The "ask" questions showed exactly the same developmental pattern identified by Chomsky (1969) with the verb *promise.* The minimal distance principle is only one example showing that syntax development in children continues beyond five years of age. There are continued transformations which have to be made, elaborated, and refined before the syntactic structures of the child have reached the point of adult mastery in terms of production and comprehension.

SEMANTIC DEVELOPMENT

Although it is possible to isolate the structure of the child's language (phonology, morphology, syntax) from semantics, many psychologists are trying to understand this relationship. How does semantics influence these structural developments?

Psychologists have recently recognized the importance of the context, or situation, in children's acquisition of meaning (Bloom, 1970; Bowerman, 1973). In her work with children, Nelson (1973) suggests that children may initially learn the meaning of words by attending to their *function*. A child learns that the word *car* refers to an object which moves, which the child rides in, and which has a baby seat in which to sit—all of which are highly important situational or functional uses. Thus, word meaning may not exist apart from the context in which the words are used. This is very similar to Piaget's explanation of how the child acquires concepts in general: through overt manipulation and direct activity a concept becomes an internalized part of the child.

Another account of the development of semantic information in children can be seen in the *semantic feature theory* of Eve Clark (1973). Clark feels that the child initially learns that words have very concrete, perceptual features or attributes. For example, to a child a *horse* may mean any living object with four legs. As the child uses the word and hears it used by others, *horse* gradually acquires additional qualifying features. These features might include attributes such as large, animal, neighs, that differentiate it from cows, fat people who crawl, and St. Bernard dogs. Clark has extensive evidence that it takes some time for children to develop semantic categories which match those of adults. Children's errors usually involve either *over-extensions,* such as a child calling a large St. Bernard a "horse," or *under-extensions,* like calling a small pony a "dog."

Palermo has proposed a third process, called *prototype theory,* which may explain children's acquisition of semantics. Palermo assumes that the child's cognitive development provides the basis for semantic development. At the basis of language is a *core meaning* which we intend to express and which we recognize when others speak. This abstract meaning can be represented in language by two prototypes: nouns and verbs. *Prototypes* are relations among "abstract perceptual, functional, and affective factors" (Palermo, 1978, p. 246). While these look like the deep structural relations presented by Chomsky, it is possible that some are learned through experience (as Nelson and Clark suggest) and that others may be innate. Perhaps certain perceptual prototypes are innate for children, such as recognition of contour or shape, which merely require that the child learn the appropriate label or word to express the prototype. There may be innate categories of perception and cognition which determine how we see and think about our environment (Rosch, Mervis, Gray, Johnson, & Boyes-Braem, 1976). We may see and respond to selected aspects of our environment because of the way the perceptual-cognitive systems are constructed biologically. At least some such category limitations appear to be present in humans. For example, we cannot hear high-frequency sound waves or see the infrared part of the color spectrum. Geometric categories like circles and rectangles may be prototypes with basic core meaning (Rosch, 1973). Prototypes are assumed to be at the cognitive base of children's semantic development by Palermo (1978). If this is so, then the puzzle of how children can use a single word to represent a number of different meanings may be closer to being solved.

Children also begin to discover the meaning of words by seeing how they fit into the context of a sentence. Younger children are dependent on normal sentence structure context with its familiar word order patterns. For example, Love and Parker-Robinson (1972) found that children imitate nonsense material better if it is placed in the context of a sentence than if it is arranged randomly. They presented four- to six-year-olds with nonsense strings that did or did not have functors (prepositions, conjunctions, or adverbs) embedded in either normal sentence form or arranged randomly. Examples of these statements are:

1. Normal sentence arrangement
    a.   With functors: "The kiv bixed the yag."
    b.   Without functors: "Kiv bixed yag."
2. Random arrangement
    a.   With functors: "The bixed kiv in the yag."
    b.   Without functors: "Bixed kiv yag."

When functors were present, children found it easier to imitate nonsense statements arranged in the normal sentence fashion than when random arrangements were used. When functors were not present, children did not differ in their ability to imitate the normal sentence and random arrangement presentations. Children thus appear to rely on *contextual cues* for processing and imitating language-type material.

THE FUNCTIONS OF LANGUAGE

Piaget and Language Development

In Piaget's well-known book, *The Language and Thought of the Child* (1926), he devoted considerable attention to egocentric speech. In listening to children use language, he recognized that the preoperational children (younger than six or seven) were unable to take the role of listener. *Egocentric speech,* then, involves language which takes place in the presence of others but without much exchange of information or ideas. Children may take turns in speaking, but they often talk only about their own ideas. For example:

Billy: Did you know that Susie came to my house last night?

Neal: This is a big red fire truck.

Billy: She made cookies for us and then we ate them all up. Do you like cookies from the oven?

Neal: The fire truck is going to the fire. Ding. Ding. Ding. Look out! Here it comes.

Piaget also recognized that as children got older there was evidence of *socialized speech*. That is, sometimes children made an effort to communicate with another peer. There was an active attempt to share ideas and recognize the perspective of the other. Children would begin to explain things and avoid using personal pronouns or names which the listener would not understand. For example, in the above exchange an older child might explain that Susie is a neighbor who babysits for the child. The transition from egocentric to socialized speech is gradual, not abrupt. In fact, Piaget found evidence that older children sometimes employed examples of egocentric speech.

Piaget describes three classes of egocentric speech: repetition, monologue, and collective monologue. The term *repetition* applies to speech in which the child repeats words for personal pleasure. Children may just enjoy the way a word sounds. A child who hears a cuckoo clock strike may begin to say, "Cuckoo, cuckoo, cuckoo." In some instances words are made up or invented and have no real communicative function. Three-year-old Pamela enjoyed saying to her parents, "I want any Wheeo . . . , Wheeo . . . , Wheeo . . . , Wheeo. . ." The repetition of such words, without communicative meaning, is called *echolalia* by Piaget. Echolalia is also applied to the repetitive speech of disturbed children seen in clinical settings who repeat one word or phrase over and over again. *Monologue* refers to children speaking aloud to themselves to help them carry through some activity—even though other children are present. An example can be seen in the speech of Billy as he tugs his wagon up the steps: "I want it up here. I'm gonna go home." In the *collective monologue* children take turns speaking, but direct their speech to themselves. Consider the following exchange among three children in a sandbox:

Billy: "This is a big semi going up a hill." (He pushes the truck in the sand.)

Anne: "I don't want shoes." (She takes off her shoes and throws them outside the sandbox.)

Charles: "I'm gonna stay here all night. I don't want to go home."

Not only are the statements unrelated to each other, they are directed at each individual child's ongoing behavior.

Egocentrism begins to diminish as the child comes to realize that others have a different perspective, a different set of experiences, and a different perception of the world. These realizations set the stage for socialized speech. For Piaget *socialized speech* consists of: (1) adapted information, (2) criticism, (3) commands, including requests or threats, (4) questions, and (5) answers. In the first category, *adapted information,* children use information offered by another person. For example, consider the following exchange:

Bill: "I'm gonna shoot a bad man."

Jim: "You can't, he'll shoot you!"

Bill: "I can!"

Jim: "No, you can't."

Criticism, the second category, is often used by the child to attain feelings of superiority. Such statements as, "My dog is smarter than yours 'cause he can do more tricks" often lead to arguments or quarrels among children. In the third category, *commands,* children expect someone to follow their instructions: "Jimmy, you get your truck off my road." The remaining two categories, *questions* and *answers,* are exchanges which often involve adults. For children asking questions is easier than giving answers. The favorite question "Why?" seems to be almost a reflex for young children. The child's ability to answer questions, however, involves far more complex skills. Piaget, after studying children in the early school years, has found some clear deficiencies in their communicative ability. Egocentrism appears to limit their ability to adapt their language to the perspective of the listener. We must also remember, however, that most peer listeners are as egocentric as the child who is speaking.

Learning About Listeners

Although Piaget has indicated that children do not readily take the listener's perspective into account, there is some evidence that children are often aware of the listener. Sometimes children can adjust their language to try to ensure successful communication. Shatz and Gelman (1973) asked four-year-olds to describe how to operate a toy to an adult, a two-year-old, or a four-year-old listener. They documented the measured length of utterances (MLU) used with each of the respective listeners.

Table 8-1
AVERAGE AMOUNT OF SPEECH BY FOUR-YEAR-OLDS AND MEAN MLU TO ADULT AND YOUNGER NONSIBLING LISTENERS*

		Listener
Measure	**Adult**	**Younger Nonsibling**
Average Amount	67.7	34.1
Mean MLU	5.4	4.0

Source: M. Shatz and R. Gelman. "The development of communication skills: Modifications in the speech of young children as a function of listener," *Monographs of the Society for Research in Child Development* (Copyright 1973 by the Society for Research in Child Development, Inc.) 38, 5, no. 152, p. 11. By permission.

*Each cell total is based on 16 communication periods between speakers and listeners.

Figure 8-4 shows that the children tended to use shorter statements when talking to young children than when talking to adults. Table 8-1 shows that the children seemed to accommodate their language, both in terms of style and complexity, to the listener.

If accuracy of information is evaluated in children's communication, however, additional difficulties can be seen. It is not until children reach nearly seven or eight years of age that they begin to be moderately successful in communicating information (Glucksberg, Krauss & Higgins, 1975). It seems that the more complex the information to be communicated (such as how to solve a problem or how to sort complex objects with many different attributes) the less successful younger children are in such tasks. Glucksberg, Krauss, and Weisberg (1966), for example, asked nursery school children (four to five years old) to provide labels to help in an abstract block-sorting task. The labels which the children established were not effective in helping another person correctly identify specific blocks, although they were helpful for the child who produced them originally. Asher (1976), working with second, fourth, and sixth graders, also found that younger children had considerable difficulty in communicating to others how to solve a complex game. Meissner (1978) compared the performance of kindergartners and second graders on a task that required them to describe a set of concepts such as: at the top, next to, behind. Kindergarten children had more difficulty in communicating this task to other children than did the second graders.

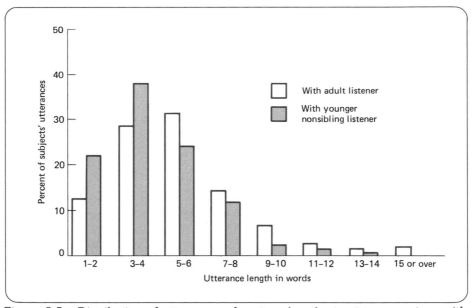

Figure 8-5. Distribution of utterances of various lengths in sixteen sessions with adults and nonsiblings. (From M. Shatz and R. Gelman, The development of communication skills: modifications in the speech of young children as a function of listener. *Monographs of the Society for Research in Child Development.* 1973, 38 [5, Serial No. 152], p. 12. By permission.)

In one study children's listening skills were found to be improved through teaching or training. (Cosgrove & Patterson, 1977). Children who were four, six, eight, and ten years old were taught to be more effective listeners by having them plan for the information that was to be presented. For all but the youngest of the children, such training improved their ability to be more accurate in a sorting task. By planning the children processed and stored information more successfully than children without training.

Two general points may help to clarify the research on children's communication skills (Flavell, 1977). First, as we noted above, Piaget's observations of children were more realistic assessments of what they were actually doing in their everyday communications. As research studies move away from lifelike situations and begin to rely on artificial situations that the child has probably never encountered, conflicting research evidence should not be surprising. Secondly, it is necessary to see that some tasks have been very demanding conceptually, while others are highly simplistic. The more complex tasks should put younger children at a disadvantage. Thus, while *some* aspects of children's language may have egocentric characteristics, clearly children do not always have difficulty communicating with others. Brainerd, for instance, notes that recent research studies have not supported Piaget's characterization that the young child's speech is largely egocentric. While egocentrism declines with increasing age, it does not dominate the language of young

Figure 8-6.   Children do not always have difficulty in communicating with others.

children. Brainerd notes, "the observed proportion of egocentric utterances never reaches 50% in even the very youngest of subjects" (Brainerd, 1978, p. 123).

LANGUAGE AND THOUGHT

There are many disagreements among psychologists as to the influence of language on children's thinking. Most agree that language can aid children's ability to remember and organize information and experiences (Flavell, 1977).

Probably the most extreme position on this issue is that thinking would not be possible without language. Russian psychologists such as Luria (1961) and Vygotsky (1962) support this viewpoint. Initially, the child's behavior is controlled by the speech of adults in the environment; thus, the overt language of others regulates the child's behavior. Gradually children become less dependent on verbal commands and begin to produce these verbal commands *overtly* on their own. What the child has heard adults say becomes what the child says *out loud* to guide his or her own behavior. The language of others becomes the spoken language of the child. We have all heard three- and four-year-olds talking to themselves as they play alone or try to solve problems. One three-year-old, Denise, was heard to say to herself as she put a puzzle together, "Now put the blue one over here. Then the red one goes up on top." Over time the child's overt language becomes *internalized,* and this self-produced language becomes totally covert. Vygotsky then sees children developing an *internal dialogue* through the steps outlined above. This sequence describes how language comes to control behavior and aid the child's problem-solving. Eventually, inner speech is used in all reasoning about complex problem-solving.

Bruner (1964) is another prominent psychologist who believes that it is language that permits children to realize their full potential as competent, successful problem solvers. In his developmental stage approach, he sees the child initially using thought which is limited to motoric or trial-and-error solutions. The child then moves towards thinking which is limited by immediate perception and finally to thinking which is language-based and thus totally abstract. Bruner sharply disagrees with Piaget on the relation between thought and language. Bruner sees the development of language as the basis for the development of thinking. Piaget, of course, sees the relationship as exactly the opposite: the child's cognitive skills make language possible. Language, as an abstract representational system, comes about late in the child's development. Initially, according to Piaget, the child utilizes motor activity, perceptual strategies, and direct experience to solve problems. Out of these interactions language emerges and serves to further the thinking skills of the child. Clearly, for Piaget language is not necessary for thinking.

One other orientation to the problem of language and thought can be seen in the research on verbal mediation in children (Kendler & Kendler, 1970). According to this orientation, it is *verbal mediation,* or covert dialogue, that permits children to develop more sophisticated problem-solving skills than other nonhuman species.

Like Luria and Vygotsky, the Kendlers see verbal mediation at the basis of higher level problem-solving. From their research (1970), they have identified a developmental trend in children's learning. Younger children, below the age of five, are likely to solve problems using stimulus-response associations common to other organisms. Children above the age of seven, however, are more likely to rely on verbal mediation as a technique of problem-solving with the same tasks. Flavell and his co-workers have indicated that such developmental differences are usually the result of younger children failing to produce an appropriate verbal mediator (Keeney, Cannizzo, & Flavell, 1967; Flavell, Beach & Chinsky, 1966). For example, if children are told how to organize a series of pictures or words using a single conceptual category (furniture, toys), their ability to remember the items presented increases. These organizational categories, required by younger children, are found to be produced spontaneously by older children who are more efficient thinkers with better memories. The older child uses such verbal mediators covertly, without any direct instruction to do so.

If verbal mediation and language can have an impact on our thought, are there also influences on our ability to formulate ideas? Both Benjamin Whorf (1956) and Edward Sapir (1958) believe that language influences how we perceive and structure our world. According to their work on this general question, it is our language which determines our perception. A classic example suggests that Eskimos have over twenty different words to describe a variety of different types of snow. In other languages, however, there are only a few words for snow. The Eskimo, because of the greater number of categories to describe snow, must have a greater ability to see different kinds of snow compared to speakers in other languages who have fewer categories. Without the appropriate language category, perceptions are limited.

While this is an intriguing notion, there is some doubt as to its validity. For example, Rosch (1973) worked with a New Guinea tribe which had only two color words in its language. Despite this limited language to describe colors, subjects did not have difficulty in recognizing the differences among the basic primary colors. In this case, limited language did *not* limit their perception. Despite having only two color names, these tribal members could distinguish a range of colors as easily as other speakers who had more elaborate color category names.

LANGUAGE AND CULTURE

Social Class and Language

A variety of investigators have tried to see if language is influenced by the different experiences and backgrounds of children raised in middle- and lower-class environments. Bernstein (1961) suggested that differential socialization experiences produce different language codes. The lower-class child develops a restricted language code as the result of controlling and restrictive socialization practices in the home. The child may be ordered to "Do what I said . . . or else!" or "Come inside the house right now!" By contrast, middle-class families use a more elaborated code. A child may be told, "Please help me out today and rake up the leaves" or "If you don't come inside the house, how will you get your homework done tonight?" The elaborated code is seen to be more abstract and personal and permits expression of precise meaning.

Hess and Shipman (1968) provide some support for the work of Bernstein. They had middle-class and lower-class mothers try to teach their four-year-old children to copy a design using an "Etch-a-Sketch" toy. Middle-class mothers provided more information to their children and used a more complex, intricate language when compared to lower-class mothers. Lower-class mothers used simple, direct language which provided minimal information to their children.

Although Bernstein's theory is provocative there is not much additional support for it in the research literature. Higgins (1976), for example, has reviewed a substantial number of studies, most of which do not support social class differences in children's language and cognitive performance. In fact, Higgins notes that the global formulation of socialization suggested by Bernstein may obscure the precise processing strategies which underlie social class differences. We must also be concerned with the generalizability of Bernstein's work. Bernstein worked with adolescents and analyzed their language skills from their ability to write or discuss topics in small groups. Also, his work was done in England, not in this country. Given these difficulties, it is hardly surprising that his work has not been strongly supported.

Language and Poverty

One of the reasons for poor children's lack of success in school is traced to their so-called deficient language. This assumption may be examined by studying the size of children's vocabularies, since vocabulary size is one index of cognitive development. It is also the foundation for expressing ideas and comprehension. One group of investigators studied the vocabulary of urban children growing up in poverty environments. Alexander, Stoyle, and Kirk (1968) compared the vocabulary scores of individual three- and four-year-old children with their ability to apply labels to concrete stimuli. Children had to name objects depicted in line drawings to assess their productive vocabulary. Almost 75% of the children were found to be below the norms for their age. After an academic year in a Head Start program the children showed significant progress and improvement in vocabulary scores. The preschool program added to their opportunities to learn new words, form new experiences, and see new objects. It was concluded that with increased vocabulary the children may have improved their overall language skills and thus enhanced their capacity for further learning.

One problem with studies of this type is the issue of cultural standards or norms. It may be that poor children fall behind middle-class children using standard middle-class dialect. According to Ginsburg (1972), poor children's language is not deficient or inferior to standard norms but is only different. Labov (1972) also argues that differences in the language of black children do not necessarily mean that their language is inferior. He notes that the dialect of black children is as rich, varied, and full of meaning as is that of middle-class white children. He finds black language is structured and that children follow very carefully a set of logical rules or transformations that permit them to express meaning. Often our perception of dialectical differences is that they represent inferior language, because the rules are not the same ones used by the dominant majority of speakers in our society, as can be seen in Table 8-2. Labov, however, feels that most people fail to recognize that there are rules underlying black children's language and view it instead as haphazard and impoverished.

Does the language of black children need to be changed? Most psychologists recognize that within our culture there are strongly held attitudes towards social class. When two adults engage in conversation it takes only a few seconds of speech to identify each speaker's social class (Entwisle, 1970). Thus, how we speak will determine how we are evaluated by others. If dominant members of the culture erect barriers to individuals from the lower class, it is not because of their supposed language or cognitive deficits; rather, it is due to an ability to identify such individuals as part of the lower class through clues such as language. Language does not make cultural barriers, but language is one basis for establishing cultural barriers.

The need to change language in black children needs careful consideration. Consider the rationale from the perspective of some black children as they listen to black activist, Stokely Carmichael. Then consider whether we need to change children's dialectical differences to make them more like standard dialects. The chil-

Table 8-2
EXAMPLES OF DIALECT DIFFERENCES AMONG BLACK AND WHITE ELEMENTARY SCHOOL CHILDREN

Standard English	Black Dialect
didn't do	didn't done, ain't done
Is that a fire truck?	That a fire truck? Ain't that a fire truck?
Where are you going?	Where you be going? Where is you going?
has	have, got
I'm nice.	I nice. I be nice.

Source: N. Anastasiow, L. Shapiro, D. Hoban, and D. Hunter. *An exploratory study of the language of Black inner-city elementary school children* (Unpublished report, Institute for Child Study, Indiana University, 1971), p. 11. By permission.

dren were asked to compare sentences in black nonstandard dialect with standard ones such as those in Table 8-2.

Stokely: Does anybody you know use the sentences on the left [black dialect]? Are they wrong?

Alma: Both sentences are right as long as you understand them.

Zelma: In terms of English they are wrong.

Stokely: Who decides what is correct English and what is incorrect English?

Milton: People made the rules. People in England, I guess.

Stokely: Will society reject you if you don't speak like on the right side of the board [standard dialect]?

Gladys: You might as well face it, man! What we gotta do is go out and become middle class. If you can't speak good English you don't have a car, a job, or anything.

(Adapted from Wasserman, 1970, pp. 142–143.)

As the children can see, much of the rhetoric for changing black children's dialect to standard dialect is really a matter of the dominant members of society influencing the minority members. Changing language has far-reaching implications for one's sense of self-identity, heritage, and cultural role.

It is interesting to note that children who use a black nonstandard dialect may not be at a disadvantage in comprehending standard dialects. Levy (1972), Copple and Suci (1974), and Anastasiow and Hanes (1974) have all found that both dialects are equally well understood by children who use a black dialect. While the educational setting usually demands that black children develop standard English, perhaps the educational setting needs to change to accommodate such dialectical differences.

If we consider the Mexican-American child, whose language skills are often restricted to Spanish, it seems that the schools have begun to recognize the problem. A language difference must evidently be dramatic before the school will alter its teaching and instructional demands (Entwisle, 1975). Hopefully, no one would argue that the Spanish-speaking child must "sink or swim" and be educated solely in English. Rather, if learning English is as important as learning academic skills, children should be taught both. We would not want to limit the learning of Mexican-American children by forcing them to be instructed only in English.

Often our monocultural schools have denied the pluralism of American life, however. Ramirez and Castaneda (1974) show that learning, school performance, and the attitudes of the school towards Mexican-American children have far-reaching consequences (illustrated in Table 8-3). Our ability to deal effectively with Mexican-American children means far more than just school success. If we demand that these children use only English in the school, we deny the importance of their cultural heritage. When we forcefully refuse to accept Spanish in the classroom, children feel that we are devaluing their Mexican-American background. At the

Figure 8-7.   Our schools have often denied the pluralistic language and cultural heritage of many children. (Paul Conklin/Monkmeyer Press Photo Service)

Table   8-3
CULTURALLY DEMOCRATIC EDUCATIONAL ENVIRONMENTS AND CURRENT EDUCATIONAL PRACTICES: A COMPARISON

	Majority of Existing Educational Environments	**Culturally Democratic Educational Environments**
Mexican-American culture	Viewed as inferior and damaging, thus: 1. Children are not permitted to speak Spanish 2. Mexican and Mexican-American heritage is not included in the curriculum 3. Teachers are not given instruction on values of Mexican-American culture	Viewed as a valuable resource which should be reinforced and developed further through: 1. Bilingual education 2. Inclusion of Mexican and Mexican-American heritage in the curriculum 3. Acquainting teachers with Mexican-American cultural values

Table   8-3 (Continued)

	Majority of Existing Educational Environments	Culturally Democratic Educational Environments
Socialization styles	Seen as interfering with child's development; thus, Mexican-American parents are not encouraged to participate in the educational process	Seen as valuable teaching styles which must be used as a basis for developing teacher-training materials, such as Culture-Matching Teaching Strategies; parents are actively involved in educational process; community culture and school culture are integrated
Personality characteristics of children	Seen as deviant and unacceptable; thus, many children are tracked or placed in classes for the educationally handicapped or educable mentally retarded	Seen as a reflection of child's learning style, human-relational style, incentive-motivational style, and communication style; thus, is the basis on which culturally democratic educational environments must be developed
What is changed and how?	The child is encouraged to behave in accordance with values and life-styles of school culture through pressure from the school and community, through monocultural teaching strategies, curriculum, and assessment	The educational system is changed through: 1. New teaching strategies and curriculum 2. Parent involvement 3. New assessment practices
Results	1. Low self-esteem in Mexican-American children 2. Negative view of Hispanic culture and language by non-Mexican-American children 3. Suspicion and conflict between Mexican-American and non-Mexican-American children, school personnel, and parents	1. Bicultural identity in Mexican-American children 2. Self-esteem in Mexican-American children 3. Intercultural understanding between Mexican-Americans and non-Mexican-Americans 4. Higher academic achievement

Source: M. Ramirez and A. Castaneda. *Cultural Democracy, Bicognitive Development, and Education* (New York: Academic Press, 1974), pp. 105—106. By permission.

234

same time, such children begin to see that the socialization practices in their homes, their personality characteristics, and their orientation to life itself are viewed as inferior, deviant, and deficient. Ramirez and Castaneda feel that encouraging Mexican-American children to use English in the classroom, if successful, may have far-reaching negative consequences to which we are insensitive: low self-esteem, negative view of their unique cultural background, and distrust of the school in general. A seemingly simple change in language has far greater implications on the Mexican-American child's life than we have previously recognized. Our insistent demand that all nonstandard dialects, such as those of black children, be changed appear to produce similar negative consequences. Who should change—the child, the school, or our society?

SUMMARY

Productive language allows us to represent the complex abstract ideas which are the foundation of our society. We discovered that both biological and environmental factors play an important role in children's language development. The relationship between the meaning and structural components of language was presented. We also traced the development of syntax and semantics. Semantic development may be viewed in terms of semantic features, the context, or prototypes. Piaget's perspective on the child's transition from egocentric to socialized speech was presented. His formulations do not appear to be strongly supported however, in more recent research studies.

The intriguing relationship between language and thought was examined from the standpoint of Luria and Vygotsky, Bruner, and the verbal mediational theorists. Finally, we looked at the influence of social class and ethnicity on language, discussed the rationale for changing nonstandard dialects, and considered the implications of such change.

RECOMMENDED READINGS

Curtiss, S. *Genie: A Psycholinguistic Study of a Modern-Day "Wild Child."* New York: Academic Press, 1977.

A fascinating account of the psycholinguistic development of an isolated "wild child". The running account of her progress is intriguing, and the analysis of her language skills highly revealing.

Ginsburg, H. *The Myth of the Deprived Child.* Englewood Cliffs, N.J.: Prentice-Hall, 1972.

A variety of general issues, one of which is language, are related to the development of children from poverty backgrounds. Ginsburg provides convincing support that cultural differences have been mistakenly interpreted as cultural deficits.

Palermo, D. S. *Psychology of Language.* Glenview, Ill.: Scott, Foresman, 1978.

An excellent basic introduction to the data and newer theories of language. Excellent treatment of the relationship of cognition and language.

9

Personality and Social Development in Early Childhood

In the years between two and five the child's world continues to expand beyond the limited environment of home and family. Each day brings new people, new friends, new objects, and new situations to explore and discover. Social interactions and peer relationships become more complex as children learn how to enjoy others and how to tolerate their behavior. Group experiences such as neighborhood play groups, day-care, and nursery school mean the development of new social skills. Through these experiences the child learns how to sustain relationships and develops an increased capacity to behave independently. Gradually children learn the reciprocal roles needed for harmonious social interactions.

PERSONALITY AND SOCIAL LEARNING

Egocentrism and Social Learning

As we have already seen, Piaget believes that young children's understanding of their world is limited by their egocentric thought. As they develop there is progress in realizing that not everyone shares the same perspective on the world—socially, experientially, and cognitively. In the preoperational stage of development, young children up to the age of seven have difficulty in understanding and accepting the views of others.

Piaget and Inhelder (1948/1967) have provided some evidence of children's egocentrism at this stage of development. Children were shown a miniature landscape of three mountains and were asked to place a doll at a number of different locations. Each child was then asked to describe what the doll could see in order to determine the child's ability to take the perspective of the doll. Children younger than seven described the doll's visual experience in terms of their own. Thus, preoperational children are still egocentric and believe that their view of reality is shared by everyone.

A gradual reduction in egocentric thought appears to occur as the child's peer interactions increase. The give-and-take required for successful social interactions highlights the alternative perspectives which other children have. We find that the child's social interactions help reduce egocentric thought. Adults generally are not successful in helping children overcome egocentrism (Piaget & Inhelder, 1948/1967). Adults are perceived as powerful and controlling. They make strong demands and often limit the child's behavior for reasons which are poorly understood or poorly explained to the child. Thus, the child may see the world of adults as self-centered and devoid of alternative views. Social relations among peers, however, allow children to explore alternative views, to deal directly with differences of opinion, and to find means for their solution. Very often children have to confront the effects of their actions on their peers. As they play they see that their own views and past experiences may be quite different from those of other children.

238

Children's Play

Psychologists have not been able to agree on a clear definition of play. Play can stand for so many different kinds of activities, in so many different kinds of situations that a generally accepted definition appears impossible. The importance of play in children's development is a problem difficult to resolve.

When we look at the behavior of children, however, we discover that most children spend countless hours at play in the course of their development. Freud and Piaget both consider play to be a valuable and important activity for children. Freud and other psychoanalytic theorists see play as a means of releasing tension and expressing feelings such as anger, anxiety, or frustration. Piaget takes a somewhat different view. He and others (Sutton-Smith, 1967) emphasize the cognitive processes revealed in play. They feel that play permits children to explore through fantasy many cognitive responses which may not be possible in their own environment. By substituting fantasy for reality the child will not have to pay the price of actually carrying out his or her actions. Children may pretend to be naughty or disobey a parental rule without fear of punishment. Consider a child playing the role of a circus lion tamer who draws the rapt attention of a large audience. Symbolic play of this type has as its primary goal the "satisfaction of the ego" (Piaget,

Figure 9-1.   Play, free from adult demands, can be a form of problem-solving and a means of exploration. (David Strickler/Monkmeyer Press Photo Service)

1962). Piaget also views symbolic play as "egocentric thought." Such play represents the child's struggle to deal with reality. Play becomes a *means* of dealing with the conflict between the child's own perception of the world as he or she wishes it to be and the way it is in reality. Through fantasy the child can go beyond the limitations imposed by the real world of parents, peers, and personal fears to experiment with highly creative, independently derived solutions to problems. The conditions in which play occurs enable children to experiment; in real life there are dangers and risks, while in fantasy there are none. There is no possibility that a make-believe lion will suddenly devour the youthful lion tamer. Thus play is exploration free from adult demands, and serves as a valuable activity to help stimulate the child's overall intellectual development.

Play and Problem-Solving

Some investigators have examined the contribution of play to general problem-solving ability in children. Rosen (1974) assumed that disadvantaged children who were given a chance to use sociodramatic play would improve their problem-solving ability. *Sociodramatic play* requires that children take different roles and coordinate their behavior with the roles of others. There is usually a theme such as playing policeman, fireman, or doctor. Rosen facilitated the sociodramatic play of kindergarten children by increasing the complexity of their play activities. She attempted to make the play of the children lead to new ideas and themes. If she saw a group of children playing house, for example, she pretended to be sick in order to have them deal with a rather complex problem-situation. Overall, the study showed that such sociodramatic play helped children in solving problems in cognitive tasks. In this sense the study showed that play can facilitate cognitive development.

Other studies have found that symbolic play may improve children's conservation skills (Golomb & Cornelius, 1977). Using a group of 30 children, none of whom displayed conservation skills, a training program was provided in which one of two types of play experiences was presented. Half of the children received training in *pretense play,* or pretend play. For instance, children were asked to pretend that a block was a firetruck. The rest of the children were given *constructive play* such as doing puzzles or drawings. At the end of five days of play training the children's conservation skills were reassessed. More than 75% of those given pretense play training showed improvements in conservation. Among those given constructive play training, however, only one instance of conservation improvement was found. Pretense play, as a form of higher level symbolic activity, can have a positive influence on children's cognitive abilities.

In a similar manner, Lieberman (1965) found a strong relationship between children's play and creativity. She rated kindergarten children on a number of behaviors related to "playfulness." These behavioral dimensions included (Sutton-Smith, 1967):

1. How often is there spontaneous physical movement and activity in the child's

play? Some children show great exuberance, jumping or waving their arms in excitement as they play.

2. How often is there expression of joy in the child's play? This may be shown by the child smiling, verbalizing (e.g., "This is a great game"), or even just quietly singing or humming a tune.

3. How often is there humor in the play? For example, does the child see some play activities as funny, or is there laughter as the play continues?

After rating each of the kindergarten children for playfulness according to these categories, Lieberman examined the extent to which this dimension was related to creativity. She found that children who were rated high on playfulness were also high on creativity. That is, they were better at giving suggestions, developing summary titles for short stories, and thinking of unusual toys, animals, or foods. Play apparently helps develop the ability to be creative, to produce novel responses, and to see the world in different and unusual ways.

Types of Play

The typical play activities of preschool children have been categorized according to the degree of social interaction. As we can see from the descriptions given in Table 9-1, only parallel, associative, and cooperative play seem to involve other children directly.

Barnes (1971) compared the pattern of today's preschool children's play with that of an earlier sample (Parten, 1932) from the 1930s using these six categories. His results indicate that the play of three- and four-year-olds has changed significantly over the past forty years. He finds that the play of today's children is much less socially oriented than the earlier sample. As Figures 9-2 and 9-3 show, there are significant increases in today's three- and four-year-olds' unoccupied, solitary, and onlooker categories of play while there are corresponding decreases in the categories of associative and cooperative play for three- and four-year-olds. While parallel play shows some decline, the differences are not significant compared to the earlier sample of children. Barnes (1971) speculates that perhaps today's children have more toys that encourage solitary play than did children of earlier generations. Alternatively, today's children spend many hours watching television, which is likely to reduce the amount of time they have to develop their social skills in free play situations.

Play Therapy

Play has also been used by clinical psychologists to diagnose and treat children with a variety of disturbances. Anna Freud, for example, has used play therapy to help diagnose children's conflicts. The play which children undertake may provide

Table   9-1
TYPES OF PLAY

Types of Preschool Children's Play	Behavioral Definition
Unoccupied Play	The child is not involved with other children; often watches passively the ongoing activies of others or walks aimlessly about.
Solitary Play	The child is not involved with other children; independently plays alone; playing with toys is the primary goal.
Onlooker	The child observes other children at play and often comments or laughs at what is seen; more active involvement than in unoccupied play.
Parallel Play	Children are able to play next to one another or nearby with the same toys or engage in the same activities; however, their play is still independent and they do not share their play with each other.
Associative Play	Children play next to each other and use a variety of social exchanges to show their recognition of peers; e.g., there is communication like asking questions of each other, showing off their accomplishments, using each other's toys.
Cooperative Play	Children are involved in complex social organizations with shared common goals or themes. There is reciprocal role-taking such as taking turns, a shared sense of identification with the group, leaders, and often formal rules that govern play in games like tag and hide-and-go-seek.

(left margin, vertical:) Increasing Social Interaction

Source: Parten, 1932; Parten & Newhall, 1943.

important insights into their particular unresolved emotional conflicts (Freud, 1946). While adults may be able to express their problems verbally, children have limited skills in this regard and usually limited insights. Thus, a therapist must be sensitive to the themes and activities expressed by children in their play, for example, aggression, parental hostility, dependency, or death.

Alternatively, play can serve a *therapeutic* function in helping a child to overcome an emotional problem. A child who is having difficulty coping and needs counseling often participates in a situation which includes play therapy. The play therapy is designed to help the child see not only conflicts but also alternative ways of coping with the conflicts. A child, for example, who may feel guilty about hostile wishes towards a parent can be helped to see that such feelings are acceptable and be given ways of both resolving the conflict and dealing with these feelings in play therapy. Such *directive play therapy* is usually of short-term duration.

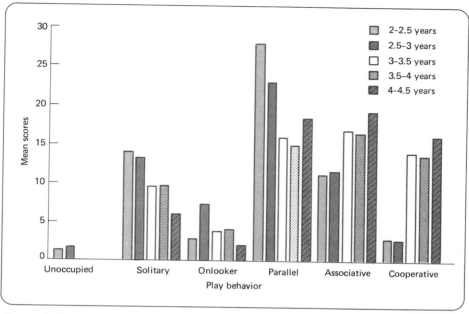

Figure 9-2. Preschool children's play norms: 1932. (Figures 9-2 and 9-3 from K. E. Barnes, Preschool play norms. *Developmental Psychology,* 1971, 5, 99–103. Copyright 1971 by the American Psychological Association. By permission)

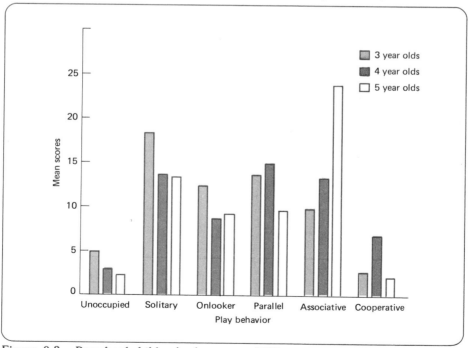

Figure 9-3.   Preschool children's play norms: 1971.

Still another technique of play therapy is the *non-directive* approach of Virginia Axline (1947). Non-directive play therapy helps to establish an environment in which the child is free to express his or her feelings and act without fear of negative evaluation. The goal in this longer-term therapy is to enable the child to develop self-realization. Such goals are clearly difficult to reach and may take years to accomplish with any individual child. Nevertheless, the approach is valuable and often produces highly successful results. Axline notes the following metaphorical description of one child's struggle for self-realization through non-directive play therapy: "I think *every* child should have a hill all his own to climb. And I think *every* child should have one star up in the sky that is all his own. And I think *every* child should have a tree that belongs to him. That's what I *think* should be" (Axline, 1964, p. 105).

THE IMITATION OF MODELS

Children seem to be particularly influenced by models in their environment, such as peers, parents, teachers, and television characters. Virtually every aspect of the child's social behavior has been found to be sensitive to modeling. In school, for example, young children readily acquire and use indiscriminately the forbidden four-letter words of older peers. Children also imitate the language of their parents and display it in the most unlikely situations. At a first-grade talent show one little boy told a terrible ethnic joke to the audience. Afterwards, upon questioning from his unsuspecting teacher, he revealed that this joke was heard at the family dinner table and was a direct imitation of his father.

Modeling and Social Behavior

Any observation of children in group settings is likely to provide further support for the principle that significant others serve as effective role models for children. Bronfenbrenner (1970) and Bandura (1973) both note that the role of modeling in children's development has been one of the most significant findings in psychological research over the past decade. We are often concerned about the negative behaviors which children may copy from models in the environment, such as aggression or hostility. Recognition of this powerful process, however, could serve a beneficial function in developing children's prosocial behaviors. With appropriate emphasis from parental role models or television heroes, children could be influenced positively to share, cooperate, and help others (Bronfenbrenner, 1970).

Children do not imitate *every* behavior to which they are exposed. What factors determine the effectiveness of models in influencing children's behavior? Behavior selected for imitation must stem from a person who commands high status, is perceived to be powerful, and controls resources in the environment (Bandura, 1973). Thus, both peers and adults who display these characteristics will be *perceptually salient,* or stand out, in the child's mind as models worthy of imitation. Copying a model's behavior may not be a conscious act for children. Also, the particular

Figure 9-4. Children often model adults who have high status, power, and control of resources. (United Nations photo by O. Monsen)

behaviors which are modeled may often be somewhat superficial aspects of a person's behavior which are easily identified by the child. Bandura's research (1973) notes that models which are nurturing or provide rewards for the child are most likely to produce imitation. The most prominent models in a child's life are his or her parents, peers, siblings, and teachers. They are usually most nurturant and rewarding to the child.

Based on a study of adolescents (Rosekrans, 1967), Bronfenbrenner recognizes the powerful influence of peers on imitative behavior. When children perceive that a model is highly similar to themselves, the modeling influence will be quite strong. Bronfenbrenner feels that peers may be even more potent models for children than parents.

Bandura, however, does not believe that children must decide between peer or adult models. His research (Bandura, Grusec, & Menlove, 1966) indicates that children attempt to average, or develop a kind of middle-of-the-road position, when peer and adult models display conflicting behavior. One fact is clear—the more that models are in agreement and the greater the number of models displaying similar behavior, the greater the chances that children will display imitative behavior (Bandura, 1973).

Not all modeling is so random. Adults and peers may both use rather punitive techniques to insure that a particular behavior is imitated. Teachers may demand that children say "Please" and "Thank you." Peers may ridicule a child for his or her manner of speaking or way of dressing. Children often insist that their toys match exactly those of their friends or those they have seen in television commercials. When parents are unaware of the meaning of these requests, they may discover that their selection of toys brings great disappointment to their children rather than joy and happiness.

Children pay attention to the reinforcements or punishments which a model receives. Children appear to be quite sensitive to the vicarious rewards or punishments experienced by the models in their environment. Bandura, Ross, and Ross (1963) showed children a model who displayed aggressive behavior toward a "Bobo" punching doll. Children who saw the model rewarded for aggressive behavior were more likely to imitate the aggression than children who did not see the model rewarded. Furthermore, if the model was punished for the aggressive behavior, the children were less likely to display modeled aggression. Thus, children may or may not imitate behavior as a function of the response consequences to the model (Bronfenbrenner, 1970; Bandura, 1973). Through vicarious reinforcement, children may increase or decrease their willingness to imitate *overtly* the behavior of models in their environment.

Figure 9-5 illustrates the three phases of observational learning which we have been discussing. The diagram accounts for both the direct imitation of behavior by children and their non-imitation or counter-imitation.

Modeling in the Classroom

Children's willingness to imitate the models in their environment has been used effectively to reduce both unwanted behavior such as social isolation and increase social interaction. One study of nursery school children shows how modeling may be used by teachers (Keller and Carlson, 1974). Teachers were asked to rate each of the children in their class on three behavior categories: (1) interaction, (2) giving positive reinforcement, and (3) receiving positive reinforcement. On the basis of these ratings two groups of children were identified: a group of *isolates* and a control group composed of *non-isolates*.

The isolate group was shown videotapes of preschool children engaged in social interactions such as "imitation, smiling, laughing, token-giving, or physical contact signifying affection." A sound track described the actions and social behavior of the peer models. The control group was shown nature films. The group of isolates showed a significant increase in giving and receiving reinforcement. The frequency of isolate behavior was reduced in these children, and a corresponding increase in their social interaction was found. These children modified their social behavior by imitating the actions of the models on the videotapes.

Long-Term Significance of Modeling

One of the most interesting questions related to imitative behavior is whether experimental effects are long-lasting. Will brief exposure to a model have an impact on children's behavior beyond the limited number of days or weeks of an experi-

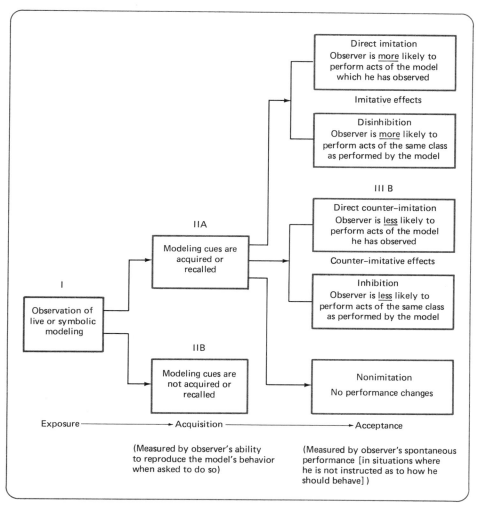

Figure 9-5. The observational learning model. (From R. M. Liebert and R. W. Poulos, Television as a moral teacher. In T. Lickona, ed., *Moral development and behavior* [New York: Holt, 1976], p. 286. Reprinted by permission.)

ment? Hicks (1965) explored this question with preschoolers who were shown a movie of an aggressive model. Not only were the children evaluated for imitative aggression immediately after the film presentation, but they were also reevaluated after a period of six months. Children exposed to the aggressive model displayed more aggression both immediately after viewing the model and six months later than control children who had never seen the model. The aggressiveness displayed after six months was considerably less than that observed immediately after viewing the aggressive model. Although we may question whether this long-term effect is unique to the area of aggression, the potential for models in the child's environment to produce long-lasting effects seems strong.

Modeling behavior may also initiate responses in children which will be carried on in their development. In one study (Halverson and Waldrop, 1974), 2½-year-old children were presented a "barrier" situation in their nursery school classroom. At the end of the first week of school, the children found a fence in their class which surrounded and blocked a number of desirable toys. The teachers served as models for the children by showing excitement over the toys and by showing how to tear down the fence. The children needed only two demonstrations before they took the fence apart.

One of the most salient findings from this study was obtained when the children's behavior with the barrier was related to their personality and coping styles five years later. The preschoolers who had spent a longer time knocking down the fence, had handled more of the fence boards, and had gone immediately to the toys were discovered to be brighter, more imaginative, more socially oriented, and better able to cope with new situations when they were tested at 7½ years of age. Halverson and Waldrop (1974) believe that, "Children who demonstrate an ability early in life to be agents capable of producing change in their environment appear in middle childhood to be active, vigorous, and competent."

The study just described suggests that certain personality characteristics persist into middle childhood and that models were necessary releaser stimuli for successful coping with the barrier. Once the behavior was "released" by the models, the children could follow their own individual styles of coping with the barrier.

Concern for Others

Concern for others is an essential ingredient for successful human interaction and is, indeed, the foundation of any society. The development in children of concern for others represents a reduction in egocentrism.

Concern for others, part of a more general concept called *altruism,* has been studied from a number of different perspectives. The two most common methods of studying children's concern for others are to examine: (1) their willingness to give to another (donate charity, relinquish tokens, give up money earned in an experiment), or (2) their willingness to help another child in apparent distress (Bryan, 1975). Interestingly, the effects of modeling as a way of increasing children's concern for others has provided different patterns of results when donations versus rescuing were compared.

We generally expect that a nurturant or warm model will produce more imitative behaviors in children when compared to a neutral or cold model (Bandura, 1969a). The impact of the warmth of the model on children's willingness to donate to others, however, has not been supported. Studies by Grusec and Skubiski (1970) and Rosenhan and White (1967) both reported that warmth of the model failed to increase the donations provided by third- and fifth-graders.

When rescuing another person in distress is assessed, the warmth of the model does have a strong influence on children's altruism. Staub (1971) had kindergarten children interact with either a model who was warm and friendly or one who was neutral and displayed no nurturance. For half of the children the model went to an adjoining room to help a child when mild distress sounds were heard—a tape recording of a child crying. The model said, "I'd better go and see what's the matter. I'll be right back." When the model returned from the adjoining room the child was told that a girl had fallen and needed some help in getting up. The children in the neutral modeling group were told that another child was playing in the room next to them.

All of the children were then left alone. A loud crash was heard, followed by the sounds of a child crying in distress in the next room. Children were observed to see if they were willing either to leave their room to help the child in distress *(active help)* or to tell the experimenter what they had heard upon her return *(volunteer information)*. Providing help to another was a function of both modeling and nurturance (see Figure 9-6).

In a related study, Yarrow, Scott, and Waxler (1973) investigated children's awareness of other people's distress. Rather than simply expose the children to a model who does or does not behave nurturantly for a short time, the warm or cold models interacted with the children for a period of six weeks. In addition, the chil-

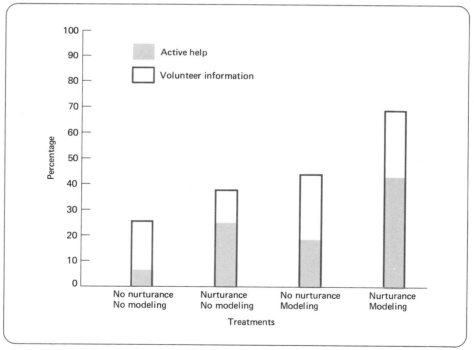

Figure 9-6.   Percentage of active help and volunteering information in all treatment groups, boys and girls combined. (From E. Staub, A child in distress: the influence of nurturance and modeling on children's attempts to help. *Developmental Psychology,* 1971, 5, 128. By permission.)

dren were given identical teaching about altruism from the nurturant and non-nur-turant models. This teaching involved the use of play materials called *dioramas* in which the model showed altruism symbolically with toy actors while verbally describing the actors' motivations and consequences of the behaviors. For exam-ple, one scene showed a baby bird that had fallen from a nest. In an alternative training procedure, children were shown real-life situations of distress with confed-erates in addition to the procedures just described. For example, in one situation an adult "accidentally" banged her head on a table and pretended to be in pain. The experimenter then put her hand on the "victim's" shoulder and comforted her. Thus, altruism was modeled either in "lesson form" with the dioramas alone or in combination with "real-life" experiences.

The investigators found that modeling in lesson form "effectively increased helping responses in the same kind of setting." With training in lesson form only, children did not transfer altruism to other situations and did not increase their ability to see distress in others in a series of pictures. Children who had experienced both the lessons and the "real-life" experiences, however, showed more generalization of altruism and more recognition of distress in a series of pictures. The nurturance or non-nurturance of the model was not a factor in these children's altruism. The conclusion drawn by Yarrow, Scott, and Waxler is that "the optimal condition for the development of sympathetic and helpful behavior was one in which children observed an adult manifesting altruism at every level—in principle and practice, both toward the child, and toward others in distress" (1973, p. 251).

Parents who are altruistic toward others but unresponsive to their own children will not help their children to be altruistic because of the inconsistency shown. Yarrow, Scott, and Waxler believe that both teaching and the provision of real-life examples are essential. Nurturance by itself is not enough—children also need direct teaching, verbalization of principles and ideals, explanation, and consistency in the values and actions of models.

The warmth or nurturance of a model appears to produce different effects on children's willingness to help others and to donate or give to others. Bryan (1975) suggests that with donation the warmth of a model seems to highlight for the child that it is permissible to behave as he or she wishes—that is, children feel free enough to choose not to donate to others. In the case of helping another, the warmth of the model appears to increase the child's empathy with the person in distress and leads to an increase in the willingness to provide help.

IDENTIFICATION

The importance of the parent-child relationship in helping children acquire cul-turally appropriate behavior has been given special attention. Beginning with Freudian or psychoanalytic theory, *identification* has referred to the process through which a child emulates the personality characteristics of a significant person or persons in his or her life. This process, of course, may also be described in terms of modeling. Bandura (1969b) sees the similarities between children and adults as the result of children modeling their parents' behaviors. A young boy enjoys developing skills which his father has, such as constructing a house for their pet dog. Similarly a girl gains satisfaction in helping her mother around the home or in learning to be a skilled tennis player. Identification involves a continuous series of exchanges in a highly emotional context between child and parents.

Both psychoanalytic and modeling theorists see identification as a major factor in the socialization of the child. It is through identification that the child begins to perceive certain personal attributes and behavior as worthy of the approval and acceptance of others (Bandura, 1969b). Such approval provides the child with a sense of security as a person and provides additional motivation to try to master the challenges encountered in everyday living. Identification, in this sense, helps the child to acquire successful behavior patterns without the need for direct teaching from adults. According to Sears, Rau, and Alpert (1965), the process of identification establishes a variety of responses including sex-role appropriate behavior, the capacity for guilt, and internal self-control.

Identification originates from the normal bonds of affection between children and their parents according to both psychoanalytic and social learning theorists. Thus, identification is actually the continuing of attachment bonds to parents established during infancy. Psychoanalytic theory says that identification grows out of the Oedipal complex in the early childhood period. A boy has possessive feelings about his mother but is unable to displace the powerful father; he identifies with the father who is perceived to be successful in achieving goals. For girls the Electra complex is experienced as the basis for identification. Because of the fear of competing with her mother for the love and affection of her father as well as supposed envy over her lack of a male sex organ (penis envy), a girl develops an almost ambivalent form of identification with her mother. Social learning theorists say that identification is further strengthened by reinforcement. If the child engages in behavior which is similar to that of the parents, the behavior is generaly approved of and rewarded. Parents are significant models, and through direct reinforcement they help the child to develop identification and imitative behaviors. While in the early years children are likely to emulate parental behavior and attitudes, older children may come to value the norms of their peers.

AGGRESSION

Most definitions of aggression include any behavior which involves physical or verbal attacks on another person. Some psychologists believe that aggression is *action* motivated by hostility. Other psychologists believe that it is important to separate aggressive behavior that occurs with hostility from that which is lacking in hostility. We can illustrate the differences as follows. Two nursery school children are playing together in a sandbox until one wants a toy truck which the other has. The child who wants the toy truck hits the other child and takes the truck. The child who hits is said to be behaving aggressively but without a hostile motive. The motive is to get the truck. On the other hand, if one child strikes another without provocation or without any other goal in mind, then hostility may be seen as motivating the aggressive action.

Children's aggressive behavior is often related to problem-solving. In the example above, one way of obtaining the toy truck held by the other child is to behave aggressively. While this is clearly an instance of aggression, it is also an example of successful and effective problem-solving behavior. While we may react negatively to children's aggression, we should keep in mind that aggression is one effective way of coping with problems in a complex and highly competitive society.

Some investigators see aggression as part of a broad class of behavior termed "assertive." Assertive behavior includes both motor and verbal responses which force, compel, or demand that one person respond to another (Patterson, Littman, & Bricker, 1967). Such demands, in general, are intended to coerce one person to conform to another. Demands are often successful in producing a particular response. If our attempts to be assertive are reinforced through successful outcomes, we are more likely to be assertive in the future.

Origins of Aggression

While it is difficult to categorize or define aggression, it seems clear that all species have the capacity to behave aggressively. Some ethological theorists (Lorenz, 1974) have suggested that there must be an innate tendency for aggressive behavior, an innate instinct to fight. Aggression has evolutionary significance and helps animals to acquire food, defend their territories, and protect their young. The aggressive instinct serves to energize an individual internally and is not dependent on the environment. Lorenz sees aggression as innate, although it is possible to reduce or control aggression within our society.

Freud (1930) also believed that aggression stemmed from innate causes or instincts. In his early writing Freud considered aggression the result of the blocking of the libidinal impulses (sexual energy) of the life instinct (Eros). Later, he thought that aggression came directly from a second instinct (Thanatos, or the death instinct) which was the direct opposite of Eros (Baron, 1977). Aggression is the attempt by individuals to channel the death instinct from personal self-destruction out toward others. If unchecked and not directed outwardly, the death instinct would inevitably destroy the individual. Thus, aggression is often viewed as a healthy response since it permits the catharsis or release of destructive impulses. This concept of catharsis has been the source of considerable controversy (Baron, 1977).

Most psychologists, in exploring the interpersonal nature of children's aggression, have not tended to accept ethological or innate theories of aggression (Baron, 1977). Instead, they have accepted drive theory, which states that aggression is based on an aggressive motive or drive: "a heightened state of arousal that can be reduced through overt acts of aggression" (Baron, 1977, p. 21).

The earliest formulation of drive theories of aggression can be seen in the work of Dollard, Doob, Miller, Mowrer, and Sears (1939), who hypothesized that aggression was the result of frustration. *Frustration* was considered to be the blocking of any ongoing, goal-directed behavior. Frustration produced an aggressive drive or instigation towards aggression which could then lead directly to an aggressive behavior. We could probably find many everyday circumstances in which this *frustration-aggression* hypothesis would appear to have some merit. Certainly, teachers have often observed children who, when frustrated, become aroused and angry and behave aggressively towards one of their peers.

The difficulty with the frustration-aggression hypothesis is that while it may explain some aggressive behavior, it appears to be incapable of explaining a large variety of other aggressive acts. A number of investigators have noted that while frustration sometimes leads to aggression, there are many other ways in which children respond when frustrated and there are many times when frustration does not produce aggression at all (Bandura, 1973; Berkowitz, 1969; Geen & O'Neal, 1976).

Eventually Miller (1941) and Sears (1941) came to the realization that the frustration-aggression hypothesis needed revision. They suggested that aggression was but one of many possible responses to frustration. Furthermore, they suggested it was possible to inhibit or control aggressive responses through punishment or fear. If aggressive acts can be inhibited, then aggression can be directed not towards the frustrating situation or individual but towards other persons. The concept of displaced aggression (Miller, 1948) seems to account for a number of aggressive acts which do not easily fit the limited frustration-aggression theory. The frustration-aggression hypothesis appears to be a modification of Freudian theory, but without instinctual drives. Aggression is not considered to be innate but dependent on the instigation of frustrating experiences. The idea of displaced aggression seems to be an important and necessary refinement.

The role of learning in children's aggression is a matter of continuing debate. Bandura (1973) has emphasized three components of aggressive behavior: (1) how aggressive behaviors are learned or acquired initially; (2) what stimuli or situations are likely to produce aggression; and (3) what accounts for the ongoing display of aggression over time, i.e., what maintains aggressive behavior in an individual? Bandura has rejected the idea of instinctual drives formulated by Freud and Lorentz and instead emphasizes the importance of modeling and reinforcement.

Bandura (1973) suggests that aggression is a learned behavior and as such is not different from any other social behavior which the child acquires. Social learning in children occurs through two processes: (1) *direct reinforcement*—for some children aggression works and is rewarding and (2) *social modeling*—children may acquire a new behavior through observing the behavior of other persons in their environment (Baron, 1977). Much of the available research summarized earlier in this chapter provides considerable support for the impact of models on the social development of children. We will briefly examine the social learning position.

The display of aggression may be related to any number of situational cues or experiences. Baron notes that events which are likely to increase the occurrence of aggression include: " . . . direct provocation from others, exposure to live or filmed aggressive models, heightened physiological arousal, environmental stresses such as heat, noise, or crowding . . ." (1977, p. 170). The list could certainly be extended.

What accounts for the maintenance of aggression is contained in the general factors which Bandura has identified as responsible for the acquisition of aggression. When aggression is rewarded, socially sanctioned by others, and produces successful results, there will be an increase in its probable occurrence (Bandura, 1973).

Clearly, from Bandura's perspective, significant people in the child's social world (parents, teachers, and peers) are potential models for the development of children's social behavior in general and aggressive behavior in particular. Role models provide children with a chance to see how to act aggressively, when to act aggressively, or when to display self-control. They also either directly reinforce children's overt acts of aggression or inhibit aggression through non-reinforcement or punishment.

Television and Children's Aggressive Behavior

Television is one of the possible influences on the development of aggression identified in Bandura's social learning theory. Numerous studies have found that televised models, both real and cartoon characters, can significantly increase children's aggression (Feshbach & Singer, 1970; Friedrick & Stein, 1973; Liebert & Baron, 1972; Galst & White, 1976). One of our major social concerns is the effect of television on the imitative learning of children. An illustrative study of the effect of television on children's aggression is that of Liebert and Baron (1972). They based their work on the previous research of Bandura and his associates, who found that even brief exposure to aggressive models increases children's aggression.

Liebert and Baron objected to the standard measurement procedures used by Bandura, in which children's aggression was assessed as they interacted with inanimate objects like the "Bobo" punching doll. Instead, they evaluated how children aggressed towards their peers in a group of five- to nine-year-olds. Children in the experimental group watched part of a violent television program in which there was fighting, shooting, and a knifing. A control group observed a film about non-aggressive sports. After 3½ minutes of observing, each child was taken to a room and seated before a "response box." On the box were two buttons—a green one on the right and a red one on the left. A white light was located above the two buttons, and wires led from the box to a wall. The experimenter told the children that they were going to play a game with a child in the next room who would be activating the lights. It was explained that as the child in the other room turned a handle the white light came on. The children were told that if the green button was pressed, it *helped* the other child by making it easier to turn the handle, and if the red button was pressed, it made the handle hot and *hurt* the other child. Of course, no child was actually in the adjoining room. The children who had observed the aggressive acts in the television show were much more willing to hurt the other child. Liebert and Baron concluded that exposure to aggressive models increased children's tendency to be aggressive with others. Exposure to aggression *reduced* the children's restraints on hurting another child.

There are numerous summary reports of research relating to aggression and television. These reports generally condemn the amount of violence and aggression on television and suggest some degree of parental monitoring of available programs (Surgeon General's Scientific Advisory Committee, 1972). Alternatively, the major television networks have tried to establish certain prime-time hours for family-type programs, to hopefully lessen the negative impact which television may have on children's social development.

Rothenberg (1975) feels very strongly that the link between television and children's aggression is a national scandal. He feels the evidence from the Surgeon General's report and from more than 10,000 studies shows a positive relationship between television and aggression. He makes the conclusions which are presented in Box 9-1.

SEX DIFFERENCES IN EARLY BEHAVIOR

Many children, early in their development, begin to behave in ways which are culturally defined as appropriate for their sex. Children also begin to be wary of responding in ways which are not appropriate to their sex to avoid the negative sanction of their parents, peers, or siblings. The process of acquiring the sex-role behaviors which we label as masculinity or femininity has been called *sex-typing*. Even with preschool-aged children we have sound evidence that preliminary sex-typing has occurred (Kagan, 1964). Mischel (1970) has indicated that there are sex differences in aggressive behavior in children as early as three years of age. As we have seen, boys are more aggressive than girls and this difference persists through the developmental years. Mischel (1970) also notes that similar differences in aggression are also seen cross-culturally.

Definitions of masculine or feminine behavior are, of course, the subject of much recent debate, stimulated by the women's liberation movement. The arbitrary way in which our culture has assigned particular sex-role stereotypes has been strongly criticized. Cross-cultural evidence suggests that our own cultural definitions of masculinity or femininity could be modified. Children's behavioral traits could be adapted to different sex-role standards. Margaret Mead (1935), for example, noted that among the Arapesh of New Guinea the behavior which we associate with femininity are expected of males, while females adopt behavior which we ordinarily judge to be masculine.

It appears that biological sex may not be as important in determining sex-typed behavior as are individual cultural expectations for masculinity or femininity. Never-

Box   9-1
Television and Aggression

1. *Effects on Learning.* Novel, aggressive behavior sequences are learned by children through exposure to aggressive actions shown on television or in films. . . . The following conditions encourage the actual performance of aggression: a similarity between the observed setting and the viewer's real setting; when the observed aggression "worked"; when it wasn't punished and when it was the favored and most frequent method used to attain goals.

2. *Emotional Effects.* There is a decreased emotional sensitivity to media violence, as a result of the repetition of violence in the mass media. . . . There is a decreased aggression anxiety and an increased ability to be violent with others.

3. *The Question of Catharsis.* Does watching the kind of aggression shown in the media result in "aggression catharsis," a "draining off of aggressive energy?" . . . studies have shown the opposite of catharsis, i.e., an increase in the viewers' subsequent aggressiveness. There has been no evidence that the observation of pain, horror, and suffering results in catharsis.

4. *Effects of Aggressive Behavior.* Aggression can be inhibited by (1) reminders that the aggression was morally wrong in terms of the viewer's own ethical principles, and (2) an awareness of the bloody, painful aftermath of aggression. Aggression can be facilitated by (1) the cue properties of available targets, i.e., stimuli in the postobservation period that have some association with previously observed violence, an association between the victim of the observed violence and the target of the viewer's aggression; and (2) the general state of arousal of the aggressor, e.g., when in experimental settings, the subject is verbally attacked and then exposed to film violence, he later is more aggressive than one who wasn't attacked before being exposed to film violence.

Source: B. Rothenberg, *Effect of Television Violence on Children and Youth* (Copyright 1975 by American Medical Association), pp. 1043–1046. By permission.

theless, a number of studies have found that the biological contribution of hormones does influence some sex-typed behavior.

Ehrhardt and Baker (1974) looked at seventeen girls who had a genetic defect which caused the adrenal glands to produce an excess of the male hormone *androgen.* The researchers wondered whether the excess androgen produced during the girls' prenatal development influenced any aspects of the girls' sex-typed behavior later in life. Although most of the girls had started receiving chemical therapy to correct this condition, the carry-over effects from prenatal development were still of interest.

Compared to other females in their families, the girls who had experienced excess levels of androgen in the prenatal period showed higher levels of "energy expenditure," preferred rough-and-tumble play, and were more likely to choose boys as playmates. They showed little interest in dolls and more often played with cars, trucks, or blocks. They were not interested in future roles such as bride, wife, or mother and showed either indifference to or dislike of caring for and handling infants. They were not strongly interested in appearing attractive and showed minimal concern for jewelry, makeup, hairstyles, and clothes. Most of these girls were clearly tomboys. For this group of genetic females, the effects of high levels of the male hormone during prenatal development appeared to influence some aspects of sex-typed behavior. Ehrhardt and Baker (1974) suggest that similar hormonal influences may affect the development of "temperamental differences" in males and females in general. Hormones appear to be one biological factor to recognize in children's sex-role development.

What part of children's sex-typed behavior is influenced by cultural expectations? Maccoby and Jacklin (1974) have attempted to review the evidence on sex differences from hundreds of psychological studies. Their work identifies the following myths, which have *not* been supported in psychological studies with children, regarding possible sex differences:

Myth 1—Girls are more social than boys.

Myth 2—Girls are more suggestible than boys.

Myth 3—Girls have lower self-esteem than boys.

Myth 4—Girls lack motivation to achieve.

Myth 5—Girls are better at role learning and simple repetitive tasks. Boys are better at high-level tasks that require them to inhibit previously learned responses.

Myth 6—Boys are more analytic than girls.

Myth 7—Girls are more affected by heredity, boys by environment.

Myth 8—Girls are more "auditory," boys "visual."

These eight myths appear to be part of people's general "commonsense" notion regarding sex differences and may be the basis of many of our cultural sex-role stereotypes. When Maccoby and Jacklin (1974) looked further at research for sex differences in behavior, the following differences were supported empirically.

Difference 1. Males *are* more aggressive than females.

Difference 2. Girls *do* have greater verbal ability than boys. Girls' verbal abilities seem to mature a little earlier in development than boys'. From preschool to early adolescence, however, there are no differences in verbal abilities. At about eleven years of age, girls begin to show signs of superiority in verbal ability, and this difference remains consistent.

Difference 3. Boys *do* excel in visual spatial ability. This difference, however, is not usually found until early adolescence. Prior to this time there are no systematic differences in this ability.

Difference 4. Boys *do* excel in mathematical ability. It is not until children reach approximately 12 – 13 years of age that we can clearly identify such differences.*

How do the social environments of boys and girls differ to foster such sex differences? Most studies suggest the environment exerts its influence in subtle ways

*Adapted from Eleanor Emmons Maccoby and Carol Nagy Jacklin, *The Psychology of Sex Differences,* Stanford University Press, 1974. Reprinted with the permission of the Board of Trustees, Stanford University.

Figure 9-7. The environment may foster sex-role stereotyping in both direct and subtle fashions. (Photo by Diana Blanchard)

almost from the moment the child is born. Rheingold and Cook (1975) observed that parents furnish girls' and boys' rooms differently: boys' rooms are provided more educational art materials, toy animals, sports equipment, while girls' rooms contain more dolls, flowers, and ruffles. Parents respond differently to girls and boys even as early as infancy. Lewis and Weinraub (1974) reported that boys are given more direct, physical stimulation (e.g., rocking and handling) from their mothers, while girls receive more indirect stimulation, such as talking and looking, and far less physical contact. Among older children, Rothbart and Maccoby (1966) found that fathers are generally more permissive with their daughters and more tolerant of daughters' aggression and dependency. Conversely, mothers are more permissive and accepting of this same behavior in their sons. Such cross-sex effects are often said to result from a sense of rivalry between the parent and same-sex child or from the higher expectations imposed by parents on their same-sex children (Weitz, 1977).

Even in school, girls and boys receive different responses from their teachers. The comments of nursery-school teachers to boys and girls were recorded by Serbin and O'Leary (1975). Teachers were more likely to respond verbally to boys who were behaving aggressively than to girls showing the same behavior. Exactly the opposite results were seen for dependency, however. Serbin and O'Leary also reported that girls were talked to more frequently when they were close to the teacher than when they were at some distance from her. For boys, proximity to the teacher had no effect on the frequency with which the teacher talked to them. Overall, boys were given more general attention from their teachers than were girls. Cherry reports highly similar results. Teachers seem to provide far more verbal comments to boys than they do to girls. Many of the comments directed towards boys are designed either to *control* their ongoing behavior or to gain their *attention* (Cherry, 1975).

Sex-role stereotypes are reinforced in children's books (Tavris & Offir, 1977). Boys are more often the central characters in stories, folktales, or fantasies. Television has continued to support such stereotyping. Sternglanz and Serbin (1974), for example, found that children were most likely to see males acting in constructive, helpful, and aggressive roles; females were rarely seen in such roles. Most female characters displayed high deference to others and a passive orientation. Interestingly, the only females who showed control over their environments and who possessed some status were those who had "magic" powers (e.g., witches).

EMOTIONAL DEVELOPMENT

Emotions are generally recognized as one of the most significant aspects of human experience. Our understanding of the developmental origins of emotions is very limited and tentative. We are beginning to recognize that while there is a biological basis for our emotions there are cognitive contributions as well. Some theorists believe that emotions are important in the acquisition of new skills and cognitive abilities, because pleasant feelings and emotional satisfaction can act as reinforcements. Other viewpoints, often held by clinical psychologists, emphasize the negative or unpleasant emotions such as fear or anxiety, which are encountered in disordered behaviors or psychosomatic illness.

Fear and Anxiety

It is difficult to separate the concepts of fear and anxiety. Psychologists have tended to use the term *anxiety* to refer to a global, undifferentiated emotional reaction which is brought about by a general situation. If a child, for example, is upset over separation from his or her mother, the reaction is usually called anxiety. If a child is playing in the yard however, and a large dog appears, the child's reaction is called fear. *Fear* occurs in response to a narrower class of events or objects which the child may perceive as harmful or threatening. Anxiety is a global concept while fear is a much more specific concept. No harm is immediately apparent to a child who is anxious about the return of his or her mother, especially when adequate care and security are assured by selection of a good babysitter. Yet, children do become anxious when their mothers leave.

Both fear and anxiety produce similar emotional states in the child. Physiologically both result in an increase in *adrenalin* from the adrenal glands. This hormone causes changes in respiration and heart rate, to cite a few of the general bodily changes with which we are most familiar (Brady, 1967; Kety, 1967; Bakwin & Bakwin, 1972). Sometimes the body responds adversely to persistent anxiety; that is, anxiety that lasts over a long period of time. The result of long-term anxiety may be a psychosomatic illness. An example of this type of illness is an intestinal disorder called *ulcerative colitis* (although not all ulcerative colitis is produced by anxiety). The physiological reaction to anxiety which results in ulcerative colitis is an over-production of hormones which trigger secretions in the colon. These eventually destroy the protective mucous coating of the colon, the tissues of the colon itself, and produce structural damage which may require surgery (Engel, 1955; Shirley, 1963; Alexander, 1965).

Fears

Children's fears are usually directed at specific identifiable events or objects in their environment. Most children's fears seem to fade rather quickly in the course of their development. The fears of younger children are usually centered on fantasy or imaginary characters (Bauer, 1976). Bauer found that kindergarten children were most likely to be afraid of ghosts or monsters. Older children in second and sixth grade showed more fear of events or circumstances that had some basis in reality. The six-graders feared possible bodily injury or realistic physical dangers. Fears are usually short-lived and transitory. Most children, in the course of development, work through their fears and overcome them. Some fears are so predictable that we expect to see them in almost every child.

One of the common fears of children is a fear of death. Around 7 – 8 years of age, children begin to develop the cognitive capacity to understand the meaning of death, its finality. Children at this age may not express their concerns directly. Often, they are fearful about the possible death of their parents. Psychoanalytic child psychologists believe that such fears stem from fears about the child's own death (Anthony, 1967). Death fears, like any other fears, are not easily minimized or discounted by parents. Attempts to reduce children's fears by ridiculing, belittling, or ignoring them generally do not help the situation (Salk, 1972). Tactics which are effective include talking about the fears, removing possible misconceptions, and giving the child emotional support (Salk, 1972; Shirley, 1963).

Phobias

A fear that becomes very intense, disrupts a child's adjustment, and far exceeds the potential harm or threat, is a *phobia*. A phobia is more arousing, more debilitating, and more intense than a fear. Children can develop phobias to virtually anything in their environment, such as heights, dogs, buses, or old women with white hair.

One of the most common phobias which parents, psychologists, and teachers have to deal with in children is school phobia. The school-phobic child cries, begs to stay home, and often develops physical complaints in his or her attempts not to attend school. These symptoms are present on school days, not weekends, and are most dramatic and intense at 8:30 A.M. Children often complain of headaches, stomachaches, and nausea, but as the day progresses, the symptoms subside (Shirley, 1963).

There is frequently a precipitating event which precedes the school phobia, such as a new baby at home, an accident, or a threatening bully (Verville, 1967). A number of studies have found that school-phobic children share a common background (Hersov, 1960; Chazan, 1962; Berecz, 1968; Poznanski, 1973). These children tend to isolate themselves from their classmates in school and are generally sheltered from close contacts with people except those in their immediate families. They have mothers who are strongly overprotective. It appears that the real fear for these children is the separation from the mother. School-phobic children usually cannot derive as much satisfaction in school as they can in the family. Teachers are not likely to be as solicitous and protective as their mothers. Mothers of children who have developed school phobia appear to have a difficult time letting their children grow up and become independent. A few studies have found that the fathers of these children tend to be passive and inadequate.

While the school-phobic child needs to return to school, the transition can be gradual. "The longer the children's return to school is delayed, the more difficult it becomes for him to give up his pleasant existence at home for the one in which he is lonely and uncertain" (Verville, 1967, p. 265). He or she may not immediately rejoin the class but could possibly do assigned work on an individual basis (Verville, 1967). As the child spends more and more time in school the return to the classroom becomes easier.

General Anxiety

In spite of the negative aspects of anxiety and fear, we all recognize that anxiety is necessary for survival. Anxiety about potential dangerous situations or threatening conditions prepares us for either defense or flight. Thus, anxiety helps us to adapt to our environment. Anxiety and fear can help children to avoid contemporary dangers. Heavy traffic creates lots of loud noise which may frighten young children and perhaps discourage play near or on city streets. Personal achievement can be spurred by fear or anxiety. A child who is anxious about meeting parental expectations will try to learn new skills and excel in appropriate areas, such as academics or sports.

Too much anxiety, of course, can influence children's performance negatively in a number of tasks. Zigler, Abelson, and Seitz (1973) hypothesized that the intelligence test scores of disadvantaged children might be low as the result of anxiety and low motivation. They thought that the children's generally low test scores could be improved if the testing situation were altered to both heighten their motivation and reduce their anxiety. Children's test scores did improve when anxiety levels were lessened as the result of familiarity with the person administering the test. The "motivational hypothesis" suggested in the study assumes that disadvantaged children are more wary of strangers than are children from middle-class homes (Zigler, Abelson, & Seitz, 1973).

REFLECTION-IMPULSIVITY

The personality dimension of *reflection-impulsivity* has been of interest to research psychologists studying children in recent years (Kagan, 1966; Kagan & Kogan, 1970). This dimension represents a relatively consistent personality variable which can be easily assessed in children. Kagan has created the Matching Figures Test to determine whether children solve problems in a *reflective* or *impulsive* fashion. Figure 9-8 shows two of the problems from this test. Children are asked to find a match for the single standard picture from an array of six pictures. Reflective children take longer to make their choices than impulsive children. Impulsive children, who decide quickly, have been found to make more errors than reflective children. Reflective children are more likely to evaluate the problem and the available choices carefully before reaching a decision (Siegel, Kirasic, & Kilburg, 1973).

The reflection-impulsivity dimension seems to be present in children as young as two years of age. As we might expect, errors decrease as children grow older. Thus, children become more reflective and less impulsive overall. Kagan considers this personality variable to be stable; however, he also recognizes that through experience and training it is possible to modify reflectivity-impulsivity (Yando & Kagan, 1968). Teachers have been found to influence the characteristic reflectivity or impulsivity of children through their role as models for the children in their classes. The influence of such models appears to be stronger for boys than for girls

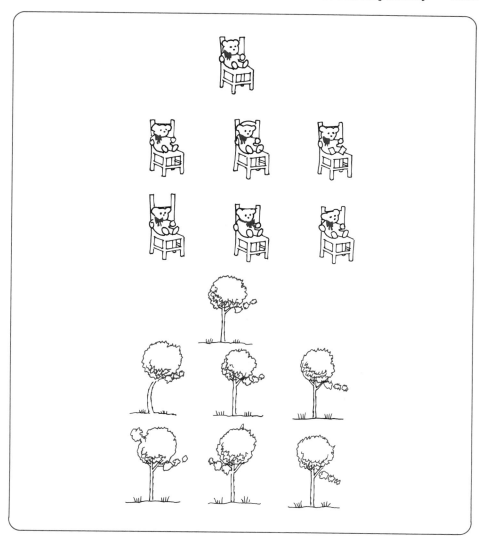

Figure 9-8.   Sample items from Matching Familiar Figures Task (MFF). (From J. Kagan, Reflection-impulsivity: the generality and dynamics of conceptual tempo. *Journal of Abnormal Psychology*, 1966, 71, 18. By permission.)

(Yando & Kagan, 1968). Kagan believes that disapproval from others acts as a deterrent to rapid response and seems to be the basis for the development of reflection. This would suggest that reflection may be associated with the development of anxiety.

The concept of reflection-impulsivity is controversial (Block, Block, & Harrington, 1974; Achenbach & Weisz, 1975). Not everyone agrees with Kagan's testing procedures or the meaning of the errors and style of responding (fast/slow). Block,

Block, and Harrington see impulsive children as the ones who are most anxious; they see the slower-to-act, reflective child as having minimal anxiety. They also feel that the concept of reflectivity-impulsivity is too broad to be measured by a single test.

Available research indicates that children can be categorized as reflective or impulsive on the basis of responses to the Matching Familiar Figures Test. Children's reflectivity-impulsivity can be modified through exposure to role models such as teachers. Two questions, however, remain unresolved in the research. First, the role of anxiety in explaining differences among children on reflectivity-impulsivity is not clear. Second, it is not known whether there is a biological contribution or foundation to this interesting personality variable.

SUMMARY

In this chapter we examined children's social and personality development. We looked at the importance of play in a number of different contexts. The importance of social learning theory (modeling, imitation, vicarious reinforcement) as a way of understanding the development of a wide range of children's behavior was emphasized. In addition, explanations of identification and aggression were considered from both psychoanalytic and social learning perspectives.

The origins of sex-role differences were considered from both biological and cultural orientations. We also looked at children's emotional development, including fears, anxieties, and phobias. Finally, the personality dimension of reflection-impulsivity was considered.

RECOMMENDED READINGS

Axline, V. M. *Dibs: In Search of Self.* New York: Ballantine Books, 1964.

A now classic description of one boy's attempts to cope with life, as seen through the eyes of his distinguished therapist. The play therapy sessions are absorbing and enlightening, as are the commentary and interpretations.

Baron, R. *Human Aggression.* New York: Plenum Press, 1977.

An excellent summary of current research and thinking into one of man's most problematic behaviors. Both developmental and social-personality viewpoints are considered.

Lips, H. M., and Colwill, N. L. *The Psychology of Sex Differences.* Englewood Cliffs, New Jersey: Prentice Hall, 1978.

An interesting collection of perspectives, both research and theoretical, on the most current controversies in this growing field. The topics include biological contributions, aggression, socialization, and achievement.

Maccoby, E., and Jacklin, C. *The Psychology of Sex Differences.* Stanford, California: Stanford University Press, 1974.

An excellent synthesis of literally hundreds of research studies on sex differences in both children and adults. The extensive annotated bibliography is particularly helpful.

5

MIDDLE
CHILDHOOD

10

Cognitive Development in Middle Childhood

In this chapter we will consider cognitive processes and trace the cognitive attainments of middle childhood. We have already seen in Chapter 5 how the infant becomes increasingly aware of the environment, as well as increasingly able to think and learn. What additional changes in children's reasoning and logical thought occur in middle childhood? We will study isolated facets of children's cognitive abilities, such as memory, perception, or conceptual categories. Real children, however, are not so compartmentalized and use all of these components simultaneously to solve problems in their environment.

THE ENVIRONMENT: MODES OF REPRESENTATION

In the course of development children may adopt a variety of ways of representing their world. Psychologists have been interested in which types of representation are most characteristic of children at different ages.

Imagery

If you were asked to visualize a bright red apple or a suspension bridge, you would probably have little difficulty forming an image of these objects. Children represent much of their world in this fashion, especially during the preschool years. By middle childhood, however, imagery has become a less common technique of representation.

Bruner (1966) is one theorist who sees imagery as having an important role in cognitive development. Initially infants use an *enactive,* or *motoric,* mode of representation to think; that is, their thoughts lead directly to action or overt behavior. When an infant sees an attractive toy, we know it because the infant reaches to try to bring it closer. With *enactive representation* the child is limited to the here and now. A second stage becomes evident in children around two to three years of age. This stage is labeled *iconic,* or *image,* representation (Bruner, 1966). With iconic representation children can use images to represent persons, events, and objects that are not in the immediate environment. The child's thought is thus freed from direct experience. Imagery is an effective abstract way for children to think. Bruner notes a third stage called *symbolic representation,* which provides an even more efficient, abstract thinking style. At this stage children who are five to seven years old can use language to represent abstract events, ideas, and thoughts. Symbolic representation based on language, according to Bruner, is the basis for the higher level problem-solving ability that emerges in middle childhood. Note, however, that older children and adults retain the ability to utilize both imagery and symbolic modes of representation.

While the ability to utilize imagery and symbolic representation may coexist, certain kinds of imagery may decline markedly in development. Some kindergarten children, for example, have the capacity to experience *eidetic images* while older

Figure 10-1. Imagery, as a form of symbolic representation, plays a major role in children's cognitive development. (Ott/Monkmeyer Press Photo Service)

children (nine years of age and above) rarely display this mode of representation (Giray, Altkin, Vaught & Roodin, 1976). Eidetic images are images that are experienced as if the real object or picture which elicited them is still present. Children who have eidetic imagery can project on a blank screen a picture that was presented previously to them. Children report that they actually "see" an eidetic image exactly matching the former picture. When asked about the eidetic image, children scan the blank screen where the image appears to them, as if the original picture were still there. They see this image as having positive coloration, identify its location as "outside on the screen" rather than in their heads, and describe it as an ongoing, contemporary event (e.g., they use the present tense). These children can identify virtually every detail of the image with great accuracy, and these images persist on the average for 45 seconds (Doob, 1970; Giray et al., 1976).

Eidetic imagery does not appear to be a common ability among older children or adults (Cutts & Moseley, 1969). In one investigation with subjects ranging in age from five to eighteen years, eidetic imagery was found to decline systematically over the age ranges from five to eight years (see Figure 10-2). No other systematic relationships were found in eidetic ability among any of the older subjects over the age range nine to eighteen (Giray et al, 1976). These data seem to support Bruner's ideas regarding the developmental importance of imagery as a way of representing reality.

Conceptual Categories and Rules

Children may also represent their environment in terms of basic categories. Some of these conceptual categories are clear-cut to us (for example, triangles; the "middle-sized" one) while others have meaning only for the child ("Be wary of

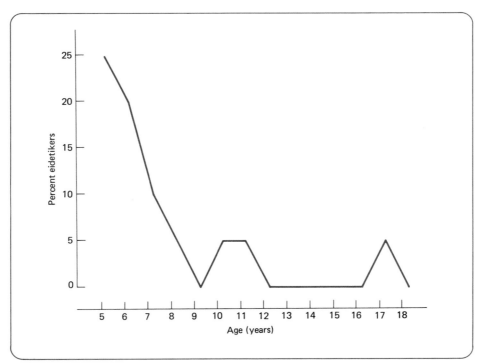

Figure 10-2.   Incidence of eidetic imagery as a function of age. (From Giray, Altkin, Vaught, and Roodin, The incidence of eidetic imagery as a function of age. *Child Development*, 1976, 47, 1209. By permission.)

men with moustaches"). Conceptual categories are derived from the child's recognition of physical or abstract-symbolic similarities among objects and experiences in the environment.

Thus, children search for ways to organize or structure their environment—for perceived psychological similarity—by constructing conceptual categories (Elkind, 1969). They also recognize that some conceptual categories are related to each other (cars, trucks, buses, and vans are all vehicles). Rules describe a set of systematic relationships among conceptual categories. What do each of the following pairs of objects have in common: hammer/saw, cake/bread, car/bicycle, and coat/blanket? In the case of hammer/saw there is a conceptual rule (tool), while for cake/bread the rule is food. Rules can be applied by children again and again in situations which are quite different from one another. Bruner (1973) has called the process by which children generalize and utilize previously acquired rules and concepts in new situations *scanning.* Scanning involves developing hypotheses about a new problem by examining it closely for similarities to other problems children may have faced in the past. It may take several "scans" before the child finds the right rule or concept to fit a particular problem.

Robert Gagné has also recognized children's unique ability for generalizing rules from one situation to another. Such *transfer of training,* along with the ability to *differentiate* or discriminate one stimulus from another, and a well-developed memory or *recall* ability are necessary prerequisites for complex problem-solving and higher-order learning. Gagné does not believe that children develop concepts and rules by chance experience or insight. Concepts and rules are the result of the successful application of transfer of training, differentiation, and recall, which follow a *cumulative developmental sequence* (Gagné, 1970).

Gagné's *cumulative learning model* is presented in Figure 10-3. In contrast to the work of Piaget, the cumulative learning model shows that children's cognitive development is the result of cumulative, sequentially ordered learning. Each of the lower steps must be successfully learned, in sequence, before a child can attain more advanced ones. Before a child can attain a complex rule (e.g., coordinating two or more rules) he or she must learn simpler individual rules. Before a simple rule can be acquired (e.g., relating two or more concepts), the two basic concepts must be learned. And before concepts can be acquired, children must have learned how to discriminate among stimuli. Such discriminations, according to Gagné, are based on learning to link verbal-motor responses, such as using the verbal label *red* and selecting out all of the red blocks from an array. The most basic learning in the cumulative learning sequence is the associative or stimulus-response type. Gagné has arranged the basic elements of cognition in a hierarchical way, with learning providing the basis of children's cognitive development.

COGNITIVE PROCESSES

While the role of environmental factors in children's cognitive development has been extensively studied, the role of maturation has received far less consideration.

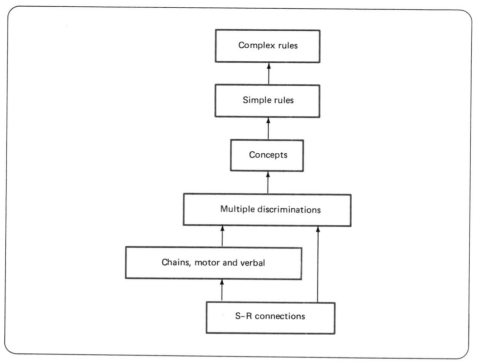

Figure 10-3.   A general sequence for cumulative learning. (From R. M. Gagne, Contributions of learning to human development. *Psychological Review*, 1968, 75, p. 182, Figure 1. By permission.)

White (1965), however, has identified the years between five and seven as particularly important ones in the development of the child's central nervous system. It is not until middle childhood that higher level cognitive processes begin to be seen. Before this time children seem to be responding on a more simplistic (stimulus-response) basis association. By the time children have reached five to seven years of age their behavior is marked by a "new level of function": "We might generally characterize the higher level of function as 'cognitive'" (White, 1965, p. 213). For White and Piaget, cognitive development is dependent on the maturation of the child's central nervous system. By seven years of age children are capable not only of responding in complex, abstract, cognitive ways but are also able to inhibit the simpler associative responses characteristic of much younger children. He suggests that a primitive layer of associative responding is overshadowed by a more mature layer of cognitive functioning. Cognitive functioning is the result of completion of central nervous system development which occurs between five and seven years of age. White's list of cognitive abilities that result from neurological development include:

1. Use of language as a mediator or guide for children's behavior; abstract rather than concrete use of language
2. Maintenance of invariant dimensions of stimuli by children even though the stimuli undergo change
3. Representation of actions internally which permits planning, directed behavior rather than trial and error, and allows inference
4. More responsiveness to visual and auditory distance receptors and less responsiveness to near receptors involved in emotion, touch, or pain. (1965, p. 210)

While development of the central nervous system is an important factor in such changes in children's behavior, we must also remember that by five to seven years of age most children have started school and the formal process of education. The environmental impact of school experiences may exert an effect equally important to the effect attributed to maturation. Clearly, both influences must be recognized to obtain an adequate picture of the development of children's cognitive processes.

Perception

Most psychologists agree that perception is an important cognitive process to study in children. However, there is some disagreement as to whether the process is active or passive. Probably the most well-developed *activist theory* of perception has been proposed by Eleanor Gibson (1969). In the course of development children continually change their ways of organizing and attending to the world. Children do not acquire or substitute "a new response to stimulation previously responded to in some other way" (Gibson, 1969, p. 77), but rather they seem to become more and more aware of stimuli in their environment which they have previously ignored. Children's perception shows an increase in recognition of detail and specificity over time. They become increasingly able to differentiate and respond to salient aspects of the environment.

What keeps children from being overwhelmed by the multitude of perceptual stimuli which directly affect their senses every second? Gibson has proposed that a *selective-attention* process is responsible for controlling the flow of perceptual stimuli to the child. What is this process of selective attention like? Pick, Frankel, and Hess (1975) have recently reviewed experimental studies on selective attention.

Selective attention can be influenced by what the child highlights from his or her own viewpoint (child-controlled) or by environmental events that emphasize particular stimuli or attributes (environmental control). In the case of child-controlled selective attention we notice that certain features of the environment seem to be particularly salient. These salient features change as the child develops. For example, at three years of age John may be particularly attentive to dogs and see them wherever he goes, even before his parents notice them. At the age of eight, however, John may be particularly interested in sports cars and quickly point out Jaguars, Corvettes, and Triumphs. Such child-control of selective attention can also be seen in developmental changes to stimulus features. Children show definite preferences when asked to match visual objects which vary on the basis of color or form. For young children color is the basis for judging whether two objects are similar, while shape or form tends to be the basis for the judgments of six- and seven-year-olds (Suchman & Trabasso, 1966). Children also have rather well-developed hierarchies of dimensional preference and dimensional dominance which are different from one child to the next (Odom & Guzman, 1972; Smiley, 1972). Such "preexisting attentional dispositions . . . may be important in influencing what the child processes, learns, and remembers in a task situation" (Flavell, 1977, p. 168).

The environmental control of children's selective attention has also been investigated. In one study children from nursery school, first grade, and fifth grade were shown a number of stimulus pictures (Appel, Cooper, McCarrell, Sims-Knight, Yussen, & Flavell, 1972). These children participated in a memory task with two different sets of instructions. They were told to look carefully at a set of pictures but were not told that they would be asked to recall them. In a second condition, they were told that they were to memorize the pictures because they were to be recalled. These two types of instruction, *looking* vs. *remembering,* were compared for the three age groups. First- and fifth-graders remembered more pictures when told to memorize than when told to look. For preschool children remembering was not found to be a function of the type of instruction. For children from nursery school age to fourth grade instructions to visualize items, however, did seem to improve the ability to recognize these items later (Millar, 1972; London & Robinson, 1968; Robinson & London, 1971). With increasing age, instructions seem to help children focus their attention on relevant aspects of problems.

Developmentally, children become increasingly able to direct and control their own attention. They become better and better able to focus, for themselves, on the important features of a problem and successfully avoid distracting, irrelevant features (Flavell, 1977). Pick and Frankel (1974) have noted that second-graders are not nearly as flexible as sixth-graders in modifying or changing the focus of their selective attention processes. Sixth-graders easily and quickly focus on different aspects of new problems, discarding earlier successful strategies of attention in favor of more appropriate, more efficient ones.

Further evidence in support of this view can be seen in research on children's perception of part-whole relationships. Elkind, Koegler, and Go (1964) used the two-dimensional drawings shown in Figure 10-4. These drawings were based on familiar objects such as a heart derived from the combination of common independent parts, i.e., the placement of the two giraffe necks. Four- and five-year-olds focused on only the independent parts and reported seeing, for instance, only two giraffes. Seven-year-olds *alternated* in their perceptions of these drawings, shifting their attention and reporting not only the two giraffes but also the heart formed by their necks. Nearly 60% of the 8-year-olds and 78% of the 9-year-olds attended to

Figure 10-4.   Illustrations used to evaluate whole versus part perception. (From D. Elkind, R. Koegler, and E. Go, Studies in perceptual development, II: part–whole perception. *Child Development,* 35, 1964, 81–90. Copyright 1964 by the Society for Research in Child Development. By permission.)

both part and whole at the same time. They reported, for example, "I see a heart formed by giraffes' necks."

Memory

Memory is a fundamental part of our cognitive processes. By memory we mean the condition that continues to affect us after a stimulus is no longer present

(McGaugh, 1973). After we store experiences in our brain, we can then use them to respond appropriately to the demands of the same or similar stimulus-situations in the future (Anderson, 1975). There is evidence that a residue of events and stimulation is stored within the brain. Some of our memories affect us throughout our entire lives, while others are brief and relatively unimportant.

Biological Bases of Memory.   The search for a specific place in the brain which stores our memories has been discouraging. For example, laboratory studies of rats' brains, in which limited areas were destroyed, have not revealed a specific memory site. Some studies have nevertheless found that certain regions of the brain are necessary for memory, although no one single storage center for memories has been found (Carlson, 1977).

Penfield (1959) reported that the *temporal lobe* of the brain, in patients undergoing surgery, produces vivid memories of past experiences when stimulated. The temporal lobe of the brain appears to interpret our various memories. Another brain site that is involved in memory is the *hippocampus*. In the case of head injury or accidental destruction of the hippocampus, memory ability is significantly reduced. Individuals with hippocampal damage do not appear to be able to learn anything new or to identify people except those met before the damage (Carlson, 1977). Damage to the hippocampus does not destroy old memories, but it interferes with the storage of new ones.

Some investigators believe that memory may have a biological basis. They have found that new kinds of experiences, such as training in a maze-learning task, increase RNA (ribonucleic acid) in mice. These biological changes are somewhat brief, however. The possibility that there is a specific molecule for memory has also been suggested, and investigators have attempted to transfer memories from one animal to another. Such studies use worms (planaria) that are trained, to see if this training can be transferred to untrained worms (McGaugh, 1973). In early studies, worms that had been trained were destroyed, and their remains were fed to naive, untrained worms in the hope that some kind of memory transfer would occur. Unfortunately, there was no difference in subsequent learning between worms fed a regular diet and those whose diet was supplemented by trained worms! To summarize, since memory involves the lasting effects of a stimulus on an individual, we must hypothesize that significant changes occur in the brain somehow. Our knowledge regarding these changes, however, remains quite incomplete.

Types of Memory.   We may divide memory into two types, which are usually called *short-term memory* and *long-term memory* (Posner, 1973). An example of short-term memory can be found in intelligence testing when a child is asked to repeat a series of digits immediately after hearing them. Short-term memory is said to persist for about 30 seconds; beyond this time limit we are dealing with long-term memory. Long-term memory may last for minutes, or throughout an individual's lifetime.

We can study both how children store information to be remembered *(storage)* and how such information is retrieved from memory *(retrieval)*. Recently, Emmerich and Ackerman (1978) have found that information storage is far more important than information retrieval for children in the third through fifth grades. Two basic responses that have been used to study memory involve *recall* and *recognition* of previously presented material (Flavell, 1977). A study of children's *recognition* memory will illustrate the procedure. A group of first-graders was shown 40 slides of unfamiliar landscapes and cityscapes by Entwistle and Huggins (1973). When their memories were tested a week later, children could easily recognize whether a particular slide had been seen before or not. In a similar investigation, preschool children shown a series of pictures in a recognition memory task were almost perfectly able to identify whether they had seen the picture on a previous occasion one month earlier (Brown & Scott, 1971). When the stimulus materials were a list of words read aloud, however, second-grade children were found to be less accurate (Poteat & Kasschau, 1969). Thus, children's recognition memory for visually presented materials is better than that for orally presented materials (Pick, Frankel & Hess, 1975).

A more complex response used in studying memory is to ask children to actively *recall* items from a previously presented series. A number of interesting processes have been found to influence children's recall. These processes may help us to understand how children become more efficient and accurate in recalling information as they develop.

One process that influences children's ability to recall is *organization*. When we present a list of words to a child and ask that the list be recalled, younger children seem to try to remember the list of words exactly as it was presented, while older children spontaneously organize words which are related to each other (Halperin, 1974). However, we can improve the recall of younger children by giving them instructions to help them organize or group words together. Even third grade children show improved recall when instructed to group or cluster words on the basis of their meaning (Liberty & Ornstein, 1973).

Another process that helps children to recall information is that of *categorization*. When given a list of words to remember, the series with words that are categorically related, such as tools or colors, is remembered better than a series with unrelated items (Zupnick & Forrester, 1972). By analyzing the order in which words are recalled we can see that older children make use of such categories while younger preschoolers tend not to derive such categories.

Another process which helps the recall of children is *elaboration*. Rohwer (1970) found that a word which is to be recalled at a later time is less likely to be forgotten when it becomes part of an elaborated phrase or idea. For example, we might ask children to remember a series of word pairs like dog—moon, tree—car, oil—street. The word pairs will be remembered better, according to Rohwer, if children elaborate the pairs into a phrase or sentence: the *dog* jumped over the *moon*, the *tree* is next to the *car*, the *oil* spilled onto the *street*. Simply trying to remember individual word pairs in isolation is not very effective. Odom and Nesbitt (1974) found that if elaboration involves actions the word pairs are remembered even better. To remember the pair dog—moon, they suggest using such elaboration phrases as "the dog is jumping over the moon." Action-based elaborations not only provide a semantic context to help a child's memory but also provide better, more vivid images of the words themselves. Elaboration, then, can also occur through imagery.

Still another process which is related to memory in children concerns their ability to *rehearse* during the period intervening between presentation of stimuli and subsequent recall. As we have seen in Chapter 8, by the age of seven, some children will spontaneously create and utilize verbal mediation to help them remember. Younger children, however, are unlikely to create such verbal mediators spontaneously (Flavell, Beach, & Chinsky, 1966). Flavell (1970) has noted that there are a number of possible ways other than verbal in which children could mediate or rehearse to improve their memories. Imagery would be one type of mediation, and overt or covert motor responses would be another (Bandura & Jeffrey, 1973). For those who play a musical instrument, in fact, motor rehearsal is a well-recognized tactic for learning songs or passages "by heart." Rehearsal strategies such as verbalization, imagery, or motor responses, however, may only be used spontaneously by children after they have been well-developed and well-practiced (Flavell, 1977).

A final process related to children's memory has been called *metamemory* (Flavell, 1977). Metamemory refers to what children think they know about their own memory and memory-related skills. Such knowledge about our own memory shows developmental trends. It has been shown that older children develop metamemory (awareness) of their own memory strategies and can recognize effective from less effective memory strategies. Moynahan (1973) asked children from three elementary school grades to judge which of two lists would be easier for them to learn—a list of unrelated items or a list of semantically related items which could be grouped into categories such as articles of furniture, types of foods, etc. She found that both third- and fifth-graders could recognize that the unrelated items would be more difficult to learn than the list with related items. First-graders, however, saw the learning of the two lists as equally difficult.

The implication of studies on children's metamemory is that children's knowledge of their own memories may *interact* with some of the processes identified above. Wellman (1978) has suggested that children's "memory monitoring" of potential strategies may partially explain the efficient memory systems of older children, while the lack of "memory monitoring" may help us understand the relatively inefficient memories of younger children.

Memory and Inference.   In real life children's memory is applied to more than just the simple recall or recognition of isolated words or pictures. Piaget suggests that children not only relate their past memories to the demands of the present, but also actively attempt to reason how present and past are related. When children store and retrieve information from memory, they are actually *reconstructing* their experiences. Piaget, Flavell, and others believe that children must infer from these reconstructions in order to utilize their memories effectively (Flavell, 1977). We do not just store information and experiences but represent such entities in our memories; we do not just retrieve information or experiences but rather our representations of these events.

Donaldson (1976) suggests that the ability to utilize memory is related to the growth of internal cognitive control. As children develop they are increasingly able to direct their attention voluntarily, to resist irrelevant aspects of problems, and to manipulate symbols covertly, or mentally. These attainments are necessary for the process of inference. Inferential abilities may come about in children only as they develop increased awareness of their own thinking (Donaldson, 1976). Thus, just as metamemory may be related to children's selection of efficient memory strategies, conscious awareness of themselves as thinkers may underlie their inferential abilities.

One of the consequences of the view that memory is a reconstructive process is that as children develop increased consciousness of their own thinking and more sophisticated cognitive skills, their past memories may be altered. What children infer about the past, in other words, may be influenced by what they are like in the present. Piaget and Inhelder (1973), for example, showed three- to eight-year-old children an array of ten sticks which were arranged in systematic order from smallest to largest. The children were asked to draw the array one week later and also eight months later. Children showed better drawing of the array after eight months than after one week! The observed improvement in reproducing the array after a long period of time does not fit with most experimental studies of memory (Flavell, 1977).

Generally, shorter time intervals result in superior recall when compared to longer ones. The reason for the improvement in recalling the array after eight months, according to Piaget and Inhelder, was the overall acquisition of general knowledge by the children during the eight-month interval. A more accurate representation of the array was possible because children acquired knowledge of ordering relations, or *seriation,* moving from smaller to larger. With this new knowledge children were able to make better inferences about what they had previously seen. Without this new knowledge of ordering relations, children's inferences about what they had seen were less accurate. Liben (1977) found similar results with children 8.5 years of age.

Let's examine another study which is based on the ideas of reconstruction in memory and the importance of inferences. Paris presented the following story to school-age children:

Linda was playing with her new doll in front of her big red house. Suddenly she heard a strange sound coming from under the porch. It was the flapping of wings. Linda wanted to help so much, but she did not know what to do. She ran inside the house and grabbed a shoe box from the closet. Then Linda looked inside her desk until she found eight sheets of yellow paper. She cut up the paper into little pieces and put them in the bottom of the box. Linda gently picked up the helpless creature and took it with her. Her teacher knew what to do. (1975, p. 233)

Following the reading of the story, the children were then asked the following series of eight questions:

1. Was Linda's doll new?
2. Did Linda grab a matchbox?
3. Was the strange sound coming from under the porch?
4. Was Linda playing behind her house?
5. Did Linda like to take care of animals?
6. Did Linda take what she found to the police station?
7. Did Linda find a frog?
8. Did Linda use a pair of scissors?

Questions 5–8 are the ones of most interest to us because they cannot be answered from anything which was directly presented in the story. The children responded correctly to these latter questions, thus supporting the importance of the concept of constructive processes in memory. The answers which children derived to questions 5–8 came from their ability to make inferences from the limited information given in the story. For instance, the answer to question 6 must be inferred: children already know teachers are not likely to be found in police stations. Paris has identified that reconstruction and inference play an important part in children's memories.

Hypothesis Formation

When we study the formation of hypotheses in children, we are interested in how present experiences and past memories are used to derive possible solutions to problems. Flavell (1977) has considered the process of hypothesis formation as *applied cognition*.

The process of hypothesis formation is studied developmentally by examining the way in which children of different ages learn a rule to solve a complex problem. In particular, how do they derive likely solutions of hypotheses and at the same time rule out unlikely alternatives? Children not only try out hypotheses, but they also must reject some in favor of others. The process of hypothesis-testing involves the logical process of inductive reasoning. *Inductive reasoning* describes the process in which we consider individual facts and derive a general conclusion from them; it is reasoning from the particular to the general. Inductive reasoning underlies construction of the concepts and rules children use to comprehend their environment. In virtually every situation children try to discover specific rules or concepts to help them in coping with the multitude of new challenges they face.

A number of psychologists have been interested in how children derive hypotheses from their experiences (Gohlson, O'Connor & Stern, 1976; Levine, 1975). Usually a problem is presented to children in which they have to figure out a correct solution so that they can be right 100% of the time. We might, for example, present pairs of shapes so that a child has to learn that SQUARE should always be chosen, as in the series of stimulus pairs below:

1. red circle/blue SQUARE
2. blue circle/red SQUARE
3. blue SQUARE/red circle
4. red SQUARE/blue circle

We would be sure to assign the SQUARE an equal number of times to left and right on the cards and continue to present the sequence of cards (1–4) until the SQUARE was always chosen by the child, e.g., 10 times in a row. What hypotheses might a child apply to this problem? What ways might children have of analyzing this problem to discover, inductively, the correct solution?

Hypothesis 1.   Children might try to solve the problem by using position only. For example, Hypothesis 1a could be to choose the shape on the left, Hypothesis 1b to choose the one on the right. Hypothesis 1c might be to *alternate* position choices—left, right, left, right, etc.

Hypothesis 2.   Children could consider that color might be the basis of the solution to the problem. They could try Hypothesis 2a and always choose red or Hypothesis 2b and always choose blue. Or, they might alternate color choices in Hypothesis 2c: red, blue, red, blue.

Hypothesis 3.   Children might consider that form is the basis of the solution. They could use Hypothesis 3a and select circles from each of the stimulus pairs or Hypothesis 3b (the correct one) and chose SQUARE each time.

In other words, children can be thought of as selecting from a large array of possible hypotheses, testing potential solutions, ruling out those that do not work, and eventually choosing the correct one (Hypothesis 3b). Using any of the other hypotheses would not allow for successful solution of the problem 100% of the time.

We can expect kindergarten children to be more likely to use a "position-alternation" hypothesis (e.g., Hypothesis 1c in the example above), in which they simply switch or alternate from left to right (Rieber, 1969). Second- and fourth-graders appear more likely to adopt non-positional hypotheses as they attempt to solve problems. Older children are better able to deal with more complex hypotheses to solve more complex problems (Gohlson & Danziger, 1975). Older children are both quicker to discard incorrect hypotheses and more likely to stay with hypotheses that are successful (Mims & Gohlson, 1977; Phillips, Levine & O'Brien, 1978). Sixth-graders seem to be uniformly more skilled in hypotheses formation than younger children.

Decision-Making

Probably the highest level of mental processes is decision-making. Once we have tested alternative hypotheses and determined which one best fits a particular problem, we mus. then utilize the information to guide our behavior. This part of cognitive activity is the end result of our thinking and reasoning. Since children are thinking as well as behaving, we expect that their decisions to respond or not respond in particular ways will be influenced by their own thoughts. When a child is in a new situation and applies a rule or concept acquired from past experience, we may speak of his or her reasoning as *deductive.* Deductive reasoning involves working from a general principle or rule to reach a decision about a specific situation. We might illustrate the process of deductive reasoning by looking at five-year-old Gina, who has already learned that bees have stingers which can hurt. When Gina is on the playground swing, she hears a buzzing near her ear. She looks behind to discover a bee and makes the inference that this bee, like others, has a stinger. She makes a decision to get out of the swing as fast as possible and move away from the bee. Her behavior is controlled by an active decision-making process. Based on what she knows from past experience, Gina deduces that it is best for her to leave the swing—immediately.

PIAGET'S CONCRETE OPERATIONAL PERIOD

It is in middle childhood that the capacity to use logical thought with concrete problems emerges. For Piaget, children's concrete operational thought is evolved from the progressive attainments of the earlier preoperational period discussed in Chapter 7. You may remember that the child's cognitive abilities improved during the preoperational period as the result of the acquisition of language. There was also a decline in egocentric behavior during the preoperational period and a consequent increase in children's social awareness. Nevertheless, children were still restricted in their thought processes. The preoperational child finds it difficult to move beyond his or her immediate perceptual experience into the realm of complex, abstract cognitive operations.

Why do children develop increasingly more complex, abstract operations during the concrete operational period? Piaget's view is that children become dissatisfied with their past preoperational solutions. Children begin to recognize the inadequacy of these solutions and the errors which these primitive solutions produce. Children are always attempting to attain a state of equilibrium with the environment and their cognitive skills. In working towards this ideal balance children seek coherence, stability, and ever more effective ways of coping with reality. Striving for equilibrium requires the child to modify his or her own cognitive structures, for example, from those of the preoperational period to those of the concrete operational period.

Schemata, or operations, are considered the components of the cognitive structure that permit adaptation to the environment. The more schemata or intellectual operations a child possesses, the more adaptive and successful the child's problem-solving will be. In the course of development some schemata become displaced while others become coordinated as part of more advanced cognitive structures. For example, the behavioral schemata used by infants to control their actions become part of the operations of middle childhood which control thought/action through the processes of assimilation and accommodation. You may recall from Chapter 5 that *assimilation* is the process through which the child incorporates new information from the environment into previously existing cognitive structures (schemata, operations). *Accommodation* takes place when the child either modifies an existing cognitive structure so that new stimuli will fit into it or forms an entirely new cognitive structure. Each stage of cognitive development permits a better, more logical fit between the demands of the environment and the child's ability to cope with those demands. Equilibrium, of course, is a goal which is sought, but usually never attained.

The thought processes of the concrete operational child are increasingly more logical in dealing with realistic problems. The ability to think logically about concrete problems slowly emerges in the middle childhood years from seven to eleven. Piaget and his associates emphasize that the age limits, or boundaries, are only rough approximations and are not fixed or absolute for every child from every culture or subculture. Piaget also emphasizes that the cognitive attainments which he describes as a series of developmental stages, are really continuous and gradual—not static and fixed. There is a tendency, however, to think of stages as discontinuous, abrupt, and clearly separable from each other. Stages in development could be better thought of as an "intellectual idealization" which helps us to organize and represent changes in a convenient manner (Toulmin, 1971).

In the years from seven to eleven the *quality* of the child's thinking changes and exceeds the capability shown in the period of preoperational thought. Improved understanding of causation, reality, and time is evident. Although children's ability to think improves, logical thought is not as abstract or complex as it is in the next period where it reaches its highest level. Thought processes in the concrete operational period are of value primarily in dealing with *observable* (concrete) objects and events. Hypothetical or abstract, verbal problems are still too difficult. If a verbal problem is made more concrete by the addition of objects, however, children can solve the problem. A child might have trouble solving an arithmetic problem stated simply as "Add 3 and 5," whereas the child's understanding increases when requested to add 3 toy cars and 5 toy cars arranged in view on a table.

Egocentrism

During middle childhood egocentrism continues to decrease as a result of social experience. In this period the child acquires new awareness of the viewpoints and concerns of others and can compare and contrast his or her personal thoughts with those within and outside the family (Piaget & Inhelder, 1969). As a result of finding satisfaction and similarity in peer relationships, the child's confidence in personal judgment grows.

It is important to take into account the child's increased use of language with peers and adults. Piaget emphasizes that this social interaction represents a resource for the child of refinements of ideas and concepts handed down by earlier generations. Thus, egocentrism may also be reduced through social transmission.

While children borrow from this cultural reservoir liberally, at times they reject some ideas because of their "mental level." The rejection may be counteracted to a limited extent in the family, since in the process of interchange children find that new thoughts are contradicted or approved and discover a vast world of ideas beyond their own. As a result of this interchange with others, the child is " . . . forced to accept an ever-increasing number of obligatory truths, ready-made ideas and true norms of reasoning" (Piaget, 1966). Social experience and interaction reduce the child's intellectual egocentricity, and the child gains greater freedom in thought processes. The development of logic, in fact, depends upon cooperation with others. Cooperation also contributes to a knowledge of rules and norms that conform to "a morality of thinking imposed and sanctioned by others."

Figure 10-5. Egocentrism continues to decrease as a result of children's social experiences. (David S. Strickler/Monkmeyer Press Photo Service)

Decentration and Perception

During the concrete operational period additional progress is made in *decentering,* or giving up the tendency to center attention on one element while excluding other important elements. The problem that the preoperational child had in taking into account all of the essential properties of a stimulus is no longer apparent. Recognizing the essential characteristics of a stimulus enables the older child to understand conservation. The child no longer centers attention on the level of beads in a tall or wide glass as an indication of quantity but can remember that the quantity is always the same no matter in what shape it is stored.

For preoperational children, the area on which they fixate the longest usually becomes magnified in importance (height or length). Piaget believes that this increased importance causes the child's perception to be in error. For the young child, however, this erroneous perception is as real as if the part had actually been expanded. When children begin to decenter, they make use of new information. They *coordinate* different centers or points of fixation so that the new information leads to a reduction of perceptual distortion (Piaget, 1969). We find that the child's overall perception, in the concrete operational period, is improved as the result of decentering and coordination. This period of development therefore permits thought to be based on the essential features of the stimulus.

Logical Operations

Logical operations are defined by Piaget as internalized acts—derived through interaction with the environment and as a result of assimilation and accommodation. A mental operation can be carried out in thought as well as in action; it can be reversed; it involves some conservation; and it always takes place in relation to a logical system. Examples of logical operations include reversibility, seriation, and classification (Piaget, 1969).

Reversibility. The illustration in Chapter 7 of the child's inability to reverse the "act of lengthening" should be recalled. In that example a child was shown two rows of ten checkers placed side by side so that their equivalence was easily apparent. After the child examined the rows, the spaces between the checkers were lengthened so that one row was made longer. At the preoperational level, the child believes that more checkers are present, and Piaget explains that the child at this level of thought *cannot* reverse the act of lengthening to see that the checkers are still the same in number. In the concrete operational period, however, children understand that the checkers remain the same in number in spite of the perceptual appearance of taking up greater space. Thus, concrete operational children, after constructing two equivalent sets of checkers, perceive the rows as equivalent even though the arrangement is altered. They are capable of decentering, using extended information, and attending to both important dimensions: the length of the row and the space among the checkers. They realize that a relation exists between length and density, and they understand that as length increases, density decreases. Such an understanding is a form of reversibility (Ginsburg & Opper, 1978; Wadsworth, 1971). *Reversibility* is an operation in which an increase in length counteracts an increase in space so that a reversal is made mentally back to the original condition—to perceive an equal number of checkers in each line. Thus, concrete operational children can imagine the reversal of an event and can mentally change a situation back to its original condition.

Seriation.   Another logical operation which occurs during the concrete operational period is *seriation*. This operation consists of an ability to arrange elements in relation to increasing or decreasing size. Suppose that Allen (five years of age), Bill (seven years of age), and Cathy (nine years of age) each play with a wooden model train that has respectively 5, 7, and 9 cars. Allen's train is 2 cars shorter than Bill's. Allen, a preoperational child, can easily perceive that his train is shorter than Bill's. He goes to another part of the room and sees Cathy's train and discovers that her train is longer than Bill's. (Allen's own train is out of sight behind a table.) If Allen is asked to compare his own train with Cathy's while his is out of sight, he will not be able to answer correctly. (His reasoning, however, ought to be: A is less than B; B is less than C; and therefore A is less than C). Instead, Allen runs to get his train in order to compare it with Cathy's. Allen thus illustrates that he cannot *mentally* order the trains or other elements in a series (Piaget, 1967).

The acquisition of seriation ability generally follows a pattern of horizontal décalage similar to that found for conservation. Children first become able to deal with the seriation of length at about seven or eight. Seriation of weight is attained at about nine years, and that of volume at about eleven or twelve.

Classification.   Before the middle childhood years children have difficulty in classifying objects and in relating classification systems to one another. Piaget (1966, 1967) used beads in an experiment to illustrate children's approaches to classification. If a mixture of brown and white wooden beads is shown to children (7–12 years of age) the children will, of course, be aware that the objects belong in the general classification of *beads*. They also will be aware of the two classes present in the box—15 brown and 5 white beads. It is important, in Piaget's thinking, to note that in this period the child becomes aware of classes within classes or supra-classes and sub-classes. Supra-classes would be all-inclusive, such as beads or wooden; sub-classes would be brown beads or white beads.

In the preoperational period children can classify the brown and the white beads. If they are asked whether there are more wooden beads or more brown beads in the box, they will say that there are more brown beads than wooden beads in the box. On the other hand, concrete operational children (7 and older) will say that there are more wooden beads than brown beads in the box. Consequently, Piaget concludes that preoperational children cannot perform the logical operation of classification. Concrete operational children, however, can both add

Figure 10-6. The logical skills of concrete operational children continue to emerge in middle childhood and are revealed in Piagetian tasks such as the conservation problem. (Sybil Shelton/Monkmeyer Press Photo Service)

classes and reverse the process of classification. That is, they can add the classes of *brown* and *white* to *wooden*. They can also reduce the added classes involving color to the general class of *wooden*. This shows that children in middle childhood have the capacity to classify.

The Attainment of Conservation

One of the most extensively researched problems in Piaget's concrete operational period is that of conservation (see Chapter 7). Perhaps more than any other task, conservation tasks seem to provide striking support for Piaget's contention that children differ qualitatively in their development of thought processes or cognitive operations. The preoperational child, when faced with two equal amounts of water, one of which is poured into a container which is either wider or taller than the original (see Figure 10-7) will be convinced that the amounts of water are now *different*. In the case of the taller container, the child typically says, "It's higher up, so there must be more." From Piaget's viewpoint, the preoperational child's thinking is dominated by perception.

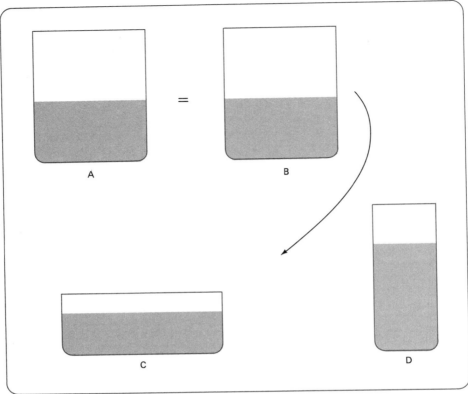

Figure 10-7. Conservation of liquids: (1) The child is asked if A and B are equal. (2) The child is then shown B transformed or poured into container C *or* D. (3) The child is questioned as to whether there is still an amount in C or D equal to that in A. (4) Piagetian explanation requires that the child justify his responses. (5) Outcomes: *Pre-operational* children judge the amount in A to be different from that in C *or* D (more in C, less in D). *Concrete operational* children judge the amount in A to be the same as that in C *or* D; they can justify their response.

Children in the concrete operational stage can readily solve the conservation problem on the basis of logic, not appearance. Children may recognize: (1) that the amount of material does not change when we change the shape of its container—matter is *invariant;* (2) that the operations could be reversed mentally and there would still be the same amount of material—*reversibility;* or (3) that whatever had been gained in height or lost in width was compensated for by a change in another dimension—*compensation/coordination.* Any of these explanations is acceptable for a Piagetian understanding of the conservation task. Concrete operational children, who are successful in their conservation task performance, have derived a solution which is qualitatively different from that of preoperational children.

Children can conserve some materials but not others. Piaget calls this lack of ability to transfer *horizontal décalage*. Even though a child may have the necessary logical understanding to master conservation of liquid material, these same mental operations do not necessarily transfer to all problems (Ginsburg & Opper, 1978). Piaget notes that there is about a two-year lag in concrete operational children's mastery of liquids (seven years of age), weight (nine years of age), and volume (eleven years of age).

We might contrast the concept of horizontal décalage with that of *vertical décalage*. While horizontal décalage refers to the lack of transfer from one type of problem to another within a particular stage, vertical décalage refers to the lack of transfer that may occur from one stage to another. Even though a child can reason logically about a concrete problem in the concrete operational period, the same type of logical skills cannot be transferred when the problem is presented verbally or abstractly. This gap between thinking skills which the child can apply successfully at the concrete operational level but not to verbal-abstract problems is called *vertical décalage*. Not until the formal operational period in adolescence is the vertical décalage overcome, and the child able to transfer general concrete operational logic to verbal-abstract problems.

The marked difference in the preoperational and concrete operational child's solution to the conservation problem provides behavioral evidence for Piaget's theory that there are qualitative changes in the child's cognitive structures, which influence the child's view of reality. These changes in cognitive structures influence the child's beliefs and conceptual understanding of every part of the environment.

In one set of investigations, a Piagetian approach to children's understanding of death was studied (Childers & Wimmer, 1971; Melear, 1973; White, Elsom & Prawat, 1978). These studies found that children's cognitive development was related to some aspects of their understanding of death. Children seem to acquire initially the understanding that death happens to all of us and is unavoidable—no one can escape it; it is universal. Later they realize that people who are dead cannot be brought back to life—death is irrevocable. Children's knowledge regarding the irrevocable nature of death would seem to be directly analogous to their knowledge of conservation (reversibility). This idea was not supported by the research, however. Children's knowledge of conservation was related only to their knowledge of the *universal* nature of death. The *irrevocable* nature of death was not significantly related to conservation (White, Elsom, & Prawat, 1978).

Children's Understanding of Causality

Piaget has found that children do not understand the concept of causal relationships (A produces B) until quite late in the concrete operational period. Young children believe that any two events which follow each other closely in time are causally linked. Piaget calls such linkages *juxtaposition* (Ginsburg & Opper, 1978). With juxtaposition children are just as likely to accept the idea that A produces B as they are to think that B produces A. As long as the two events occur close together in time, they can be linked by juxtaposition and seen as causally related.

Support for juxtaposition has come from studies in which the verbal questioning method (Piaget's *clinical method*) has been used. Piaget found the following juxtaposition responses indicative of children's failure to comprehend causality (Phillips, 1975):

1. The man fell from his bicycle because _____?
   Child: Because he broke his arm.
2. I teased that dog because_____?
   Child: Because he bit me.
3. I've lost my pen because_____?
   Child: Because I'm not writing.

For these children, the juxtaposition of two events is interpreted as causality. At about nine to ten years of age Piaget finds that children can understand simple causality as more than just juxtaposition.

The Question of Stages

Piaget has represented the major intellectual developments of children as following a sequence of stages. The successive attainment of increasingly complex, logical abilities is the result of interaction with the environment and its demands. Any theory of developmental stages must consider the extent to which the observed sequence is dependent on maturation (biological factors), experience (learning), and the interaction of the two. It is often extremely difficult to make this assessment. Piaget, of course, is an interactionist on this issue.

Some examples from studies of children's reasoning will help to define the problem. It has been suggested that children understand the concept of "more" before they acquire the concept of "less." This has been found to be the case for children of three and four years of age (Palermo, 1973, 1974). When asked to show which of two liquids, weights, or lines was less than another, older children made fewer errors than younger children. Since younger children have greater difficulty in understanding "less," they should also show correspondingly more difficulty in cognitive tasks which require the use of the word, such as conservation tasks.

Some investigators maintain that the understanding of "less" is dependent on the child's maturational level (Trehub & Abramovitch, 1978). They suggest that children's confusion of the terms "less" and "more" arises from the younger child's *nonlinguistic* preference for arrays with more items or elements. Trehub and Abramovitch found that preschoolers showed a preference for arrays with more objects in them. When asked to point to either of two arrays of objects, children consistently pointed to the one with more. Such a perceptual basis for children's preferences may be based on maturation. Kavanaugh (1976), however, has questioned whether the choices given to children in experiments on understanding "more" or "less" might influence the results.

Does the sequence of children's understanding of "more" before "less" depend on nonlinguistic factors brought about by changes in the child's developing nervous system (maturation) or does it depend on the child's experiences (learning) with the terms themselves? In the latter instance, children may understand the word *more* earlier in their development because the word is part of their experiences; thus maturation may not be of much importance. Mothers ask their children to eat "a little more"; children learn to say "more" for cookies or candy and are asked to "quiet down a bit more." Mothers rarely use the word *less* in conversations with their children. We do not say "Be less careless" but "Be more careful." While the sequence of "more before less" can be observed, it is not *easy* to determine the basis of this sequence. The issue of whether we have found an innate sequence in human cognitive development or are merely seeing one thing *learned* before another remains unsettled.

In evaluating the concept of stages in cognitive development Piaget has emphasized two major criteria (Brainerd, 1978): invariant sequences and cognitive structure. According to Piaget, stages in cognitive development should follow an invariant sequence which holds for all children, in all cultures. The invariant sequence which he suggests is then said to be universal. No child skips a stage or acquires a more advanced stage before a less advanced stage. It is certainly evident, however, that the average chronological age at which a particular stage is acquired may vary from one culture to another or from one subculture or social class to another (Piaget, 1970). As long as the sequence remains intact, the stages are said to be invariant. Research has generally been supportive of this aspect of Piaget's theory (Buck-Morss, 1975).

Studies which attempt to teach or train children at an earlier stage to behave like those at a more advanced stage are of particular interest. According to Piaget, such training should not be successful, because children must develop cognitive abilities in a specific, invariant sequence. Thus, "according to Piagetian theory (e.g., Inhelder, Sinclair, and Bovet, 1974), children's ability to learn conservation concepts is constrained by their current stage of cognitive development" (Brainerd, 1978, p. 39). If a particular cognitive structure is missing or not yet developed, then certain tasks will not be mastered by the child.

Successful training has been found under only two general conditions. First, children apparently can be taught some advanced cognitive skills if these skills require rather simple judgments, rather than the complex verbal explanations often seen in Piaget's own work. Second, such successful learning generalizes only to problems that are highly similar to the ones initially taught. For example, if we train children to conserve with red liquids, there should be lots of generalization to conservation tasks in which blue or yellow liquids are used but less generalization to conservation tasks of number or matter. Training studies present problems for Piaget's emphasis on the importance of cognitive structures in development.

For Piaget cognitive operations do not exist in isolation but arise from a common set of cognitive structures. The cognitive structures of earlier stages are said to be qualitatively different from those of later stages. Piaget's own experiments provide the behavioral evidence for this aspect of the theory. If children's problem-solving behaviors change qualitatively in the course of development, then the structures assumed to underlie these behavioral changes must also undergo stage-like changes according to Piaget.

While few psychologists can dispute the fact that there is indeed evidence for the qualitiative changes in children's overt problem-solving behaviors seen in Piaget's experiments, some psychologists question whether these qualitative changes stem from *internal* changes in the child's cognitive structures (Brainerd, 1977; Bruner, 1973). That is, Piaget's theory has been criticized but rarely have his observations or behavioral evidence been questioned. You may recall the work of Gagné (1970) mentioned in the beginning of this chapter. He believes that the behaviors reported by Piaget may be better explained as the results of a cumulative, hierarchical arrangement of learning.

If one measure of the worth of a theory is the amount of research and debate which it generates, then few could argue that Piaget has had and will continue to have a major impact in developmental psychology.

SUMMARY

We have examined a number of theorists' (Bruner, Gagné, White, and Piaget) explanations for the cognitive attainments of middle childhood. In addition, we have discussed the developmental course of such cognitive processes as perception and memory. We saw that these abilities, as well as hypothesis-formation and decision-making are important in children's development. Piaget's views on the development of concrete operations was considered in detail. A variety of logical operations such as reversibility, seriation, and classification was presented. We briefly examined the cognitive operations underlying conservation attainment as well as the child's improving ability to comprehend causality. Finally, we considered the meaning of *stages* and the importance of two lines of research—invariant sequence and training studies—for the stage concept in Piaget's theory.

RECOMMENDED READINGS

Brainerd, C. J. *Piaget's theory of intelligence.* Englewood Cliffs, N.J.: Prentice-Hall, 1978.

A high-level but clear presentation of Piaget's views. Considerable time is spent examining research studies to see the extent to which Piaget's theory has been supported empirically. Appropriate critical appraisal of the theory is presented.

Flavell, J. H. *Cognitive development*. Englewood Cliffs, N.J.: Prentice-Hall, 1977.

A text which covers virtually *every* approach to the study of children's cognitive development. Adequate coverage is given to Piaget although the theory does not dominate the presentation.

Furth, H. G., and Wachs, H. *Thinking goes to school: Piaget's theory in practice.* New York: Oxford U. Press, 1974.

A fascinating account of the implementation of Piagetian principles of cognitive development in a classroom situation. The project is described from both the standpoint of theory—method—and actual day-by-day operation and is particularly easy to read and follow.

Luria, A. R. *The mind of a mnemonist*. New York: Basic Books, 1968.

One of the extensive case histories of an individual's "photographic" memory. Luria describes a series of ongoing experiments conducted to see if there were any limits to this individual's ability to remember.

11

Personality and Social Development in Middle Childhood

The years of middle childhood, from approximately six to twelve, reflect the child's involvement with and growing awareness of an ever larger environment. Children move from the security of the family and neighborhood to the unfamiliar and novel. Children who take a school bus for the first time and see their world slowly disappear from view, perhaps wonder if they will ever return home. They meet unfamiliar people such as teachers or peers whom they must trust. The child moves further into other social groups such as Little League, Boy Scouts or Girl Scouts, and summer camp. There is a gradual reduction in the dependence which children place on their parents. Children in middle childhood develop their abilities to behave independently and to handle competently time spent away from the family "nest."

With increasing independence from home and family, children have the opportunity to participate directly in life—to see things, do things, touch things, even take apart and destroy things. The world is fascinating and exciting for children. There are always new and wonderful places to explore as the world reveals its intricate mysteries to each child. Adults patiently try to answer questions of great importance: Why is the sky blue? Where do clouds come from? Why do birds build nests? Where does the sun go at night? How does the moon stay up in the sky?

As we have seen, children's social interactions with both peers and adults pro-

Figure 11-1. Children increase their involvement with the larger environment as they move beyond the family and home.

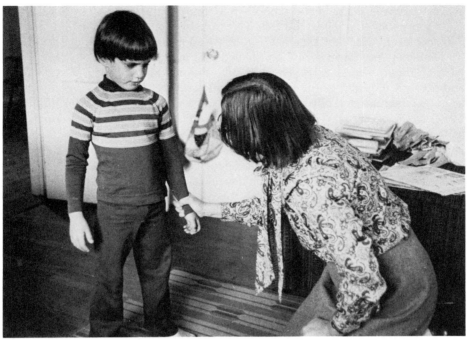

Figure 11-2. Physical development is rapid during middle childhood and may serve as the basis of positive evaluations from the peer group. (Michael Kagan/Monkmeyer Press Photo Service)

vide a valuable means for change. Social exchanges allow children to understand their culture, their family, and their particular place in the social order. These interactions allow children to begin to see and understand their uniqueness. As they discover what it means to be human, they find that there are social rights, duties, and responsibilities—central themes for these years.

Peers begin to have greater social influence in children's development during middle childhood. The impact of the peer group is understandable since the child spends less and less time in the home. We know from observation that peers, both in school and in play groups, invent secret passwords, establish clubs, have special signs, share certain jokes, and generally carry on activities which derive special significance because they are free from adult control. When we see children at this age it is difficult to believe that their behavior fluctuates from one situation to another. Parents, for example, may see only the "quiet" side of their child's behavior in the home. A teacher's description of a loud, boisterous, aggressive child, however, may lead parents to ask, "Are you sure you are talking about our Billy?" Barker and Wright were the first to recognize the importance of observing children in many different situations in order to understand their behavior more completely. In the book *One Boy's Day* (1951), they illustrated how behavior differs in various activity groups at home and at school. They found that it was necessary to understand the situation in which the child was studied; e.g., roles may be adopted on the playground which are different from those adopted in the home or school.

Generally, psychoanalytic theorists find that middle childhood involves a quieting of the instinctual urges. They describe the period as *latency* (Freud, 1938) and see it as the calm before the storm of adolescence. It is a time when children learn cultural rules and obligations and develop a *personal* set of values (Baldwin, 1967). In the psychoanalytic framework, there are no new conflicts developing, but earlier conflicts are becoming better and better resolved. With the acquisition of personal values, for example, the child's superego becomes more organized and well-defined. The lack of additional, new conflicts contributes to children's increased tolerance of others. Children develop skill and tact as methods for dealing with peers who block their goals. They become more and more reluctant to use force or "tattletales" as tactics of control.

Both Baldwin (1967,1969) and Maddi (1976) disagree with the psychoanalytic view that middle childhood is quiescent in terms of new conflicts and sexual interest. Problem behaviors do occur, and rebelliousness is common in the latter part of middle childhood. While boy-girl relationships are usually antagonistic, there is some interaction and interest in the opposite sex. This interest may be expressed initially as rivalry between same-sex play groups; such as who can run faster—boys or girls? Such competition may be linked to identification with the same sex parent. By the end of this period there is preliminary cross-sex interest, but these early interactions are transitory and impersonal. There is none of the intense personal involvement characteristic of adolescence. Cross-sex interest and relations in late middle childhood are tentative, casual, and experimental. In sum, rebelliousness, early cross-sex rivalry, and later cross-sex interactions contradict the psychoanalytic description of this developmental period (Baldwin, 1967).

Erik Erikson describes the period of middle childhood in somewhat different terms. As explained in Chapter 2, this is a time of basic conflict between a sense of "industry versus inferiority." Erikson sees children as basically industrious, deriving great pleasure from their ability to become active and competent participants in the process of living. Independent behaviors, however, lead to a careful evaluation of their skills and abilities. Often children experience self-doubts *(inferiority)* as they attempt to meet the expectations and obligations imposed by family and school. Erikson sees middle childhood as a paradox. On the one hand, industry brings pleasure and satisfaction to children because they respond independently and achieve success, acquire new skills, and develop increased control over their environment. On the other hand, even though these newly acquired talents bring competence, children quickly discover that some others are more adept in these abilities.

GROWTH AND DEVELOPMENT

To adults such as parents, grandparents, and teachers, the most noticeable change during middle childhood is the even, steady, and continuous process of physical growth. The average height for six-year-olds is about 46 inches (not quite 4 feet tall), but by the time he or she has reached the threshold of adolescence, the average twelve-year-old is almost 5 feet tall and weighs nearly 100 pounds. For some children, of course, adolescence begins much earlier than the teens, and in these children the "growth spurt" may occur between the tenth and twelfth years. We are discussing only average expectations. Since the growth spurt marks the beginning of sexual maturity, it would be inaccurate to characterize middle childhood as a stable period of growth for all children (Tanner, 1970).

Changes in Physical Growth and Development

It is important to recognize the influence of biological factors underlying physical growth. Children of similar ages in a classroom will display a wide range of heights. Yet, when an individual child's growth in height is plotted over time, there is relatively stable, consistent growth. Evidence from a number of studies (Bayley, 1954; Tanner, 1970) indicates that as children grow older their height tends to become much like their parents; there is a genetic similarity in physical stature between children and parents.

We also see the role of heredity on the differential growth patterns of boys and girls. At the beginning of the period of middle childhood, boys are slightly larger than girls, but by the end of the period the tendency is reversed. Boys tend to have more bone and muscle while girls tend to have more fatty tissue (Breckinridge and Murphy, 1969).

Less observable changes in the child's overall body functioning and internal organs accompany the steady changes in height and weight in these years. For example, the observed changes in body growth reflect the corresponding growth of the reproductive organs as well as the testes and ovaries. In elementary school-children the rate of chemical reactions taking place in the cells *(cell metabolism)* is nearly twice that of adults. By the end of middle childhood, however, the rate has decreased and approximates that of adults. Thus, even physiological processes are altered.

Environment and Physical Growth and Development

The relationship of environment to physical growth or body make-up is not simple. Individual variability in growth may be influenced by nutrition as well as a number of other factors (Maresh & Beal, 1970). Sex differences in the amount of food consumed appear pronounced during the latter period of middle childhood. Boys consume more food on the average than girls (see Figure 11-3).

Socioeconomic factors may influence growth indirectly. Children who live under conditions of extreme poverty may be at risk when we consider health hazards such as disease, injury, or malnutrition. Fortunately, such environmental factors must be extreme before they will alter children's inherited pattern of physical growth. Children's growth is usually affected adversely only when detrimental

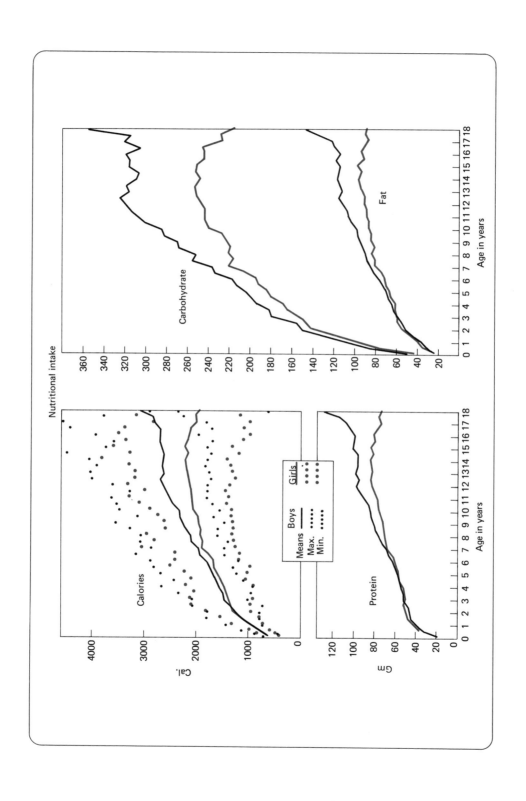

environmental influences have occurred and persisted over a long period of time. Even if a child's physical growth has been retarded, appropriate intervention can reestablish natural growth patterns (Krogman, 1970). Our ability to redirect physical growth is clearly greater with younger children. The most common cause of physical retardation appears to be poor nutrition. It is also one of the easiest causes to correct through a diet enhanced by nutrients, calories, and proteins (Bailey, 1970). Groups like the World Health Organization of the United Nations are increasingly attempting to offset such nutritional deficiencies.

With an adequate environment, the general health of children shows improvement during middle childhood. There is a decrease in the rate of acute illnesses, although chronic illness becomes more prevalent (Vaughn, 1975). The number of injuries in the home decreases as the child continues to explore the larger environment on his own. A corresponding increase in injuries occurs away from the home—in climbing trees, playing on school gym equipment, or in organized sports like football. Injuries away from home continue to increase in number throughout the school years.

Psychological Effects of Physical Growth and Development

Children have predictable reactions to their own physical development. Many of these reactions are the result of socialization or culture rather than biology. Boys are often more adept at activities which require the use of large muscles (football or basketball), while girls seem to perform better tasks requiring the use of fine muscles (drawing, painting, or writing). These reactions, of course, do not reflect innate sex differences. They mirror our society's differential encouragement of activities which are sex-typed. Given appropriate support, the pattern of physical interests could be redirected.

Nevertheless, because of the sex-typed activities present in our society advanced physical maturity for boys is often an asset. Being taller, stronger, and bigger provides boys an advantage on the playground or in sports. This advantage serves to enhance further their status within the peer group which usually values athletic skills. Any delays in physical development or less-than-average stature and size usually present problems for boys. Childhood nicknames, such as "Shrimp" or "Shorty," are good indicators of the type of social reactions from the peer group with which physically underdeveloped boys must contend.

Advanced physical maturity, especially during middle childhood, may present problems for girls. Unlike boys, girls with advanced physical development may feel isolated and uncomfortable with their less-well-developed age-mates. Frequently advanced physical development results in the presence of secondary sex characteristics, such as breast development. Often these changes contribute to girls' feel-

Figure 11-3.   Mean intake of calories, carbohydrate, fat, and protein of boys and girls, showing range of caloric intake. (From M. Maresh and V. Beal, A longitudinal survey of nutrition intake, body size, and tissue measurement in health subjects during growth. *Monographs of the Society for Research in Child Development,* 35 [whole No. 140], p. 35. Copyright 1970 by the Society for Research in Child Development. By permission.)

ings of self-consciousness and separation from their peer group. Once past elementary school, however, adolescent girls who have shown advanced physical development appear to be at an advantage (Faust, 1969). With peers who are similarly developed, advanced physical development becomes an asset, rather than the liability it was previously. Thus, the effects of advanced physical development for girls are far more complex than for boys.

Why should physical development and the diverse body builds of children produce psychological reactions at all? Sheldon (1940) originally assumed that people have characteristic reactions to specific body types. Thus, our personalities may be partly the result of how others respond to us—in particular, to the way we look. Sheldon recognized three basic body builds: (1) a round body type, or *endomorph*, like the pear-shaped appearance of Santa Claus; (2) a thin, angular body type, or *ectomorph*, like the "pencil-shaped" appearance of Abraham Lincoln; and (3) a muscular body type, or *mesomorph*, like the "V-shaped" appearance of Muhammad Ali. In general there is only limited support for Sheldon's notions that these body builds are associated with specific personality characteristics. That is, all fat children are not jolly nor are all tall, thin children "intellectual."

Walker (1962), however, found that children's body type was partially related to teachers' ratings of their behavior. Those children who were rated by their teachers as most active and aggressive were found to have a muscular or mesomorph type of body build. In another study, older children and adolescents were shown to have clear preferences for pictures of mesomorph body builds over the other two types (Lerner & Korn, 1972). Staffieri (1972) also reported that both boys and girls have developed strong preferences for the "ideal" mesomorph body type by five years of age. Children who fit this physical image are clearly at an advantage in the peer group.

Perhaps a more limiting body type for children to deal with is the endomorph. Nicknames developed by each generation of children show that negative concepts are frequently part of peer evaluations: "Fatty Fatty," "Tub-O-Lard," or "The Blob." Being fat is not strictly the result of overeating but involves inherited factors as well. Many physicians recognize that the best time to begin to reduce weight is during infancy and the preschool years (Heald & Khan, 1976), which means education of parents. Overweight children often develop predictable reactions, such as defensive joking or denial of the problem. Most endomorphs do not receive the overwhelming support and positive acceptance of the peer group that mesomorphs receive. For boys there will be difficulties in competing in physical activities and group sports, while for girls there will be difficulties because of the cultural standard for physical attractiveness—thin and trim.

THE ROLE OF THE FAMILY IN PERSONALITY AND SOCIAL DEVELOPMENT

The family as a social unit exists in every society on earth. The family is the major link between the child and society. It perpetuates the social order and provides continuity in socialization between the child and larger social institutions such as the school, church, or government. Because of the importance of the family as an initial socializing agent, there is cyclical concern for its stability and impact. Is the family likely to decline in importance or in the effectiveness of its socialization? The impact of communal living, assigning sex education to the schools, and urban renewal are often taken as signs of the reduced importance of the family.

The family is sensitive to the activities of other structures in our society. Its important role in the socialization of children has remained relatively intact for centuries, however. Generally, other social institutions seek the support and approval of the family in order to maintain their status and impact (Blood, 1971). In addition to general socialization the family also serves the primary needs of all members: for food, shelter, and reproduction of our species. On a psychological level the family provides a source of affection and genuine concern for all members. It sustains individuals' beliefs in the value and importance of their existence. In our own society, the family unit consists of two generations—parents and children. In other societies and at other times in our own history, however, an extended family unit could be identified. Extended family units consisted of either three generations (including grandparents) or of more distantly related relatives.

In modern society the income generated by the parents or the vocational occupation of the head of the household defines social class. Social class provides a rough gauge of where the family lives, the quality of living, and the status of the family in the community. Families from higher social class groups are able to provide a host of benefits to their children. Roff, Sells, and Golden (1972) have found support for the general advantages experienced by children from higher income families as compared to those with lower family income. Their data show that higher social class is associated with: "loving, warm" parents rather than "rejecting" ones; mothers who are "matter-of-fact" in child-rearing rather than punishing or demanding; and general agreement on child-rearing principles by mothers and fathers. Children from these social classes show higher IQ test scores, more positive self-concept, fewer health problems, and are rated by their teachers as more outgoing, friendly, and considerate (Roff, Sells, & Golden, 1972).

The Influence of Parents

Beginning with Freud, psychologists have maintained a strong interest in the role of parents on children's personality and social development (Baumrind, 1971; Becker, 1964; Schaefer, 1965; Sears, Maccoby & Levin, 1957). Most research has assumed a unidirectional model of causality, saying that parents influence their children. Although different techniques are used from one study to another, there seems to be general agreement as to the pattern of personality and social characteristics produced by particular types of child-rearing. The research also suggests looking at the general child-rearing approach or atmosphere rather than any specific parent behavior in isolation.

The parent atmosphere or general child-rearing approach has been defined by two dimensions (Becker, 1964; Schaefer, 1959, 1961): (1) warmth-acceptance vs. cold-rejectance, and (2) autonomy-permissiveness vs. control-restrictiveness. *Warm-accepting* parents provide understanding and emotional support for their children. They respond positively to their children's appropriate behaviors ("Good, I'm pleased that you cleared the table tonight"). They are generally approving and accepting of their children and allow their children's needs to take precedence over their own. Such parents easily express physical affection (hugging, kissing) and typically provide an explanation for discipline. The *cold-rejecting* parent shows the opposite characteristics.

In examining the second dimension we can focus on *restrictive-controlling* parents. Typically, they impose a large number of rules in the home which their children are expected to follow. The rules involve virtually every aspect of the child's behavior, from proper table manners to neatness and care of the furniture. Most importantly, the rules are enforced rigidly and inflexibly. For example, when bedtime is set at 8:30 P.M. there is no bending of the rule to permit an extra five minutes of TV or yet another drink of water. These parents expect their children to be obedient and to follow directions with no backtalk, sarcasm, or muttering. Restrictive-controlling parents do not usually tolerate aggression in their children. At the other end of the dimension are parents who are *autonomy-permissive* in orientation. They display the direct opposite patterns in relationships with their children (Becker, 1964; Schaefer, 1959, 1961).

The general child-rearing atmosphere in the home is represented by the joint combination of these two dimensions (e.g., the four quadrants described in Figure 11-4). In order to see how children develop under these different combinations, it is helpful to study the extreme ends of the two dimensions. But we should remember that few parents will be either as extreme as we portray or as uniformly consistent as we illustrate. Our descriptions should be thought of as representing the most typical child-rearing atmosphere which is provided for the child. The child-rearing atmosphere provided by the four possible combinations of these two factors results in very different types of children. We can briefly look at each of these combinations.

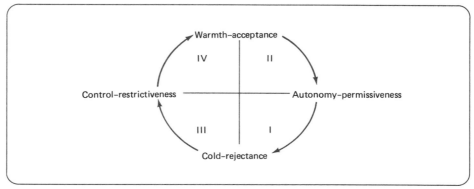

Figure 11-4. The dimensions of parent behavior. (Adapted from Becker, 1964, Schaeffer, 1959, 1961.)

I. Cold-Rejectance with Autonomy-Permissiveness.   Parents who provide this type of child-rearing atmosphere typically have children who show acting out behaviors, rebelliousness, and patterns of delinquency. There is a tendency for these children to be "loners" or social isolates. They often have emotional problems and are rather immature. These effects appear to result from the excessive freedom which is provided by non-caring parents. Children feel rejected and often emotionally starved.

II. Warmth-Acceptance with Autonomy-Permissiveness.   A rather different pattern emerges in children's personality and social development when freedom is provided but is coupled with emotional concern. Children are given love and a high degree of emotional acceptance. Parents are unable or unwilling to set limits for their children. Rules are rarely developed or enforced. The results of this child-rearing atmosphere of "over-indulgence" are self-centered children; usually the "spoiled child" has experienced this type of child-rearing. Children fail to develop adequate impulse control and place their needs and desires above those of others. The ability to get along well with peers is obviously impaired.

III. Cold-Rejectance with Control-Restrictiveness.   This atmosphere appears to be associated with children who tend to be conforming and submissive. Such children are rarely leaders, but rather followers. It seems that these children readily accept or bend to the will of others. As a result, they appear to be passive, shy, and anxious to win the approval of both peers and adults. Although parents control or dictate their children's every response, children do not feel warmly accepted by such emotionally distant parents. Thus children continue to need the structure and direction of others as a guide for their behavior. And, by following such guidelines, the child develops feelings of acceptance and approval. We would not expect very high self-concept or the capacity to make independent decisions in such children.

IV. Warmth-Acceptance with Control-Restrictiveness.   Under this child-rearing atmosphere we see children's personality has many of the overtones described in III above. The independence of the child is threatened by highly controlling parents who expect their children to "toe the mark." With the warmth and acceptance, however, children perceive their parents as concerned and involved. In fact, such parents are often seen as too involved with their children, and the term "overprotective" is used to describe this type of child-rearing atmosphere. Overprotection leads to highly dependent children who are extremely cooperative with peers and adults in general. At least in the early elementary grades, teachers enjoy having such docile children in class. They are seen as "model" children who do not show extreme behaviors. They are not likely to be too compliant or too rebellious, too loud or too quiet—rather they are moderate. Such children are not generally very independent, responsible, or creative.

Guidelines for Parents

Is there an "ideal" parent atmosphere for children's personality and social development? The recommendations of child-care experts who write specifically for parents (Ginott, Salk, Spock) appear to provide some general agreement. Often these experts stress that children should develop traits of responsibility, self-initiative, achievement, goal-direction, and independence. To foster these characteristics in children they advocate that parents provide an atmosphere of Warmth-Acceptance coupled with *moderate* Autonomy-Permissiveness (Quadrant II in Figure 11-4). The key to success is that parents must not be too permissive, too lax, or too indulgent; otherwise the "spoiled child" will emerge. Parents are strongly encouraged to exert some controls over their children, to make demands on their children, and to establish norms for their children's everyday behaviors.

These recommendations, as parents soon discover, are difficult to implement in an absolute sense. It is difficult to find the right blend of freedom and control within a framework of Warmth-Acceptance. Some parents begin to rely on the individual assessment of each of their children for clues as to what they should do. This type of concern and evaluation represents a major shift in conceptualizing parent-child relations (Bell, 1971): Children can influence their parents to adopt particular child-rearing styles. The model suggested by Bell is seen as bi-directional or *interactionist* in nature. As such it contrasts sharply with the one-way or unidirectional model we evaluated previously (Figure 11-4).

Bell (1971) notes that the child is an integral part of the child-rearing atmosphere or style adopted by parents. Parents have to determine which behaviors must be controlled because they occur too often (upper-limit control) and which because they do not occur often enough (lower-limit control). We could apply this bi-directional model to the "ideal" parental atmosphere advocated by child-care experts. Successful parents are those who constantly monitor their children's development and recognize when controls should be tightened or loosened. Parents may have to make different decisions regarding the control of children, even within the same family. Similarly, successful parents see that even the same child needs different control strategies as he or she gets older.

Baumrind (1971), in exploring the "ideal" parental atmosphere, has made similar suggestions. She was interested in the parental antecedents of competence in young children. Competence was seen as encompassing both social responsibilities (relating well with others) and independence. Her findings suggest that competence is fostered by "authoritative" parents. *Authoritative* parents are moderately controlling and, at the same time, concerned about their children. They are genuinely interested in their children's development and present needs. They are warm but firm in their demands for obedience to rules and are seen as supportive. Competence failed to emerge when parents displayed *permissive* approaches or *authoritarian* approaches towards the child (Baumrind, 1971). The *permissive* approach describes parents who make too few demands, use too few controls, and have too few expectancies for their child's behavior. On the other hand, the *authoritarian* parent is far too demanding, rigid, and controlling. Baumrind sees competence as emerging from authoritative parents who are neither too lax nor too demanding of their children. She also supports the bi-directional model (Bell, 1971) as a factor in promoting competence.

Authoritative parents alone recognize that their child-rearing style must take into account the age or maturity of the child and that they cannot be inflexible. They do not choose a global style and use it in most parent-child encounters as do the authoritarian or permissive parents. Instead, we find that authoritative parents are uniquely willing to take the time to evaluate each child-parent situation. They evaluate on an individual basis the needs of each of their children and the demands of the given situation (Baumrind, 1971).

Is any type of child-rearing atmosphere particularly negative? Again, there appears to be some moderate consensus that inconsistency in most forms is rather detrimental to children's personality and social development. Extreme parental inconsistency suggests to a child that there is no predictable relationship between the child's behavior and the parent's responses. This is sometimes seen in the background of severely disturbed, schizophrenic children (Zax & Cowen, 1976). In order to develop a clear, rational understanding of the social environment, children must see that it has order and predictability. Thus, consistent parent responses to children are desirable.

Inconsistency in discipline is also found in virtually every instance of child abuse (Parke & Collmer, 1975). Not only do abusive parents provide an inconsistent approach, they also employ harsh physical punishment as well. It has been repeatedly observed that child-abusive parents were abused by their own parents (Parke & Collmer, 1975). Through the rather simple processes of modeling and imitation, tactics used by one generation of parents may be adopted by the next generation as well. Attempts to deal with child abuse have centered on breaking this cycle for one generation. Groups such as Parents Anonymous provide support and guidance for parents who are child abusive.

Father Absence

One way to determine the specific influence of any factor in children's personality development is to look at what happens when that factor is missing or lacking. Research shows that when fathers are absent from the home during a child's early development the consequences on the child's personality are far more detrimental than when the absence occurs after the child is five years old (Lynn, 1974). Baggett (1967) reported that adjustment was influenced by the reason for the father's absence. For males, father absence due to death was not as detrimental as absence due to divorce, separation, or desertion. For females, father absence due to death interfered with overall adjustment and was about as detrimental as absence due to other reasons. In all cases, children were no more than eight years of age when the father absence occurred.

Hetherington (1972) also examined the effects of father absence on adolescent girls. She compared the personalities and behaviors of girls from intact homes with those who experienced father absence due either to death or divorce. Father absence altered the interactions of these girls with other males, producing one of two extreme reactions. In cases of divorce, girls actively and aggressively sought the attention and physical attention of men. In cases of father absence due to death, however, the reaction of the girls was active avoidance of male peers and a preference for other girls as companions.

These differences were further supported in an interview situation. When a male interviewer was present, daughters of divorcees displayed nonverbal signs of openness and acceptance: relaxed positions in the chair, leaning forward as they talked. However, the opposite pattern emerged in the interviews of girls whose fathers had died. They assumed rigid postures, sat upright in the chair, and tended to draw away from the male interviewer. In interviews, Hetherington (1972) found that both groups of father absent girls expressed more insecurity about their ability to relate to males than girls from intact homes. Each group of father absent girls adopted a different way of dealing with this insecurity in relating to males: with divorce over-involvement was found, and with death avoidance was more typical.

Interviews with the mothers of these girls revealed that father absence led to maternal overprotection. The earlier the father absence had occurred, the more overprotection mothers were likely to display. Divorced mothers as a group tended to express more negative orientations towards life and themselves.

Father absence has also been found to interfere with the sex-role development of boys (Burton, 1972). Father-absent boys tend to show conflict and uncertainty regarding appropriate masculine orientations (Lynn, 1974; Lynn & Sawry, 1959). Some studies show that this results in boys assuming a "super-macho" role as overcompensation. In other research, however, boys may appear more feminine in orientation. For example, on standardized tests like the SAT boys from intact homes typically show higher quantitative (math) than verbal (English) scores. Boys who experienced father absence, however, have a pattern that is reversed: higher verbal than quantitative scores (Carlsmith, 1964; Hetherington & Deur, 1972).

Birth Order

The particular place which a child occupies within the family system may also influence his or her personality and social development. One of the more fascinating ways to study such influences is to look at ordinal position. The social structure of the family has been of interest to psychologists since the early work of Alfred Adler (1931), who derived general personality types which should emerge from one's ordinal position in the family.

Today we see that some of these characteristics tend to persist. The firstborn child is a true experiment for new parents. Most parents, after this first attempt, become less anxious and more secure, easygoing, and consistent in their childrearing (Lasko, 1954). The firstborn is closest to the parents, and no other child in the family experiences the same period of exclusive association. The firstborn child is at least for some time an only child. The general findings among firstborns suggest that these children are adult-oriented: successful, serious, studious, leaders, academically skilled. In their personalities, however, we see a need to seek out the approval and company of others, moderate anxiety, and a conservative outlook (Altus, 1966; Belmont & Marolla, 1973; Warren, 1966). Middle children are said to feel emotionally rejected, since they have never experienced the luxury of an exclusive relationship with their parents as did their oldest brother or sister. They are seen as seeking emotional support outside the family, from their friends, and thus must become socially skilled. They typically choose to be successful in areas in which they will not have to compete with the firstborn. The results of some studies suggest that middle children do not excel in academically oriented areas. Last born children remain in the eyes of themselves and other family members perennial "babies." Because they are last born they receive extra consideration and attention from both their older siblings and their parents. It is hard for the youngest child to want to grow up since there are many satisfactions derived by remaining within the family. It is also hard for parents to see their last born child grow up and mature.

While these general statements obviously need to be qualified by the sex of the child occupying any ordinal position and the spacing of the children in the family (Sutton-Smith & Rosenberg, 1969), there are additional problems in these generalizations. First, it is important to discover the specific effects which are the result of parent-child interactions and those which are the result of sibling-sibling interactions. Also, many of the above generalizations may hold only in small families on which most of the research was done or for a particular period in our cultural history. Schooler (1972, 1973) notes that many of the earlier birth order-personality relationships have not been supported in more recent studies. For example, in the 1960s firstborns were found to be overrepresented in psychological studies when volunteers were solicited. They were thought to be more willing to respond to social pressure or social influence (Sampson & Hancock, 1967). By the 1970s the susceptibility of firstborns to social influence was more difficult to see, however. That is, fewer and fewer studies have found firstborns more likely to volunteer for research investigations (Roodin, Broughton, & Vaught, 1978; Roodin & Vaught, 1974; Rosenthal & Rosnow, 1975).

Firstborns, in exclusive interaction with their parents during early infancy, may receive more stimulation and verbal interaction from their parents than children who come later. Later born children may not receive the quality, intensity, or depth of parent involvement, perhaps for no other reason than lack of time and energy. Breland (1974), for example, feels that intellectual abilities and birth order are related. He found that as children were further and further removed from their parents (as birth order increased) their scores on standardized tests of achievement were lower and lower. Not only did firstborns tend to score higher than children from other ordinal positions, but children from last born positions had a tendency to score lower than children from higher ordinal positions.

It has been similarly suggested that when the spacing of siblings is compressed so that older and younger children differ by only a few years, lowered intellectual abilities will be found among the younger children. In contrast, families who permit broader spacing between siblings will promote greater intellectual abilities (Zajonc & Markus, 1975; Zajonc, 1976). With closer spacing, the siblings just ahead of the younger children will be less developed themselves. They will be more like the younger children than like their more effective parents; the verbal stimulation and general enrichment provided by older siblings will be less effective than that provided in families with wider spacing. In families with wider spacing, younger children will experience greater intellectual advances since their older siblings will be more similar to parents. In fact, Zajonc and Markus have found that with extremely broad spacing younger siblings benefit most intellectually. It seems that the greater the opportunity for adult or adult-like interaction the more children's intellectual abilities will advance. Thus, we see the importance not only of spacing of siblings within the family but also of family size.

Siblings

Sutton-Smith and Rosenberg (1969) have found that older siblings have a significant influence on the sex-role development of younger brothers and sisters. We see that a younger brother has at least two masculine models: father and older brother. Younger brothers are usually more masculine in orientation than their older brothers. Similarly, younger sisters are typically more highly feminine than their older sisters. They, also, reflect the impact of having multiple feminine models in the family: older sister and mother. Similarly, older cross-sex siblings influence their younger counterparts. Older brothers seem to "masculinize" a younger sister, while older sisters serve to "feminize" younger brothers.

Sutton-Smith and Rosenberg (1969) also reported that interacting with younger siblings of the same sex produces *reactive effects* on an older brother or sister. They found that older boys are rarely as masculine as their younger brothers and older girls are analogously rarely as feminine as their younger sisters. Similar reactive effects on older siblings are seen in cross-sex situations. Older boys become more masculine when younger sisters are part of the family and older girls become more feminine with younger brothers. Exactly why this type of reactive role is assumed by the older child has not been determined.

Within the family children may develop specialized roles in order to meet their needs for self-recognition and individuality. No child enjoys being compared or evaluated with another sibling. We have already seen that, in order to avoid such comparisons, middle children are unlikely to assume the roles previously adopted by the first born. In an older study, Bossard and Boll (1955) investigated the development of roles in families in which there were six or more siblings. They discovered that children in each family attempted to specialize and evolve distinctive roles. Within these large families they discerned eight unique roles which children usually adopted (Table 11-1). As we can see from their work, roles are actively chosen by children as a means of expressing their individuality. Some of these roles should be relatively easy to employ outside the family and will bring few role conflicts or problems of adjustment. The studious role, for example, is a good illustration. Other roles, however, may require more difficult problems of adjustment. Conflict may arise when a child must give up the satisfactions derived from playing a particular role within the family and assume an alternative one demanded by some societal institution like the school. The role of the spoiled child is a good example of this

Table 11-1
EIGHT TYPES OF ROLES ADOPTED BY CHILDREN FROM LARGE FAMILIES TO GAIN RECOGNITION AND ATTENTION

1.	Responsible	Typically oldest children who willingly serve as parental substitutes. They are both looked up to and seen as bossy by their siblings.
2.	Popular, Sociable, Well-Liked	Typically the second born. A style of responding in which personal charm is employed.
3.	Socially Ambitious	The social butterfly. Children who are interested in social contacts with non-family members. Usually adopted by girls in 3rd, 4th, or 5th birth order.
4.	Studious Role	Children who do well in school and are quiet, hardworking, and methodical. Withdraw from siblings.
5.	Self-Centered Isolate	Children who are secretive and stubbornly antisocial toward siblings and/or life. Often away from home.
6.	Irresponsible	Children who are largely able to sit back and withdraw from family responsibilities
7.	Unwell	Children with physical, chronic, or hypochrondriacal illness. They may have learned to utilize their illness to gain special favors or to justify their failures.
8.	Spoiled	Usually the last born, for whom overindulgence has been provided by family members.

Source: Adapted from J.H.S. Bossard and E.S. Boll, "Personality Roles in the Large Family," *Child Development*, 1955, **26**, pp. 71–78.

problem. In smaller families siblings may adopt more than one of the roles identified by Bossard and Boll. With multiple roles, adjustment to the larger society may be a bit easier, especially if part of one's role-orientation can still be maintained within the family.

School Performance

7:30. – 7:38 – 8 minutes – 313–318.

In our society one of the best predictors of school success is the family's position in the social structure. Middle-class children are much more successful in school than children from the lower social classes. In other countries, however, the relationship between social class and school success may be more complex. In a recent study, children's school success and school attendance was studied in a rural setting in Guatemala (Irwin, Engle, Yarbrough, Klein, & Townsend, 1978). School was not legally required for children and therefore provides an interesting contrast to our own culture. Children's school performance in the early grades was not found to be related to the social class of families. Success in school was related to the intellectual abilities of the children prior to their enrollment. In this rural setting, it seemed that parents carefully assessed each child's potential to profit from school and were more likely to send only children whom they thought would benefit from the experience. Social class was found to be related only to the age at which children were initially enrolled in school.

Why is social class a good predictor of school success for children in our own society? Ginsburg (1972) feels that the socialization experiences of middle-class children best fit the demands of the typical middle-class school. He feels that many prerequisites for success in school, such as sensitivity to others, ability to delay gratification, willingness to follow directions, and ability to profit from verbal instructions, are developed best by middle-class parents. The transition to the school is therefore simple and straightforward for these children, since our schools tend to be similarly middle-class in their orientation.

Middle-class parents lean towards Baumrind's (1971) authoritative child-rearing approach. Numerous studies have found a relationship between an authoritative parental atmosphere and school performance. Success is most likely when children have been given moderate autonomy from their parents in a warm and open atmosphere. School success is also encouraged when parents demand excellence from their children. Additionally, we find that school success is fostered by parents who emphasize the positive aspects of their children's successes and who provide more positive than negative feedback (Fesbach, 1973). In general, the authoritative approach leads to a positive self-concept which is still another factor in children's school success. Thus, the process of socialization is assumed to underlie, in part, the relationship between school success and social class.

Mothers from different social classes do employ different behaviors in interaction with their children. In some studies mothers were asked to teach their children a specific task: how to build a house, how to copy a design, or how to sort blocks (Bee, Van Egeren, Streissguth, Nyman, & Leckie, 1969; Brophy, 1970). Brophy (1970) found that lower-class mothers did not provide as much preliminary instruction, information, or preparation (e.g., orientation to the task and verbal instructions) to their children as did middle-class mothers. Although middle-class and lower-class mothers gave equivalent feedback, once their children made a response, middle-class children were far more "prepared" for the task to be performed.

Hess and Shipman (1968) also found maternal behaviors were related to social class. Black mothers from different social classes were asked to respond to a hypothetical question about their preschool children: "Let's imagine your child is old enough to go to school for the first time. How do you think you would prepare him? What would you do or tell him?" Two general responses were evident: (1) middle-class mothers tended to prepare their children with *instructives* in which rules were justified or explained; or (2) lower-class mothers focused on *imperatives* in which rules were simply expressed as a series of commands. We can illustrate these two types of responses:

1. *Instructives:* First of all, I would take him to see his new school. We would talk about the building, and after seeing the school I would tell him that he would

meet new children who would be his friends and who would work and play with him. I would explain to him that the teacher would be his friend, would help him and guide him in school, and that he should do as she tells him to, that she will be his mother while he is away from home.

2. *Imperatives:* I would tell him he going to school and he have to sit down and mind the teacher and be a good boy, and I show him how when they give him milk, you know, how he's supposed to take his straw and do, and not put nothing on the floor when he get through. (Hess and Shipman, 1968, p. 96. By permission.)

Hess and Shipman reported that imperatives were nearly three times more prevalent in the responses of mothers from lower classes than from middle classes. Clearly such differences suggest there are differences in the general orientation to school which parents from different social classes provide for their children.

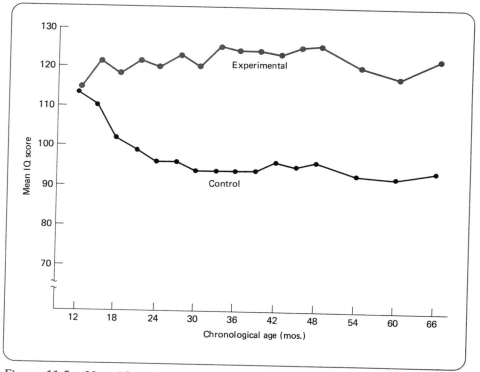

Figure 11-5.   Mean IQ performance with increasing age for the experimental and control groups. (From R. Heber and H. Garber, The Milwaukee project: a study of the use of family intervention to prevent cultural–familial mental retardation. In. B. Z. Friedlander, G. M. Sterrit, and G. E. Kirk, eds., *Exceptional infant: assessment and intervention.* Vol. 3. New York: Bruner/Mazel, 1975, p. 429. By permission.)

Heber and Garber (1975) have also suggested that socialization experiences provided by parents with low intelligence may limit children's intellectual abilities and ultimate school success. In order to enhance children's development, they instituted a model program that initially identified mothers with low intelligence. Working with mothers who had IQ test scores of 80 or below, they developed an intervention program that began when the children were six months old. The mothers were considered culturally-familial retarded, which is retardation that arises from minimal environmental stimulation rather than brain dysfunction or organic factors. Heber and Garber attempted to provide added stimulation and environmental enrichment experiences both for the children and their parents. Infants were not only seen in the home and sent to day-care through preschool years, but their mothers also received instruction in homemaking skills, occupational training, and child-training classes. By focusing on the total environment of the child and initiating the program early, Heber and Garber demonstrated dramatic success with these "high risk" children, who were themselves likely to have low IQ scores and poor school achievement. As this longitudinal program unfolded, they found that, compared to control children (siblings in the same family or other children from the same social class and neighborhood), children who initiated the program showed much higher levels of intellectual ability. For example, children in this program showed scores nearly 20 to 25 points higher on IQ tests than children who did not participate in the program. Figure 11-5 illustrates that as the children have gotten older these differences have become even greater. At the last reported testing period (66 months) the experimental children in the Milwaukee Project obtained average IQ test scores of 122 compared to the control children's scores of 91—a difference of 31 points (Heber & Garber, 1975). With such early and broad-based intervention, we can certainly expect that the chance for these children's success in school has been greatly improved.

The ethnic background of the family may have a significant influence on children's school success. Lesser, Fifer, and Clark (1965) carefully assessed the verbal abilities, general reasoning skills, numerical abilities, and spatial-relations skills of children from first-grade classes. One-fourth of the 320 children in the study represented one of the following ethnic groups: Chinese, Black, Jewish, and Hispanic. As Figure 11-6 shows, sharp differences in the pattern of mental abilities were found within each of these ethnic groupings. Hispanic children tended to perform better on spatial relations and poorer on verbal ability tasks. Black children showed good verbal abilities but relatively poorer numerical abilities. Chinese children showed consistent skills in reasoning, numerical, and spatial tasks but poorer performance in verbal areas. Jewish children showed more skill in verbal tasks and poorer performance on problems of reasoning and spatial relations. To understand Figure 11-6 it is necessary to examine the skills revealed for each ethnic group, rather than to compare the level of performance from group to group.

Birns and Golden (1973) have raised the possibility that the sex of the child results in different socialization experiences within the family, which in turn influences the pattern of mental abilities. Schratz (1978) investigated this possibility in a study based on the work of Lesser, Fifer, and Clark. She noted that boys typically

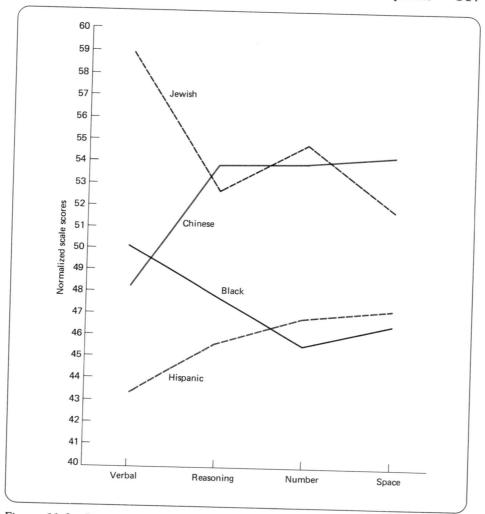

Figure 11-6. Pattern of mental ability scores for ethnic groups. (From Lesser, Fifer, and Clark, Mental abilities of children from different social classes and ethnic groups. *Monographs of the Society for Research in Child Development,* 1965 [Serial No. 102], p. 64. Copyright 1965 by the Society for Research in Child Development.

outperformed girls on all of the measures used by Lesser, Fifer, and Clark, regardless of ethnic background. But both sexes displayed similar patterns of mental abilities within ethnic groupings. Schratz worked with children who were older in order to test the possible effects of ethnicity *and* sex on mental abilities. Her subjects were from third, fourth, fifth, and ninth grades. Three ethnic groups were used: Black, Hispanic, and white children. She obtained information on children's mathematical abilities and on spatial-relational abilities. The importance of looking at both sex and ethnicity was confirmed only for the oldest children (ninth-graders). Hispanic girls obtained significantly higher spatial relation scores than Hispanic boys, and a similar but lower tendency was found among Black adolescent girls. Adolescent Hispanic girls also obtained significantly higher mathematical ability scores than Hispanic boys. No other differences in abilities were found due to either sex or ethnic background among any of the children at any other ages.

CONTINUING DEVELOPMENT OF THE CHILD'S IDENTITY

Patterns of childrearing, family relationships, peer interactions, and the impact of the school experience all continue to have an influence on the development of children's sense of identity. During the years of middle childhood, youngsters become increasingly aware of their own sex and uniqueness as persons. A sense of identity continues to evolve over time. Some investigators feel that a sense of identity develops in a manner which is highly similar to Piaget's notions about cognitive development (Kohlberg, 1966; Emmerich, Goldman, Kirsh, Sharabany, 1977; Marcus & Overton, 1978).

One investigation of this approach to the development of children's identity was undertaken by Guardo and Bohan (1971), using semi-structured interviews. They selected four dimensions of identity to study in children from kindergarten through third grade. The first dimension, *humanity,* was assessed by asking children if they could take the identity of an animal. Most children said they could not. Younger children reasoned that their own appearance (not having four legs, a tail, or fur) prevented this from occurring, while older children reasoned that they were human and could never become animals. Thus, humanity was a component of their identity which was firmly established. The second dimension, *sexuality,* was tested by asking children if they could become, or identify with, an opposite-sex sibling or peer. Boys at all ages gave more negative answers than girls. Girls, however, showed a decreasing number of negative responses as age increased. Girls seemed more sensitive to this aspect of identity and gave many conditional answers. That is, they said that if some intervention like an act of God occurred, then the change could take place.

Information regarding the third dimension, *individuality,* was obtained by asking children if they could become a sibling or peer of the same sex. Responses showed consistent age differences. The oldest children gave the fewest negative answers and the most conditional replies ("Maybe, if . . ."). Younger children argued that such a change would be possible when physical differences in appearance or behavior were removed, but older children did not use such reasoning. Older children relied more on an external agent or event which could bring about the change: "Well, . . . if there was a machine . . ."

Children's view of the fourth dimension of identity, *continuity,* was obtained by asking them how long they had been the boy or girl that they were now. Older children were more likely to say "always" while younger ones said they "didn't know." Older children were seen as having a sense of continuity with their past. Guardo and Bohan (1971) suggest that children's sense of identity is dependent on developmental processes. Their analysis shows that children's identity varies qualitatively according to age. In general, younger children appear to think about themselves in concrete, visible, behavioral terms. Older children recognize their identity and its experiential basis more relatively. They can deal with a range of possibilities concerning their identity which younger children cannot.

Marcus and Overton (1978) have also studied the development of children's sexual identity. They were specifically concerned with children's ability to see themselves *consistently* as boys or girls. Kindergarten, first- and second-graders were questioned to see if constancy or stability in sexual identity was related to other cognitive abilities as suggested by Piaget. Once a consistent sexual identity has been established, it may become a basis for organizing other features of children's masculine or feminine behaviors (Kohlberg, 1966).

Marcus and Overton asked children questions related to their understanding of their own sexual identity. They also assessed each child's cognitive abilities through a conservation task. They found a sequential pattern in children's sexual identity and cognitive abilities. At the earliest point in the sequence children have no consistent sexual identity and none of the cognitive skills necessary for conservation problem-solving. Next, a limited understanding of sexual identity was seen despite the fact that children did *not* have the skills necessary to solve conservation problems. The limited knowledge which children first possessed about their sexual identity was related to *motive*. That is, children understood that wishing to be a member of the opposite sex was not sufficient to change their sexual identity. Although they could successfully deal with motives, other aspects of their sexual identity were not yet comprehended. For instance, if the physical appearance of a child was altered to make a boy look more like a girl, or vice versa, children were likely to be misled by the physical changes. Marcus and Overton found that only when children had developed the cognitive skills needed to solve conservation problems did their understanding of the constancy of sexual identity become complete. In other words, the cognitive abilities underlying conservation are needed in order to complete a child's concept of the constancy of sexual identity.

The importance of sexual identity constancy as an organizer of other related behavior can also be seen in another study (Ullian, 1976). Six-year-olds who did not have a firm sexual identity strongly believed that their status as boys or girls could only be preserved through appropriate sex-role behavior. However, eight-year-olds who had attained constancy in their sexual identity were far more tolerant of inappropriate or cross-sex role behavior. They did not feel that cross-sex role behavior threatened their sexual identity as boys or girls. We see that cognitive factors underlie children's sexual identity. Furthermore, with a firm sexual identity children appear to be able to organize and restructure their thinking about the importance of sex role appropriate behaviors.

THE DEVELOPMENT OF SELF AND PEER PERCEPTIONS

For both children and adults, social interactions are a mirror in which they see themselves. The opinions, reactions, and attitudes of others help children to reflect on why and how they are perceived in characteristic ways. Such dependence on others in the social environment is both beneficial and detrimental. Social interaction is necessary to sustain us and fulfill our basic needs, which may be so important that when others threaten or deny them we experience anxiety, frustration, depression, hostility, and hopelessness.

Social exchanges provide us with pleasure and satisfaction in another sense. It is through social exchange that children gain affection, develop feelings of belonging to a group, and develop social competence—which, in turn, favorably influences the way they see or feel about themselves. Children recognize the importance of *actively* searching for favorable responses from others. In a study of several hundred children from six to eleven years of age, investigators found that children considered by teachers to be "leaders" were more active and aggressive than children who were nonleaders (Harrison, Rawls, & Rawls, 1971).

In another study, Kaspar and Lowenstein (1971) were interested in how activity is instigated in children's peer groups. They identified peers who were "activity instigators" and studied their influence on more quiet, less active children. Boys from six to eight years of age were observed in an unstructured play situation, and their level of motor activity was recorded. The data showed that motor activity increased whenever there was peer interaction, regardless of the child's initial level of activity. This suggests that some contagion is at work in peer settings. When two boys with sharply divergent activity levels interacted, the less active boy increased his activity to approach the level of the more active boy. The influence was never the other way. Thus, active children instigate activity in less active ones.

These findings suggest that *activity* as well as aggressiveness are important parts of the social values of our society and are reflected in the social behavior of children. Clearly children who possess these valued traits will be more positively evaluated by others in the social environment.

THE SOCIAL ENVIRONMENT AND RACIAL IDENTITY

The social environment and children's social exchanges are significant factors in the development of racial identity. By the age of four children are sensitive to the physical differences in appearance between themselves and other members of society (Stevenson, 1967). As we saw in the case of sexual identity (Marcus & Overton, 1978), there are cognitive factors which underlie children's developing sensitivity to dimensions of physical appearance. Children often mirror the emotional attitudes of their parents. Thus, in one study (Alexander & Anderson, 1957) Cheyenne Indian children perceived the social world as primarily hostile at a time when the adults around them were particularly concerned with the disintegration of their society and their eventual welfare. The children reflected the unhappiness of the adults, who were trying to resolve conflicts regarding tribal customs and the demands for cultural change and assimilation. The children's response to the perceived hostility in the social environment was one of submission and denial of feelings.

Ramirez and Castaneda (1974) suggest that the children of Mexican-American parents experience problems in adjustment as they attempt to cope with their racial identity. Among the adolescents interviewed, they found two characteristic responses. One group of students identified with and emphasized the similarities between themselves and the white, middle-class majority: "I don't want to be known as a Mexican-American, but only as an American." This type of identification resulted in many disagreements with parents but improved relationships outside the home in the peer group. Another group of students emphasized their identification as exclusively Mexican-American: "I am proud of being a Mexican-American." This type of racial identification resulted in minimal parent conflicts in the home but in feelings of alienation from the peer group. The two styles adopted in this case reflect the choices which are forced on virtually every child from a different racial background. Ramirez and Castaneda (1974) argue that our society, and especially our schools, have not permitted a third type of racial identification to emerge: *bicultural identity.* They would like to see children benefit from their unique backgrounds as both Mexican and American. For the Mexican-American child, the identification which Ramirez and Castaneda advocate emphasizes the advantages of being both American and of Mexican descent: "I feel very rich and fortunate because I have two cultures rather than just one." This type of identification has yet to emerge fully among any of our racial groups—Black, Mexican-American, American Indian, Chinese, Hispanic. It is hoped, however, that as we remove the negative racial stereotypes from our society children will show corresponding increases in pride in their unique bicultural heritage.

Racial awareness in children is often related to prejudice and negative evaluations by the peer group. Prejudice is said to be partially related to the parental atmosphere adopted in the home. Using Baumrind's (1971) parent typology, we see that prejudice is most likely when an *authoritarian* atmosphere prevails. Recall that authoritarian parents employ strong control over their children, maintain an emotionally cold, rejecting attitude, and provide little room for compromise on the many rules which they expect their children to follow. Prejudiced children not only model their parents' inflexible stance, but also appear to react to others in the social environment with a similar narrowness and cold, hostile approach. Some psychologists view prejudice as a way of building up a shattered and weak self-concept. The authoritarian parent atmosphere cannot help but develop children with feelings of powerlessness, inadequacy, and low self-worth.

While the development of racial prejudice in children evolves from early experiences, there are many strategies which can be employed to lessen or reduce such attitudes. One way of reducing racial prejudice is through increased contact and social exchange. Children discover that responding to their peers on the basis of race interferes with successful relationships or limits the effectiveness of group func-

Figure 11-7.   Racial prejudice may be reduced through increased contact, exposure, and social exchange. (Nancy Hays/Monkmeyer Press Photo Service)

tioning (Radke-Yarrow, 1958). Increasing social contacts with members of other racial groups may therefore reduce prejudice and negative stereotyping. In fact, school desegregation represents the most recent effort to reduce prejudice through increased social contact (Katz & Zalk, 1978). DeVries and Edwards (1973) note that social contacts between children of different races is most effective in reducing prejudice when peer group members have equal status and when peers share common goals.

Another approach that has been used to reduce prejudice is to increase children's exposure to models from different ethnic backgrounds. It is argued that seeing Black or Mexican-American families in children's reading books or on TV will decrease children's negative stereotyping. The secondary consequences of increased exposure to models is that children from different backgrounds will be more likely to view their own sense of racial identity in a positive light. These secondary benefits have been reported in some research. Fox and Jordan (1973) found that Black children five to seven years of age both preferred and identified with children from their own racial group. These results are in sharp contrast to earlier studies (Clark, 1955) in which Black children tended to identify with white society and preferred to play with white rather than black dolls. Simple exposure to racially different models seems to result in more positive racial attitudes and less prejudice among both Black and white children (Bogartz & Ball, 1971).

Katz and Zalk (1978) have identified two additional techniques which can be adopted to modify racial prejudice among children. They have attempted to increase the *perceptual salience,* or differentiation, of faces depicting different racial groups. Through training, children can develop sensitivity to faces of individuals from different racial groups. (Katz, 1973). More importantly, with such training they found that racial prejudice and negative stereotyping show corresponding declines. Simple positive reinforcement has also been found to be effective in modifying racial prejudice among children (Williams & Morland, 1976).

Katz and Zalk recently compared the effectiveness of each of these approaches in reducing racial prejudice among children from second- and fifth-grade classes. They found that all of the techniques were effective in reducing racial prejudice. The longest lasting results however, were seen with perceptual salience training and increased exposure. The short-term gains after two months were far more impressive in general than the long-term gains after six months.

SUMMARY

In this chapter we have traced the child's personality and social development. We recognized that physical growth is influenced by various environmental factors and has important implications for children's psychological development. The impact of the family on children's personality and social development was considered from a number of perspectives: parents, birth order, brothers and sisters. The importance of parental attitudes, father absence, and a number of precursors of school success were also emphasized. We also explored children's growing sense of identity by looking at the development of sex-role identity. Finally, the significance of peer and self-perceptions was considered. The processes underlying racial identity and experimental studies on racial prejudice were also considered.

RECOMMENDED READINGS

Elkind, D. *The child and society.* New York: Oxford U. Press, 1979.

A series of essays in applied child development which focus on the child in numerous social environments: family, school, church, and therapeutic settings.

Lomax, E. M. R.; Kagan, J.; and Rosenkrantz, B. G. *Science and patterns of child care.* San Francisco: Freeman & Co., 1978.

The concept of early experience within the context of child-rearing is considered. There is a good deal of emphasis on the relationship of early theorists to specific child-rearing philosophies and approaches.

Salk, L. *What every child would like his parents to know.* New York: Warner Paperback, 1972.

This book contains most of the questions which parents are likely to confront in dealing with the typical problems of child-rearing. The author's advice is often based on cogent syntheses of the research literature.

Moral Development and Problems of Development

Young children are dependent on the moral standards of their parents and teachers. Few three- or four-year-olds will do the "right" thing and voluntarily share their toys or take turns with another child. Initially, advice and direction from adults is a major external factor which influences the morality of children. Younger children do not appear to have an abstract, internal system of rules to guide their moral sense. Thus, they are dependent on the system of adult morality. Interestingly, however, children do not understand the morality of adults as we might think. Piaget (1965) has found that in the course of development children distort moral principles in characteristic and predictable ways.

By middle childhood children are much more reliant on their own personal judgments of morality. They have developed an internal moral system which, although incomplete when compared to that of adults, enables them to respond independently on the basis of their own sense of right and wrong. The dependence on the morality of other adults (*external control*) has been overcome by the development of a personal morality that is unique to the child (*internal control*). How does such morality develop in children?

THE PSYCHOANALYTIC VIEW

When children can tell right from wrong on their own, they are considered to have *internalized* a set of moral standards. The development of internalized standards, according to the psychoanalytic view, is the result of the child's identification with parents and the discipline which they use to control the child's behavior. Parents may use physical punishment, threats of physical punishment (e.g., "You'll get a spanking if you keep jumping on the couch"), or threats of a psychological nature which are based on withdrawal of love (e.g., "Daddy doesn't like you when you write on the wallpaper"). Through discipline the child develops the ability to tell what parents expect, reward, and value in his or her behavior, as well as what parents disapprove of and dislike. Children continue to identify with their parents, try to please them, and become more and more like them. Children's morality thus follows closely the standards of their parents and, ultimately, that of society.

The reason for children's adoption of moral standards, in the psychoanalytic view, is to avoid the uncomfortable feeling of guilt. When a child can recognize the moral standards of his or her parents, we say that his or her *superego* or, in everyday terms, *conscience* has been developed. The superego allows us to recognize ourselves as we should be (*ego-ideal*) and the unacceptable behaviors which parents have not approved (*conscience*). When we fail to act as we should, we experience a feeling of general anxiety which we call guilt. Since younger children have not internalized a consistent set of moral standards, they do not experience guilt. With the development of the superego, older children are made aware that they have violated a moral standard by feelings of guilt. In time children try to avoid the uncomfortable feelings of guilt and respond more and more to a consistent set of moral standards. Psychoanalytic views of moral development consider that the capacity to experience guilt is an important sign that the child's superego has been

Figure 12-1. Psychoanalytic theorists consider the ability to experience guilt a major step in the acquisition of a conscience. (Photo by Mary M. Duncan)

well formed. The child is then capable of internally controlling and directing his or her own behavior and the demands of the id. Appropriate identification with parents, internalization of their moral standards, and the capacity to experience guilt are all signs of children's normal psychological development.

Research derived from the psychoanalytic view of children's moral development centers on the affective-emotional reactions of children. This research looks at how the child expresses guilt after a transgression: confession, self-punishment, remorse, or the degree of expressed anxiety (Aronfreed, 1976). The child's emotional reactions provide the best index to his or her moral development; avoidance of the unpleasant emotional state of anxiety (guilt) is the basis for children's moral standards.

THE SOCIAL LEARNING VIEW

The major difference between the social learning view of moral development and the psychoanalytic view is in the conceptualization of the process of identification. In the social learning view (Bandura, 1969), the development of morality is explained by the processes of learning. Bandura and other theorists feel that children are deliberately shaped by their parents through rewards, punishments, and

Figure 12-2. Moral behaviors may be acquired through the processes of reward, imitation, and modeling, according to social learning theorists. (Photo by Mary M. Duncan)

indirectly through the processes of imitation and modeling. Moral development, like the development of any social behavior, is *learned.*

We have already discussed some of the important components of the social learning process that underlies children's acquisition of aggression in Chapter 9. These same processes underlie all social behavior, including morality. For example, rewards by parents are important in the social learning view. A child who displays self-control and allows another child to share a favorite toy may receive verbal reinforcement ("That's good, Jimmy; it's nice that you could share your truck with Bobby") from his parents. Conversely, children are often punished or not rewarded for deviant, unacceptable behavior that does not conform to that of their parents. A child who says, "No, Marilee can't have a turn on the swing; I want to stay on all by myself, all morning," may be scolded by her mother and told to "Go inside the house, and stay in your room!"

As in the case of aggression, children may learn moral standards through modeling and imitation of their parents. We expect that children will be most likely to be influenced by parents who are nurturant, warm, and apparently competent (Bandura, 1969). When these factors are absent or only minimally present, the degree to which children will imitate and model parental morality will be reduced. The tendency among most children will be to develop moral standards which are similar to those of their parents. The process of social learning is basic to understanding how discipline (rewards and punishments) and modeling help to develop appropriate moral behaviors in the child.

The social learning view is based on an analysis of the child's responses or behavioral reactions to moral standards. The most commonly assessed behaviors are general measures of self-control, such as the ability to withstand temptation or the tendency to lie or cheat. For example, children may be observed to see whether they can resist a highly tempting situation when there is almost no chance of their being detected. Are children who are left alone in a room with a large bowl of candy able to resist helping themselves, despite being told that the candy is "not for you?" The social learning view of morality has largely concentrated on the development of behavioral self-control. The child's actual, overt moral responses or their absence are what concern psychologists within this framework.

THE COGNITIVE DEVELOPMENTAL VIEW

The focus of the cognitive orientation is on moral thought. Thus, the ability of children to make moral judgments and to indicate their understanding of these judgments in response to verbal questioning is basic to the cognitive-developmental view. Probably the two most well-known theorists studying the development of moral thinking and judgment in children are Piaget (1965) and Kohlberg (1969, 1976). In their explanations of morality both apply developmental *stage progression theory* to children's moral thinking. They believe that morality does not develop all at once, but rather unfolds in a series of stages. Earlier stages are integrated and replaced by successively more advanced ones; the stages show evidence of increasingly more mature moral thinking. We have learned that such stage progressions assume the sequence observed in children's moral thinking to be invariant, marked by an orderly process of attainment with no skipping of stages. Moral stages are said to be the result of underlying structural reorganizations of the child's cognitive abilities. Let us look at Piaget's and Kohlberg's approaches to see how children's moral thought is qualitatively different from that of adults.

Piaget

Children's moral thinking, for Piaget, involves the gradual recognition that there are rules in society which must be valued; these rules are based on concepts of justice and fairness. Before we can look at children's moral understanding, we must see how Piaget views the moral thinking of adults. For him, "All morality consists of a system of rules, and the essence of all morality is to be sought for in the respect which the individual acquires for these rules" (Piaget, 1965, p. 13).

Piaget investigated the development of morality by studying how children understand the rules of childhood games. We all remember such games from our pasts such as Tag, or Hide-and-Seek. Piaget studied, as one illustration, the game of marbles as Swiss boys played it some 30 years ago. He was particularly interested in how the rules of the game were viewed by children of different ages, since the rules for any game are handed down from generation to generation as "moral realities" and are preserved by children's respect for the rules themselves. Older children typically teach younger children the rules. Through this tradition, younger children believe that rules can never be changed or altered. If a five-year-old is asked if the rules for marbles are the same in different countries, cities, or nearby schools, the response will be that rules are fixed forever, for all players. Rules may never be changed because they have been created by people more powerful and authoritative than the child. Piaget calls this idea a belief in *moral absolutes*.

Piaget's discovery of moral absolutism in children is based on his analysis of: (1) how children *practice* the rules of their games, and (2) their *consciousness* of the rules which they follow. Piaget described, for example, how children who think of rules as moral absolutes play a marble game called Squares. A square is drawn in the dirt and then a number of marbles are put inside of it. Children take turns trying to knock the marbles out of the square with a special marble, which is kept just for this purpose. One rule which children follow is called *consecration*: when a child says to the other players a particular plan or operation for eliminating marbles. A simple consecration which we can recognize is the decision about who goes first. As soon as a player says "Firsts," all opponents abide by the decision to allow the player to begin the game. The only defense other players have against consecration

Figure 12-3. Piaget examined children's morality by assessing their knowledge of the rules of various games, such as marbles. (David Strickler/Monkmeyer Press Photo Service)

is the rule of *interdiction*. In the case of interdiction, a player can say a word which automatically negates the use of a consecration. To prevent a player from having "Firsts," another player must say "No firsts." An interdiction will only work if it is uttered *before* a consecration. Children who think about rules as moral absolutes regard all rules as *obligatory* (the practice of the rules) and *inviolable* (their consciousness or understanding of the rules), so that they may not be changed in any way.

Thinking about rules as moral absolutes is only one sign for Piaget that until nearly eight or nine years of age children are in a stage of *moral realism*. In this early stage of morality, children believe all rules must be obeyed; rules are always obligatory and applied despite extenuating circumstances or unusual situations (Piaget, 1965, p. 111). The child in the stage of moral realism believes that if any rules are broken then punishment must be experienced. Conversely, if some accident occurs to an individual, such as falling off a bicycle, cutting a knee, or being hit on the head by an errant snowball, children believe that the disaster must have been "earned." Thus, children display a strong belief in "immanent justice" in the stage of moral realism. Accidents and common disasters do not occur by chance— they are always deserved (e.g., a rule must have been broken).

The stage of moral realism has three features. First, it is *heteronomous;* children believe that any action is morally "good" if it conforms to a rule. Second, moral realism directs children to follow the *"letter of the law" rather than its spirit.* That is, no provisions for extenuating circumstances nor for any moderation in applying rules can be made. Third, children display a belief in *objective responsibility;* they believe that "good" can only come about when you are obedient and follow the rules and "bad" is the result of violating the rules. Thus, children are extremely objective in evaluating moral behaviors—rules are either obeyed or not. There is no need for children to make subjective judgments of a person's motives or intentions. To determine goodness or badness, children simply examine whether the rules were followed or not.

Piaget's method of studying objective responsibility involved presenting pairs of stories to children, who were asked to judge "Which character is the naughtiest, and why?" The story pairs always contrasted a *good*-intentioned child who produced *lots* of damage with a *bad*-intentioned child who produced only a *little* damage:

Story A

A little boy who is called John is in his room. He is called to dinner. He goes into the dining room. But behind the door there is a chair and on the chair there is a tray with fifteen cups on it. John couldn't have known that there was all this behind the door. He goes in, the door knocks against the tray, bang go the fifteen cups and they all get broken!

Story B

Once there was a little boy whose name was Henry. One day when his mother was out he tried to get some jam out of the cupboard. He climbed up onto a chair and stretched out his arm. But the jam was too high up and he couldn't reach it and have any. But while he was trying to get it, he knocked over a cup. The cup fell down and broke. (Piaget, 1965, p. 122)

Piaget, we might note, deliberately chose stories which involve the consequences of a child's "clumsiness." He felt that children typically encounter the wrath of adults because of their childish clumsiness, such as in breaking or dirtying objects in the house. We can look at the typical answers of a seven-year-old girl to see how moral realistic thinking influences her judgments to these two stories.

Q: If you were their mother, which one would you punish most severely?
A: The one who broke the cups.

Q: Is he the naughtiest?
A: Yes.

Q: Why did he break them?
A: Because he wanted to get into the room.

Q: And the other?
A: Because he wanted to take the jam.

Q: Have you ever broken anything?
A: A cup.

Q: How?
A: I wanted to wipe it, and I let it drop.

Q: What else have you broken?
A: Another time, a plate.

Q: How?
A: I took it to play with.

Q: Which was the naughtiest thing to do?
A: The plate, because I oughtn't to have taken it.

Q: And how about the cup?
A: That was less naughty because I wanted to wipe it.

Q: Which were you punished most for—for the cup or for the plate?
A: For the plate.

Q: Listen, I am going to tell you two more stories. A little girl was wiping the cups. She was putting them away, wiping them with the cloth, and she broke five cups. Another little girl is playing with some plates. She breaks a plate. Which of them is the naughtiest?
A: The one who broke five cups. (Piaget, 1965, 123–124)

The responses of this seven-year-old indicate the nature of moral realism. Her judgment of "naughtiness" in the stories is based solely on the amount of damage which each of the two girls produces; she centers on their *objective responsibility*. The different intentions (good vs. bad) which underlie each child's actions are ignored in her judgment. She evaluates the stories rather simply: greater damage is more naughty than less damage.

Interestingly, she has also faced a similar problem in her own home and shows a more mature understanding of morality when asked to evaluate her own behavior. She does not stress objective responsibility (amount of damage) but rather sees the importance of intentions (it is naughtier to break one plate while playing than five cups while trying to dry them). When asked to reason about the very same problem presented verbally, however, she returns to the stage of moral realism and concentrates on damage. This is a good example of the *vertical décalage* discussed in Chapter 10.

Piaget is not surprised to discover that children may be more mature moral thinkers when evaluating their own concrete behavior than when evaluating the sophisticated verbal problems used in his experiments (Rybash & Roodin, 1978). Children can readily tell whether "Glen meant to trip me and make me fall" or whether "It was only an accident." Despite the ability to focus on intentions in real-life situations, children still respond to the verbally presented problems of Piaget as moral realists and see only the damage done. It is the order in which moral development stages are acquired which is important to Piaget, not the chronological ages corresponding to these acquisitions. We may find many children younger than eight or nine who use intentions in evaluating their friends' moral behavior. "If the child had witnessed the scenes we describe to him, would he judge them in the same manner? We think not. The stories that were told to them lag in time behind the direct evaluations of daily life." (Piaget, 1965, p. 120).

Regardless of whether children are evaluating verbal or behavioral dilemmas, there is a transition from moral realism to a more advanced stage of moral thinking called *autonomous morality,* in which rules are viewed in a less rigid manner. Rules are considered to be based on mutual agreement and can therefore be changed by mutual consent. Piaget finds that by age nine or ten most children can evaluate moral problems using *subjective responsibility;* they begin to take the motives or intentions underlying behavior into account.

What are the early signs of the stage of autonomous morality? Initially, children discover that reciprocity is fundamental to the working of rules. They see that rules are only effective if people agree to accept them. Rules are not made by some external authority (God, parents) never to be changed; rather they are the result of agreed-upon conventions among individuals. Children also discover, a bit later, that mutual respect among people is a necessary part of autonomous morality. As children realize that others have feelings, rights, and needs like their own, they begin to understand more deeply the origin and meaning of rules. Thus, both *reciprocity* and *mutual respect* provide early signs for Piaget of autonomous morality.

Children in the stage of autonomous morality are characterized by reductions in moral absolutism and immanent justice (i.e., punishments must always be administered for rule violations). The stage of autonomous morality is also marked by an increased awareness of peer expectations as well as an ability to sympathize and to show affection and gratitude. These skills may be best described as increases in "role-taking" ability. Role-taking abilities are directly related to the moral developmental stages attained by children (Selman, 1976).

As we have seen, Piaget maintains that egocentrism limits children in many spheres throughout their development, including morality. Egocentrism underlies children's thinking in the earlier stage of moral realism; younger children believe that other people view the world as they do. A significant step in moving away from moral realism towards autonomous morality is therefore the reduction of egocentrism. As Hoffman (1970) explains, psychoanalytic and social learning theories consider moral values to be the result of parental teachings which become a part of the child's own value system. Piaget, on the other hand, maintains that such social interactions and exchanges do not establish a value system directly in the child, but the system is incorporated into the child's existing cognitive structure. For Piaget, children's moral development is, like other spheres, a sphere in which they play an *active* part. As children relate to their peers and parents, they discover the differing perceptions and beliefs which others have. The mutual cooperation, give-and-take of ideas, and sharing of perspectives that are necessary for social interaction help children actively construct the increasingly complex cognitive structures of which morality is an integral part. As cognitive structures become more complex and elaborated through social experience, the child's morality progresses from a stage of moral realism to one of autonomous morality.

There is a similar developmental sequence when the moral understanding of children's concepts of justice or "fairness" is examined (Piaget, 1965). Up until about seven or eight years of age, children do not have a concept of justice except as it relates to adult authority. The child feels that any ideas of justice must be subordinated to adult authority: "whatever conforms to the dictates of adult authority is just" (Piaget, 1965, p. 315). Children are constrained by the morality of adults. The punishments administered by adults for not following the rules are always seen by children as just or fair. Piaget finds that children have a general *unilateral respect* for adults and adult decisions. Unilateral respect overrides their own abilities to make judgments of the fairness or justice of these decisions.

During the period between eight and eleven, however, children begin to show signs of *progressive egalitarianism*. It is then that children begin to show evidence of their own ability to evaluate morality, independent of adult authority. Children seem to be primarily concerned with both *equity* and *reciprocity* in accepting the legitimacy of punishments. Punishments may not be administered harshly just because a child has violated a rule, but rather the punishment must "fit the crime." Children can see the difference between appropriate punishments and arbitrary punishments, e.g., those that are far in excess of the rule which has been transgressed. Children, however, tend to be limited to notions of "equal justice for all." Fairness implies treating all individuals alike.

By 11–12 years of age the child is capable of tempering equality, so that it is not the only basis for determining justice. The child's tempering of egalitarian justice with "considerations of equity" represents a significant change in his or her perception of justice. The child can apply notions of equity (viewing individuals with equal shared interests and responsibilities) in a situational context. Although earlier equality was the basis for justice, children now determine whether all individuals *deserve* equal treatment. For example, there may be extenuating circumstances which indicate that justice should not be applied. In groups of children, some may be more responsible for damage than others. In other words, the child recognizes that rules cannot be applied equivalently to all individuals, without some assessment of the situation, circumstances, and motives or intentions underlying behavior.

Piaget concludes that moral development does follow a sequential progression. As children participate in successful social interactions with peers and give up their unilateral respect for adults and adult morality, their moral thought changes. They move from the limited perspective of moral realism to the stage of autonomous morality. Autonomous morality is marked by the recognition of mutual respect, cooperation, and reciprocity in all social exchanges and is the basis for mature comprehension of rules, punishments, and justice.

Kohlberg

An approach very similar to that of Piaget can be found in the cognitive developmental theory of moral thought developed by Lawrence Kohlberg (1963, 1969, 1976). Following the basic ideas of Piaget, Kohlberg has attempted a more detailed

Figure 12-4.   Children's answers to complex stories help theorists such as Kohlberg understand the processes underlying children's moral thinking.   (Ellen Kirouac/Monkmeyer Press Photo Service)

Table 12-1
KOHLBERG'S SIX MORAL STAGES

Level and Stage	What Is Right	Reasons for Doing Right
LEVEL I PRECONVENTIONAL *Stage 1* —Heteronomous Morality	To avoid breaking rules backed by punishment, obedience for its own sake and avoiding physical damage to persons and property.	Avoidance of punishment, and the superior power of authorities.
Stage 2 —Individualism, Instrumental Purpose, and Exchange	Following rules only when it is to someone's immediate interest; acting to meet one's own interests and needs and letting others do the same. Right is also what's fair, what's an equal exchange, a deal, an agreement.	To serve one's own needs or interests in a world where you have to recognize that other people have their interests, too.
LEVEL II CONVENTIONAL *Stage 3* —Mutual Interpersonal Expectancies, Relationships, and Interpersonal Conformity	Living up to what is expected by people close to you or what people generally expect of people in your role as son, brother, friend. "Being good" is important and means having good motives, showing concern about others. It also means keeping mutual relationships, such as trust, loyalty, respect, and gratitude.	The need to be a good person in your own eyes and those of others. Your caring for others. Belief in the Golden Rule. Desire to maintain rules and authority which support stereotypical good behavior.
Stage 4 —Social System and Conscience	Fulfilling the actual duties to which you have agreed. Laws are to be upheld except in extreme cases	To keep the institution going as a whole, to avoid the breakdown in the system "if everyone did it," or the

where they conflict with other fixed social duties. Right is also contributing to society, the group, or institution.	imperative of conscience to meet one's defined obligations.

LEVEL III POST-CONVENTIONAL, or PRINCIPLED *Stage 5*—Social Contract or Utility and Individual Rights	Being aware that people hold a variety of values and opinions, that most values and rules are relative to your group. These relative rules should usually be upheld, however, in the interest of impartiality and because they are the social contract. Some nonrelative values and rights like *life* and *liberty*, however, must be upheld in any society and regardless of majority opinion.	A sense of obligation to law because of one's social contract to make and abide by laws for the welfare of all and for the protection of everyone's rights. A feeling of contractual commitment, freely entered upon, to family, friendship, trust, and work obligations. Concern that laws and duties be based on rational calculation of overall utility, "the greatest good for the greatest number."
Stage 6—Universal Ethical Principles	Following self-chosen ethical principles. Particular laws or social agreements are usually valid because they rest on such principles. When laws violate these principles, one acts in accordance with the principle. Principles are universal principles of justice: the equality of human rights and respect for the dignity of human beings as individual persons.	The belief as a rational person in the validity of universal moral principles, and a sense of personal commitment to them.

Source: Adapted from Lawrence Kohlberg, "Moral Stages and Moralization," in T. Lickona, ed., Moral Development and Behavior (New York: Holt, Rinehart, 1976), pp. 34–35.

examination of moral development by studying children between ten and sixteen years old. Like Piaget, Kohlberg presents moral dilemmas to children; however, his stories are extremely complex and have no single absolutely correct response. Kohlberg has studied the way in which children reason about the moral dilemmas as well as their attempts to understand the basic issues which are involved.

Kohlberg's theory represents the development of children's moral orientations (moral ideology and moral reasoning) as following a sequence of three major levels: (I) Preconventional, (II) Conventional, and (III) Post-Conventional or Principled. Each level is composed of two distinct stages; thus, there is an invariant hierarchy of moral development consisting of a sequence of six stages. Earlier stages must be acquired before higher stages can be attained; however, not all persons reach the highest stages. Through these six stages, Kohlberg sees that children gradually develop the concept of justice: "He defines justice as a primary regard for the value and equality of all human beings and for reciprocity in human relations, and considers it a basic and universal standard" (Sanborn, 1971, p. 14). The stage sequence, along with the typical moral orientation of each of the six stages, is described in Table 12-1. The child's understanding of what is *right* for each of the moral stages as well as the *reason* or motivation for acting at each stage is presented as well.

The first level is designated the *Preconventional Level,* and two stages are seen within this level. Stage 1 involves obedience and punishment—the child depends upon a superior power, is egocentric in behavior, and fears punishment. Stage 2 is characterized by a naive hedonism—the child tends to define behavior as moral if it is personally satisfying.

The second level is the *Conventional Level,* in which moral behavior is defined as behavior which contributes to the social order and our cultural expectations. Control of the child's behavior is perceived as external since the significant expectations come from adults who are important to the child. Within this second level of morality, Stage 3 is one in which the child is oriented toward helping others and being aware of their approach. Stage 4 is one in which the child shows respect for authority and adopts the views of others; the child believes that if one is good, one will receive a reward.

The third moral level is the *Post-Conventional* or *Principled Level.* An essential characteristic of this level is that control of a person's behavior is perceived as internal—decisions about right and wrong come from the child's own thought and judgment. Within this level, Stage 5 is characterized as one in which standards of right and wrong are described in terms of rational laws that provide the bases of judgments of what is right. The child continues to believe that if the needs of an individual conflict with the law, the law must still be obeyed. In Stage 6, the control of conscience is emphasized; behavior is controlled by ideals and that which is labelled "moral." The individual's conforming behavior develops from observing the behavior of others. In essence, for individuals in this stage, morality stems from the conscience.

These six stages have been studied in two ways by Kohlberg. Originally, he assessed 25 basic *aspects* which the child held towards morality or justice. Each of these aspects or factors was revealed from an analysis of the child's verbal reasoning about the moral dilemmas. The aspects included the child's orientation toward rules, conscience, welfare of self, welfare of others, sense of duty, role-taking, punitive justice, positive justice, and motives (Kohlberg, 1976). Using this *aspect scoring* approach Kohlberg found, like Piaget, that not all of a child's moral judgments conformed to a single moral stage. Kohlberg's descriptions of the child's stages of moral development were appropriate for about 50% of the moral responses to the series of dilemmas presented (Sanborn, 1971). Therefore, a stage may be thought of as the child's most typical (*modal*) moral orientation, rather than as a description of all of the child's moral thinking.

The second approach used by Kohlberg to score the children's responses to moral dilemmas is called *intuitive*. It was developed to overcome problems in the earlier aspect scoring system. The intuitive scoring of children's moral responses to Kohlberg's dilemmas is based on *what* the child values, judges, or focuses on in the stories rather than *how* he or she reasons about the issue itself. In other words, Kohlberg finds that at each of the six stages children reason about different types of issues. The degree to which children see issues as important, or even present, is the basis of the intuitive approach. Kohlberg has identified the following issues, values, or moral institutions which may be used by children in their attempt to develop an understanding of the moral dilemmas which he presents: (1) laws and rules, (2) conscience, (3) personal roles of affection, (4) authority, (5) civil rights, (6) contract, trust, and justice in exchange, (7) punishment and justice, (8) the value of life, (9) property rights and values, (10) truth, and (11) sex and sexual love.

We may illustrate the difference between these two approaches by looking at Kohlberg's now famous moral dilemma—*Heinz and the Drug:*

In Europe a woman was near death from a special kind of cancer. There was one drug that the doctors thought might save her. It was a form of radium that a druggist in the same town had recently discovered. The drug was expensive to make, but the druggist was charging ten times what the drug cost him to make. He paid $200 for the radium and charged $2000 for a small dose of the drug. The sick woman's husband, Heinz, went to everyone he knew to borrow the money, but he could only get together $1000 which is half of what it cost. He told the druggist that his wife was dying, and asked him to sell it cheaper or let him pay later. But the druggist said, "No, I discovered the drug, and I am going to make money from it." So Heinz got desperate, and broke into the man's store to steal the drug for his wife. (1969, p. 379)

We see the typical Stage 1 responses of a child asked to evaluate this story in Table 12-2. These responses are the ones which Kohlberg would analyze for Type of Moral Reasoning, i.e., the aspect scoring system. This approach may be contrasted with the intuitive scoring system illustrated in Table 12-3, which centers on how the issue of the value of life is conceptualized at five of Kohlberg's stages.

Table   12-2
ASPECT-SCORING RATING SYSTEM: TYPICAL STAGE 1
STATEMENTS TO THE DRUG STEALING DILEMMA

Stage 1 Responses

1. *Rules:* Thinks Heinz should not steal the drug, since it is bad to steal whatever the motive; it's against external law and is a violation of the superior power of the police.

2. *Conscience:* Concern about the wrongness of stealing is in terms of fear of punishment.

3. *Altruism:* Heinz thinks about his own welfare, not that of other people, like his wife.

4. *Duty:* Duty is only what he has to do, a husband doesn't have to steal for his wife.

5. *Self-Interest:* Yields to power and punishment where rational self-interest would say to stick up for himself or to try to get away with it.

6. *Role-Taking:* Since Stage 1 doesn't see things from other people's point of view and doesn't expect them to see things from his, he expects punishment for stealing, no matter why he did what he did.

7. *Justice:* Justice in punishment is simply retribution for committing a crime, for breaking the law.

Source: Lawrence Kohlberg, ''Moral Stages and Moralization,'' in T. Lickona, ed., *Moral Development and Behavior* (New York: Holt, Rinehart, 1976), p. 42.

For Kohlberg, regardless of the scoring system used, the cognitive-developmental approach provides the best understanding of the sequential attainments of morality. Like Piaget, Kohlberg (1976) emphasizes that these attainments are partially the results of intellectual development, or cognitive structures, and partially the results of social role-taking. Recent studies have begun to confirm the importance of role-taking as a necessary condition for the acquisition of moral stages (Selman, 1976).

Selman

Selman indicates that social role-taking is necessary for the development of Kohlberg's moral stages; however, the fact that a child possesses particular role-taking skills will not be the single determinant of his or her moral stage of development. For Selman, children's role-taking abilities follow an invariant developmental sequence similar to the one found by Kohlberg for moral development. The similarities can be seen in Table 12-4. As the role-taking skills of the child unfold, corresponding development in moral maturity can be expected.

The role-taking stages identified by Selman indicate an increasingly complex understanding of social relations. Role-taking skills were determined by responses to both standard questions and open-ended questions based on a complex story. Younger children might be read stories like the one about Holly below. Children (four to ten years old) are asked to decide what Holly must do—climb the tree and save her friend's kitten or keep her promise to her father and not climb trees.

Table   12-3
INTUITIVE SCORING TO THE DRUG-STEALING DILEMMA

Stage	What Is Life's Value in the Situation?	Why Is Life Valuable?
Stage 1	Wife's life has no clear value here to husband or others when it conflicts with law and property. Does not see that husband would value his wife's life over stealing.	Does not give a reason and does not indicate understanding that life is worth more than property.
Stage 2	It is its immediate value to the husband and to the wife, herself. Assumes the husband would think his wife's life is worth stealing for, but he isn't obligated to if he doesn't like her enough. Life's value to a person other than its possessor depends on relationship; you wouldn't steal to save the life of a mere friend or acquaintance.	Each person wants to live more than anything else. You can replace property, not life.
Stage 3	Life's value is its value to any good, caring, person like the husband. The husband should care enough to risk stealing (even if he does not steal), and a friend should care enough to save the life of a friend or another person.	People should care for other people and their lives. You're not good or human if you don't. People have much more feeling for life than for anything material.
Stage 4	Even though he or she may think it wrong to steal, understands the general rule of *sacredness* of human life or the rule to preserve life. Sacredness means all other values can't be compared with the value of life. The value of life is general; human life is valuable no matter what your relationship to the person is, though this doesn't obligate you to steal.	Life is valuable because God created it and made it sacred. Or life is valuable because it is basic to society; it is a basic right of people.
Stage 5	Recognizes that in this situation the wife's right to life comes before the druggist's right to property. There is some obligation to steal for anyone dying; everyone has a right to live and to be saved.	Every person or society logically and morally must place each person's individual right to life before other rights such as the right to property.

Source: Lawrence Kohlberg, "Moral Stages and Moralization," in T. Lickona, ed., *Moral Development and Behavior* (New York: Holt, Rinehart, 1976), p. 42.

Table 12-4
PARALLEL STRUCTURED RELATIONS BETWEEN SELMAN'S SOCIAL ROLE-TAKING AND FIVE OF KOHLBERG'S MORAL JUDGMENT STAGES

Social Role-Taking Stage	Moral Judgment Stage
Stage 1 Egocentric Viewpoint (average age range 3–6)	*Level I—Preconventional* **Stage 1 Heteronomous Stage**
Child has a sense of differentiation of self and others but fails to distinguish between the social perspective (thoughts, feelings) of other and self. Child can label other's overt feelings but does not see the cause-and-effect relation of reasons to social actions.	Judgments of right and wrong are based on good or bad consequences and not on intentions. Moral choices derive from the subject's wishes that good things happen to self. Child's reasons for his or her choices simply assert the choices, rather than attempting to justify them.
Stage 2 Social-Informational Role-Taking (average age range 6–8)	**Stage 2 Individualism, Instrumental Purpose, and Exchange**
Child is aware that other has a social perspective based on other's own reasoning, which may or may not be similar to child's. However, child tends to focus on one perspective rather than coordinating viewpoints.	Child focuses on one perspective, that of the authority or the powerful. Child understands, however, that good actions are based on good intention. Beginning sense of fairness as equality of acts.
Stage 3 Self-Reflective Role-Taking (average age range 8–10)	*Level II—Conventional* **Stage 3 Mutual Interpersonal Expectations, Relationships, and Interpersonal Conformity**
Child is conscious that each individual is aware of the other's perspective and that this awareness influences self and other's view of each other. Putting self in other's place is a way of judging his or her intentions, purposes, and actions. Child can form a coordinated chain of perspectives, but cannot yet abstract from this process to the level of simultaneous mutuality.	Moral reciprocity is conceived as the equal exchange of the intent of two persons in relation to one another. If someone has a mean intention toward self, it is right for self to act in kind. Right defined as what is valued by self.
Stage 4 Mutual Role-Taking (average age range 10–12)	**Stage 4 Social System and Conscience**
Child realizes that both self and other can view each other mutually and simultaneously as subjects. Child can step outside the two-person dyad and view the interaction from a third-person perspective.	Right is defined as the Golden Rule: Do unto others as you would have others do unto you. Child considers all points of view and reflects on each person's motives in an effort to reach agreement among all participants.

Table   12-4 (Continued)

Stage 5	Social and Conventional System Role-Taking (average age range 12–15+)	Level III —Post-Conventional or Principled
		Stage 5 Social Contract or Utility and Individual Rights
	Person realizes mutual perspective-taking does not always lead to complete understanding. Social conventions are seen as necessary because they are understood by all members of the group (the generalized other) regardless of their position, role, or experience.	Right is defined in terms of the perspective of the generalized other or the majority. Person considers consequences of actions for the group or society. Orientation to maintenance of social morality and social order.

Source: R. L. Selman, "Social-Cognitive Understanding: A Guide to Educational and Clinical Practice," in T. Lickona, ed., *Moral Development and Behavior* (New York: Holt, Rinehart, 1976), p. 309.

Holly is an eight-year-old girl who likes to climb trees. She is the best tree climber in the neighborhood. One day while climbing down from a tall tree, she falls off the bottom branch but does not hurt herself. Her father sees her fall. He is upset and asks her to promise not to climb trees any more. Holly promises. Later that day Holly and her friends meet Shawn. Shawn's kitten is caught up in a tree and can't get down. Something has to be done right away, or the kitten may fall. Holly is the only one who climbs trees well enough to reach the kitten and get it down, but she remembers her promise to her father. (Selman, 1976, p. 309)

Look at how a child in Stage 1 of Egocentric Role-Taking deals with the dilemma:

Q: What do you think Holly will do—save the kitten, or keep her promise?
A: She will save the kitten because she doesn't want the kitten to die.

Q: How will her father feel when he finds out?
A: Happy, he likes kittens.

Q: What would you do if you were Holly?
A: Save the kitten so it won't get hurt.

Q: What if Holly doesn't like kittens? What will she do?
A: She won't get it.

Q: What if her father punishes her if she gets the kitten down?
A: Then she will leave it up there.

Q: Why?
A: Because she doesn't want to get in trouble.

Q: How will she feel?
A: Good, she listened to her father. (Selman, 1976, p. 303)

In this example, the child assumes that all people would focus on rescuing the kitten. When the child is reminded about the promise which was made, however, then this becomes the only perspective for looking at the problem. There is an inability to coordinate the conflicting perspectives, and the child focuses on either the rescue or the promise, not both.

For older children (ten years old and above), more complex dilemmas are presented, such as "Heinz and the Drug" problem presented before. In dealing with these dilemmas, older children at Stage 5 (Role-Taking) can see that the problem involves a general social system rather than just the limited view of two people who may mutually be obligated to each other. In the example provided by Selman (1976), we see that children's role-taking is based on wide-ranging concepts of law, morality, and a generally agreed upon set of principles or common perspectives which all members of a social group share. This type of role-taking is found only in Stage 5 (Social and Conventional System Role-Taking) by Selman.

Q: What do you think the judge would do in Heinz's case?
A: I'm afraid he'd have to convict him. When Heinz stole the drug, he knew it was wrong from society's point of view. He also knew that if he were caught he'd be convicted because he'd realize the judge would have to uphold the law.

Q: Why?
A: The judge has to think about the way it would look to everybody else. If they see Heinz getting no punishment, they might think they can get away with stealing. Heinz should realize this and take some form of punishment.

Q: Would the judge think Heinz was right or wrong to do what he did?
A: The judge is not supposed to be a philosopher. Even if the judge thought Heinz was morally right, from the legal point of view the judge has to consider the law of the people. (Selman, 1976, p. 307)

RESEARCH ON MORAL DEVELOPMENT

The diversity of responses in each of the three explanations of moral development (see Table 12-5) suggests that there is little relation among children's moral behavior, moral thinking, and moral feelings (Hoffman, 1970; Lickona, 1976). This is characteristic of adult morality as well. We often find that our expressed moral beliefs are not a good guide to our own behavior. Parents recognize this separation of morality into different systems, often asking children to "Do what I say, not what I do." The recent Watergate trials offer further support that "knowing" what is right does not necessarily lead to moral behavior.

Research interest has tended to be limited to one of the three orientations, rather than to continue to search for relationships among moral responses. Nevertheless, research has led to a recognition that a number of factors may influence children's morality, as illustrated in Table 12-5. Surprisingly, whether we focus on feelings, thought, or behavior, children's morality does not show a great deal of consistency from one situation to another (Burton, 1976; Lickona, 1976). There appears to be a rather complex set of variables which influence children's morality. These variables assume differential importance depending on the type of moral responses studied. For example, we can examine the importance of moral reasoning in obedience to authority.

In a classic study, Milgram (1963, 1974) found that college students would conform to the demands of an authority figure and ''shock'' a supposed victim to help him to learn. Moreover, most students willingly followed orders and administered apparently higher and higher levels of electric shock when instructed to do so by the experimenter. Kohlberg (1965, 1969) conducted further moral reasoning assessments of 32 of the subjects who participated in Milgram's original experiment. In general, those subjects who refused to continue to administer stronger levels of shock and terminated their participation in the study were found to be at more advanced moral stages. Subjects at Stage 6 were most likely to discontinue their participation in the study. When questioned, subjects at both Stage 6 and Stage 5 displayed a far different definition of the situation than those at lower stages of moral reasoning. The subjects at Stage 6 seemed to feel that they themselves had to make an *individual* decision regarding the experimenter's demand for continued shock and their participation in the study. Stage 5 subjects who continued in the study appeared to accept the fact that a ''contract'' between themselves, the supposed victim, and the experimenter had been established prior to the start of the experiment. Stage 6 subjects, however, denied the validity of this prior contract and individually tended to refuse to follow the experimenter's orders to provide

Table 12-5
FACTORS INFLUENCING THREE DIMENSIONS OF MORAL DEVELOPMENT IN CHILDREN

Moral Behavior (Social-Learning)	Moral Thought (Cognitive-Development)	Moral Feelings (Psychoanalytic)
Probability of reward-punishment	Intelligence	Empathy
Fear of detection	Cognitive structures	Perception of motives
Risk-taking	Verbal skills	Parental socialization practices
Motivation	Social Experience	
Modeling	Role-taking	Degree of identification
Past history of reward		

increasingly stronger levels of shock (Kohlberg, 1965, 1969). Obedience to authority was more typical of subjects at lower stages of moral reasoning.

Most research in recent years has been designed to explore the ideas of the cognitive-developmental orientation expressed by Piaget or Kohlberg. Three basic questions have been addressed:

1. Validation: Is the structural account of moral development adequate? Are the stages which have been found universal, invariant, and accurate descriptions of moral thought?

2. Methodology: Are the developmental stages of Piaget and Kohlberg the result of specific variables, techniques of measurement, or stimuli which might account for the sequences which they have reported?

3. Training and Experience: To what degree are the moral stages modifiable through deliberate training or influenced by specific types of experiences?

Validation

One way of validating the structural approach of Piaget and Kohlberg is to see if there are corresponding cognitive-developmental attainments which parallel the moral stages. According to the structural account of Piaget, for example, such correspondence or concomitance in development should occur. Lee (1971) attempted to relate the child's moral development with corresponding changes in the child's cognitive abilities. She wanted to see if the child progressed through the stages of intellectual development (preoperational, concrete operations, and formal operations) at the same times that the moral stages of realism and autonomy were acquired. Lee tested children aged 5–17 on a series of Piagetian tasks and compared their performance to their level of moral judgment. The series of Piagetian tasks included, for instance, conservation of mass and liquid. Another task was called "projected space." Children were shown a large pink rock, a flat blue rock, and a tall green rock to represent mountains. On top of each of the respective "mountains" were a red house, a covering of snow, and a red cross. A screen with three sides was placed around this scene so that a doll could be positioned to look through a window on each of the sides. In the task, children were asked to judge the perspective which the doll saw from the windows by selecting out a correct photograph (see Figure 12-5).

Another task consisted of a ruler balanced on a supporting ball: a balance task. Children were asked to balance this primitive scale when weights were placed on one end of the ruler. Children could either place equal weights on the opposite side or could move the weights nearer or further from the center to achieve balance. In addition, other cognitive tasks were presented as well as Piaget's traditional moral conflict stories. The themes of these stories involved authority, peer cooperation, and altruism.

Lee reported that her findings generally supported Piaget's predictions: there was concomitance in children's moral and cognitive development. She validated Piaget's theory of similarity of moral thinking and cognition. Children in the pre-operational period based their morality on authority; in the concrete operational period they based their moral judgments on reciprocity; and in formal operations they related their formal judgments to social realities and ideals.

The question of validation can also be seen in research on the invariance of Kohlberg's developmental stages. Cross-cultural studies in both complex and more primitive societies show the same type of stage sequences in moral thinking as initially identified by Kohlberg (1969). A three-year study of Bahamian children eight to seventeen years old (White, Bushnell & Regnemer, 1978) supported the invariant sequence of Kohlberg's stages, although no subjects advanced beyond Stage 3 reasoning. Further support for the notion of invariance can be seen in Kohlberg's cross-sectional study in our own country (see Figure 12-6). As Figure 12-6 shows, the prevalence of more basic stage reasoning declines as age increases. In addition, a recent longitudinal study of Kohlberg's stages (Kuhn,

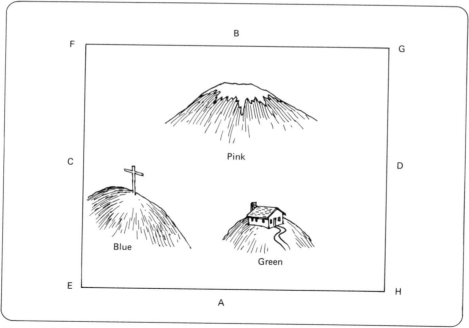

Figure 12-5.   Diagram of mountain scene in space projection task. The letters refer to positions from which to view the mountains. (From L. C. Lee, The concomitant development of cognitive and moral codes of thought: a test of selective deduction from Piaget's theory. *Genetic Psychology Monographs,* 1971, 83, 93–146. By permission.)

1976) shows a step-wise pattern of change which reflects invariance. Earlier stages are progressively subsumed into more advanced stages. Kuhn found general support for Kohlberg's sequences at least for the early stages of his model.

Methodology

The question of methodology is an important one. Many research investigators feel that other variables might be responsible for the developmental stages which Piaget and Kohlberg have found. They are reluctant to accept the stage notion of the cognitive-developmental theory of morality without careful consideration of these factors. Keasey (1977) found, for instance, that five-year-olds made more mature moral responses when asked to imagine that the dilemma happened to themselves rather than to a story character. By assuming the role of the central character, children could concentrate on intentions.

The complexity of the stories which Piaget has used has also been questioned. King (1971) and Imamoglu (1977) both noted that the reasons for children's apparent stage-like moral judgments may reflect only their difficulty in understanding the difference between an accident and an intentional outcome. King found four-, six-, and nine-year-olds increasingly able to recognize others' intentions in a series of films. Imamoglu noted similar findings in working with children five to twelve years old with a verbal presentation procedure.

To overcome complexity, investigators have used single stories rather than story pairs. Rybash, Sewall, Roodin, and Sullivan (1975) found that kindergarten children could make more mature moral responses when stories were presented to them one at a time rather than paired as Piaget required. Other investigations have also found that judgments of a single story are considerably easier than judgments of story pairs. Single stories result in more mature judgments from even the youngest of children (Nummendal & Bass, 1976; Feldman, Klosson, Parsons, Rholes & Ruble, 1976).

The problem of the complexity of Piaget's stories is related to the importance of memory. Memory may account for the relative importance of damage for the younger child and intention for the older child. Feldman and associates (1976) used a single story presentation in which children were asked to rate story characters for naughtiness. They found that younger children often forgot the story details which were presented first (typically, the *intentions* in Piaget's dilemmas) and remembered the details which were presented most recently (*damage*). Austin, Ruble, and Trabasso controlled for memory in a study which used story pairs similar to that of Piaget. Children (kindergarten to third grade) had to recall all story details before assessing the naughtiness of the characters. Using this procedure, *no* age differences were found in assessing damage and intention. The authors concluded that perhaps "differential recall may have been responsible for age effects in prior studies" (Austin, Ruble, & Trabasso, 1977).

Numerous investigators have reported that Piaget's story pairs do not really distinguish between damage and intention-based judgment. More than damage

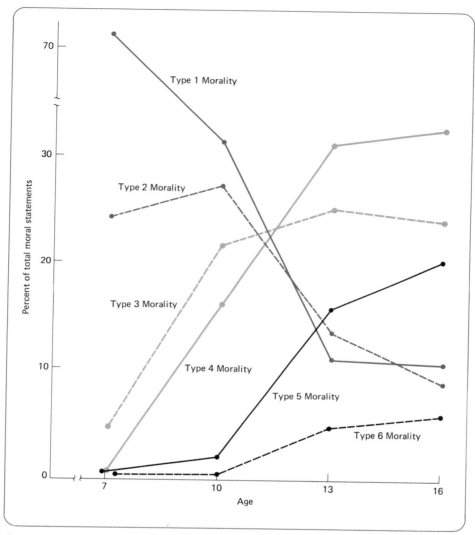

Figure 12-6.   Mean percent of total moral statements of each of six moral judgment types at four ages. (From L. Kohlberg, Development of moral character and moral ideology. In M. L. Hoffman and L. M. Hoffman, eds. *Review of Child Development Research, Vol. 1.* Copyright 1964 by the Russell Sage Foundation. By permission.)

and intentions alone are varied in the story pairs (Gottlieb, Taylor, & Ruderman, 1977; Karniol, 1978; Shantz, 1975). For instance, Piaget has confounded *type of intent* (good or bad motivation) with *degree of responsibility* (accidental or intentional). Thus, it is difficult to determine if children are focusing on the intentions (good or bad) of a character or his or her responsibility for the outcome (accidental or intentional). Another problem is that high damage is always the result of good intentions, while low damage is always the result of bad intentions. Piaget never considers children's relative valuation of bad intentions that produce high damage nor good intentions that produce low damage. Karniol (1978) also points out that in Piaget's stories children must infer that a rule exists and has been broken (bad intentions), such as when the child is getting some jam. Younger children may not see this as a forbidden act with bad intentions; this is especially likely given their concrete thinking. We also see that in both Piaget's story types the damage that results is really the result of clumsiness or carelessness (Karniol, 1978). On closer inspection of the story pairs it seems that children are really asked to evaluate two accidental acts. Unless the stories deliberately specify the reasons for the behaviors, the rules which are violated, and the degree of a child's responsibility for the damage, it is difficult to understand whether intentions increase in importance in children's moral development.

Story content has also played a role in the work of both Piaget and Kohlberg. Looking first at Piaget, we find that the type of damage which characters produce is evaluated differentially by children (Berg-Cross, 1975). Berg-Cross found that six-year-olds judged characters who produced damage to persons more harshly than characters who produced property damage. Elkind and Dabek (1977) elaborated on the importance of type of damage in a study with kindergarten, second-grade and fourth-grade children. They found that children at all ages judged physical damage to people more harshly than damage to property. Children also evaluated characters more negatively when they intentionally, rather than accidentally, produced equal damage. The implication is that children, even at age five, can recognize and use intentions in their moral evaluations. However, their damage judgments are not content-free. Damage to another person is more incriminating than damage to inanimate objects.

Kohlberg's stages appear to some to have similar methodological problems. There are difficulties in that children with higher measured intelligence tend to have higher levels of moral development (Kohlberg, 1963). Also, the scoring of the responses to the moral dilemmas is difficult and requires considerable training and experience (Kurtines & Grief, 1974). There are content-related problems similar to those we see in Piaget's stories. On retesting, subjects do not necessarily display the same kinds of moral reasoning to the same moral dilemmas (Kurtines & Grief, 1974; Rubin & Trotter, 1977). The stages also do not seem to lead to predictions of what individuals will do in real-life situations (Kurtines & Grief, 1974). Finally, some evidence appears to show that, at least for some individuals, the stages are not fixed; movement above and below one's modal stage is possible (Kohlberg, 1976; Kurtines & Grief, 1974). Whether these shifts are the results of scoring errors or problems in Kohlberg's theory is not clear.

Training and Experience

The importance of experience or deliberate training on the cognitive developmental sequences identified by Piaget and Kohlberg remains a fascinating field for study. Turiel reasoned that exposure to more advanced moral reasoning (one stage higher than already achieved) would modify children's current stage of moral development. This type of experience was more successful in modifying children's moral reasoning than exposure to moral reasoning which was one stage below the level of reasoning which the child had attained. Turiel (1966) thus found support for the sequence suggested by Kohlberg. In a later study (Rest, Turiel, & Kohlberg, 1969), children were given moral reasoning which was either one stage above, two stages above, or one stage below their own. Children were found to judge the highest stage as "best" and the stage below their own "worst." Their comprehension, however, of the more advanced stages was somewhat inadequate. Recent evidence indicates that children may simply judge more complex language to be preferable to simpler language—which lessens the impact of the two studies above (Moran & Joniak, 1979). The apparent preferences for higher stage responses may be the result of a preference for using the more complex language exhibited in the higher stages.

A few studies have attempted to provide "moral education" in the classroom based on the principles of Kohlberg (Reihman, 1978). In these studies, deliberate training through a moral education program in the classroom typically produced sequential development along Kohlberg's stages (Beyer, 1976; Blatt & Kohlberg, 1976; Galbraith & Jones, 1976). Control children, who did not receive such training, did not show improvements in moral understanding and did not show an increase in the rate at which stages were acquired. A relatively common training procedure used in moral educational studies is seen in Table 12-6, which describes the processes that teachers follow in their classrooms (Galbraith & Jones, 1976) to guide moral development along Kohlberg's stage sequences.

Other investigators have induced change in moral levels in children through modeling (Bandura, 1969; Keasey, 1973) as well as role-taking (Arbuthnot, 1975), and these changes are apparently long-lasting. Changes were evident in children

Table 12-6
THE PROCESS OF MORAL EDUCATION IN THE CLASSROOM

Confront a Moral Dilemma	State a Tentative Position	Examine the Reasoning	Reflect on an Individual Position
Present the dilemma	Reflect on an individual position	Examine reasons in a small group	Summarize reasoning
State the circumstances	Establish individual position	Examine different reasons on the basis of:	State a reason
Define terms	Establish class position	a) Issues	
State the problem for the main character	Establish reasons for position	b) Analogous dilemmas c) Consequence d) Previous dilemmas	

Source: Adapted from R. Galbraith and T. Jones, "Teaching Strategies for Moral Dilemmas," *Social Education,* 1975, pp. 16–22.

after more than two weeks (Keasey, 1973) and in some cases after three months (LeFurgy & Woloshin, 1969). Such effects, of course, raise questions about the cognitive-developmental theory of morality. For example, change due to mere exposure or imitative modeling is not expected if moral development is structurally based.

The role of parents has been somewhat underemphasized by both Kohlberg and Piaget, who see peer interactions and role-taking in peer groups as the major factors underlying morality. Nevertheless, some studies have found that parents play a significant role in the development of children's morality. Hoffman and Holstein both note that children who experience frequent verbal explanations from parents in the course of socialization are more mature in their moral behaviors, thoughts, and emotions than children without this kind of parent interaction. This type of socialization, called *induction,* permits children to draw conclusions about their own behaviors (Hoffman, 1970). Holstein (1972) suggests that induction may encourage moral development because parents appear seriously interested in the dilemmas which their children confront. They show a willingness to discuss but not solve these dilemmas for their children. Both Holstein (1972) and Hoffman (1970) find that induction allows the child to see that parents can empathize and adopt his or her perspective in their concern for the child's dilemmas. Clearly, some types of parents—those who use induction—have an important influence in their children's moral development.

SUMMARY

The development of morality was considered from three different theoretical perspectives: psychoanalytic, social learning, and cognitive-developmental. The majority of recent research has concentrated on the cognitive-developmental view, and we closely examined the work of three representative lines of work undertaken by Piaget, Kohlberg, and Selman.

The contribution of current empirical studies on children's moral development was also presented. These studies were evaluated in terms of the validity of the cognitive-developmental view and the relative importance of specific training or experience. We also considered some of the methodological factors which partially underlie the developmental trends in morality identified thus far.

RECOMMENDED READINGS

DePalma, D. J., and Foley, J. M. (eds.). *Moral development: current theory and research.* Hillsdale, N.J.: Lawrence Erlbaum, 1975.

This book consists of a series of papers emphasizing the nature of empirical studies designed to help us understand the dimensions of moral development in children. The variety of orientations and task situations designed to assess "morality" in children is particularly revealing.

Lickona, T. (ed.). *Moral development and behavior.* New York: Holt, Rinehart, 1976.

A broad-based collection of original papers dealing with current theoretical perspectives, research, and social issues in the area of moral development.

Wright, D. F. *The psychology of moral behavior.* Baltimore: Penguin Books, 1971.

A brief, readable account of the major theories of morality, coupled with separate chapters on empirical studies in specific content areas. The issue of how to apply our knowledge of children's morality is also considered.

6

ADOLESCENCE

13

Physical and Social Development in Adolescence

CURRENT VIEWS

Looking back on our own adolescence, we are reminded that this developmental period is an ambiguous one in our modern society. Because their role is not clearly defined adolescents experience uncertainty and anxiety as they search for a place in the social order. We all remember the conflicts of this period, especially as we see younger siblings, cousins, and family friends attempting to resolve dilemmas similar to those we encountered. Many times trivial conflicts assume monumental importance because our society provides vague and undefined techniques to help adolescents reconcile their roles as adult or child. One way of dealing with such conflict is to vacillate between the two roles.

Historical Perspectives

In the past, the length of adolescence was considerably shorter than the ten to twelve years which are devoted to this period today (Bakan, 1971). Adolescents and children in earlier times were expected to contribute to the family's economy. On rural farms, devoid of mechanized equipment, every available family member helped to harvest the crops. Imagine the reaction parents of this era would have had to their adolescents' requests for a few months of free time to "get their heads together!" The luxury of an extended period in which to grow up was simply impossible. Adolescents were expected to assume clearly identifiable adult roles as rapidly as possible. The requirements and expectations imposed by society were clear, straightforward, and easy for adolescents to discern.

Thus the transition from childhood to adulthood was relatively simple and direct. Bakan (1971) notes that as education became compulsory for children, labor needs were supplemented by advanced technology, and health care and longevity improved, our society was able to devote longer and longer periods to the adolescent quest for identity. Despite this increased time, however, the process of becoming an adult has become more confusing and more anxiety-producing.

It may be that passing through this developmental period is far more difficult than ever before. Coleman (1974) notes that adolescents may have more difficulty in assuming adult roles because they are given minimal responsibilities by their parents, are unable to assume work roles because of compulsory education, and are economically dependent on the family for an extended period of time. In earlier periods of our history, these conditions were absent.

Idealized Perspectives

Some authorities see the period of adolescence in highly stylized form. Often adolescents are characterized in largely negative terms—as a force to be controlled and continually socialized (Haan, 1972). On the other hand, adolescents may be seen as a very powerful, positive force for society—the basis for social change

358

(Kenniston, 1975). Both of these positions are obviously far too extreme to accurately represent this period of development. Large segments of our society, however, tend to hold one or the other of these views of the "younger" generation. For example, many times adolescents are described as flighty, moody, unpredictable daydreamers by adults (Haan, 1972). Others see only the beneficial results to society which this age group produces and wonder why we don't profit from their fresh perspective on life's problems (Yankelovich, 1972). Consider the initial reactions of American youth to the Vietnam War and their continued distrust and resentment towards the policies of then President Nixon. We discovered that these adolescent views were based on a solid foundation and were subsequently easily and rapidly absorbed by the adult generation.

It appears that the orientation most frequently encountered by adolescents is more often negative than positive. Adolescents are often seen as overcritical, antisocial, and unappreciative of the attainments and life struggles of their parents. Adolescents never seem to be able to get away fast enough from those awful one-way parent lectures that begin "Why, when I was your age . . . " or "Do you know what I had to do to get . . . " Perhaps adolescents generalize our society's interest in newness and change and reject out-of-hand the established roles and values of their parents.

While not all adolescents nor all adults are one-sided in their orientations, it is rare for young people to move towards adulthood with assurance, confidence, and a sense of personal accomplishment. Idealizations of this period only limit our understanding of what actually occurs.

Adolescent Conflicts

The extent to which adolescents experience conflicts and difficulties in development is a matter of sharply divergent opinion among psychologists (Murray, 1971). Some psychologists see adolescents as engaged in a battle to survive this period of "storm and stress," while others think adolescents move through this phase of life with few problems and stresses. Bandura (1964) has presented a number of reasons for the popularity of storm and stress notions of adolescence. Based on his interviews with adolescent boys, he concludes that most adolescents easily pass through this phase of life with a minimum, not a maximum of problems. Adolescents accept their parents' values with no hint of rebellion, repression, and emotional upheaval.

Why do we *expect* to find adolescents experiencing great conflict at this time? Bandura (1964) thinks that the popular media have dramatically emphasized the problems of this developmental period. No one would go out of their way to read a newspaper story with the bold headline "Johnny Reaches Puberty" and the normative details which follow. But people are much more likely to read a story titled "Johnny Threatens School Teacher with a Knife." Bandura's conclusion is that the unusual events of adolescence, those which illustrate the storm and stress idea, receive more attention and publicity than the less novel but more frequently successful transitions experienced by most adolescents. He also reminds us that many of the foremost theories which emphasize storm and stress have been developed by those who see the atypical, deviant adolescent. For instance, there are many therapists whose understanding of this period may be based almost entirely on the cases which are brought to them for evaluation and treatment. This is a biased sample from which to attempt to draw general, normative conclusions. Such cases represent instances of unsuccessful coping with the adolescent developmental period. Since therapists see few successful adolescents, who have *not* encountered problems in coping, Bandura believes we ought to be concerned about the theories developed from such atypical samples (1964).

Descriptions of adolescence as a period of great stress may be seen in terms of the self-fulfilling prophecy. That is, expecting all adolescents to experience stress, rebelliousness, and emotional turmoil may help to maintain and encourage these behaviors (Bandura, 1964). Adolescence, like any other period in human development, involves both conflicts and adjustment. It is unfortunate that our society has overemphasized the problems which characterize these years. As you will see, there are many adolescents whose experiences are marked by mastery, success, and a sense of satisfaction. For them adolescence is a developmental period handled efficiently and effectively and marked by a relatively small number of problems (Douvan & Adelson, 1966). Through the self-fulfilling prophecy, however, both adolescents and adults may be sensitized to problems which become magnified in importance at this time. By expecting to find problems, both adolescents and adults may help to create them.

Rites of Passage

In more primitive societies the process of reaching adulthood is aided by the presence of tribal rituals or *rites de passage*. These rites may be simple and completed in an evening or very elaborate and require many weeks (Muuss, 1975a). The timing of these rites of passage for girls is usually based on the onset of the *menarche* (first menstruation). Because no comparable biological indicator of development exists for boys, the rites for boys may be based on other criteria such as age. The rites of passage for both sexes are usually dramatic and, once experienced, provide full acceptance into adult society. For instance, the following rites of passage for girls have been described among the Tukuna Indians of South America:

> . . . immediately upon onset of menarche the young girl hides from men by going into the seclusion hut, where she stays for three months in complete isolation. In preparation for the festivities the girl's body is painted. During the three days of ceremonies, dancing, and merrymaking the girl's hair is plucked from her head. Immediately after the ceremony the young woman is permitted to marry, but there is no wedding feast. The puberty ritual is the most significant ceremony in her lifetime, changing her status from that of a child to a marriageable woman. (Muuss, 1975a, p. 474)

For boys, ceremonies often entail feats of strength or tests of endurance, pain, suffering, and humiliation. There are often elements of bodily mutilation, such as scarring of the face, piercing the ears, and ritualistic circumcision (Muuss, 1975a). Adult males reveal tribal customs, hunting tactics, religious ceremonies, and other secrets to the young initiates. Boys are told the tribe's origins, the history of the major families in the village, or the genealogy of past tribal chiefs.

Such rites of passage are important because they are the only means by which children can attain adult status in these societies. Anthropologists have speculated that the rites themselves also help to solidify and stabilize sex roles (Young, 1962), especially for boys. Rogers (1969, 1977) feels that the rites of passage may help boys establish sex-role identity but are not as crucial for girls. The majority of anthropological studies suggest that rites of passage for boys are far more elaborate and extensive than for girls (Bettleheim, 1962). Other studies have noted that the harshness of these rites varies from culture to culture. Following psychoanalytic theory, Burton and Whiting (1961) developed the idea that such rites help boys to resolve finally Oedipal conflicts which may have arisen through sleeping with their mothers during infancy. These authors noted that male rites of passage are particularly harsh in societies where such sleeping arrangements continue for an extended period of time; the longer the mother and son slept together, the harsher were the rites of passage imposed by adult males in the society. During these rites the strongly aggressive, powerful adult males instill fear, anxiety, and submission in their younger counterparts; a strong sense of same sex identity is insured. These rites are seen as overcoming the potential interest and cross-sex identification of sons with their mothers once and for all.

Do we have such rites of passage in our own modern society? Although there are many indicators which mark the passage of adolescents into adult life, no single ritual assumes the importance found in more primitive cultures. Some of our most notable rituals have only symbolic value, since no real change in the adolescent's status can be discerned. In this category are such religious ceremonies as confirmation, Bar Mitzvah, or even social events like a "Sweet Sixteen" party. We also find that attainment of a certain age entails differential legal obligations and privileges—the right to vote, to drive a car, to drink, to join the army. As others have noted (Muuss, 1975a), we must look to adolescents themselves to see if they interpret these rites of passage as significant marker events separating the world of childhood from the world of adulthood.

For many adolescents, events that have special significance do not receive the attention of the adult generation: using the family car for the first time, having a first date, taking a drink or getting drunk, trying their first cigarette, getting high, their first kiss, petting, or intimate sexual relationship. Within the family, other rites are equally important signs of impending maturity, such as the first shave for boys or girls' first use of make-up. Other more visible events may be seen as rites of passage as well. Graduation from high school or college is one such event—the pagentry and pomp and circumstance may signify the beginning of economic independence for adolescents. It may also mean the beginning of independent living away from the family home, in a college dormitory or in an apartment or commune.

While none of these events are recognized by themselves as major rites of pas-

Figure 13-1. Adolescents attach special significance to events that mark their transition from childhood to adulthood. (Mimi Forsyth/Monkmeyer Press Photo Service)

sage in our society, taken together they suggest to adolescents that adult status is being attained. In comparison to many primitive societies where rites of passage provide a clear discontinuity between child and adult status, in our society the transition consists of a series of small and highly discrete rites. Today's adolescents perhaps need a series of reminders that they are making progress towards adulthood, because of the extended developmental period and because of the ambiguity of the adolescent role. With a multiplicity of such rites, adolescents can monitor in a more continuous fashion their progress.

THEORETICAL EXPLANATIONS OF ADOLESCENT BEHAVIOR

Psychoanalytic View of Adolescence

As we learned in our previous discussion of psychoanalytic theory in Chapter 2, when the body's endocrine system begins to change, the period of latency in middle childhood is over. The biological changes which signify the start of adolescence are important events for psychoanalytic theorists. These biological changes are assumed to be responsible for a reawakening of many earlier emotional conflicts. For Freud, the advent of adolescence means the reappearance of the sexual urges and childhood Oedipal conflicts. Freud reminds us that the basic instincts of the id are never totally eliminated, but merely repressed or suppressed. The infantile impulses of the id which have been successfully held in check by the superego during latency resurface during adolescence. Although these sexual urges have been controlled effectively through a harmonious balance between id, superego, and ego, the biological changes underlying adolescence upset the balance. Specifically, these changes heighten adolescents' libido and libidinal energies. It is only through a major resolution, paralleling that required in the Oedipal conflict, that the adolescent can again strike a balance between id, superego, and ego. Psychoanalytic theorists see the need during adolescence for individuals to control again the sexual instincts and energies of the id to solidify and provide balance in the personality.

If adolescents successfully resolve these urges, then the earlier oral, anal, phallic, and latency stages become merged into a fifth developmental stage—the genital stage. The genital stage for Freud involves the ability to move beyond the narcissism of infancy and develop love relationships beyond one's own self. This permits the biological processes of reproduction essential for maintenance of our species (Freud, 1938).

Freud (1905) considered that adolescent sexuality develops in three ways: (1) through stimulation of the genitals directly, (2) through internal tension and the need for physical release, and (3) through internal thoughts which trigger sexual excitement. Unlike five-year-olds, adolescents in the genital stage have already developed and can explore interests and relationships beyond the family unit. They can direct their sexuality and libidinal energies to persons outside the family unit (Baldwin, 1967). The peer group then becomes an important source of emotional support and provides the opportunity for feelings of independence from parents. In addition, the tentative emotional relationships and deeper love relationships of adolescence are developed in this nonfamily setting. The search for significant relationships beyond the family is called the *primary accomplishment*. Primary accomplishment encompasses both the recognition of our own personal sexuality as well as our need to find a "love object" (Freud, 1938).

Freud described the nature of the adolescent's initial affectional bonds outside the family unit. Adolescents are at first highly attracted to a member of the same sex, such as an older family friend, a favorite teacher, or a special older peer. These brief attachments represent the beginnings of the adolescent's sexual awareness and possession of sexual feelings which have been effectively repressed until this time (Baldwin, 1967). These early affectional, homosexual attachments (i.e., along same-sex lines) must be supplanted by successful cross-sex emotional attachments. Only then is the primary accomplishment of adolescence considered to have been attained.

Freud's view of adolescence emphasizes the biological and instinctual elements of sexuality which resurface and must be resolved. Other psychoanalytic writers, however, including Freud's daughter Anna, have viewed adolescence from a slightly different perspective (Miller, 1974). Anna Freud (1948) considered that although the adolescent's problem in controlling sexuality may appear to be a repetition of the conflicts of the phallic stage, these problems are also different in a number of ways (Gallatin, 1975). For instance, Anna Freud saw that the adolescent had matured and developed more sophisticated techniques for dealing with the heightened drives of this period. In particular, she recognized that by adolescence the superego was well-developed and had become a powerful inner mechanism for controlling behavior. Successful coping with the id-oriented impulses of adolescence was based on very different mechanisms than those available to the younger child attempting to reconcile the Oedipal conflict. Anna Freud's major contribution to the study of adolescence was her identification of the developmental gains the child had accomplished during latency in controlling his or her own behavior. She recognized that new ego defenses or techniques of coping with heightened id impulses were available (Freud, 1938). Thus, Anna Freud saw that the basic struggle in adolescence, striking a balance between the increased demands of the id and the demands of the superego, involved different processes from those employed in coping with similar conflicts during the phallic period (Gallatin, 1975). For instance, since the superego was now well-developed, children can see themselves as "good" or "bad" after giving into or withstanding the impulses of the id.

The capacity for self-evaluation represents an important difference between the adolescent and the child, who relied on parents for such information. Coping with these conflicting demands involves approaches that were previously unavailable. The adolescent might choose to see how long he or she could control a particular impulse or examine the degree to which he or she could withstand giving in to a particular need (Freud, 1936). As Gallatin suggests, such self-denial, or *asceticism,* may arise because the id appears so strong and so powerful that any form of gratification is somehow suspect (1975, p. 69). Anna Freud also recognized that the intellectual skills of the adolescent, vastly superior to those of the young child, could be used in coping. These skills could be employed in defensive reactions such as *intellectualization* to help cope with the heightened demands of the id: "By casting his own struggles in the form of an abstract argument, the adolescent could manage to gain some distance from it" (Gallatin, 1975, p. 71).

Anna Freud felt that successful resolution of adolescent conflicts was dependent on three additional factors: (1) the strength of the id impulses, which vary because of genetics from one person to another; (2) the strength of the ego and superego which are developed prior to adolescence; and (3) the characteristic ego defenses previously employed to control the impulses of the id—and their resultant success or failure (Gallatin, 1975). Anna Freud's orientation to adolescence emphasized not only the conflicts which arise between id, ego, and superego but also the unique defenses which may help to attain a balance between these demands. Like other psychoanalytic writers, she found a parallel between the demands of the id during the phallic period and those seen in adolescence. She had, however, a unique view of the important role of the ego defenses which separates her from other psychoanalytic theorists. Many consider Anna Freud's view of adolescence far superior to any other psychoanalytic account (Miller, 1974).

Cultural-Anthropological View of Adolescence

The cultural-anthropological view of adolescence developed in reaction to the psychoanalytic emphasis on the biological factors which trigger new impulses and desires. Both the importance of biological factors and the description of adolescence as a period of storm and stress were directly challenged by the cultural-anthropological view (Havighurst, 1976). The works of Margaret Mead (*Coming of Age in Samoa,* 1939a; *Growing up in New Guinea,* 1939b) and Ruth Benedict (*Patterns of Culture,* 1934) were among the earliest to question the importance which psychoanalytic theories placed on biological explanations of adolescent behavior. The basic emphasis of the cultural-anthropological viewpoint is on the role of cultural factors in understanding adolescence. For Mead and Benedict adolescent behavior is more dependent on cultural teaching than it is on biological factors.

Both Benedict and Mead support the notion that development is a continuous process not isolated into separate stages. In particular, they question the validity of the adolescent period as *inevitably* a time of great anxiety. Mead, for example, studied children growing up in Samoa. She reported that they participated in virtually every aspect of society and were permitted from an early age to observe most aspects of adult behavior. Children were able to witness directly sexual intercourse, illness, death, and the birth process in this island society. Sexual interest and activity was considered a natural part of growing up, and few restrictions were imposed on this or other kinds of behavior. She found that most children masturbated during childhood and by adolescence were actively pursuing sexual relations.

Mead reported that there were no sharp discontinuities between the roles of child and adult. In the course of development girls carried out the responsibilities of other females in the society, such as caring for younger brothers and sisters; while boys learned about fishing and how to manage a canoe. As Samoan children entered adolescence then, no basic changes in roles took place. Although responsibilities were perhaps increased, the transition from adolescence to adulthood was gradual, smooth, and continuous. Parents, who had provided virtually total freedom for their children, did not try to control their offspring, and the result was minimal conflict with authority. As Mead noted, in Samoa, "Adolescence represented no period of crisis or stress but was instead an orderly developing of a set of slowly maturing interests and activities" (1939a, p. 157). The transition to adulthood was gradual and continuous and flowed from the earlier experiences of childhood.

Samoans had, according to Mead's description, derived salient benefits from these socialization practices. First there was minimal concern over sexuality in the society; neither guilt nor attempts to be secretive were found. Child-parent interactions were relatively conflict-free and casual. Samoans had little interest in deriving personal prestige or endless collections of personal possessions. The emphasis was on a low-key, casual, and unhurried life-style. Moreover, Mead discovered that there was little interest in competition nor anxiety about achievement so often encountered in Western society.

Although Mead represented Samoan life as idyllic and conflict-free, she was not totally enamored of the Samoan life-style. She reported that emotional relation-ships among Samoans were relatively superficial and did not seem to involve the intensity of commitment which we would expect to find fulfilling. She pointed out that long-lasting relationships were extremely rare; casual encounters and casual relationships were the norm. Samoans were encouraged to adhere to traditional styles of thinking and behaving, and there was a general intolerance of any unique, individual differences in Samoan society.

Benedict emphasized the importance of continuities and discontinuities in West-ern culture (1960). A *continuity* represents a traditional belief or way of believing which persists from one developmental period to another. *Discontinuities,* on the other hand, require change in beliefs as old forms of behavior become discarded in favor of new ones. Benedict noted that in Western society there were far more discontinuities than continuities in development. For instance, in childhood we encourage play and enjoyment with no responsibility for self-support. Later, as work roles assume greater importance, the earlier beliefs of childhood are no longer appropriate. Other examples of discontinuities include: (1) the change from the submissiveness of childhood to the dominance of adulthood, and (2) the shift from repression of sexual feelings to open expression and satisfaction. Whether there is a separate stage of adolescence and whether this period is marked by conflict depends primarily on the ways in which a culture provides for the transition from one developmental period to the next. Despite the biological changes associated with adolescence, a smooth, natural transition may be expected where cultural continuities exist.

The cultural-anthropological view provides a sharp contrast to the psychoana-lytic approach. Clearly, the biological changes associated with adolescence do not always result in psychic conflict and emotional turmoil. As we saw in the work of Mead, Samoan society provided opportunities for the adoption of adult roles at very early ages. Under these conditions, adolescence occurred with a minimum of problems, conflicts, and emotional stress. There is thus support for a continuous, rather than discontinuous, approach to development. There is little evidence for adolescence as an inevitable time of storm and stress.

Adolescents as Marginal Persons

Some theorists perceive adolescence as a time of marginality. Based on the work of Lewin (1948), *marginality* refers to individuals who have no real sense of belonging and who have no reference group with whom they identify. Lewin (1959) saw adolescence as a period in which there was an important change in reference groups. The shift from the reference group of the child to that of the adult took time and left the adolescent in a transitional period without a sense of group membership. This marginal existence described the seemingly endless search among adolescents for a personal identity, physical self-concept, and a coherent value system. Adolescent marginality, with membership and identification as nei-ther child nor adult, brought about feelings of uncertainty and ambiguity.

The results of this transitional existence as a marginal member of society are predictable. Marginality produces emotional instability, personal conflict, increased uncertainty, and self-hate (Muuss, 1975b p. 127). The concept of marginality, in part, helps us understand the adolescent attempt to derive new meaning from life, to undertake religious search or conversion, and to redefine his or her role within the family and within the larger society.

Experimental evidence in support of adolescent marginality is minimal. In one study, Bamber (1973) asked adults and adolescents living in Ireland to complete a questionnaire involving items designed to assess marginality: "I act decisively," "I wish I were more skillful," "I am sure about my place in any social situation." Subjects also completed a personality inventory and assigned adjectives they considered appropriate for three developmental periods: childhood (7–12), adolescence (13–19), and adulthood. The study thus relied in part on the reports of adolescents who were currently experiencing this supposed transitional period.

The results of the study provide little evidence that adolescents view their existence as marginal. They tended to see only two developmental periods: childhood or adulthood. More importantly, adolescents saw themselves as part of the world of adults, not between worlds. The responses of adults, however, reflected three distinctly different developmental periods: childhood, adolescence, and adulthood. There was no overall evidence for an adolescent marginal personality. Younger adolescent girls, however, displayed personality dimensions which were somewhat marginal (e.g., neuroticism and low extraversion). Bamber concluded that to characterize adolescence as a "marginal time" is an oversimplication of the complexities of adolescence.

Emphasis on Individuality in Adolescence

The theoretical approach of Carl Rogers, emphasizing the importance of the individual, grew out of his clinical experiences and role as a therapist. Although Rogers does not specifically deal with adolescence, his general interest in the process of development and personality growth provides a useful way of conceptualizing this period. Rogers does not adhere to a stage theory, but rather views all development as oriented towards the achievement of a "fully functioning person" (Rogers, 1961, 1962). His views of the process of *becoming* can easily be seen in any adolescent's search for a sense of identity and attempt to assume a valued role in adult society.

For Rogers, success in achieving the goal of becoming a fully functioning person depends in part on our willingness to be *open to experience*. If we can develop and maintain openness, our ability to function effectively as a person is enhanced. If we fail to develop this openness, we will be defensive, distorting experience and failing to grow from it. Adolescence seems to be an important time for developing this openness (Rogers, 1964).

Adolescents do, at times, appear willing to experiment with new ideas and to experience different aspects of life. This provides a sharp contrast to younger children who tend to rely on others (e.g., their parents) to guide their behavior, make their choices, and interpret their experiences. One of the most significant changes in adolescence should be the shift to a personal, uniquely individualistic value system which can then be used to interpret the flow of life experiences (Rogers, 1964). Not all adolescents, however, accomplish the development of a unique, personal set of values. Many adolescents merely continue to parrot the values, attitudes, and beliefs of their parents. Those adolescents who fail to develop a personal system of ideals are typically defensive; they protect themselves from new experience and the possibility of further growth thoughout their lives. They cannot profit from and realistically understand their own experiences. Thus, they distort reality and develop stereotyped, narrow methods of problem-solving. By accepting the view of their parents or the dominant cultural position, adolescents can only experience the process of living indirectly. They hold attitudes towards experience and life which are not their own. If adolescents develop and maintain an openness to experiences, however, they can see life in a totally different fashion. Based on their personal reactions, adolescents can begin to see creative solutions to social problems which are different from those found by the older generation. Thus, openness to experience provides the basis of change and growth not only for the individual but for society as well.

A second principle emphasized by Rogers is that we should begin to perceive ourselves as *processes* rather than static entities. Adolescents recognize that they change as they become involved in living. Most importantly for adolescents, behavior can be thought of in terms of both present and future perspectives. As we will see, for Piaget this represents a major change in intellectual development. Adolescents begin to see that their behavior can be adapted to fit the immediate situation or can be altered to fit into a more expanded time frame. Rogers is describing the dynamic process of living: adolescents recognize for the first time that they are not totally the products of their past experiences. He emphasizes that we construct or structure our ongoing experiences: the structure of experience is devised from the experience itself (Rogers, 1961).

A third principle is that of *trust* in our own capacities. Our behavior should develop from our own personal judgment and resources—right or wrong. This helps evolve a mature view of accepting responsibility for success and failure which are necessary for each adolescent's growth. Through both success and failure, adolescents learn to size up situations more effectively, understand the demands of others, comprehend their own needs, and accept the outcome of their action or inaction. As they learn from past experience, more accurately understand the present, and predict the future consequences of their behavior, they find themselves growing and developing a sense of achievement and accomplishment. Perhaps this trust is best seen in the adolescent quest for experiencing life directly. Rogers certainly feels that trust in our own capacities cannot be developed without direct experience.

By being open, seeing living as a dynamic process, and by trusting their personal capacities, adolescents can move toward satisfying, full lives. Rogers thinks that these are difficult goals which require great courage on the part of the individual. Have we established conditions in society which permit adolescents to move towards the goal of becoming a "fully functioning person?''

Erikson's Theory of Psychosocial Development

Erik Erikson has attempted to understand adolescence within a broad-based psychosocial theory of human development which we briefly reviewed in Chapter 2. His "Eight Stages of Man" are presented in Table 13-1. The table shows that Erikson has conceptualized development as a series of basic crises throughout the entire life span. The period of adolescence (Stage 5) is described as a time of *identity* vs. *identity diffusion*. Erikson has based his work in part on the psychoanalytic formulations of Freud. His work differs from the psychoanalytic tradition in many ways, however. For example, personality development is seen as a continuous lifelong process. The crises are presented as critical choice points from infancy to old age. Each crisis requires tremendous energy and shifting of perspective in order to be mastered successfully. Not only does Erikson view the individual's own growth and inner dynamics as crucial to the process of development, he also recognizes the equally important contribution of the larger social environment. His theory involves a broadly based psychosocial perspective which is not seen in the psychoanalytic tradition.

While Freud derived his theory from studying the neurotic personality, Erikson's theory evolved from a study of the normal, "healthy" personality (Erikson, 1968). He began to see the importance of the inner forces *and* cultural forces which are at work in the development of a coherent ego identity (Thomas, 1979). The process by which we attain this sense of identity is assumed to be biologically based (Erikson, 1968); Erikson used the term *epigenetic principle* to refer to this developmental progression. In Erikson's theory, the epigenetic principle underlies all development, since "everything that grows is governed by a present construction plan" (Thomas, 1979). Erikson states: "Out of this ground plan the parts arise, each part having its time of special ascendency, until all parts have arisen to form a functioning whole" (1968, p. 92).

We will examine only his approach to the period of adolescence: identity vs. identity diffusion. Erikson himself has viewed this stage as perhaps most crucial to the formation of ego identity. The problem in adolescence is to develop a sense of personal identity at a time in which there are many rapid changes in physical appearance, emotional and psychological perspectives, and in evaluations from the larger society.

Coping with the identity crisis of adolescence depends on how successfully the earlier four stages were resolved. Erikson attaches special significance to the adolescent period, and society also recognizes the uniqueness of this developmental stage by permitting a lengthy "psychosocial moratorium" in which adolescents are given the freedom to work through the crisis of identity. The moratorium granted adolescents is not seen at any other point in development. A *psychosocial moratorium* is "a period of delay, granted to somebody who is not ready to meet obli-

Table 13–1
ERIKSON'S EIGHT DEVELOPMENTAL STAGES

Stage Number	Column A Psychosocial Crisis	Column B Radius of Significant Relations	Column C Psychosocial Modalities	Column D Freud's Psychosexual Stages	Column E Approximate Ages in Years
I	Trust versus Mistrust	Maternal person	To get To give in return	Oral-Respiratory, Sensory-Kinesthetic (Incorporative Modes)	0–1
II	Autonomy versus Shame, Doubt	Parental persons	To hold on To let go	Anal-Urethral, Muscular (Retentive-Eliminative)	2–3
III	Initiative versus Guilt	Basic family	To make (going after) To "make like" (playing)	Infantile-Genital, Locomotor (Intrusive, Inclusive)	3–6
IV	Industry versus Inferiority	"Neighborhood" and school	To make things (completing) To make things together	Latency	7–12 or so

Stage Number	Column A Psychosocial Crisis	Column B Radius of Significant Relations	Column C Psychosocial Modalities	Column D Freud's Psychosexual Stages	Column E Approximate Ages in Years
V	Identity and Repudiation versus Identity Diffusion	Peer groups and out-groups; models of leadership	To be oneself (or not to be) To share being oneself	Puberty and Adolescence	12–18 or so
VI	Intimacy and Solidarity versus Isolation	Partners in friendship, sex, competition, cooperation	To lose and find oneself in another	Mature Genitality	The 20s
VII	Generativity versus Self-Absorption	Divided labor and shared household	To make be To take care of		Late 20s to 50s
VIII	Integrity versus Despair	"Mankind" "My kind"	To be, through having been To face not being		50s and beyond

Source: Adapted from E. H. Erikson, Identity and the Life Cycle Psychological Issues, 1959, **1**, p. 166 copyright © 1959 by International Universities Press. By permission of W. W. Norton & Co., Inc.

gations or forced on somebody who should give himself time to do so'' (Erikson, 1956, p. 5). At no other time is the individual given as much time to examine, think, imagine, and experiment with his identity. Erikson sees the psychosocial moratorium as permitting adolescents the opportunity to deal with the following seven areas.

1. *Time perspective vs. time diffusion.*   The adolescent must begin to see him or herself as having clear roots in the past and a potential existence in the future. These past and future perspectives must be integrated.

2. *Self-certainty vs. apathy.*   The adolescent must discover that his or her actions are evaluated by others and that evaluations of others matter to him. There may be doubts about our abilities, but we cannot escape by failing to act. Our own actions and the evaluations of others bring about a sense of self-certainty and confidence in our own identities and contribute to a sense of who we are.

3. *Role experimentation vs. negative identity.*   The adolescent must not be afraid to experiment with new and different roles. Adolescence is a time for trying out adult roles, without the need for personal commitment.

4. *Anticipation of achievement vs. work paralysis.*   The adolescent must begin to apply his or her sense of industry to some work-related tasks. These help provide the feedback that is needed to select work roles which are suited to our particular unique abilities.

5. *Sexual identity vs. bisexual diffusion.*   The adolescent must resolve conflicts which surround his or her sex-role identity. The preliminary, tentative commitments of adolescence provide a proving ground for heterosexual relationships which involve intimacy.

6. *Leadership polarization vs. authority diffusion.*   The adolescent must accept the responsibility of assuming leadership roles when appropriate. There must also be a recognition that bowing to the authority of others is sometimes necessary for successful social interaction.

7. *Ideological polarization vs. diffusion of ideals.*   The adolescent must develop a personal value system which will enable him or her to make individual decisions for the remainder of his or her life. (Erikson, 1959)

These adolescent tasks require an extensive period of time and reflection, which our society has provided in the psychosocial moratorium. Yet, the psychosocial moratorium is not always successfully utilized by every adolescent.

A moratorium sometimes fails when individuals have defined themselves too early and are committed to adult society before they are ready or when they have strong feelings of inadequacy from being left to the uncertainty of their developmental period and their time for an eventual progression in development. They will find themselves fully at a loss as to who they are, who they want to be, and who they are in the eyes of others. (Maier, 1978, p. 116).

Thus adolescents must be cautious that their attempts to resolve the problems of identity do not result in commitments which are superficial and illusory. Successful resolution of the identity crisis may take far longer than the teenage years, and often very creative people seem to require a long psychosocial moratorium (Cartwright, 1979). From Erikson's study of historical figures like Luther and Ghandi, he sees that often creative individuals do not have a simple, readily identifiable role to assume in society.

Erikson's theory has been studied experimentally and generally supported in terms of the sequence of order in which crises are attained (Ciaccio, 1971). Waterman, Geary, and Waterman (1974) have also shown that Erikson's stage of identity vs. identity diffusion is particularly appropriate for describing college students. Only about 25% of a sample of freshmen had attained resolution of this fifth stage of development. By the time they were seniors, however, almost 45% of the sample had achieved some degree of identity. Interestingly, more than 30% of students showed evidence of identity diffusion throughout all four years of college.

PHYSICAL DEVELOPMENT AND CHANGE

Initially, our only realization that we have reached adolescence is a specific change in our body such as the emergence of breast buds or the first pubic hair—pigmented and standing all alone. These changes may bring either embarrassment or delight. Adolescents often share the changes in their physical development with their peer group and compare the rate of growth and appearance of their bodies.

Adolescent growth involves changes in body size, sexual organs, and secondary sex characteristics. Most research on adolescent growth supports the theoretical position that it is in fact a continuous process (Faust, 1977; Tanner, 1970). Tanner (1973) sees little evidence for discrete stages in physical growth; even the sequence of crawling to walking is continuous rather than composed of separate, isolated stages. Consequently, physical growth is best considered as a "series of many successive processes, overlapping one another" (Tanner, 1970). Physical growth may appear to be rather stage-like because of the *disjunctive* scales which we use to isolate the successive steps in a sequence (Wohlwill, 1973). Yet, for Tanner (1973) and others, these sequences are really "conjunctive," since the changes are hierarchically arranged and integrated sequentially throughout development.

Physical growth unfolds at different rates in different individuals. These differences are the result of the interaction of both genetic and environmental events (Tanner, 1973). The complexity of the interrelationships is so great that it seems impossible to determine the relative importance of genetic and environmental forces. Yet, since the growth process is initiated by biological events, genetic factors are of immense importance in the determination of growth (Tanner, 1970).

Before we examine these biological events, let's briefly look at the role of environmental factors in physical development. Nutrition seems to be a significant environmental influence on adolescent growth. Many studies report a positive cor-

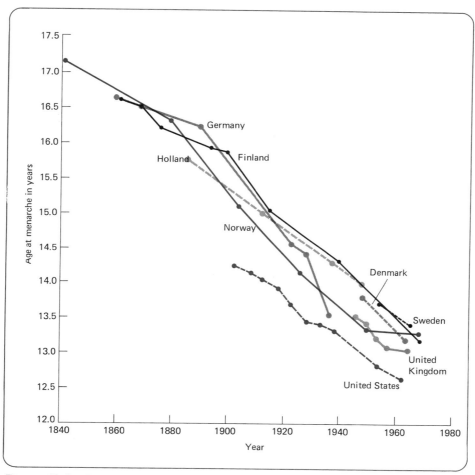

Figure 13-2. The age of menarche in the U.S. and seven countries of western Europe has declined greatly from what it was 120 years ago. For example, in the mid-1840s, an average Norwegian girl began menstruating at 17. Today she is just over 13. (From J. M. Tanner, *Growth at adolescence.* 2nd. ed.; Oxford: Blackwell Scientific Publications. Redrawn for *Scientific American,* 1973, 229, p. 40. By permission.)

relation between social class and physical developmental indicators such as height or age at menarche (Tanner, 1961; 1973). The diets of adolescents from advantaged social class backgrounds often contain more of the proteins and calories necessary for growth than the diets of those from lower social classes. Tanner (1961) also notes that advantaged adolescents are more likely to have good medical care, healthy exercise, and sleep. These factors are directly related to advanced rates of physical growth among adolescents in all societies, and they help adolescents to realize their full genetic potential for physical development.

The very same factors (improved environmental and social conditions) have also been implicated in the *secular trend* in the age of menarche described in Figure

13-2. This figure shows that there has been a considerable change in the timing of first menstruation over the last 100–150 years. Girls today are reaching menarche nearly 4–5 years earlier than they did in earlier generations. While some have questioned whether this trend would ever stop, evidence suggests the progression towards earlier and earlier menarche has begun to taper off (Eichorn, 1975; Tanner, 1973).

Demographic data in our own country indicates that there are substantial differences in caloric intake among adolescents from different social classes and ethnic backgrounds. Table 13-2 shows that the difference in caloric intake is substantial and related to both poverty and ethnicity. These figures take on additional significance when we recognize that in adolescence the recommended caloric intake for boys has been established at 2,700–3,000 calories and for girls 2,300–2,700 calories (Smart and Smart, 1978).

In many other ways, adolescent nutrition is far from ideal. Junk foods, snacks, and late night eating often provide many "empty calories" rather than the proteins, vitamins, and other nutrients essential for growth. You may be interested to compare your own eating patterns to those of a group of college students who recently responded to an open-ended questionnaire. Most of the students were living in college dormitories and subscribing to a prepaid meal plan (see Table 13-3). Are your breakfasts and lunches similar to theirs? If these dietary patterns were maintained over a long period of time, we would expect to see malnutrition, frequent illness, and other physical deficiencies emerging. When these students were asked why they often skipped meals the two most common explanations were: (1) "I'm dieting and have to watch my weight/figure," and (2) "I just don't have enough time to eat." Interestingly, saving money was not mentioned by a single one of the students as a factor in their food selections.

Table 13-2
MEAN CALORIC INTAKE PER DAY AMONG WHITE AND BLACK ADOLESCENTS FROM POVERTY AND NON-POVERTY BACKGROUNDS

	Non-Poverty	Poverty
White	2,423	2,076
Black	2,164	1,877

Source: Adapted from S. Abrahams, F. W. Lowenstein, and C. L. Johnson, *Preliminary Findings of the First Health and Nutrition Examination Survey, United States, 1971–1972.* (Washington, D.C.: U.S. Government Printing Office, DHEW Publication No. [HRA] 74–1219–1, 1974).

Table 13-3

EATING PATTERNS OF COLLEGE STUDENTS AT BREAKFAST AND LUNCH

Breakfast	Percentage*
protein (eggs, bacon, ham)	12
cereal	38
fruits	15
toast	44
sweets (donuts, candy)	25
sandwich	8
nothing (juice, coffee, or soft drink only)	66
Lunch	
protein (meat, fish, cheese)	35
salad	27
fruit	5
ice cream	18
yogurt	12
sweets (candy, fruit pie, cake)	31
nothing (juice, coffee, or soft drink only)	42

*Figures total more than 100% since students could respond with more than a single item at meals. (Roodin, 1978)

Changes in Body Size

Growth in body size may be studied *cross-sectionally,* and average increments per age may be derived. Alternatively, growth may be studied *longitudinally,* and the rate of growth of an individual may be charted from year to year or at more frequent intervals. Scientists recognize that the longitudinal method of study provides a better and more accurate representation of the *rate* of adolescent growth. With the longitudinal method, an adolescent *growth spurt* can be identified. The growth spurt seen in adolescence refers to the rapid acceleration of an individual's physical development which is universal and which occurs about two years earlier in girls than in boys (see Figure 13-3). The adolescent growth spurt can be seen as a distinct series of phases (Faust, 1977). There is a period of peak velocity (rate) for height called the *height apex.* It occurs at about 12 years of age for girls and about 14 years for boys (Tanner, 1973). From this point the beginning and end of puberty in terms of the growth spurt can be seen (see Figure 13-3). The timing of the onset of puberty as well as the length of time needed to complete the period of puberty show wide fluctuations among adolescents.

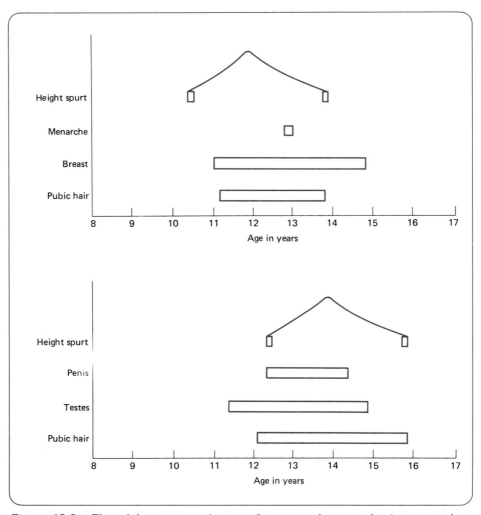

Figure 13-3. The adolescent growth spurt: Sequence of events of puberty in girls at various ages is diagrammed for the average child. The hump in the bar labeled "Height spurt" represents the peak velocity of the spurt. The bars represent the beginning and completion of the events of puberty. Although the adolescent growth spurt for girls typically begins at age 10.5 and ends at age 14, it can start as early as age 9.5 and end as late as age 15. Similarly, menarche can come at any time between the ages of 10 and 16.5 and tends to be a late event of puberty. First pubic hair appears after the beginning of breast development in two-thirds of all girls.

Sequence of events of puberty in boys is also shown in various ages for the average child. The adolescent growth spurt of boys can begin as early as age 10.5 or as late as age 16 and can end anywhere from age 13.5 to 17.5. Elongation of the penis can begin from age 10.5 to 14.5 and can end from age 12.5 to age 16.5. Growth of the testes can begin as early as age 9.5 or as late as age 13.5 and end at any time between the ages of 13.5 and 17. (From J. M. Tanner, *Growth at adolescence.* 2nd ed.; Oxford: Blackwell Scientific Publications, 1962. Redrawn for *Scientific American*, 1973, 229, p. 43. By permission.)

Faust (1977) has reported that early-developing girls are generally short in both overall height and leg length. They also have narrower shoulders and hips and weigh less than late maturers. Faust found late-maturing girls were considerably taller when puberty began and had greater hip and shoulder width than early maturers. Early maturers had longer periods of puberal growth than late maturers. Despite these differences, no relationships were found between early and late maturity and subsequent adult physical appearance. These general descriptions appear to apply to adolescent boys as well (Faust, 1977). As we have mentioned in Chapter 11, the timing of physical maturity has important consequences for adolescents' evaluations of themselves, their skills, and their self-concepts. Early maturity is generally an advantage for boys, since it provides more successful peer interactions in competition, athletics, and strength. For girls, however, early maturity is far less advantageous. Late maturity seems more difficult for boys to cope with successfully (Faust, 1969; Jones, 1957).

The rapid growth that takes place among girls and boys during puberty is substantial. The average girl of 13 is about 5 feet 2 inches tall and weighs about 100 pounds. Four years later she has gained about 2 inches in height and more than 17 pounds in weight. The biggest gain in weight usually occurs after menarche. At 14 years of age, the average boy is 5 feet 4 inches tall and weighs 105 pounds. By 17, however, he is about 5 feet 8 inches in height and weighs about 137 pounds.

Puberty and Sexual Maturation

There are many changes in the reproductive organs which are associated with the adolescent growth spurt (Figure 13-3). These changes cannot be understood without some perspective on the biological events which produce them. Tanner (1970) points out that it is the brain which initiates the events of puberty. The *hypothalamus* stimulates the anterior portion of the pituitary gland, which then releases a number of hormones. These hormones may be related to general body growth (*somatotrophin*), cellular growth of metabolism (*adrenocorticotrophic hormone*), or the development of the sexual organs (*luteinizing hormone* and *follicle stimulating hormone*). The latter two hormones, although present in both boys and girls, have different effects on their development. In the case of girls these hormones stimulate the growth of the ovaries and ovulation and increase the amount of *estrogens* (female hormones) in the bloodstream. The very same hormones are responsible in boys for the production of sperm cells in the testes, development of the seminiferous tubules, and increasing the amount of *androgens* (male sex hormones) in the body.

Secondary Sex Characteristics

At puberty boys and girls also begin to develop secondary sex characteristics (see Figure 13-3). The pattern of appearance of these characteristics is interesting.

In boys, *testosterone,* one of the androgenic hormones produced in the testes, begins to influence the development of secondary sex characteristics. The first outward sign of puberty in boys is the increase in the growth of the testes, followed by the appearance of pubic hair and growth of the penis. These secondary sex characteristics also involve the appearance of facial and axillary hair.

In girls, the estrogens influence the development of secondary sexual characteristics. The first signs of puberty in girls is a change in the size of the breasts, which is quickly followed by the appearance of pubic hair. These changes usually precede menarche by about one year. Internally, the uterus and vagina are developing at about the same time, accompanied by maturation of the ovaries. Menarche is one of the last growth changes to occur.

Adjustment to Physical Change

All adolescents must make psychological adjustments to changes in their body's characteristics, appearance, and functioning. The hormones which bring about menarche in girls are at first released unevenly and produce irregular menstrual cycles. These irregular cycles require major adjustments to different emotional levels. Both boys and girls have to deal with other concerns as well—heightened sexual drives, acne and pimples which arise from increased activity of the sebaceous glands, new body odors produced from actively functioning sweat glands, and a clear change in body image. Some investigators have suggested that becoming used to a new body image may be far more stressful to adolescents than we have realized (Dryer, Hulac, & Rigler, 1971).

Adjustments to new body images are among the major concerns of adolescents. Menarche has been found to be an event which helps girls cope with these changes in body image (Koff, Rierdan, & Silverstone, 1978). Human figure drawings done by adolescent girls were studied on two occasions separated by an interval of six months. The investigators compared the drawings of adolescents who were premenarchal and those who were post-menarchal on both testings with those who had reached menarche during the six-month interval. They found that post-menarchal girls drew figures which were more sexually differentiated. With the advent of menarche, girls were more likely to portray females when asked to "draw a person." Other data showed that premenarchal girls were less accepting and less satisfied with female body parts than post-menarchal girls. The study suggests that one of the major events which helps adolescent girls to adjust to their new body image is the onset of menarche. Once menarche was attained, girls seemed to be able to restructure and define their sexual identity and body image (Koff, Rierdan, & Silverstone, 1978).

Adolescents generally worry about their overall physical appearance. They seem concerned about how they appear to others, perhaps sensitized by extensive advertising programs in the mass media. They must cope with their egocentric concerns and learn that they are the only ones critically evaluating their acne, facial hair, breast size, and weight. Adolescents make such assessments to see how well they match social physical ideals; it is one of their chief preoccupations. Elkind (1967; 1978) suggests that adolescents are reacting to an "imaginary audience" as they assess how they appear to others.

Adolescents often overemphasize or distort a particular part of their appearance. Each adolescent seems to feel that nature has been particularly unkind in at least one physical trait. Adolescents usually identify some aspect of their appearance which cannot be "protected" from the view of the imaginary audience. Frequently the face is singled out for special criticism; they bemoan the size of the nose, the shape of their ears, or the positioning of their teeth. No adolescent is ever content with his or her appearance, and they often say with certainty: "My eyes are too close together, my forehead is too large, my chin sticks out too far, and my mouth is too small." Such egocentric preoccupations are difficult to overcome (Elkind, 1978). Once the adolescent realizes that others in the social environment do not share his or her concerns or critical stance, this type of egocentrism is reduced (Elkind, 1967; 1978).

VALUES, ATTITUDES AND BELIEFS

Generational Differences

There is no question that the world in which our parents were raised is vastly different from our own. The recognition of this fact, as Keniston (1971) and others have noted, tends to magnify the differences among generations rather than emphasize the similarities among parents and adolescents. While generational differences may influence psychological functioning (Baltes, Reese, & Nesselroade, 1977), such as type or amount of information, it may be erroneous to continue to emphasize a "generation gap" in terms of attitudes and values.

Tolor (1976), for instance, compared the values of 2,908 high-school students, college students, and parents. He assessed their support of traditional attitudes towards family life, work, and higher education. There was little support for a large generation gap in the data, although high school and college groups were less traditional in their attitudes than the parent group. The group that differed most from the parent group was the college-age sample, not the younger adolescents. High-school students were closer to the attitudes of the parent group than were college students. Although the study was not longitudinal, Tolor suggests that adolescents continue to be influenced by parents through high school and to show similar attitudes and values. It is in college that the sharpest divergence in attitudes from parents occurs. Then there is a shift back to more traditional values and attitudes once the college years are over, as individuals assume work roles and a more structured place in society (Tolor, 1976). Although there may be differences in attitudes between adolescent and parent, these differences are not as great as many have suggested. The generation gap may appear large because of the freedom which adolescents have to express their growing individuality. Rogers (1977) notes that such *behaviors* as long hair, dress styles, and living together are highly visible and dramatic differences between adolescents and the older generation. Nevertheless, the fundamental values and attitudes held by adolescents and parents are more similar than dissimilar.

Adolescents continue to be concerned about conventional or traditional goals (Conger, 1972; Keniston, 1971), such as vocation, marriage, and income. Other values, however, are also assuming increased importance among adolescents today. The need for personal satisfaction from living, the importance of the quality of life and the environment, and the emphasis on meaningful personal relationships (as opposed to superficial ones) are hallmarks of today's generation of youth. Each adolescent generation seems to develop its own theme for living, decade by decade. For instance, the adolescents in the sixties were generally seen as "radical" (Lee, 1970).

The Peer Group

Adolescent peer groups are a major institution in our society for adolescent experimentation. Free from the participation of critical adults, adolescents can develop stylized behaviors, practice skills, and experiment with roles which contribute to their personal identities. Adolescents often conform rigidly to the demands of the peer group, adopting similar clothing, musical preferences, language patterns, and styles of expression. Being similar to the peer group contributes to a sense of belonging, emotional security, and feelings of independence. The irony, of course, is that adolescents have shifted their earlier dependence on parents to the peer group. Independence has not really increased until conscious decision-making and responsibility for personal decisions occur (McCandless, 1970).

Peers are usually attracted to each other because they share common interests, social goals, and values (Gray & Gaier, 1974). Adolescents usually develop peer relationships with those who share similar backgrounds and come from the same social class (Dunphy, 1963). These are certainly among the significant factors in determining a "best" friend at this time. Fasteau (1975) suggests that among boys friendships are more superficial than among girls. The need to appear "macho" prevents adolescent boys from sharing many of their fears and problems. Among girls, however, there appears to be much more intimacy and sharing of feelings, hopes, and dreams. Exchanging secrets, evaluating dates, parents, classmates, and expressing fears appear to be more socially sanctioned among girls.

Mitchell (1976) argues that intimacy and the sharing of goals, hopes, fears, and problems helps adolescents to see themselves as similar to their peers. The peer group may accomplish this goal far more successfully for girls than for boys. Predominant adolescent attitudes among boys deny weakness, emphasize competition, and stress success (Fasteau, 1975).

Peers and Sexuality

As peers continue to interact, the beginning of heterosexual dating occurs. Studies of dating suggest that the initial interest in the opposite sex is related to the myriad changes associated with the adolescent growth spurt. Girls will exhibit this interest about two years in advance of boys.

Early dating and later dating appear to have entirely different functions (Feinstein & Ardon, 1973; Place, 1975). These differences are presented in Table 13-4. Early dating patterns suggest that the entire experience is an experimental testing ground in which both girls and boys develop their "techniques." They kiss, try petting, and see if they can spend an evening successfully entertaining, talking, and coping with a total stranger. Interestingly, once these skills are mastered, dating becomes more intense, involves more sexual intimacy, and is emotionally demanding. Many psychologists think that late dating often leads directly to marriage (Feinstein & Ardon, 1973; Place, 1975).

Keniston (1975) observed that adolescence may be followed by a period of youth in which some individuals continue to prepare for adulthood. In this period

Figure 13-4. Adolescents are concerned about their physical appearance and their evaluations by others. (Mimi Forsyth/Monkmeyer Press Photo Service)

Table   13-4
COMPARISON OF EARLY AND LATE ADOLESCENT DATING

Early Age	Function*	Description†
Level 1 (13–15)	Recreation	Dating for friendship and tentative heterosexual intimacies (kissing, petting)
Level 2 (14–17)	Socialization	Dating to develop new relationships and become proficient at relating to opposite sex— many, brief relations in which to practice skills
Late Age		
Level 3 (16–19)	Status Attainment	Dating to establish longer-term intimate relations with significant members of the opposite sex: greater intimacy and sexual experimentation
Level 4 (18–25)	Courtship and Selection for Marriage	Using the dating relationship in order to "identify with a love object" and to permit the choice of a marital partner—sexual intimacy and strong commitment to a single individual

Source: Adapted from D. M. Place, "The Dating Experience for Adolescent Girls," *Adolescence,* 1975, **10**, pp. 157–174; and S. C. Feinstein and M. S. Ardon, "Trends in Dating Patterns and Adolescent Development," *Journal of Youth and Adolescence,* 1973, **2**, pp. 157–166.

*Place, 1975.

†Feinstein and Ardon, 1973.

following traditional adolescence, dating relationships are often marked by one-to-one relationships by couples who are strongly committed to each other, live together, and share experiences and expenses but who remain unmarried. Macklin, (1972; 1974) has studied extensively such cohabitation arrangements, which are commonly seen among people 18–35 years old. Her research examined the experiences of college students. Cohabitation was adopted as a way of establishing emotionally satisfying relationships, experimenting with a relationship before making a permanent committment, sharing sexual intimacy in a meaningful relationship, and avoiding the superficial sham of traditional dating. Students generally found such relationships to be significant growth experiences and emphasized the degree of maturity and self-understanding which were derived from cohabitation. Such arrangements were not free of conflict, however; Macklin found that many of the problems were similar to those experienced by young married couples: problems with parents, problems relating to each other, sexual problems, and problems centered on the living arrangement (lack of privacy and money).

Sexual Attitudes and Behavior

There is a growing body of research which suggests that adolescent attitudes and behaviors towards sexuality have undergone significant change over the last two decades (Godenne, 1974; Hunt, 1974; Lucke & Nass, 1969; Sorenson, 1973). There has been a lessening of concern about formerly repressed topics, such as masturbation, homosexuality, premarital intercourse, and communal living. The prevailing attitude is one of open discussion of sexual matters among the peer group and a great deal of permissiveness as people approach college age. The attitudes which seem to underlie adolescents' orientation are mutual trust, open acceptance of individuals, and freedom of personal choice in the area of sexuality. Among girls, for instance, the prevailing attitude is that with appropriate emotional commitment premarital sexual intercourse is a natural outgrowth of mature relationships. There is minimal condemnation or negative evaluation for such behavior (Hunt, 1974), which represents a sharp change from past attitudes. Interestingly, with this change in attitude the "double standard" ("It's O.K. for boys but not for girls") is rapidly disappearing among older adolescents of both sexes (Hunt, 1974).

Figure 13-5. Adolescent sexuality often involves an ethic-based emotional commitment, trust, and mutual acceptance. (Sybil Shelton/Monkmeyer Press Photo Service)

It may still, however, be found among younger (15 years and younger) adolescents and those from lower social class backgrounds (Kerckoff, 1974; Sorenson, 1973).

Most surveys of adolescents have reported a decline in the age at which first intercourse occurs and an increase in the number of adolescents experiencing premarital intercourse (Hunt, 1974; Robinson, King, & Balswick, 1972; Sorenson, 1973; Verner & Stewart, 1974). Such data are usually compared to Kinsey's classic studies conducted 25–30 years ago. Today most research suggests that 50% of college females and 75% of college males will have experienced sexual intercourse prior to their graduation (Hettlinger, 1974; Luckey & Nass, 1969). These data show considerably more change for females than for males, when compared to earlier studies. Again, there appears to be a lessening of the negative sanctions (double standard) for girls' participation in sexual intercourse.

While studies suggest that the patterns of adolescent sexuality are clearly different from earlier generations, it would be incorrect to conclude that promiscuity and total abandon characterize today's youth. Sorenson (1973), for instance, notes that premarital sexual intercourse is viewed by adolescents as permissible only within the bounds of "love" and a meaningful relationship. Other authorities (Godenne, 1974) feel that the change in today's generation of adolescents involves honesty, openness, and frank discussion of sexuality far more than actual behavior. While many authorities emphasize the detrimental consequences of sexual relationships which occur too early, some take a more positive stance and see these experiences as the basis for genuine success in later relationships such as marriage (Kirkendall, 1974). Those adolescents who are able to handle successfully the range of problems which go hand-in-hand with deep emotional relationships seem to develop a realistic appraisal of marriage rather than the romantic or idyllic fantasies which are often portrayed by parents, peers, and the popular culture (Kirkendall, 1974).

We have seen that the age at which adolescents are initiating sexual intercourse is occurring earlier and earlier. Sorenson (1973) reported that of the 54% of adolescents (13–19 years old) who had experienced sexual intercourse, more than two-thirds had begun by the age of 15. Although the popular press would have us believe that promiscuity is also a problem, survey data contradicts this belief. Sorenson (1973), for example, found that only 24% of the adolescents in his study experienced sexual intercourse with more than 6 different partners. In fact, sexual intercourse was usually experienced with only one individual and in the context of a love relationship. At an emotional level, most young adolescents are concerned over their sexual relations and experience some difficulty in coping with guilt (Conger, 1973). Few twelve-, thirteen-, or fourteen-year-olds appear psychologically able to cope with this type of behavior.

Most adolescents are inadequately prepared to accept the responsibilities that go along with sexual activity. Numerous surveys have found that the sexual information of adolescents is often nonexistent or incorrect where pregnancy is considered (Green & Lowe, 1975). Despite attempts to provide sex education in the schools and to develop parents' awareness of their children's early need for sexual information, national figures tell us that we are doing too little, too late. Consider-

Table 13-5
FREQUENCY OF BIRTHS TO UNMARRIED ADOLESCENTS

| | Number of Births | | Percentage of Births | |
	Under 15	15–19	Under 15 (%)	15–19 (%)
1973	10,900	204,900	85	34
1971	9,500	194,100	82	31

Source: Adapted from C. P. Green and S. J. Lowe, "Teenage Pregnancy: A Major Problem for Minors," *Zero Population Growth National Reporter*, 1975, **7**, pp. 4–5. By permission.

able misinformation is still conveyed within the peer group. The result is increased pregnancies among adolescents (see Table 13-5). At least two major factors must be carefully considered in evaluating the trend towards the increase in adolescent pregnancies: (1) lack of information and (2) legal obstacles.

Most adolescents simply deny the facts of life, or so it seems. Both boys and girls appear to have an almost magical or egocentric belief in the *personal fable* (Elkind, 1967; 1978) that negative events in life happen to others and never to them. The infrequent use of contraceptives supports this common adolescent belief that pregnancy will "never happen to me." Sorenson found that 53% of adolescents aged 15–19 had not used contraceptives the last time they had sexual intercourse. When asked why they failed to use preventive measures, adolescents frequently blamed the other partner, as if contraception was a matter of concern to only one of the sexual participants. Boys, for instance, said that contraception was the "girl's responsibility, since she was the one who took the Pill." When asked how they were able to prevent pregnancy, 56% of the sample who were engaging in sexual intercourse gave explanations which were in error. Kantner and Zelnich (1972, 1973) found incorrect explanations by adolescent girls about pregnancy such as: (1) I have sex too infrequently to get pregnant; (2) I am too young to get pregnant; (3) You only get pregnant if you *want* a baby; and (4) You can only get pregnant when you're having your period.

Adolescents appear relatively unaware of the variety and safety of potential contraceptive methods and rarely evaluate the techniques which they use, if any. Nearly 75% of adolescents who use contraceptives (Kanter & Zelnich, 1973) chose either a condom, the Pill, or withdrawal (a most unreliable technique). One of the obstacles toward providing information and inexpensive contraception can be found in the attitudes which adolescents themselves hold. Adolescents usually seek out information and services such as Planned Parenthood long after they have become sexually active. Often the first service which these agencies provide is a pregnancy test! Traditional morality may be contributing to the problem (Green &

Lowe, 1975); adolescents do not seek out information and contraceptive devices before they initiate sexual intercourse because they may fear the appearance of deliberateness, planning, and rationality. Rather than face such issues head on, they wait for the inevitable in an ill-prepared, ill-advised scenario which results in "Oh no, I may be pregnant!"

Do adolescents who engage in premarital intercourse differ from those who do not? Shirley and Richard Jessor (1975) were interested in comparing the characteristics of virgins and nonvirgins. In a recent study, they asked adolescents from grades 10, 11, 12, and college to complete a self-report questionnaire. The results suggested that those who begin sexual activity are less conventional in their values and less controlled by parents and peers, gain more support from their peers, and show less involvement with conventional institutions than those without sexual experience. Adolescents with sexual experience seemed to value and emphasize their independence and were not seen as dependent on either parents or peers. Similarly, nonvirgins were more likely to have engaged in unconventional behavior such as trying alcohol or marijuana (Jessor & Jessor, 1975).

SUMMARY

In this chapter we have dealt with a wide range of topics related to adolescent development. After a brief look at some current views of adolescence—idealized perspectives, conflicts, and rites of passage—we presented a number of theories that explain adolescent behavior. The psychoanalytic and cultural-anthropological theories of adolescence were presented and compared. The concept of adolescence as a time of marginality and individual growth was also considered. Erikson's theory and concern for the crisis of identity vs. identity confusion was discussed.

We described many of the physical changes associated with adolescence, as well as adjustments to these physical changes. The development of attitudes, values, and beliefs was studied, in particular the importance of the peer group in the areas of dating and sexuality. Finally adolescent sexual attitudes and behaviors were discussed primarily from a normative basis.

RECOMMENDED READINGS

Gallatin, J. E. *Adolescence and individuality.* New York: Harper & Row, 1975.

A well-written and comprehensive treatment of major theoretical views of adolescent development. Erikson's work is given especially fine treatment.

Hunt, M. *Sexual behavior in the 1970s.* New York: Dell, 1974.

A well-designed study of the typical patterns of early sexual behaviors in the United States. There is also extensive treatment of marital and extramarital sexual behaviors as well.

Thornburg, H. D. *Contemporary adolescence: readings.* Monterey, Calif.: Brooks, Cole, 1975.

A particularly fine selection of original studies and reviews of current thinking in a wide variety of areas of importance to those trying to understand today's adolescent. School, sex, drugs, family, work, and delinquency are some of the issues presented.

14

Cognitive Development, Identity, and Experience

COGNITIVE DEVELOPMENT

Piaget's theory of cognition provides an important link between the emerging goals and aspirations of adolescents and their search for identity. Many of the unique accomplishments of adolescence—identity formation, development of an ethical system of values, political and moral ideology, and vocational choice—may in one way or another be related to the capacities acquired at this fourth stage of cognitive development.

The Period of Formal Operations

For Piaget cognitive maturity is realized during the period of formal operations (about 11–16 years of age). This is the final stage in which the child's earlier cognitive structures undergo qualitative change. The period of formal operations is characterized by the *capacity* to think in the abstract, without the need for concrete referents. This kind of thinking has been referred to as the capacity to "think about thinking" (Looft, 1971), "the relationship of reality to possibility" (Berzonsky, 1978), or "reflective abstraction" (Brainerd, 1978). Adolescents can think scientifically using inductive reasoning, reasoning which involves deriving generalizations or broad principles from a limited number of facts. The formal operational period is also marked by the capacity to think using hypothetico-deductive reasoning. This is reasoning in which we derive conclusions "from premises which are *hypotheses* rather than from facts" which are verified from direct experience (Brainerd, 1978, p. 205). Hypothetico-deductive reasoning thus is heavily dependent on language. It is only in the stage of formal operations that adolescents can begin to reason about problems without concrete referents according to Piaget (Inhelder and Piaget, 1958). For instance, verbal problems like the following are not usually successfully solved by children younger than twelve:

Bill's hair is lighter than Fred's.
Bill's hair is darker than John's.
Who has the darkest hair, Bill, Fred, or John?

In formal operations the adolescent is no longer tied to either his or her immediate perception or own past experience or personal knowledge. Adolescents can move far beyond their own experiences and imagine a world of possibilities and events which they have never directly encountered. They can imagine things which could never really happen as well as events which they wish would happen. Looft (1971) characterizes adolescent thinking as involving this capacity to imagine possibilities.

We will look at some of Piaget's experiments to see why he characterizes adolescent thinking as formal operational and based on logic, abstractness, scientific reasoning, propositions, and possibility. His experiments have been designed to

Figure 14-1. Adolescents enjoy the process of discussion: thinking about their own thoughts and those of others and imagining a world of new possiblities. (Conklin/Monkmeyer Press Photo Service)

reveal the qualitative way in which the operations of adolescence (formal) differ from the operations of middle childhood (concrete). Much of the distinction is in the unique capacity of adolescents to internalize actions totally—to mentally act or reverse their own thoughts.

Combinatorial Thought

The capacity to think using propositions or combinatorial reasoning is best illustrated by the problem of colorless liquids (Inhelder and Piaget, 1958). Five bottles of colorless liquids are placed before the child: no. 1 contains sulfuric acid, no. 2 contains water, no. 3 contains oxygenated water, no. 4 contains thiosulphate, and no. 5 (a smaller bottle) contains potassium iodide. With the child watching, the experimenter adds several drops from bottle 5 (potassium iodide) to glasses containing various mixtures of the colorless solutions (e.g., 1 and 3, 2 and 4, etc.). One of the combinations (1 and 3) reacts to the potassium iodide and turns yellow. The child is then asked to repeat the experiment and produce the yellow color by combining the liquids in any way he or she likes. Children at the concrete operational stage attempt to solve the problem in a haphazard fashion. They may combine no. 5 with no. 1, then 2, then 3, and 4. Finding that no change in color results, they may then switch to combining all four liquids with no. 5, and then might try random combinations of liquids (e.g., 2 and 3, 2, 1, and 4). With adolescents, however, Piaget reports a more systematic attempt to solve this same problem. Adolescents will add elements of the problem in a combinatorial fashion beginning with one element at a time, then two, and so on, carefully checking to see that no "permutations or combinations" have been omitted. This ability to construct all possible combinations and permutations of a problem is taken as evidence that formal operations has been attained.

Proportion

In the concrete operational period children understand that a small weight can balance a large one if they place it further from the center (or fulcrum) than a larger weight. They can solve the problem of equalizing weight and length (distance from the fulcrum) by experimentation. However, it is not possible for concrete operational children to represent weight and length as proportions. With the onset of formal operations, Piaget finds that the concept of proportionality is understood by adolescents as a general principle. Adolescents see the relationship between weight and length and can solve balancing problems in an abstract manner. In dealing with proportions they recognize that objects that are twice as heavy may be offset by objects that are twice as light by placing them twice as far from the center of balance (fulcrum). Such general principles are acquired in the formal operational period and can be applied successfully to any number of problems without the need for the trial-and-error experimentation characteristic of the concrete operational child.

The Pendulum Problem

The adolescent's shift to qualitatively different modes of thinking is also highlighted in the pendulum problem. The task is designed to have children determine the reason for the rate of speed or frequency of oscillation of a pendulum. The speed of the pendulum's swinging is related only to the *length* of the string which holds it. The shorter the string the faster the oscillations; the longer the string the slower the oscillations. In addition to the length of the string, three other potentially related factors are presented: (1) the weight of the object at the end of the string, (2) the height or level at which the pendulum is first pushed, and (3) the force with which the object is pushed. Younger children in the concrete operational stage do not behave like scientists in determining what controls the speed of the pendulum's swing. Their "experiments" are not capable of deducing the factor responsible since they often vary two or three of the factors at the same time. In the formal operational stage, however, children solve the task in a more systematic, scientific fashion. Piaget finds adolescents evaluating each of the potential factors, one at a time, in order to determine their impact on the frequency of oscillation. It is only in the period of formal operations that adolescents approach the problem as careful scientists, successfully employing the inductive method. The following example illustrates this type of thinking:

> Eme (15;1), after having selected 100 grams with a long string and a medium length string, then 20 grams with a long and a short string, and finally 200 grams with a long and a short, concludes: *"It's the length of the string that makes it go faster or slower; the weight doesn't play any role."* She discounts likewise the height of the drop and the force of her push.   (Inhelder and Piaget, 1958; p. 75)

Structural Change in Formal Operations

What accounts for the changes in adolescent thinking? According to Piaget the key attainment responsible for the qualitative change in adolescent thinking is a new intellectual structure, the INRC group. This group consists of four rules or operations: Identity (I), Negation (N), Reciprocity (R), and Correlativity (C). The INRC group, borrowed from mathematics, describes how each of the four operations permits a special type of reversibility (Brainerd, 1978). Most importantly the INRC group allows the adolescent to operate on or reverse his or her own symbolic thoughts. Ideas and hypotheses can be created and transformed on a completely abstract level. Thus the INRC group explains the way in which adolescents manipulate their own thinking and operate on hypothetical propositions, free from the constraints of the immediate concrete situation (Ginsburg and Opper, 1978).

During the formal operational period adolescents also develop the ability to use *propositional logic*. The simplest form of propositional logic which the adolescent can use is called binary. *Binary propositional logic* involves the ability to evaluate simultaneously the truth or falsity of two statements such as:

Proposition A: Person X was an artist.

Proposition B: Person Y was an inventor.

These two general propositions may be considered together in one of four ways: (1) both are true, (2) both are false, (3) A is true but B is false, or (4) B is true but A is false. If we consider the total number of ways in which these propositions can be considered (Table 14-1) we find a total of 16 possibilities. The ability to derive the 16 possibilities, or outcomes of binary propositional logic has special significance. The 16 possibilities correspond to 16 basic relationships which logicians have identified (Hunt, 1961) and are considered by Piaget to form a set of 16 corresponding mental *operations*. The 16 propositional operations (presented in Table 14-1) permit the adolescent to internalize actions and are themselves capable of being reversed (Brainerd, 1978).

The 16 propositional operations and the INRC group underlie the qualitative differences that separate the thought of the adolescent from that of the concrete operational child. As Brainerd notes, "Piaget has . . . taken the most elementary branch of symbolic logic, and put it inside the adolescent's (and adult's) head as a system of mental operations" (1978, p. 221). We must remember, of course, that the ability to utilize the 16 operations and to use the INRC group are only *repre-*

Table   4-1
THE SIXTEEN OUTCOMES FROM COMBINING TWO BINARY PROPOSITIONS

	Outcome	P = true Q = true	P = true Q = false	P = false Q = true	P = false Q = false
1.	Affirmation ($P * Q$)	true	true	true	true
2.	Disjunction ($P \lor Q$)	true	true	true	false
3.	Reverse Implication ($P \leftarrow Q$)	true	true	false	true
4.	Implication ($P \rightarrow Q$)	true	false	true	true
5.	Nonconjunction (P/Q)	false	true	true	true
6.	Affirmation of P (P)	true	true	false	false
7.	Affirmation of Q (Q)	false	false	true	true
8.	Equivalence ($P \equiv Q$)	true	false	false	true
9.	Denial of $Q \sim (Q)$	false	true	false	true
10.	Denial of $P \sim (P)$	false	false	true	true
11.	Nonequivalence $\sim (P \equiv Q)$	false	true	true	false
12.	Conjunction ($P \cdot Q$)	true	false	false	false
13.	Nonimplication $\sim (P \rightarrow Q)$	false	true	false	false
14.	Nonreverse implication $\sim (P \leftarrow Q)$	false	false	true	false
15.	Nondisjunction $\sim (P \lor Q)$	false	false	false	true
16.	Negation $\sim (P * Q)$	false	false	false	false

Source: C. J. Brainerd, *Piaget's Theory of Intelligence.* Englewood Cliffs, N.J.: 1978, p. 223. By permission.

sentative of the adolescents' cognitive structures. Ginsburg and Opper state that the two acquisitions are "not intended to imply that the adolescent understands logic in any explicit way. Most adolescents do not know propositional logic . . . Piaget does not use logic to describe the adolescent's explicit knowledge, but to depict the structure of his thought" (1978, p. 196).

Research on Formal Operations

Recent research evidence indicates that considerable caution is needed in dealing with this stage of Piaget's theory (Berzonsky, 1978; Brainerd, 1978; Ennis, 1978; Lunzer, 1978; Neimark, 1975). Many studies suggest that neither adolescents nor adults consistently use the formal operations potentially available to them (Berzonsky, 1978; Neimark, 1975). Thus we have the paradox that even though new intellectual structures may have developed, sometimes concrete operational problem-solving may still be seen among adolescents and adults who are capable of formal operational thought. Although the *capacity* to think logically, abstractly, and hypothetically about propositions may be present, it doesn't necessarily lead to formal operational problem-solving in any given situation (Brainerd, 1978; Ginsburg and Opper, 1978; Neimark, 1975).

Perhaps part of the difficulty is in the particular bias of the tests typically used to assess this fourth stage of development. The tasks are clearly from the domain of "science" and most familiar to those who are "better educated" (Ginsburg and Opper, 1978). In particular, without the requisite educational background and cultural experience, such formal tasks as those employed by Piaget put large groups of adolescents at a distinct disadvantage. Evidence from cross-cultural studies suggests that in more primitive societies (less schooling, less Westernization) formal operational thought is rarely attained (Aston, 1975). The formal operational stage is neither universal across cultures nor systematically attained even by those within Western societies (Neimark, 1975).

Piaget (1972) believes that in most advantaged societies experiences, role taking, and specific training do provide adolescents the capacity for formal thought. Berzonsky (1978) notes that "this capability, however, may not be applied all pervasively to all problems; specific interests and vocational specialization may be determining factors." Thus adolescents' use of formal operational thinking may be content- or task-specific (Berzonsky, 1978; Dulit, 1972; Piaget, 1972). Whether an adolescent or adult displays formal operational thought is dependent on his or her experiences, interests, vocational training, and, of course, the task used in the assessment.

Research supports the fact that formal operations are content-specific (Bart, 1971; Martorano, 1977). Martorano (1977) asked sixth-, eighth-, tenth-, and twelfth-grade girls to complete a series of ten typical Piagetian tasks dealing with formal operations. None of the age groupings showed evidence of consistent intra-individual consistency in the use of formal operations across ten different tasks. One interpretation of such data is to recognize that there are considerable performance differences in the tasks themselves, such as cognitive complexity, degree of structure in the instructions used to introduce the tasks, and familiarity with the "contents" of the tasks themselves.

Thus the failure to use formal operational thinking in a consistent manner across a number of tasks may be related to performance factors rather than to the failure to develop the necessary cognitive structures of this fourth stage. If this is true, then perhaps adolescents' performance on many of Piaget's formal problems is far more modifiable through training or experience than it is at other stages. Many studies have in fact demonstrated that adolescents and even preadolescent concrete thinkers can be readily trained to use scientific, abstract thought (Brainerd, 1978). Siegler, Liebert, and Liebert (1973), for example, trained fifth-graders (10–11 years old) in Piaget's pendulum problem. After pre-testing, the children were given a combination of training experiences. They were provided a conceptual framework for solving this kind of problem, were shown how to use a stopwatch to measure the speed of the pendulum's swings, and were shown how to reason about similar problems. The latter "analogy" training involved their discovering a single factor responsible for some particular event. The training program was successful and significantly improved the performance of the children on the formal operational problem dealing with the pendulum. Their logical thinking skills were dramatically altered as a result of training. In another study Tomlinson-Keasey (1974) posed a similar question. Three groups of females (mean ages of 11.9, 19.7, and 54 years) participated in the study. After determining their level of formal operational thought, a short-term training experience was provided to help the women solve such tasks as the pendulum problem and the balance-proportionality problem. Afterwards two types of assessments of the effectiveness of training were conducted. An immediate assessment (directly after training) revealed that subjects from all three groups showed significant improvements in conceptual performance on similar tasks. Thus training produced immediate measurable improvements. A subsequent *delayed* assessment of these gains after one week demonstrated, however, that the training was short-lived and task-specific: when different tasks analagous to those used in training were presented there was no evidence that the training produced permanent effects which were generalizable. Only when a task identical to one used in training was employed were any long-term gains found.

Another group of studies suggests that, counter to Piaget's claim, the ability to use propositional logic is not restricted to adolescence (Brainerd, 1978; Ennis, 1976, 1978; Lunzer, 1978). Ennis (1976) has considered that propositional logic may be of two forms: Valid and Invalid. Syllogisms can be used to illustrate these two types of propositional forms:

Valid Form: If this is Tuesday, then we must be in Paris.
             This is Tuesday.
             Correct Conclusion: Then we are in Paris.

Invalid Form: If this is Tuesday, then we must be in Paris.

This is not Tuesday.
Incorrect Conclusion: Then we are not in Paris.

A number of studies (cf. Brainerd, 1978) have shown that many concrete operational children can successfully solve and evaluate valid-form logic problems. In fact, in one study (Kodroff and Roberge, 1975) valid forms were derived by first-graders (77%), second-graders (78%) and third-graders (88%) suggesting that propositional logic is not restricted to only adolescents as Piaget has claimed (Brainerd, 1978). Reasoning about invalid-form logic problems is much more difficult, and the final conclusion which is drawn by many adolescents and children is often in error as in the example above (e.g., even though it is not Tuesday we could still be in Paris). The rate at which these problems are failed (drawing erroneous conclusions) is exceedingly high, regardless of whether children, adolescents, or adults are used as subjects (Brainerd, 1978). Thus Piaget's claim that formal thought leads to the ability to deal with propositional logic does not receive support when invalid-form problems are considered.

Wildman and Fletcher (1977) attempted an analysis of both valid and invalid form problems in order to understand why the latter were so much more difficult to solve correctly. Subjects from grades 8, 10, 12, and college were asked to reason about a number of syllogisms. The authors found that many of the incorrect conclusions drawn from reasoning about invalid form problems were based on misinterpretations of "if . . . then" statements. Most of the subjects interpreted such conditional statements incorrectly as meaning "if and only if" (Wildman and Fletcher, 1977). Clearly, the ability to utilize effectively some types of propositional logic is *not* uniformly characteristic of adolescent and adult performance.

Others have questioned Piaget's system of propositional logic and found it to be faulty. Ennis (1978) has called for a revision of the logical system or structure attributed to adolescents in the formal operational stage. A more extreme position has been advocated by Lunzer, who questions whether propositional logic underlies the attainments of the formal operational period:

> What is the role of logic in thinking?. . . . are we to assume, with Piaget, that a later development enables the adolescent to reflect on the system as a whole and that it is such reflection that facilitates effective thinking?
>
> It is at least equally possible that productive thinking is primarily analogic, that it is based, like language, on substitution within familiar frames, but that the frames as such are rarely, if ever, available in pure form. (Lunzer, 1978, p. 73)

Formal thought, thus, may not necessarily exist in "pure" form as suggested initially by Piaget (Wason and Johnson-Laird, 1972). It seems questionable to continue to "concentrate our energies either on the study of logical process or on the teaching of logic as an aid to effective thought" (Lunzer, 1978, p. 74).

IDENTITY FORMATION

The Problem of Identity Formation in Adolescence

Most theorists agree that the major accomplishment of adolescence is the consolidation, formulation, and charting of a personal identity. In looking at the process of constructing our individual identities we are reminded that an extremely complex network of dynamic interactions is at work, involving both hereditary and environmental factors. While theorists pay lip service to these complex, dynamic relationships in theories of development, all too often their experiments examine narrow, isolated segments of the person which do not provide an understanding of the whole system. Lerner (1978) has considered this problem characteristic of most developmental studies.

Looking at adolescent identity we realize that no single factor can be understood in isolation from another. A complete picture of adolescent identity requires us to look simultaneously at the dynamic interactions of a number of developmental processes: physical maturation, social experiences, and cognitive growth. Lerner (1978) thinks that at one level development involves experiences and interactions with a person's own biological maturation (timing, rate, etc.), such as personal reactions to the physical changes in adolescence. At another level development involves the specific interactions a person has with the environment, such as social experiences. Based on a dialectical viewpoint, however, Lerner recognizes that there are interactions not only within each level but also across levels. It is just such a complex, interactive viewpoint that is needed to understand the development of identity in adolescence. Lerner's concerns represent one important direction for developmental theorists to consider in the future.

For some theorists, identity formation has roots in early infancy, while for others it is a continuing process which evolves throughout an entire life. Most experts agree that adolescence is a time of major identity consolidation (Blos, 1970). Many consider that today's adolescent has a particularly difficult time in developing a coherent identity (Blos, 1971; Keniston, 1975). With rapid social change, improved technology, and new information adolescents may develop a distrust of adults, whose values, beliefs, and information are seen as out-of-date. As a result, adolescents do not know where to turn. They become alienated and unsure of how to resolve the problems associated with identity.

Others, however, see the development of identity as a basic problem for every generation of adolescents and stress the continuity in the process of resolving identity confusion. Carl Rogers (1961) feels that a sense of identity involves seeing ourselves as we really are: (1) who we have been, (2) who we are today, and (3) who we will become. Thus, a sense of identity can only be attained when we discover and chart our own destiny in life. In order to do this every generation of adolescents must move beyond what others wish them to become and beyond the fantasies of what they imagine they could become. If successful resolution of personal identity occurs we become "what we truly are" according to Rogers.

Factors Influencing the Development of Adolescent Identity

Cognitive Development.   Despite criticism of Piaget's theory of formal operations, many of his ideas are intuitively appealing to those who are attempting to understand the process of adolescent identity. For example, the capacity to think in the abstract about hypothetical situations suggests one possible vehicle for vocational choices. The idealism of youth and their willingness to entertain new ideas, values, and belief systems also seem dependent on formal operational thinking. The resolution of the adolescent identity crisis is, at least in part, aided by the development of new modes of thinking in which "reality becomes secondary to possibility" (Ginsburg and Opper, 1978). Among adolescents fantasy, daydreaming, and "what if . . . " thoughts are common. Adolescents evolve potential solutions to problems in their lives and choose, through combinatorial reasoning, the best one among the many which are possible. For example, Cynthia might consider what to do if . . . "I am not asked to the senior dance." She could mentally construct a range of solutions:

1. I could ask Mary to try to fix me up with a date.
2. I could call Clyde (a casual friend) and see if he could find me a date.
3. I could see if any of the boys in my English class are looking for someone to take to the dance.
4. I could stay home that night and be miserable.
5. I could consider going alone.
6. I could arrange to visit my older sister who lives in another city.
7. I could get a job babysitting.

These solutions could then be evaluated until the most satisfactory solution, from Cynthia's perspective, is chosen.

With the acquisition of the formal operational stage, adolescents can imagine their futures, contemplate a world that could be made better, and create in their minds countless solutions to many of the social-environmental crises which currently exist: hunger, threat of nuclear war, ecology, and racial prejudice. To both recognize these problems and derive potential solutions adolescents must be able to move far beyond the limited, immediate perceptions and thoughts of the concrete operational period. The ability to project into the future—to imagine, to hope, and to dream—certainly suggest that at least part of Piaget's view of intellectual development during adolescence has a good deal of intrinsic appeal and external validity. Yet, research support has often been disappointing.

Berzonsky, Weiner, and Raphael (1975) have hypothesized that the acquisition of formal operational thought is a prerequisite to the adolescent identity crisis. They evaluated a group of 60 college women in an identity crisis interview and then compared the performance of those who experienced identity crises to those who did not. Both groups were presented a concept-attainment task and a series of syllogisms. Despite the appeal of Piaget's assumption that formal thinking aids adolescent identity formation, that assumption was not supported in this study. There was no significant relationship found among the measures of formal reasoning and the tendency to experience crises of identity. Thus, formal operational skills may not necessarily be applied to personal crisis situations or identity problems.

Chandler (1975; 1978) and Riegel (1973) have also suggested that the abstract mode of thinking found in the formal operational period may not be as helpful to personal growth and identity formation as Piaget has led us to believe. They argue that concrete, personal contradiction and inconsistency (the dialectical view) "provides the dynamic necessary to prompt all cognitive growth and development" (Chandler, 1975, p. 176). Perhaps identity crises are best resolved through concrete, specific attempts to resolve concrete, specific problems. For example, one of the conflicts which is central to individual identity is the result of further losses in egocentrism: feelings of existential despair. Adolescents discover that abstract thought does not help them reconcile the differences between their views of reality and the views of others. Reduced egocentrism helps the adolescent to see that "all persons view the world from individualized and idiosyncratic perspectives and that there is no simple criterion of objectivity by which to arbitrate this diversity of points of view" (Chandler, 1975, p. 172). The gradual recognition of the "universality of subjectivity" (Piaget and Inhelder, 1956) leads adolescents to feelings of "epistemological loneliness" (Chandler, 1975; 1978). Out of the growing awareness of the arbitrary nature of each adolescent's unique personal perspective, a number of predictable, *concrete* behaviors are typically adopted:

1. Seek out a group of peers and maintain rigid absolute similarity of belief and conformity of behavior; e.g., the clique or crowd.

2. Find even one other person who will share your views in a kind of "intimate relationship."

3. Stereotype the world into groups who do not share your perspectives. Such outgroups include those over thirty, or those who are educated, or those who are economically disadvantaged.

4. Think abstractly as a tool to reduce differences of opinion and increasing consensus.

5. Find those who share ideological commitments such as religious experiences, conversions, or cultism.   (Adapted from Chandler, 1975).

Thus in the stage of formal operations, Chandler believes adolescents confront new problems which were absent at earlier developmental periods (epistemological loneliness). "Epistemological loneliness" is never put to rest permanently. Thus, abstract thought is no more effective in helping adolescents cope with some problems of identity than more concrete forms of thought (Chandler, 1975; 1978).

Sexuality.   Almost all theorists emphasize that part of the process of identity formation involves coming to terms with sexuality. There must be an acceptance of the self as "male" or "female." This may mean intimacy with the opposite sex, i.e., the ability to initiate or maintain close emotional relationships (Erikson, 1963). Often the search for sexual identity is incomplete (Erikson's identity confusion) or may be finalized far too early by adolescents who have not yet matured emotionally. Such premature closure of identity may help explain the high rate of divorce among young marrieds and the high incidence of adolescent pregnancy. From interviews with adolescent girls (aged 14–20) who were pregnant and unmarried, Martin (1973) found that one of the most common reasons for having become pregnant was to overcome loneliness and find someone (e.g., a baby) to be close to emotionally. Pregnancy was thus an attempt to achieve an identity as a mother. Although becoming a mother is one way of expressing intimacy, it is not a particularly sound basis for establishing identity at such young ages.

Physical Appearance.   Physical appearance also influences identity. Adolescents who seem to "fit" our cultural stereotypes of physical beauty are at an advantage. They typically have strong, positive self-concepts which continue through the middle years of adulthood (Jones, 1957; Jones and Mussen, 1958). Thus, the advantages of matching cultural ideals are long-lasting and continue to influence identity. Physical appearance is also an important factor in peer group acceptance. Cavior and Dokecki (1973) found that physically attractive adolescents were more popular in the peer group. There are clear benefits for the development of identity among physically advantaged adolescents and equally clear liabilities to those adolescents who do not fit the cultural stereotype.

Family Background.   The family is also a major factor in the development of adolescent identity. Behavior adopted by parents may be modeled directly by adolescents. Alternatively, the influence of modeling may be reactive; that is, through interacting with a parent, the adolescent may develop response styles which will be used in reacting similarly to other people in the environment. Satisfying roles may generalize beyond the family. Bandura (1973) and other social learning theorists support the view that adolescents acquire both personal behaviors as well as expectations for the behavior of others through the modeling process. Many adult roles may be defined in this manner: responsibility, caring, nurturance, and independence. The concept of modeling can help us understand the ease or difficulty which adolescents have in moving beyond the family to establish intimate relationships. Matteson (1974) studied adolescents' perceived communication patterns with their parents. These communication patterns were then related to differences in self-esteem among the adolescents. Those adolescents who had low self-esteem perceived their communications with parents as less helpful than did adolescents who had high self-esteem. Matteson also asked the parents themselves to rate their marriages. Interestingly, parents who had adolescents with low self-esteem rated their marriages as less satisfying than parents who had adolescents with high self-esteem.

In achieving an identity, adolescents begin to see a continuity to their life. There is a sense of personal sameness that characterizes their existence. Adolescents recognize that they are uniquely different from others in certain ways. They develop insight into their past socialization experiences within the family. They take pleasure in what they have become physically and look forward with anticipation to what they will attain in the future. This perspective of sameness over time is not easily achieved.

MORAL DEVELOPMENT IN ADOLESCENCE

Part of our identity involves a moral philosophy or viewpoint. In adolescence a number of important changes in this moral framework can be identified (Gilligan and Kohlberg, 1978). Remember the cognitive-structural view of morality held by Kohlberg described in Chapter 12. According to Kohlberg's approach there are three basic levels of moral reasoning: pre-conventional, conventional, and post-conventional. Each of these levels consists of two distinct stages, which results in an invariant sequence of six stages. Not everyone necessarily reaches the highest level. From a number of different studies it appears that in order to attain the level of post-conventional morality (Stages 5 or 6) adolescents must have reached the stage of formal operational thought (Kohlberg, 1976). Thus formal operations are necessary but not sufficient for the development of post-conventional moral thought (Gilligan and Kohlberg, 1978). Just as formal operations are not universally attained by all adults in our society, the highest level of moral reasoning is not commonly found in the course of development. Kohlberg and Gilligan (1971), for example, reported that only 10% of subjects over the age of 16 were capable of post-conventional moral reasoning despite the fact that over 60% of the total sample had reached the stage of formal operations. In this study all of the post-conventional moral reasoners had developed formal operations. Thus, "while individuals may show the logical operation without its parallel in moral judgment, they almost never show the moral stage without its hypothesized logical prerequisite" (Gilligan and Kohlberg, 1978, p. 126). Tomlinson-Keasey and Keasey (1974) also report a high correlation between stages of cognitive development and moral thinking. They compared the performance of a group of sixth-grade girls who had just reached the stage of formal operations with a group of college girls who were already well practiced in formal thought. The younger girls were generally unable to apply their "newly acquired abilities" to the realm of moral decisions, in contrast to the older subjects who had little difficulty. Thus the development of moral thought and moral evaluative ability lags behind adolescents' cognitive development. Cognitive development appears to be an important "mediator" of some aspects of adolescent identity.

Longitudinal studies of adolescents' moral reasoning suggest that regression to earlier levels of morality sometimes occurs (Kohlberg and Kramer, 1969). Approximately 20% of adolescents studied longitudinally have been reported to display this type of regression in their moral thinking (Gilligan and Kohlberg, 1978). Instead of progressing from the Conventional Level (Stage 4) to the Post-Conventional Level (Stage 5), this small proportion of adolescents move backward to the Pre-Conventional Level (Stage 2). The regression has been found to be only temporary, since by age 25 all of these subjects have been found to have attained the Post-Conventional Level (Gilligan and Kohlberg, 1978). Adolescents who display such regression show "extreme relativism" in their reasoning. Any moral position is defensible, they claim, as long as it stems from personal conviction; one morality is no better or worse than another. This type of regression appears to be highly similar to the adolescent's realization of the "universality of subjectivity" (Piaget and Inhelder, 1956) and the problem of "epistemological loneliness" (Chandler, 1975; 1978) previously discussed. Gilligan and Kohlberg (1978) suggest that the relativism underlying the regression to pre-conventional moral reasoning may reflect the struggle to reconcile the morality seen in everyday life with their capacity to imagine alternative moralities that might work better.

POLITICAL IDENTITY IN ADOLESCENCE

The formation of a coherent system of political beliefs represents another important acquisition of identity for adolescents. As with other aspects of identity, there is evidence that formal operational thought is a necessary but not sufficient condition for the development of particular forms of political beliefs (Tapp and Kohlberg, 1971; Merelman, 1976). With the onset of formal operations adolescents appear increasingly able "to internalize general rules, to judge consistently and to apply universal norms to individual cases" (Lonky and Reihman, 1978, p. 25). Adelson's extensive research program (Adelson, 1971; Adelson, 1975; Adelson and O'Neil, 1971; Adelson, Green, and O'Neil, 1969) suggests that it is in adolescence that abstract political ideas and individual political views become highly developed. These abstract views are drawn out of the child's earlier direct experiences with concrete parts of the political system. For example, younger children (11 years old) view the political system as composed of separate, isolated parts. Thirteen-year-olds, however, can reason about the relationship of these parts to the larger political system. They can see the relationships among the police system, speeding tickets, maximum speed signs, judges, jail, and the general meaning of the "law." Adolescents continue to evolve, at least through the age of 18, more abstract understanding of the political system as well as a more coherent personal set of political beliefs (Galantin and Adelson, 1971). In his research Adelson asks adolescents to deal with a variety of hypothetical situations much like those seen in Kohlberg's moral dilemmas. Throughout adolescence there is evidence that political beliefs become less concrete and more abstract, more internally consistent, more concerned with a sense of "future orientation," and more liberalized (Adelson, 1971; Galantin and Adelson, 1971; Hess and Torney, 1967). Younger children (ages 6–10) tend to view political ideas within a highly personal or egocentric framework. They see, for example, that people (such as *the* President) hold power and exercise it accordingly (Crain and Crain, 1976). However, it is not until the mid-teens that political ideas such as "democracy" or "the right to vote" are understood as abstract ideas, independent from the concrete or egocentric machinery in which they operate (Crain and Crain, 1976).

In adolescence the development of political beliefs follows a pattern which is similar to the one identified for moral beliefs. Kuhn, Langer, Kohlberg, and Haan, (1977) suggest that there is a moderate relationship between moral reasoning as measured through Kohlberg's procedures and belief in the "social order" (political views). Persons holding Conventional Levels of moral reasoning (e.g., rules must be followed because they exist) generally hold concrete views of the social-political order, while Post-Conventional Levels of moral reasoning are related to more abstract views of the social order (rules protect every individual's rights). In this same study social-political beliefs were more strongly related to the development of formal operational thought (e.g., the pendulum problem, colorless liquid problem) than they were to moral reasoning. Kuhn, Langer, Kohlberg, and Haan (1977) suggest that in adolescence there is a developmental order to the acquisition of a political and moral identity. Initially adolescents must acquire formal operational thought, which leads to the development of political beliefs, and finally leads to the acquisition of a moral orientation (e.g., moral stage).

Other investigators interested in the relationship between political identity and moral belief systems have studied radical or activist youth. What factors contribute to this type of political identity? The majority of studies suggest that radical political views are usually held by adolescents who have advanced moral reasoning (Carroll, 1977). Haan, Smith, and Block (1968) found differences in moral reasoning among activist and non-activist college undergraduates. The students were categorized according to their involvement in the Berkeley Free Speech Movement of the early 1960s. Those students who were subsequently arrested (activists) tended to have Post-Conventional Levels of moral reasoning. These student activists had developed a high degree of self-autonomy "as expressed through their heightened concern with interpersonal obligations" (Lonky and Reihman, 1978). Not all student activists, however, displayed this type of morality. Other activists who joined the Free Speech Movement and were subsequently arrested displayed Pre-Conventional Levels of moral reasoning. Among these student activists, the interest in joining the protest had little to do with the basic issues; their political activism was based on exercising their right to disagree with those in authority or power (especially for males). Pre-Conventional reasoners joined the demonstration because it might produce some change which they personally found desirable. Students who did not participate in the Free Speech Movement (non-activists) typically displayed Conventional Levels of moral reasoning. They had rather traditional, conservative, middle-of-the-road views in their political identities.

Fishkin, Kenniston, and MacKinnon (1973) questioned whether these relationships would hold among students who might be radical, but whose behavior might not necessarily lead them to take such extreme form as arrest. They assessed both moral reasoning as well as the political ideology of a group of undergraduate students by having them indicate their agreement/disagreement with three types of political slogans. There were slogans of the "violent radical" type (e.g., Power to the People; Bring the War Home), slogans which were "peacefully radical" (e.g., Make Love Not War; Give Peace a Chance), and still other slogans which were clearly "conservative" (e.g., I fight poverty—I work; America: Love it or Leave it). Based on subjects' responses to the slogans and their moral reasoning scores, it was found that conventional levels of moral reasoning were typical of students who were politically conservative. Somewhat similar to the results of Haan, Smith, and Block (1968), Pre-Conventional Levels of moral reasoning were held by students who supported the "violently radical" slogans but were not endorsed by those subjects with Post-Conventional moral reasoning. Rather, Post-Conventional reasoning was related to rejection of politically conservative slogans.

In a recent study Merelman (1977) assessed adolescent political radicalism and related it to a number of measures, including moral reasoning. He reported that higher levels of moral reasoning characterized twelfth-graders who were more radical in their political beliefs. For younger seventh-graders, however, no relationship was found between moral reasoning and political radicalism. Unlike other investigators, Merelman did not find formal operational skills to be related to political beliefs among the adolescents in his sample. He suggested that a more complex relationship may underlie the development of political, moral, and cognitive domains among groups of adolescent radicals than was initially proposed.

VOCATIONAL CHOICE AND ADOLESCENT IDENTITY

Choosing a career or vocation represents one of the most significant attainments among youth in our society. The importance of work in human development has been emphasized as a means of self-fulfillment, economic idependence, and identification for the person as well as a means of organizing and directing society itself. However, it is the individual meaning of work for the adolescent that attracts most attention: "In general it is primarily the inability to settle on an occupational identity which disturbs young people" (Erikson, 1959, p. 92).

Our understanding of this component of adolescent identity is somewhat incomplete. Theories of vocational choice emphasize either the factors correlated with specific career choices (a single event) or the processes underlying the selection of a career (Amatea, 1975). The latter theories typically view career selection as a series of stages and consider the broader consequences of vocational choice throughout a person's entire life.

Many attempts to describe the relations among career choices and past background of the adolescent are sociological in nature. For example, Caplow (1954) recognizes that through the "accident of birth" career choices will be influenced by sex, social class, education, opportunity within the social structure for upward mobility, and father's occupation. The importance of role models such as parents, teachers, friends, and relatives has also been noted (Pietrofesa and Splete, 1975).

Figure 14-2. Most adolescents have difficulty selecting a career. (United Nations photo)

While these models may foster interest or initial preferences for certain careers, they may also promote dislikes or rejection of certain careers (Amatea, 1975).

Often the choice of a career is considered to be a very rational, deliberate decision. Adolescents hoping to choose a vocation may compare their own individual abilities to those required for any particular career. A "match" is assumed to be based on a cognitive, rational decision. Alternatively, an adolescent's own unique personality may lead to the choice of a particular career. According to Holland (1973), at the time at which personal vocational decisions are made, each person's unique "modal personality orientation" or "personality style" is the predominant factor influencing career choice. He defines six different personality types, each of which influences the adolescent to find particular work environments most satisfying (see Table 14-2). Both personality style and an emotional decision influence the type of work environment which an individual finds most desirable. It is not necessary to accept Holland's classification system to recognize that certain careers do seem to attract people with similar personality traits.

Other theorists are concerned with the degree to which a vocation may satisfy more personal needs. The needs of the person have been presented by Hoppock

Table 14-2
HOLLAND'S PERSONALITY STYLES AND OCCUPATIONAL ENVIRONMENTS

Personality Types		Environmental Models
Type	*Description*	*Typical Occupations in Which This Type is Found*
Realistic	Persons oriented toward this role are characterized by aggressive behavior, interest in activities requiring motor coordination, skill and physical strength, and masculinity. They prefer concrete rather than abstract problem situations, and typically avoid tasks which involve interpersonal and verbal skills.	Laborers, machine operators, aviators, farmers, truck drivers, carpenters
Intellectual	Persons oriented toward this role are characterized by thinking rather than acting and emphasize organizing and understanding the world rather than dominating or persuading. They tend to avoid close interpersonal contact.	Physicist, anthropologist, chemist, mathematician, biologist
Social	Persons characterized by this role seek close personal relationships and are adept in these relationships. They avoid situations where they might be required to engage in intellectual problem solving or use of extensive physical skills.	Clinical psychologist, counselor, foreign missionary, teacher
Conventional	Persons oriented toward this style are typified by a great concern for rules and regulations, great self-control, and a strong identification with power and status. Since this person prefers structure and order he or she seeks interpersonal and work situations in which structures are readily apparent.	Cashier, statistician, bookkeeper, administrative assistant, post office clerk
Enterprising	Persons characterizing this role are verbally skilled but use these skills for manipulative and persuasive purposes, rather than for supportive purposes. They are concerned about power and status, and they work very hard to acquire it.	Car salesman, auctioneer, politician, master of ceremonies, buyer
Artistic	Persons oriented toward this style are characterized by strong manifestations toward self-expression, particularly through the arts media. Such people dislike structure, show their emotions much more easily and demonstrate relatively little self-control. They tend to be relatively introceptive and asocial.	Poet, novelist, musician, sculptor, playwright, composer, stage director

Source: E. S. Amatea, "Contribution of Career Development Theories," in R. C. Reardon and H. C. Burck (eds.), *Facilitating Career Development*. Springfield, Ill.: C. C. Thomas, 1975, pp. 24–25. By permission.

(1967) as central to an understanding of career choices. His orientation is summarized in the list below:

1. Occupations are chosen in order to meet best those needs which concern us.
2. Needs may be cognitively perceived or felt as only vague attractions, both of which influence career choices.
3. Occupational choices become more informed as we anticipate the degree to which specific careers will meet our needs.
4. Personal awareness helps in deciding whether specific careers will meet our needs.
5. Occupational choices will change when a different career appears to meet our needs more effectively.   (Adapted from Hoppock, 1967, pp. 111–112)

Sequential stage theories of career choice emphasize the processes at work in adolescent and adult development. One of the earliest of these theories viewed career choice within the following stages (Ginzberg, 1952; 1970):

I. *Fantasy Period* (to age 11)—you may be whatever you want.
II. *Tentative Choice Period* (11–17 years of age)
    A.   Interest Stage: career possibilities based on interests.
    B.   Capacities Stage: personal skills and abilities are considered.
    C.   Values Stage: personal values become important in the process of career choice.
    D.   Transition Stage: looking forward to work role or attending college.
III. *Realistic Choice Period* (17 years of age and older)
    A.   Exploration Stage: one last look at the range of alternatives.
    B.   Crystallization Stage: career choice is determined.
    C.   Specification Stage: specific job or position is taken.

In Ginzberg's work career decision making is viewed as a process rather than a single event or choice. Although critics of the theory tend to see these choices as irreversible, Ginzberg has recognized more recently that people may move into other careers during later periods of development. The ages are best seen as guidelines for typical young people in our society. For adolescents in particular the exploratory nature of their choices has been recognized by Ginzberg in his use of the term Tentative Choice Period.

Super (1957) has also evolved a stage sequential theory of the process of vocational decisions, which is similar to that of Ginzberg in many respects. For example, the stages identified appear to capture the same processes from a developmental perspective:

I. *Growth Stage* (up to 14 years of age): vocations are considered in terms of fantasy, interests, and capacity.

II. *Exploration Stage* (15–24): self-awareness and role experimentation through school, part-time work, summer leisure.

III. *Establishment Stage* (25–44): developing a permanent job within a given career: commitment to work.

IV. *Maintenance Stage* (45–64): to do whatever is needed to continue or maintain a career.

V. *Decline Stage* (65 and older): pace and demands of work may change; retirement demands new patterns of adjustment.

Super's unique contribution concerns the importance of the *self* in vocational choice. Super considers that a career choice represents the ultimate realization of an individual's self-concept. "In expressing a vocational preference a person puts into occupational terminology his idea of the kind of person he is . . . "(Super et al., 1953, p. 1). In contrast to other theories, Super's theory views vocational choice throughout the life span, not as something which only occurs during adolescence. The concept of career patterns vs. initial occupational selections is central to his theory (Amatea, 1975). With the current emphasis on second careers and mid-life crises as precipitators of career change, Super's approach appears particularly relevant. Within Super's framework, career patterns reflect the ongoing development of the self-concept. The same factors that are influential in the development of the self-concept are influential in the development of career patterns. His theory is very similar to Erikson's task of identity formation and adopting a role in society (Kroll, Dinklage, Lee, Morley, and Wilson, 1970). Successful career decisions (Super, 1957) are predicted among adolescents who display: (1) acceptance of responsibility for planning and making choices, and (2) ability to plan.

From the difficulties which adolescents encounter in career selection, numerous recommendations have been developed. Some of these recommendations have become part of the emphasis in many public schools on "career education." Most career education programs are rather eclectic, emphasizing aspects of a number of the theories which have been reviewed. General guidelines suggested by Shertzer (1977) include:

1. Study yourself, since self-awareness is the key to career planning.
2. Where would you be most comfortable?
3. Formally write your plans and ideas down.

4. Become familiar with the requirements or pathways for specific occupations that might interest you.

5. Review your career plans and progress with someone else.

6. If you choose a career which is not for you, start over.   (Adapted from Shertzer, 1977, pp. 273–276)

ALIENATION: EXPERIENCE AND IDENTITY

Most adolescents seem to have a minimum of problems in the process of evolving a personal identity and cope successfully with this crisis. Only a minority, as Keniston (1971) points out, express strong dissatisfaction, alienation, and evolve identities out of the experiences of the counterculture. Despite the fact that most adolescents look for traditional goals, emulate the values and standards of their parents, and become the stable force behind the next generation, a small number of today's youth reject elements of modern society. In their attempt to construct a personal identity, we see strong dissent among this segment of the adolescent population. The dissent can take many forms: drugs, delinquency, dropping out of school, political activism, religious cultism. Although the number of adolescents choosing such methods in their search for a sense of personal identity is small, they are highly visible and represent a significant challenge for understanding. It is difficult to find a common denominator among adolescents who identify with a counterculture, although the label "alienation" is one popular label.

Delinquency

Delinquency refers to the violation of a local, state, or federal statute by a minor. The rate of delinquency has continued to show a steady rise over the years (Deming, 1977). From 1960 to 1975 the increase in major crimes among those 18 years of age and under has risen 117.5% for boys and 425.4% for girls. Although boys are more frequently found to be delinquents, girls are increasingly more likely to engage in contranormative behavior (Deming, 1977). Types of delinquent acts are found to vary according to sex. Girls usually are less likely to commit violations of legal statutes and more often commit status offenses—offenses related to rebellious behavior such as running away from home, uncontrollable behavior in the home, or sexual promiscuity. Boys, however, are more likely to commit legal offenses such as car theft, robbery, or assault. While it is still a matter of debate, the overall increase in delinquency is often related to the greater freedom and opportunity provided to today's youth (Deming, 1977). Many see the increases in delinquency as related to the use of drugs. Often the only way to obtain money to buy drugs is through stealing; in addition, the selling and mere possession of certain drugs is also a violation of legal statutes.

Are there differences in delinquency among middle-class and lower-class ado-

Figure 14-3. Acts of delinquency are increasingly committed by adolescent girls. (Mimi Forsyth/Monkmeyer Press Photo Service)

lescents? It is apparent from official surveys that a higher percentage of lower-class adolescents are found to be delinquents. These data, however, are misleading since the legal system (family court, judges, police) is harshest on lower-class adolescents. Middle-class adolescents, although they may have committed acts similar to those of lower-class youth, are given far more leeway and are less likely to be labeled and treated as delinquents. Linden (1978) found that adolescents (seventh- to twelfth-graders) from both social classes readily admitted to similar delinquent acts when asked to complete an anonymous self-report questionnaire. Linden found that among both lower-class and middle-class boys delinquency was positively related to closeness of peer ties and negatively related to involvement with parents. Thus, the reasons for delinquency were similar for adolescents from lower- and middle-class backgrounds.

Johnstone (1978) has attempted to understand the influence that social class has on specific types of adolescent delinquency, ranging from serious to mild status offenses. His results are presented in Table 14-3. Violent acts (breaking and entering, robbery with force) and criminal delinquency (burglary, larceny, and robbery) were the only offenses found to be related to social class: lower social class adolescents were more likely to commit serious offenses. An equally strong relationship

Table   14-3
THE INFLUENCE OF FOUR PREDICTORS ON SIX TYPES OF DELINQUENCY

| | Type of Delinquency | | | | | |
| | Major Offenses | | Minor Offenses | | | |
	Violent acts	Criminal delinquency	Automobile offenses	Property offenses	Illicit drugs	Status offenses
Family status	−.11*	−.07*	.01	.01	.04	−.02
Community poverty	.13*	.07*	.01	.00	.02	−.04
Family integration	.01	−.06*	−.08*	−.12*	−.20*	−.17*
Delinquent peers	.26*	.21*	.27*	.33*	.32*	.37*

Source: Adapted from J. W. C. Johnstone, "Juvenile Delinquency and the Family: a Contextual Interpretation," *Youth and Society,* 1978, **9,** 279–313. Copyright 1978, Sage Journals. By permission. p. 310.

*Indicates significant relationship—standardized regression coefficients.

was seen, however, between these two serious offenses and the level of community poverty. Johnstone argues that serious delinquency is related to *both* economic status and the type of community in which the adolescent lives.

When the less serious delinquent acts were considered, social class and community poverty were not as important predictors as the degree of family integration. An inverse relationship was seen between minor acts of delinquency and family integration. The less serious the delinquent act, the more family disintegration was involved. The data in Table 14-3 also support the important role of the peer group: "association with delinquent peers remains the strongest predictor for all six types of delinquency" (Johnstone, 1978, p. 310).

Baumrind (1978) suggests that styles of parenting which are either strongly authoritarian or excessively permissive may lead to delinquency. Extrapolating from her framework (see Chapter 11), these two types of parental styles can be related to delinquency. Strongly authoritarian parents most clearly lead adolescents to delinquency as an active rejection of parental authority and values. Delinquency, like other acts of nonconformity, seems to be adopted as a reaction to parental over-control; adolescents appear to reject any further attempts by parents to exert control and restrict their independence. Johnson (1959) considers this type of reaction to be "individual delinquency" and views it as a rebellion against social norms. Such delinquents consider their parents to have been particularly harsh, cruel, and demanding (Glueck and Glueck, 1950).

Alternatively, excessive permissiveness also leads to delinquency. Often permissive parents are lax or inconsistent regarding discipline. This leads adolescents to develop feelings of alienation and a sense of powerlessness and lack of control over their lives. The result is an over-reliance on and over-identification with the peer group and its norms (Baumrind, 1978). Johnson (1959) calls delinquency which arises from this orientation "sociologic"; that is, the norms of the peer group and concern over peer acceptance leads adolescents to identify strongly with the peer group (Johnstone, 1978). The "other-oriented" values which are adopted by some delinquents suggest a pattern of underlying alienation: "rejection of trusting, optimistic, socially responsible . . . values; a rejection of concern for others' and one's own future welfare" (Baumrind, 1978, p. 263).

Other research studies support the importance of parent-child relationships in delinquency. Gold (1970) notes that delinquents usually perceive their relationships with their parents as hostile and feel they have been either actively rejected or ignored. Fathers are seen in a rather negative light by delinquents (Smith and Walters, 1978). In Smith and Walters' study 330 delinquents between 14 and 18 years of age were compared to a group of nondelinquents in terms of their perception of their fathers. The delinquents were all incarcerated in a state boys' school. Delinquents reported that they had minimal involvement with their fathers and that their relationships were marked by a lack of love, warmth, and emotional support. Delinquents felt alienated and isolated from society. Although delinquents may be more involved with their mothers, she was viewed as a lax, inconsistent disciplinar-

---

Box   14-1
Interview with a Delinquent Boy: Eddie Harrington

"I think my problems are due to my parents, 'specially my father, although I hate to blame him. But like, when a kid like me grows up, he kind of expects his dad and mother to be certain ways. Like, first off, he expects them to be married or not married, right? . . .

"So the next thing I think kids got a right to expect is that their father or mother got a job . . . When he isn't working, when you see him hanging around the house doing nothing—and I mean day after day, all the time—then he ought to explain it. 'Specially to me. I'm his son. And *he's* supposed to be training *me* for when I'm a man. I got to get a job some day.

"I don't see that much of my father. Lots of guys I know, they see their father all the time, and some of 'em, they never see 'em. But not only don't I know what he does, I don't even know where he goes. If I was little, you know, like a baby just walking or talking, I wouldn't care all that much. Like, I wouldn't know how a father is supposed to be. Hell, I wouldn't even know there *is* such a thing as a father. But now, I understand all of it . . .

"My father's ashamed he's out of work . . . And you know why? 'Cause he's begging. He's a street beggar."

Source: Cottle, T. J. *Children in Jail*. Boston: Beacon Press, 1977, pp. 65–67. By permission.

ian and largely ineffectual (Gold, 1970; Glueck and Glueck, 1950; 1959). Box 14-1 provides some personal insights into the perceptions and feelings of one adolescent delinquent boy towards his father. He was interviewed while in jail having been arrested for setting fires in his neighborhood.

Drugs

Among today's adolescents searching for their identity, drugs provide an increasingly popular avenue for exploration. There are many kinds of drugs which adolescents may try: alcohol, marijuana, amphetamines, barbiturates, hashish, LSD, tranquilizers, cocaine, heroin, and inhalants.

From the perspective of Proskauer and Rolland (1973), drug use among adolescents falls into three basic categories, only two of which indicate serious "drug problems." A small number of adolescents use drugs as a way of complete escape from their own inadequate personalities and personal deficiencies. Such "characterological" drug users have experienced problems throughout their early lives, long before reaching adolescence and turning to drugs. For this group of drug users, the danger is that there will never be any attempt to deal with their problems

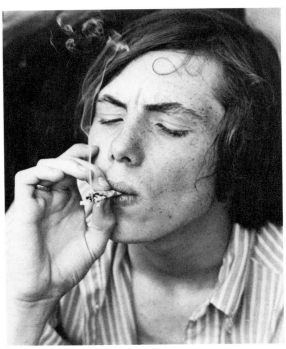

Figure 14-4. Adolescent drug use is often a means of dealing with the problems of of identity. (Paul Conklin/Monkmeyer Press Photo Service)

of personality and emotional maladjustment. Unless these fundamental problems are recognized and dealt with directly, there cannot be any resolution of the identity crisis. The total escape of the characterological drug user implies that identity formation will not be resolved and will remain incomplete and confused.

The "depressive" drug user represents a second category, also indicative of a drug problem, according to Proskauer and Rolland. Drugs are used for protection from feelings of "emptiness, hopelessness, loneliness, and worthlessness" (Proskauer and Rolland, 1973, p. 34). For this group of adolescents, depressive drug use merely prolongs and extends the eventual task of resolving the problem of identity. Depressive drug users, rather than coping with themselves and their feelings during this developmental period, turn to drugs as a way of avoiding their personal responsibilities. Such youth may be experiencing emotional depression and turn to drugs as a crutch to help them overcome their feelings of powerlessness, emptiness, and conflict. The danger in turning to drugs for such reasons is that these problems and feelings do not disappear. They remain ever-present, waiting to be resolved with finality. Depressive drug users are thus of concern, because they appear to be putting off the inevitable day of reckoning when they have to confront themselves. The longer the delay the more difficult the confrontation and resolution of the identity crisis.

The third type of adolescent drug user is seen as free of the stigma of having a "drug problem." Only in the case of the "experimental" drug user are Proskauer and Rolland (1973) less concerned. The experimental drug user simply turns to drugs because they are new and different. Experimental drug use may arise from peer-group pressures, from striving for independence, as a way of expressing freedom from parental demands and control, or from sheer curiosity. Each generation of adolescents seems to find some activity which provides them with an image of themselves as clearly different from previous adult generations. Drug use may be seen in this light. Experimental drug users do not share many of the motivational characteristics seen among depressive or characterological types. Hence, for the curious, often intellectual user, there is less cause for concern.

Why do adolescents turn to drugs at all? A frequent explanation for the strong effect of peers on adolescents' use of drugs is based on emotional distance from parents. It is assumed that adolescents who feel estranged from their parents turn to the peer group for emotional support and satisfaction. However, in a series of studies conducted on a sample of 8,306 secondary school students in New York State, Kandel and her co-workers have attempted to answer this and other related questions. Relying on anonymous self-reports from the adolescents themselves, Kandel found that the most important factors leading to the use of drugs such as marijuana were the behavior and attitude of the peer group. Adolescents were most likely to have tried marijuana and other drugs when they associated with peers who had used them (Kandel, 1973; 1974; 1978; Kandel, Single, and Kessler, 1976). The intense commitment to the peer group is said to be a prerequisite for turning to drugs such as marijuana.

Kandel (1978) explored this question among the adolescents who were part of the earlier sample reported previously. Her creative design consisted of four groups

Table 14-4

PATTERN OF DRUG USE BY TYPE OF ADOLESCENT GROUP INVOLVEMENT

| | High Peer Involvement | | Low Peer Involvement | |
Type of Drug Used	No friend uses marijuana %	Most friends use marijuana %	Most friends use marijuana %	No friend uses marijuana %
Ever used hard liquor	65	93	78	31
Ever used marijuana	5	89	75	1
Ever used other illicit drugs	9	76	54	4
Ever used tranquilizers, pills	5	68	43	2
Ever used psychedelics	0	50	29	0
Was offered marijuana	26	97	93	7
Total N ≥	(518)	(828)	(216)	(1543)

Source: D. B. Kandel, "On variations in Adolescent Subcultures," *Youth and Society*, 1978, **9**, 373–84. Copyright 1978, Sage Journals. By permission. p. 378.

of adolescents: high peer involvement with friends who did not use drugs; high peer involvement with friends who did use drugs; low peer involvement with friends who did not use drugs; low peer involvement with friends who did use drugs (see Table 14-4). The results are surprising since they do *not* support the assumption that peer involvement necessarily leads to either estrangement from parents or active experimentation with drugs such as marijuana. There were adolescents who became strongly involved with their peer group but who did not reject their parents' values and did not become emotionally distant from them (Kandel, 1978). As Table 14-5 (columns 1 and 4) shows, despite the degree of peer involvement (high or low), adolescents whose friends did not use drugs were very similar to one another. Similar parallels existed among adolescents whose friends were users of drugs like marijuana (columns 2 and 3). Thus, a high degree of peer involvement was not necessarily related to drug use unless the peer group itself was involved in drugs. Conversely, low peer involvement does not mean that drug use will be absent. As Table 14-4 suggests, it was the *level* of drug use in the peer group which was the predictor of adolescent drug involvement, not the degree of involvement with one's peers (Kandel, 1978). The data also revealed that adolescents with friends who did not use marijuana tended to display: (1) close relationships with parents, (2) relatively frequent church attendance, and (3) moderately conservative political beliefs. Kandel's study provides an insightful perspective on the role of the peer group in adolescent use of drugs. High peer involvement, positive parent interactions, and minimal drug use can co-occur. Conversely, low peer involvement, negative parent interactions, and high drug use can also co-occur.

Other research has also begun to consider that drug use among adolescents is not a unitary phenomenon. In a year-long study of 374 college students, Sadava and Forsyth (1977) investigated the impact of both personality and environmental factors on four types of drug patterns: (1) frequency of marijuana use, (2) time span as a user, (3) range of other drugs used, and (4) adverse personal consequences. Their complex analyses revealed that for each of the four drug-use patterns a slightly different weighting of personality and environmental factors was involved. For example, the pattern found among high-frequency users was, in order of importance: (1) feelings of personal isolation, (2) a lower future time perspective, (3) feelings of reduced personal control, and (4) a supportive social environment (e.g., no negative sanctions from friends). When, however, the range of drugs used was considered (poly-drug use), a different combination and weighting of factors was found. The most significant factor related to poly-drug use was the

Table 14-5

QUALITY OF INTERACTIONS WITH PARENTS BY TYPE OF ADOLESCENT GROUP INVOLVEMENT

	High Peer Involvement		Low Peer Involvement	
	No friend uses marijuana %	Most friends use marijuana %	Most friends use marijuana %	No friend uses marijuana %
High closeness to mother (index)	64	40	46	66
High closeness to father (index)	55	33	28	55
Respect parents' opinions more than friends	50	30	36	64
High on index of peer orientation	32	56	50	21
Would continue to see friends even if parents objected	62	90	82	42
Discussed personal problems with mother 1-2 times a week	39	28	30	37
Discussed personal problems with friends 1-2 times a week	59	70	68	38
Total N ≥	(534)	(830)	(210)	(1571)

Source: D. B. Kandel, "On Variations in Adolescent Subcultures," *Youth and Society*, 1978, **9**, 373–84. Copyright, 1978, Sage Journals. By permission, p. 379.

presence of an active supportive social environment (e.g., friends who provided no negative sanctions for such poly-drug experimentation).

Sadava and Forsyth also attempted to synthesize their results and identify the pattern of factors which seemed to underlie *all* four types of drug use. They found that among the students in their sample the most important influences were: (1) the presence of a drug culture environment among one's friends and the absence of negative sanctions; (2) feelings of reduced personal control; and (3) inner conflict surrounding the use of drugs, e.g., although students felt that drugs helped them to cope, they also feared the long-term consequences of their dependency on these substances.

Adolescents also appear to be turning to alcohol in record numbers (Holden, 1975). In an attempt to understand this phenomenon research studies have pointed to a number of factors underlying the popularity of alcohol. Adolescents generally turn to alcohol for reasons that are similar to those underlying their use of other drugs: peer influence, seeking new experiences, escaping negative feelings, and avoidance of personal responsibility. Since many adults use alcohol, however, additional factors seem uniquely related to adolescents' use of alcohol. For example, adolescents are most likely to drink when their parents are drinkers (Forslund and Guftason, 1970; Maddox, 1970). In some studies the factor that is most related to alcoholism among high-school adolescents is having a father who drinks excessively (Prendergast and Schaefer, 1974). Authorities feel that through modeling and observation, adolescents realize how alcohol is used (as defense) and when it is used (as a way of handling anxieties). Maddox (1970) has suggested that patterns of excessive drinking are established in adolescence, through the learning process.

Religious Cults

In recent years many youth have become immersed in a wide range of religious movements or cults. For many this represents an extreme choice of a life-style built on alienation and rejection of traditional adult values (Bodemann, 1974). Fanatical devotion to religious cults and their leaders provides a solution, although temporary, to the problem of identity for many of today's youth. No individual decisions are needed, since the cult and its leader think for everyone in the group.

We are somewhat familiar with the highly visible cults in our society as the Hare Krishna movement. The young members of this cult are seen selling flowers and pamphlets, dressed in long, flowing orange and white robes. Boys' heads are shaved with just a small topknot remaining. This group has had a large following, and its familiar chant and weaving dance have become dramatized in the rock musical "Hair."

Concern is usually directed at adolescents in religious cults whose leaders wield tremendous power and influence over converts. The Unification Church led by South Korean Reverend Sun Myung Moon has developed an extremely large and fanatical group of followers. The "Moonies" devotion to the Reverend Moon

Figure 14-5.   A mass suicide by cyanide poisoning took place at the People's Temple cult headquarters in Guyana in November, 1978. Hundreds of bodies were found, many of them of young people who had clung to each other as they died. (United Press International photo)

includes donating all worldly possessions to the group and working on his behalf by selling flowers or candy door-to-door. The tactics used to recruit cultists like the "Moonies" have come under attack. Many people view these tactics as brainwashing or "programming," to the point where young people literally have no will of their own and are unable to make individual choices. Recruiting new members to the cult involves a process called "lovebombing," which revolves around the following advice:

1. Look for lonely, isolated youth.
2. Initiate and encourage friendly conversation.
3. Invite to group dinner during which there is
   a.   sharing of personal "secrets"
   b.   tremendous acceptance of potential new "Moonie," e.g., lots of hand holding, physical contact, and love

4. Invite to a weekend retreat which includes
   a. intense group discussion of the cult
   b. physical activity (exercise, games) almost to the point of exhaustion
   c. minimal sleep
   d. no personal questions of cult members
   e. no close one-to-one relationships, allegiance only to the group
   f. assignment of a monitor who watches over new recruits every moment
5. Forceful request to break with the past and stay on in the group, e.g., don't return on Monday to work, family, friends, home, or apartment.
6. Requests for lengthier and lengthier periods of isolation.   (Woodward, Hager, Huck, Reese, Mark, and Marbach, 1978)

It is difficult for us to imagine the devotion which such brainwashing tactics can produce among members. Psychiatrists and psychologists studying the cult phenomenon are in general agreement that a series of stages can be recognized in the process. Dr. Frederick Hacker sees the process as involving an initial stage of isolation, followed by feelings of guilt regarding their previous experiences, and then a need to be "reborn like their all-knowing brothers and sisters in the new family of the cult" (Woodward, Hager, Huck, Reese, Mark, and Marbach, 1978). The final stage is the acquisition of a "new identity" which is based on a regimen similar to that seen in the initial stage of recruiting. Ultimately, the religious leader himself becomes, in the eyes of the cult members, a god. His every wish and order is followed, unquestioningly.

The capacity to think independently is actively discouraged in most religious cults. The most dramatic evidence of the success of these tactics was seen among the followers of Reverend Jim Jones and his Peoples' Temple. Under the direct orders of Reverand Jim Jones, over 900 followers committed mass suicide in Guyana on November 20, 1978. It is difficult for us to believe that cult members would be unable or unwilling to say "NO!" to this final act. Given the constant stress experienced by cultists, "sleep deprivation, hunger, constant haranguing, public beatings, and threats of death" (Krause, 1978, p. 120), the total control of Jim Jones over his followers is not that surprising. The end result is *mind control* (Krause, 1978). The cult determines what its members should do, think, believe, act, and even when they should die. Krause notes that we seem reluctant to accept the notion that human beings are ethologically innately susceptible to such techniques of persuasion. In particular, the young people in our society as well as those with marginal identities (the unemployed, the poor, the racial minorities) are particularly susceptible. Given the false sense of security, the lack of responsibility for individual decisions, a leader who is viewed as god, daily stress, and instinctive reaction to powerful tactics of persuasion, "cult members can be willing to follow their leaders even into death" (Krause, 1978, p. 120).

Suicide

During adolescence, there is a marked increase in the number of suicides (see Figure 14-6). Adolescents (fifteen to nineteen years old) account for 6.6% of the 25,000 suicides in the U.S. (Smith, 1976). Boys are three times more likely to commit suicide than girls (Smith, 1976), and boys typically choose more violent acts in comparison to the more passive methods chosen by girls (Suter, 1976). Adolescents also account for over 12% of all suicide attempts; of this figure, 90% of attempts are made by females (Suter, 1976). Suicide attempts represent an adolescent's final call for help and attention. These attempts are all too often successful, and thousands of adolescents kill themselves each year. Experts tend to interpret the statistics in light of the failure to overcome the crisis of identity. They view the failure to establish intimacy as a particularly important component of suicidal behavior.

Through analyses of both suicide attempts and actual suicides we can derive a psychological profile of the situational and personality factors leading up to the event in adolescents. Suicidal adolescents appear to have failed to identify with significant others in their environment (Corder, Shorr, and Corder, 1974). These

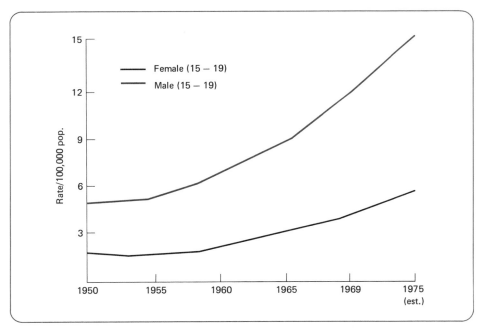

Figure 14-6. Adolescents account for 6.6 percent of the suicides in the U.S. Boys are three times more likely to commit suicide than girls. (From D. F. Smith, Adolescent **Suicide: a problem for teachers?** *Phi Delta Kappan*, **1976, 57 [No. 8], p. 541. By permission.**)

adolescents were unable to remember any feelings of closeness, emotional attachment, or identification with adults. When asked about the future, suicidal adolescents took a dim or bleak view and considered that their situation was hopeless and would not change much (Corder, Shorr, and Corder, 1974). In addition to social isolation, suicidal adolescents also displayed increasingly poor relationships with parents and personal or school crises which could not be coped with successfully (Cantor, 1977; Jacobs, 1971; Suter, 1976). The following description highlights these factors in a typical socially isolated suicidal adolescent girl:

> [her] progressively deteriorating relationship with her parents has left her with a sense of rejection, feelings of hostility, low self-esteem, and unfulfilled dependency needs. In adolescence, she turns to a boyfriend in an attempt to fulfill her emotional needs . . . built on the fear of being alone and the need to recreate the parent-child relationship in an attempt to receive the nurturance and security which were not attained in that earlier context.

> Thus, the isolated girl focuses all her energy on the relationship with a male, in the process of alienating herself from whatever girlfriends she has. If she loses the boy, or even if the romance is threatened, she may feel that she has nothing to live for; and in her terror at being alone she may attempt suicide.   (Suter, 1976, p. 150)

The girl who is still able to maintain her girlfriends during adolescence, however, is far less likely to become suicidal under similar patterns of stress (Suter, 1976). Thus, strong peer relationships and the lack of social isolation seem to reduce the chances of suicidal behaviors.

SUMMARY

We have discussed the development of adolescent identity from a number of different perspectives. The special significance of formal operational thought in the development of adolescent identity was presented. Evaluation of the formal operational stage of Piaget's theory was found to be less clearly supported than his earlier stages of cognitive development. We also explored the development of moral and political beliefs in adolescence. The process of vocational choice was presented from a number of perspectives. We briefly examined the influence of a variety of experiences (delinquency, religious cults, and drugs), and the high rate of adolescent suicide.

RECOMMENDED READINGS

Brainerd, C. J. *Piaget's theory of intelligence.* Englewood Cliffs, N.J.: Prentice-Hall, 1978.

An excellent, critical appraisal of Piaget's theory with an exceptionally fine treatment of adolescent formal operations.

Grossman, H. *Nine rotten lousy kids.* New York: Holt, Rinehart, and Winston, 1972.

A fascinating description of the techniques and results of an innovative school designed to assist adolescent dropouts. The narrative makes this book particularly fascinating.

Shertzer, B. *Career planning.* Boston: Houghton-Mifflin, 1977.

A comprehensive, but easy-to-follow guide to career choices and vocational selection. Both processes and products are given careful attention from an objective goal-oriented perspective.

Bibliography

Aaron, R. I. *John Locke* (3rd ed.). Oxford, Eng.: Clarendon Press, 1971.

Achenbach, T. M., and Weisz, J. R. Impulsivity-reflectivity and cognitive development in preschoolers: a longitudinal analysis of developmental and trait variance. *Developmental Psychology,* 1975, **11,** 413–414.

Adelson, J. The development of ideology in adolescence. In S. E. Dragastin and G. H. Elder (Eds.), *Adolescence in the life cycle: psychosocial change and social context.* New York: Wiley, 1975.

———. The political imagination of the young adolescent. *Daedalus,* 1971, **100,** 1013–1053.

Adelson, J.; Green, B.; and O'Neil, R. P. Growth of the ideas of law at adolescence. *Developmental Psychology,* 1969, **1,** 327–332.

Adelson, J., and O'Neil, R. P. Growth of political ideas in adolescence: the sense of community. In R. E. Maress (Ed.), *Adolescent behavior and society.* New York: Random House, 1971.

Adler, A. *What life should mean to you.* Boston: Little-Brown, 1931.

Aiken, H. D. (Ed.) *Hume's moral and political philosophy.* New York: Hafner, 1948.

Ainsworth, M. D. S. *Infancy in Uganda: infant care and the growth of love.* Baltimore: Johns Hopkins Press, 1967.

———. Attachment and dependency: a comparison. In J. L. Gewirtz (Ed.), *Attachment and dependency.* Washington, D.C.: Winston, 1972.

Alexander, T. An objective study of ulcerative colitis in children. *Applied Therapeutics,* 1965, **7,** 837–839.

Alexander, T., and Anderson, R. Children in a society under stress. *Behavioral Science,* 1957, **2,** 46–55.

Alexander, T.; Stoyle, J.; and Kirk, C. The language of children in the "inner city." *The Journal of Psychology,* 1968, **68,** 215–221.

Allen, J. P. B., and Van Buren, P. *Chomsky: selected readings.* London: Oxford U. Press, 1971.

Altus, W. D. Birth order and its sequelae. *Science,* 1966, **154,** 44–49.

Amatea, E. S. Contributions of career development theories. In R. C. Reardon and H. D. Burck (Eds.), *Facilitating career development,* pp. 17–36. Springfield, Ill.: C. C. Thomas, 1975.

Anastasi, A. Heredity, environment, and the question "How." *Psychological Review,* 1958, **65,** 197–208.

Anastasiow, N. J., and Hanes, M. L. Cognitive development and the acquisition of language in three subcultural groups. *Developmental Psychology,* 1974, **10,** 703–709.

Andersen, H. The influence of hormones on human development. In F. Falkner (Ed.), *Human development,* pp. 184–221. Philadelphia: Saunders, 1966.

Anderson, B. F. *Cognitive psychology: the study of knowing, learning, and thinking.* New York: Academic Press, 1975.

Anisfeld, M., and Tucker, G. R. English pluralization rules of six-year-old children. *Child Development*, 1967, **38**, 1201–1217.

Anthony, E. J. Psychoneurotic disorders. In A. M. Freeman and H. I. Kaplan (Eds.), *Comprehensive textbook of psychiatry*. Baltimore: Williams & Wilkins, 1967.

Anthony, S., and Sanberg, L. F. Actors and observers divergent attributions: a real life test using unwed mothers. Paper presented at Eastern Psychological Association Meetings, Washington, D.C., 1978.

Appel, L. F.; Cooper, R. G.; McCarrell, N.; Sims-Knight, J.; Yussen, S. R.; and Flavell, J. H. The development of the distinction between perceiving and memorizing. *Child Development*, 1972, **43**, 1365–1381.

Arbuthnot, J. Modification of moral judgment through role playing. *Developmental Psychology*, 1975, **11**, 319–324.

Aronfreed, J. Moral development from the standpoint of a general psychological theory. In T. Lickona (Ed.), *Moral development and behavior*. New York: Holt, Rinehart & Winston 1976.

Asher, S. R. Children's ability to appraise their own and another person's communication performance. *Developmental Psychology*, 1976, **12**, 24–32.

Ashton, P. T. Cross-cultural Piagetian research: an experimental perspective. *Harvard Educational Review*, 1975, **45**, 475–506.

Austin, V. D.; Ruble, D. N.; and Trabasso, T. Recall and order effects as factors in children's moral judgments. *Child Development*, 1977, **48**, 470–474.

Axline, V. *Play therapy*. Boston: Houghton Mifflin, 1947.

———. *Dibs in search of self*. Boston: Houghton Mifflin, 1964.

Baer, D. M., and Wright, J. C. Developmental psychology. *Annual Review of Psychology*, 1974, **25**, 1–82.

Baggett, A. T. The effect of early loss of father upon the personality of boys and girls in late adolescence. *Dissertation Abstracts*, 1967, **28** (1-b), 356–357. Cited in D. B. Lynn, *The father: his role in child development*. Monterey, Calif.: Brooks-Cole, 1974.

Bailey, K. V. A study of human growth in the framework of applied nutrition and public health nutrition programs in the Western Pacific region. In J. Brozek (Ed.), *Physical growth and body composition: papers from the Kyoto symposium on anthropological aspects of human growth. Monographs of the Society for Research in Child Development*, 1970, **35** (7 Serial No. 140).

Bakan, D. Adolescence in America: from idea to social fact. *Daedalus*, 1971, **100**, 979–995.

Bakeman, R., and Brown, J. V. Behavioral dialogues: an approach to the assessment of mother-infant interaction. *Child Development*, 1977, **48**, 195–203.

Bakwin, H., and Bakwin, R. M. *Behavior disorders in children*. Philadelphia: W. B. Saunders, 1972.

Baldwin, A. L. A cognitive theory of socialization. In D. A. Goslin (Ed.), *Handbook of socialization theory and research*. Chicago: Rand McNally, 1969.

Baldwin, A. L. *Theories of child development*. New York: Wiley, 1967.

Baltes, P. B.; Reese, H. W.; and Nesselroade, J. R. *Life-span developmental psychology: introduction to research methods*. Belmont, Calif.: 1977.

Bamber, J. H. Adolescent marginality—a further study. *Genetic Psychology Monographs*, 1973, **88**, 3–21.

Bandura, A. The stormy decade: fact or fiction. *Psychology and the schools*, 1964, **1**, 224–231.

———. *Principles of behavior modification*. New York: Holt, Rinehart & Winston, 1969a.

———. Social-learning theory of identificatory processes. In D. A. Goslin (Ed.), *Handbook of socialization theory and research*. Chicago: Rand McNally, 1969b.

———. *Social learning theory*. Morristown, N.J.: General Learning Press, 1971.

———. *Aggression: a social learning analysis*. Englewood Cliffs, N.J.: Prentice-Hall, 1973.

Bandura, A.; Grusec, J. E.; and Menlove, F. L. Observational learning as a function of symbolization and incentive set. *Child Development*, 1966, **37**, 499–50

Bandura, A., and Jeffrey, R. W. Role of symbolic coding and rehearsal processes in observational learning. *Journal of Personality and Social Psychology,* 1973, **26,** 122–130.

Bandura, A.; Ross, D.; and Ross, S. A. Transmission of aggression through imitation of aggressive models. *Journal of Abnormal and Social Psychology,* 1961, **63,** 575–582.

Bandura, A., and Walters, R. H. *Social learning and personality development.* New York: Holt, Rinehart & Winston, 1963.

Barker, R. G., and Wright H. F. *One boy's day.* New York: Harper, 1951.

Barnes, K. E. Preschool play norms. *Developmental Psychology,* 1971, **5,** 99–103.

Baron, R. *Human aggression.* New York: Plenum Press, 1977.

Barrett-Goldfarb, M. S., and Whitehurst, G. J. Infant vocalizations as a function of parental voice selection. *Developmental Psychology,* 1973, **8,** 273–276.

Bart, W. M. The factor structure of formal operations. *British Journal of Educational Psychology,* 1971, **41,** 40–77.

Bauer, D. H. An exploratory study of developmental changes in children's fears. *Journal of Child Psychology and Psychiatry,* 1976, **17,** 69–74.

Baumrind, D. Current patterns of parental authority. *Developmental Psychology Monographs,* 1971, **41**(1), 1–103.

Baumrind, D. Parental disciplinary patterns and social competence in children. *Youth and Society,* 1978, **9,** 239–276.

Bayley, N. Mental growth in young children. In G. M. Whipple (Ed.), *Thirty-Ninth Yearbook, National Society for the Study of Education. Part II. Intelligence: Its nature and nurture.* Bloomington, Ill.: Public School Publishing Co., 1940.

———. Tables for predicting adult height from skeletal age and present height. *Journal of Pediatrics,* 1946, **28,** 49–64.

———. Consistency and variability in the growth of intelligence from birth to eighteen years. *Journal of Genetic Psychology,* 1949, **75,** 165–196.

———. Some increasing parent-child similarities during the growth of children. *Journal of Educational Psychology,* 1954, **45,** 1–21.

———. Development of mental abilities. In P. H. Mussen (Ed.), *Carmichael's manual of child psychology.* Vol. I, 3rd ed. New York: Wiley, 1970.

Becker, W. C. Consequences of different kinds of parental discipline. In M. L. Hoffman and L. W. Hoffman (Eds.), *Review of child development research.* Vol. 1. New York: Russell Sage, 1964.

Bee, H. L.; Van Egeren, F. V.; Streissguth, A. P.; Nyman, B. A.; and Leckie, M. S. Social class differences in maternal teaching strategies and speech patterns. *Developmental Psychology,* 1969, **1,** 726–734.

Bell, R. Q. The influence of children's behavior on parental behavior in socialization. In G. G. Thompson (Ed.), *Social development and personality.* New York: Wiley, 1971.

Belmont, T., and Marolla, F. A. Birth order, family size, and intelligence. *Science,* 1973, **182,** 1096–1101.

Benedict, R. *Patterns of culture.* Boston: Houghton Mifflin, 1934.

———. Continuities and discontinuities in cultural conditioning. In J. M. Seidman (Ed.), *The adolescent.* 2nd ed. New York: Holt, Rinehart & Winston, 1960.

Berecz, J. M. Phobias of childhood: etiology and treatment. *Psychological Bulletin,* 1968, **70,** 695–720.

Berg-Cross, L. Intentionality, degree of damage, and normal judgments. *Child Development,* 1975, **46,** 1970–1974.

Berko, J. The child's learning of English morphology. *Word,* 1958, **14,** 150–177.

Bernstein, B. Social class and linguistic development: a theory of social learning. In A. Halsey, J. Floud, and C. Anderson (Eds.), *Education, economy and society,* pp. 288–314. New York: Free Press, 1961.

Berzonsky, M. D. Formal reasoning in adolescence: an alternative view. *Adolescence,* 1978, **13,** 279–290.

Berzonsky, M. D.; Weiner, A. S.; and Raphael, D. Interdependence of formal reasoning. *Developmental Psychology,* 1975, **11,** 258.

Bettleheim, B. *Symbolic wounds.* New York: Collier Books, 1962.

Beyer, B. Conducting moral discussions in the classroom. *Social Education,* 1976, 194–202.

Bijou, S. W., and Baer, D. M. *Child development: universal stage of infancy.* Vol. II. New York: Appleton-Century-Crofts, 1965.

Birns, B.; Blank, M.; Bridger, W. H.; and Escalona, S. K. Behavioral inhibition in neonates produced by auditory stimuli. *Child Development,* 1965, **36,** 639–645.

Birns, B., and Golden, M. The interaction of social class and sex on intelligence, language, personality, and the mother-child relationship. Paper presented at Biennial Meeting of the Society for Research in Child Development, Philadelphia, 1973. Cited in M. Lewis (Ed.), *Origins of intelligence.* New York: Plenum Press, 1976.

Bischof, L. J. *Interpreting personality theories.* 2nd ed. New York: Harper & Row, 1970.

Blakney, R. B. (Ed. & trans.) *An Immanuel Kant reader.* New York: Harper, 1960.

Blanton, M. G. The behavior of the human infant during the first thirty days of life. *Psychological Review,* 1917, **24,** 456–483.

Blatt, D., and Kohlberg, L. The effects of classroom moral discussion upon children's level of moral judgment. *Journal of Moral Education,* 1975, **4,** 129–161.

Block, J.; Block, J. H.; and Harrington, D. M. Some misgivings about the matching familiar figures test as a measure of reflection-impulsivity. *Developmental Psychology,* 1974, **10,** 611–632.

Blood, R. O. *The family.* New York: Free Press, 1971.

Bloom, B. *Stability and change in human characteristics.* New York: Wiley, 1964.

Bloom, L. *Language development: form and function in emerging grammars.* Cambridge, Mass.: MIT Press, 1970.

Bloom, L. (Ed.), *Readings in language development.* New York: Wiley, 1978.

Bloom, L.; Hood, L.; and Lightbrown, P. Imitation in language development: if, when, and why. *Cognitive Psychology,* 1974, **6,** 380–420.

Blos, P. The child analyst looks at the young adolescent. *Daedalus,* 1971, **100,** 961–978.

————.*The young adolescent.* New York: Free Press, 1970.

Blurton-Jones, N. (Ed.), *Ethological studies of child behavior.* London: Cambridge U. Press, 1972.

Bodemann, Y. M. Mystical, satanic, and chiliastic forces in countercultural movements: changing the world or reconciling it. *Youth and Society,* 1974, **5,** 433–446.

Bogartz, G. A., and Ball, S. *The second year of Sesame Street: a continuing evaluation.* Princeton, N.J.: Educational Testing Service, 1971.

Bolles, R. C. *Theory of motivation.* New York: Harper & Row, 1967.

Borke, H. Piaget's mountains revisited: changes in the egocentric landscape. *Developmental Psychology,* 1975, **11,** 240–243.

Bossard, J. H. S., and Boll, E. S. Personality roles in the large family. *Child Development,* 1955, **26,** 71–78.

Bower, T. G. R. The visual world of infants. In R. C. Atkinson (Ed.), *Contemporary psychology.* San Francisco: Freeman, 1971.(a)

————. The object in the world of the infant. *Scientific American,* 1971, **225,** 30–38.(b)

————. The visual world of infants. In W. T. Greenough (Ed.), *The nature and nurture of behavior: development psychobiology.* San Francisco: Freeman, 1973.

————. *Development in infancy.* San Francisco: Freeman, 1974.

————. *A primer of infant development.* San Francisco: Freeman, 1977.

Bowerman, M. Structural relationships in children's utterances: syntactic or semantic? In T. E. Moore (Ed.), *Cognition development and the acquisition of language.* New York: Academic Press, 1973.

Bowlby, J. *Maternal care and mental health.* Geneva, Switzerland: World Health Organization, 1951.

————. *Attachment and loss.* Vol. I: *Attachment.* New York: Basic Books, 1969.

————. *Attachment and loss.* Vol. II: *Separation.* New York: Basic Books, 1973.

Brackbill, Y. Continuous stimulation and arousal level in infancy: effects of stimulus intensity and stress. *Child Development,* 1975, **46,** 364–369.

Brackbill, Y.; Adams, G.; Crowell, D. H.; and Gray, M. L. Arousal level in neonates and preschool children under continuous auditory stimulation. *Journal of Experimental Child Psychology,* 1966, **4,** 178–188.

Brady, J. V. Emotion and the sensitivity of psycho-endocrine systems. In D. C. Glass (Ed.), *Neurophysiology and emotion.* New York: Rockefeller U. Press, 1967.

Braine, M. D. S. The ontogeny of English phrase structure: the first phrase. *Language,* 1963, **39,** 1–13.

Brainerd, C. J. Cognitive development and concept learning: an interpretative review. *Psychological Bulletin,* 1977, **84,** 919–939.

———. The stage question in cognitive development theory. *Behavioral and Brain Sciences,* 1978, **1,** 173–214.

———. *Piaget's theory of intelligence.* Englewood Cliffs, N.J.: Prentice-Hall, 1978.

Breckinridge, M. E., and Murphy, M. N. *Growth and development of the young child.* 8th ed. Philadelphia: Saunders, 1969.

Breland, H. M. Birth order, family configuration, and verbal achievement. *Child Development,* 1974, **45,** 1011–1019.

Brinton, C. *The shaping of the modern mind.* New York: Mentor Books, 1953.

Bronfenbrenner, U. *Two worlds of childhood.* New York: Russell Sage, 1970.

Bronson, G. W. Infants' reactions to unfamiliar persons and novel objects. *Monographs of the Society for Research in Child Development,* 1972, **37** (3, No. 148).

Brookhart, J., and Hock, E. The effects of experimental context and experiential background on infants' behavior toward their mothers and a stranger. *Child Development,* 1976, **47,** 333–340.

Brophy, J. E. Mothers as teachers of their own preschool children: the influence of socioeconomic status and task structure on teaching specificity. *Child Development,* 1970, **41,** 79–94.

Brotsky, S. J., and Kagan, J. Stability of the orienting reflex in infants to auditory and visual stimuli as indexed by cardiac deceleration. *Child Development,* 1971, 2066–2070.

Brown, A. L., and Scott, J. S. Recognition memory for pictures in preschool children. *Journal of Experimental Child Psychology,* 1971, **11,** 401–412.

Brown, R. The first sentences of child and chimpanzee. In R. Brown (Ed.), *Psycholinguistics.* New York: Free Press, 1970.

———. *Words and things.* Glencoe, Ill.: Free Press, 1958.

———. Development of the first language in the human species. *American Psychologist,* 1973, 97–106.

Brown, R., and Bellugi, U. Three processes in the child's acquisition of syntax. In J. A. Emig, J. T. Fleming, and H. M. Popp (Eds.), *Language and learning.* New York: Harcourt, Brace & World, 1966.

Brown, R., and Fraser, C. The acquisition of syntax. In U. Bellugi and R. Brown (Eds.), *The acquisition of language.* Chicago: U. of Chicago Press, 1971.

Bruner, J. S. The course of cognitive growth. *American Psychologist,* 1964, **19,** 1–15.

———. *Toward a theory of instruction.* Cambridge, Mass.: Harvard U. Press, 1966.

———. Learning and thinking. In D. E. Hamachek (Ed.), *Human dynamics in psychology and education.* Boston: Allyn & Bacon, 1968.

———. On perceptual readiness. In J. M. Anglin (Ed.), *Beyond the information given.* New York: Norton, 1973.

Bryan, J. H. Children's cooperation and helping behaviors. In E. M. Hetherington (Ed.), *Review of child development research,* Vol. 5, pp. 127–182. Chicago: U. of Chicago Press, 1975.

Buck-Morss, S. Socioeconomic bias in Piaget's theory and its implications for cross-culture studies. *Human Development,* 1975, **18,** 35–49.

Bullowa, M.; Jones, L. G.; and Bever. T. G. The development from vocal to verbal behavior in children. In U. Bellugi and R. Brown (Eds.), *The acquisition of language.* Chicago: U. of Chicago Press, 1971.

Burlingham, D. *Infants without families.* London: Allen & Unwin, 1944.

Burlingham, D., and Freud, A. *Young children in wartime.* London: Allen & Unwin, 1942.

Burton, R. V. Cross-sex identity in Barbados. *Developmental Psychology,* 1972, **6,** 365–374.

————. Honesty and dishonesty. In T. Lickona (Ed.), *Moral development and behavior.* New York: Holt, Rinehart & Winston, 1976.

Burton, R. V., and Whiting, J. W. M. The absent father and cross-sex identity. *Merrill-Palmer Quarterly,* 1961, **7,** 85–95.

Buss, A. R. An extension of developmental models that separate ontogenetic changes and cohort differences. *Psychological Bulletin,* 1973, **80,** 466–480.

————. Generational analysis: description, explanation, and theory. *Journal of Social Issues,* 1974, **73,** 431–439.

Cameron, J.; Livson, N.; and Bayley, N. Infant vocalizations and their relationship to mature intelligence. *Science,* 1967, **157,** 331–333.

Cantor, P. Suicide and attempted suicide among students: problem, prediction, and prevention. In P. Cantor (Ed.), *Understanding a child's world.* New York: McGraw-Hill, 1977.

Caplow, T. *The sociology of work.* Minneapolis: U. of Minnesota Press, 1954.

Carlsmith, L. Effect of early father absence on scholastic aptitude. *Harvard Educational Review,* 1964, **34,** 3–21.

Carlson, N. R. *Physiology of behavior.* Boston: Allyn & Bacon, 1977.

Carmichael, L. The growth of language capacity in the individual. In E. H. Lenneberg (Ed.), *New directions in the study of language.* Cambridge, Mass.: MIT Press, 1964.

Caron, A. J.; Caron, R. F.; Caldwell, R. C.; and Weiss, S. J. Infant perception of the structural properties of the face. *Developmental Psychology,* 1973, **9,** 385–399.

Carpenter, G. Mother's face and the newborn. In R. Lewin (Ed.), *Child alive!* Garden City, N.Y.: Doubleday, 1975.

Carroll, J. B. Development of native language skills beyond the early years. In C. E. Reed (Ed.), *The learning of language.* New York: Appleton-Century-Crofts, 1971.

Carroll, J. L. Cognitive and political attitudes correlates of the Defining Social Issues Test. Paper presented at the Biennial Meetings of the Society for Research in Child Development, 1977.

Cartwright, D. C. *Theories and models of personality.* Dubuque, Iowa: Wm. C. Brown, 1979.

Cavendish, A. P. *David Hume.* New York: Dover, 1968.

Cavior, N., and Dokecki, P. R. Physical attractiveness, perceived attitude similarity, and academic achievement as contributors to interpersonal attraction among adolescents. *Developmental Psychology,* 1973, **9,** 44–54.

Cazden, C. B. *Child language and education.* New York: Holt, Rinehart & Winston, 1972.

Chandler, M. J. Adolescence, egocentrism, and epistemological loneliness. In B. Z. Presseisen, D. Goldstein, and M. H. Appel (Eds.), *Topics in cognitive development.* Vol. 2, pp. 137–145. New York: Plenum Press, 1978.

————. Relativism and the problem of epistemological loneliness. *Human Development,* 1976, **18,** 171–180.

Chazan, M. School phobia. *British Journal of Educational Psychology,* 1962, **34,** 648–657.

Cherry, L. Teacher-child verbal interaction: an approach to the study of sex differences. In B. Thorne and N. Henley (Eds.), *Language and sex: difference and dominance,* pp. 172–183. Rowley, Mass.: Newbury House, 1975.

Childers, P., and Wimmer, M. The concept of death in early childhood. *Child Development,* 1971, **42,** 1299–1301.

Chomsky, C. *The acquisition of syntax in children five to ten.* Cambridge, Mass.: MIT Press, 1969.

Chomsky, N. *Aspects of the theory of syntax.* Cambridge, Mass.: MIT Press, 1965.

————. The formal nature of language. In E. H. Lenneberg, *Biological foundations of language.* New York: Wiley, 1967.

————. *Language and mind.* New York: Harcourt, Brace & World, 1968.

Ciacco, N. V. A test of Erikson's theory of ego epigenesis. *Developmental Psychology,* 1971, **4,** 306–311.

Clark, E. V. What's in a word? On the child's acquisition of semantics in his first language. In T. E. Moore (Ed.), *Cognitive development and the acquisition of language.* New York: Academic Press, 1973.

Clark, K. B. *Prejudice and your child.* Boston: Beacon, 1955.

Clarke, A. D. B., and Clarke, A. M. *Early experience: myth and evidence.* New York: Free Press, 1976.

Cofer, C. N., and Appley, M. H. *Motivation: theory and research.* New York: Wiley, 1967.

Coleman, J. S. The transition from youth to adult. *New York University Education Quarterly,* 1974, **5,** 2–5.

Combs, A. W.; Richards, A. C.; and Richards, F. *Perceptual psychology.* New York: Harper & Row, 1976.

Condon, W. Speech makes babies move. In R. Lewin (Ed.), *Child alive!* Garden City, N.Y.: Doubleday, 1975.

Conger, J. J. A world they never knew: the family and social change. In J. Kagan and R. Coles (Eds.), *Twelve to sixteen: early adolescence.* New York: Norton, 1972.

————. *Adolescence and youth: psychological development in a changing world.* New York: Harper & Row, 1973.

Copple, C. E., and Suci, G. J. The comparative ease of processing standard English and black nonstandard English by lower-class black children. *Child Development,* 1974, **45,** 1048–1053.

Corder, B. G.; Shorr, W.; and Corder, R. F. A study of social and psychological characteristics of adolescent suicide attempters in an urban, disadvantaged area. *Adolescence,* 1974, **9,** 1–6.

Cosgrove, J. M., and Patterson, C. J. Plans and the development of listener skills. *Developmental Psychology,* 1977, **13,** 557–564.

Cottle, T. J. *Children in jail: seven lessons in American justice.* Boston: Beacon Press, 1977.

Crain, W. C., and Crain, E. F. Age trends in political thinking: dissent, voting, and the distribution of wealth. *Journal of Psychology,* 1976, **62,** 179–190.

Curtis, B. A.; Jacobson, S.; and Marcus, E. M. *An introduction to the neurosciences.* Philadelphia: Saunders, 1972.

Cutts, N. E., and Moseley, N. Notes on photographic memory. *The Journal of Psychology,* 1969, **71,** 3–15.

Dale, P. S. *Language development: structure and function.* 2nd ed. Hinsdale, Ill.: Dryden, 1976.

Darwin, C. R. A biographical sketch of an infant. *Mind,* 1877, **2,** 285–294.

Dearborn, W. F., and Rothney, J. *Predicting the child's development.* Cambridge, Mass.: Science-Art Publications, 1941.

Debus, R. L. Effects of brief observation of model behavior on conceptual tempo of impulsive children. *Developmental Psychology,* 1970, **2,** 22–32.

Decarie, T. G. *Intelligence and affectivity in early childhood: an experimental study of Jean Piaget's object concept and object relations.* New York: International Universities Press, 1965.

Deese, J. The psychology of learning and the study of English. In C. E. Reed (Ed.), *The learning of language.* New York: Appleton-Century-Crofts, 1971.

Deming, R. *Women—the new criminals.* Nashville, Tenn.: T. Nelson, 1977.

Dennis, W. Infant development under conditions of restricted practice and of minimum social stimulation. *Genetic Psychology Monographs,* 1941, **23,** 143–191.

Devereux, E. C.; Shouval, R.; Bronfenbrenner, U.; Rodgers, R. R.; Kav-Venaki, S.; Kiely, E.; and Karson, E. Socialization practices of parents, teachers, and peers in Israel: the kibbutz versus the city. *Child Development,* 1974, **45,** 269–281.

DeVries, D. L., and Edwards, K. J. *Student teams: integrating desegregated classrooms.* Paper presented at American Psychological Association Meetings, Montreal, August, 1973. Cited in P. A. Katz & S. R. Zalk, Modification of children's racial attitudes. *Developmental Psychology,* 1978, **14,** 447–462.

Dodd, B. J. Effects of social and vocal stimulation on infant babbling. *Developmental Psychology,* 1971, **7,** 80–83.

Dollard, J.; Doob, L. W.; Miller, N. E.; Mowrer, O. H.; and Sears, R. R. *Frustration and aggression.* New Haven, Conn.: Yale U. Press, 1939.

Dollard, J., and Miller, N. E. *Personality and psychotherapy: an analysis in terms of learning, thinking, and culture.* New York: McGraw-Hill, 1950.

Donaldson, M. Development of conceptualization. In V. Hamilton and M. D. Vernon (Eds.), *The development of cognitive processes.* New York: Academic Press, 1976.

Doob, L. W. Correlates of eidetic imagery in Africa. *Journal of Psychology,* 1970, **76,** 223–230.

Douvan, E., and Adelson, J. *The adolescent experience.* New York: Wiley, 1966.

Dryer, A. S.; Hulac, V.; and Rigler, D. Differential adjustment to pubescence and cognitive style patterns. *Developmental Psychology,* 1971, **4,** 456–462.

DuBois, P. H. *A history of psychological testing.* Boston: Allyn & Bacon, 1970.

Dulit, E. Adolescent thinking à la Piaget: the formal stage. *Journal of Youth and Adolescence,* 1972, **1,** 281–301.

Dunphy, D. C. The social structure of urban adolescent peer groups. *Sociometry,* 1963, **26,** 230–246.

Ehrhardt, A. A., and Baker, S. W. Fetal androgens, human central nervous system differentiation, and behavior sex differences. In R. C. Friedman, R. M. Richart, and R. L. Van de Wiele (Eds.), *Sex differences in behavior,* pp. 33–52. New York: Wiley, 1974.

Ehri, L. C., and Ammon, P. R. Children's comprehension of comparative sentence transformations. *Child Development,* 1974, **45,** 512–516.

Eichorn, D. H. Physiological development. In P. H. Mussen (Ed.), *Carmichael's manual of child psychology,* pp. 157–283. New York: Wiley, 1970.

———. Asynchronizations in adolescent development. In S. E. Dragastin and G. H. Elder (Eds.), *Adolescence in the life cycle: psychological changes and social context.* Washington, D.C.: Hemisphere, 1975.

Eimas, P.; Siqueland, E.; Jusczyk, P.; and Vigorito, J. Speech perception in infants. *Science,* 1971, **171,** 303–306.

Eisenson, J.; Auer, J. J.; and Irwin, J. V. *The psychology of communication.* New York: Appleton-Century-Crofts, 1963.

Elder, M. The effects of temperature and position on the sucking pressure of newborn infants. *Child Development,* 1970, **41,** 95–102.

Elkind, D. Egocentrism in adolescence. *Child Development,* 1967, **38,** 1025–1034.

———.Conservation and concept formation. In D. Elkind and J. H. Flavell (Eds.), *Studies in cognitive development.* New York: Oxford University Press, 1969.

———. Understanding the young adolescent. *Adolescence,* 1978, **13,** 127–134.

Elkind, D., and Dabek, R. F. Personal injury and property damage in the moral judgments of children. *Child Development,* 1977, **48,** 518–522.

Elkind, D.; Koegler, R. R.; and Go, E. Studies in perceptual developmznt II: part-whole perception. *Child Development,* 1964, **35,** 81–90.

Emmerich, H. J. and Ackerman, B. P. Developmental differences in recall: encoding or retrieval. *Iournal of Experimental Child Psychology,* 1978, **25,** 514–525.

Emmerich, W.; Golden, K. S.; Kirsch, B.; and Sharabany, R. Evidence for a transitional phase in the development of gender constancy. *Child Development,* 1977, **48,** 930–936.

Engel, G. L. Studies in ulcerative colitis III: the nature of the psychological process. *American Journal of Medicine,* 1955, **19,** 231–256.

Engen, T., and Lipsitt, L. P. Decrement and recovery responses to olfactory stimuli in the human neonate. *Journal of Comparative and Physiological Psychology,* 1965, **59,** 312–316.

Engen, T.; Lipsitt, L. P.; and Peck, M. B. Ability of newborn infants to discriminate sapid substances. *Developmental Psychology,* 1974, **10,** 741–744.

Entwisle, D. R. Semantic systems of children: some assessments of social class and ethnic differences. In F. Williams (Ed.), *Language and poverty.* Chicago: Markham, 1970.

———. Socialization of language behavior and educability. In M. L. Maehr and W. M. Stallings (Eds.), *Culture, child, and school.* Monterey, Calif.: Brooks, Cole, 1975.

Entwisle, D. R., and Huggins, W. H. Iconic memory in children. *Child Development,* 1973, **44,** 392–394.

Erikson, E. H. *Childhood and society.* New York: Norton, 1950.

———. Ego identity and psychosocial moratorium. In H. Witmer and R. Kotinsky (Eds.), *New Per-*

spectives for Research, pp. 1–23. Washington, D.C.: DHEW, 1956, Cited in H. W. Maier, *Three Theories of Child Development.* 3rd Ed., pp. 115–116. New York: Harper & Row, 1978.

——. Growth and crisis of the healthy personality. *Psychological Issues,* 1959, **1**, 50–100.

——. Identity and the life cycle. *Psychological Issues,* 1959, **1** (Serial No. 1).

——. *Identity: youth and crisis.* New York: Norton, 1968.

Ervin, S. M. Imitation and structural change in children's language. In E. H. Lenneberg (Ed.), *New directions in the study of language.* Cambridge, Mass.: MIT Press, 1964.

Ervin-Tripp, S. An overview of theories of grammatical development. In D. I. Slobin (Ed.), *The ontogenesis of grammar: a theoretical symposium.* New York: Academic Press, 1971.

——. Language development. *JSAS Catalog of Selected Documents in Psychology,* 1976, **6** (4), 95 (Serial No. 1336).

Fagan, J. F., III. Infants' recognition memory for a series of visual stimuli. *Journal of Experimental Child Psychology,* 1971, **11**, 244–250.

Fantz, R. L. Pattern vision in young infants. *The Psychological Record,* 1958, **8**, 43–47.

——. The origin of form perception. In W. T. Greenough (Ed.), *The nature and nurture of behavior: developmental psychobiology.* San Francisco: Freeman, 1973.

Fasteau, M. F. The high price of macho. *Psychology Today,* 1975, **9**, 60.

Faust, M. S. Developmental maturity as a determinant in prestige of adolescent girls. In D. Rogers (Ed.), *Issues in Adolescent Psychology,* pp. 90–101. New York: Appelton-Century-Crofts, 1969.

——. Somatic development of adolescent girls. *Monographs of the Society for Research in Child Development,* 1977, **42**, (Serial no. 169) 1–90.

Feinstein, S. C., and Ardon, M. S. Trends in dating patterns and adolescent development. *Journal of Youth and Adolescence,* 1973, **2**, 157–166.

Feldman, N. S.; Klossen, E. C.; Parsons, J. E.; Rholes, W. S.; and Ruble, D. N. Order of information presentation and children's moral judgments. *Child Development,* 1976, **47**, 556–559.

Ferrier, P. E.; Ferrier, S. A.; and Kelley, V. C. Sex chromosome mosaicism in disorders of sexual differentiation: incidence in various tissues. *Journal of Pediatrics,* 1970, **76**, 739.

Feshbach, S., and Singer, R. *Television and aggression.* San Francisco: Jossey-Bass, 1970.

Fishbein, H. D.; Lewis, S.; and Keiffer, K. Children's understanding of spatial relations: coordination of perspectives. *Developmental Psychology,* 1972, **7**, 21–33.

Fishkin, J.; Kenniston, K.; and MacKinnon, C. Moral reasoning and political idealogy. *Journal of Personality and Social Psychology,* 1973, **27**, 109–119.

Fitzhardinge, P. M. The small-for-date infant. II. Neurological and intellectual sequelae. *Pediatrics,* 1972, **50**, 50–57.

Flavell, J. H. *The developmental psychology of Jean Piaget.* New York: D. Van Nostrand, 1963.

——. Developmental studies of mediated memory. In H. W. Reese and L. P. Lipsitt (Eds.), *Advances in child development and behavior,* Vol. 5. New York: Academic Press, 1970.

——. *Cognitive development.* Englewood Cliffs, N.J.: Prentice-Hall, 1977.

Flavell, J. H.; Beach, D. R.; and Chinsky, J. M. Spontaneous verbal rehearsal in a memory task as a function of age. *Child Development,* 1966, **37**, 283–299.

Flavell, J. H.; Friedrichs, A. G.; and Hoyt, J. D. Developmental change in memorization processes. *Cognitive Psychology,* 1970, **1**, 324–340.

Flavell, J. H., and Wohlwill, J. F. Formal and functional aspects of cognitive development. In D. Elkind and J. H. Flavell (Eds.), *Studies in cognitive development.* New York: Oxford U. Press, 1969.

Fling, S., and Manosevitz, M. Sex typing in nursery school children's play interests. *Developmental Psychology,* 1972, **7**, 146–152.

Forgus, R. H. Perception. In N. B. Talbot, J. Kagan, and L. Eisenberg (Eds.), *Behavioral science in pediatric medicine.* Philadelphia: Saunders, 1971.

Formentin, P.; Mack, J.; and Hockey, A. Carrier detection and assessment of dietary treatment in phenylketonuria. *Australian Journal of Mental Retardation,* 1972, **2**, 33–39.

Forslund, M. A., and Gustafson, T. J. Influence of peers and parents and sex differences in drinking by high school students. *Quarterly Journal of Studies on Alcohol,* 1970, **31** (December), 868–875.

Fox, D. J., and Jordan, V. B. Racial preference and identification of black American, Chinese, and white children. *Genetic Psychology Monographs,* 1973, **88,** 229–286.

Freeman, F. N., and Flory, C. D. Growth in intellectual ability as measured by repeated tests. *Monographs of the Society for Research in Child Development,* 1937, **2** (2, Serial No. 9).

Freud, A. *The psychoanalytical treatment of children.* New York: International Universities Press, 1946.

Freud, S. (1905) Three contributions to the theory of sex. In A. A. Brill (Ed. & trans.), *The basic writings of Sigmund Freud.* New York: Random House, 1938.

———. (1905) Three essays on the theory of sexuality. In J. Strachey (Ed.), *Standard edition of the complete works of Sigmund Freud, Vol. 7,* pp. 125–243. London: Hogarth, 1953.

———. (1923) *The ego and the id* (Rev. Ed.). Translated by J. Riviere. New York: Norton, 1960.

———. *The ego and the mechanism of defence.* Translated by C. Baines. New York: International Universities Press, 1948.

———. *Collected papers.* IV. New York: Basic Books, 1959.

Friedlander, B. Z.; Jacobs, A. C.; Davis, B. B.; and Wetstone, H. E. Time-sampling analysis of infants' natural language environments in the home. *Child Development,* 1972, **43,** 730–740.

Friedman, S. Habituation and recovery of visual response in the alert human newborn. *Journal of Experimental Child Psychology,* 1972, **13,** 339–349.

Friedmann, T., and Roblin, R. Gene therapy for human genetic disease? *Science,* 1972, **175,** 949–955.

Friedrich, C. J. (Ed.) *The philosophy of Kant.* New York: Random House, 1949.

Friedrich, L. K., and Stein, A. H. Aggressive and prosocial television programs and the natural behavior of preschool children. *Monographs of the Society for Research in Child Development,* 1973, **38** (4, Serial No. 151).

Furth, H. G. *Piaget and knowledge.* Englewood Cliffs, N.J.: Prentice-Hall, 1969.

———. Piaget's theory of knowledge: the nature of representation and interiorization. In J. Eliot (Ed.), *Human development and cognitive processes.* New York: Holt, Rinehart & Winston, 1971.

Gagné, R. M. Contributions of learning to human development. In J. L. Frost and G. R. Hawkes (Eds.), *The disadvantaged child,* pp. 272–287. Boston: Houghton Mifflin, 1970.

Galantin, J. E., and Adelson, J. Legal guarantees of individual freedom: a cross-national study of the development of political thought. *Journal of Social Issues,* 1971, **77,** 93–108.

Galbraith, R., and Jones, T. Teaching strategies for moral dilemmas. *Social Education,* 1975, 16–22.

———. *Moral reasoning: a teaching handbook for adapting Kohlberg to the classroom.* Anaka, Minn.: Greenhaven Press, 1976.

Gallatin, J. E. *Adolescence and individuality: a conceptual approach to adolescent psychology.* New York: Harper & Row, 1975.

Galst, J. P., and White, M. A. The unhealthy persuader: the reinforcing value of television and children's purchase-influencing attempts at the supermarket. *Child Development,* 1976, 1089–1096.

Galton, F. (1892) *Hereditary genius: an inquiry into its laws and consequences.* Cleveland, Ohio: Meridian Books, 1962.

Gardner, R. A., and Gardner, B. T. Teaching sign language to a chimpanzee. *Science,* 1969, **165,** 664–672.

Gaudia, G. Race, social class, and age of achievement of conservation on Piaget's tasks. *Developmental Psychology,* 1972, **6,** 158–165.

Geen, R. G., and O'Neal, E. C. (Eds.) *Perspectives on aggression.* New York: Academic Press, 1976.

Gewirtz, J. L. Mechanisms of social learning: some roles of stimulation and behavior in early human development. In D. A. Goslin (Ed.), *Handbook of socialization theory and research.* Chicago: Rand McNally, 1969.

————. Attachment, dependence, and a distinction in terms of stimulus control. In J. L. Gewirtz (Ed.), *Attachment and dependency.* Washington, D. C.: 1972.

Gewirtz, H. B., and Gewirtz, L. L. Caretaking settings, background events, and behavior differences in four Israeli child-rearing environments: some preliminary trends. In B. M. Foss (Ed.), *Determinants of infant behaviour.* Vol. IV. London: Methuen, 1969.

Gesell, A. *Infancy and human growth.* New York: Macmillan, 1928.

Gibson, E. J. *Principles of perceptual learning and development.* New York: Appleton-Century-Crofts, 1969.

Gilligan C., and Kohlberg, L. From adolescence to adulthood: the rediscovery of reality in a postconventional world. In B. Z. Presseison, D. Goldstein, and M. H. Appel (Eds.), *Topics in cognitive development,* Vol. 2, pp. 125–136. New York: Plenum Press, 1978.

Ginsburg, H. *The myth of the deprived child.* Englewood Cliffs, N.J.: Prentice-Hall, 1972.

Ginsburg, H., and Opper, S. *Piaget's theory of intellectual development.* 2nd Edition. Englewood Cliffs, N.J.: Prentice Hall, 1978.

Ginzberg, E. Toward a theory of occupational choice. *Occupations,* 1952, **30,** 491–494.

————. The development of a developmental theory of occupational choice. In W. H. VanHouse and J. J. Pietrofesa (Eds.), *Counseling and guidance in the twentieth century,* pp. 58–67. Boston: Houghton Mifflin, 1970.

Giray, E. F.; Altkin, W. M.; Vaught, G. M.; and Roodin, P. A. The incidence of eidetic imagery as a function of age. *Child Development,* 1976, **47,** 1207–1210.

Glenn, N. D. *Cohort analysis.* Beverly Hills: Sage Publications, 1977.

Glucksberg, S., and Danks, J. H. *Experimental psycholinguistics: an introduction.* Hillsdale, N.J.: Lawrence Erlbaum, 1975.

Glucksberg, S.; Krauss, R.; and Higgins, E. The development of referential communication skills. In F. D. Horowitz (Ed.), *Review of child development research,* Vol. 4. Chicago: U. of Chicago Press, 1975.

Glucksberg, S.; Krauss, R.; and Weisberg, R. Referential communication in nursery school children: method and some preliminary findings. *Journal of Experimental Child Psychology,* 1966, **3,** 333–342.

Glueck, S., and Glueck, E. T. *Predicting delinquency and crime.* Cambridge, Mass.: Harvard U. Press, 1959.

————. *Unraveling juvenile delinquency.* New York: Commonwealth Fund, 1950.

Godenne, G. D. Sex and today's youth. *Adolescence,* 1974, **9,** 67–72.

Gohlson, B., and Danziger, S. Effects of two levels of stimulus complexity upon hypothesis sampling systems among second and sixth grade children. *Journal of Experimental Child Psychology,* 1975, **20,** 105–118.

Gohlson, B.; O'Connor, J.; and Stern, I. Hypothesis sampling systems among preoperational and concrete operational kindergarten children. *Journal of Experimental Child Psychology,* 1976, **21,** 61–76.

Gold, M. *Delinquent behavior in an American city.* Belmont, Calif.: Brooks-Cole, 1970.

Gollin, E. S., and Moody, M. Developmental psychology. *Annual Review of Psychology,* 1973, **24,** 1–52.

Golomb, C., and Cornelius, C. B. Symbolic play and its cognitive significance. *Developmental Psychology,* 1977, **13,** 246–252.

Gottlieb, D. E.; Taylor, S. E.; and Ruderman, A. Cognitive bases of children's moral judgments. *Developmental Psychology,* 1977, **13,** 547–556.

Graber, T. Cranofacial and dentitional development. In F. Falkner (Ed.), *Human development.* Philadelphia: Saunders, 1966.

Graham, F. K.; Clifton, R. K.; and Hatton, H. M. Habituation of heart rate response to repeated auditory stimulation during the first five days of life. *Child Development,* 1968, **39,** 35–52.

Gratch, G. A study of the relative dominance of vision and touch in six-month-old infants. *Child Development,* 1972, **43,** 615–623.

Gray, D. F., and Gaier, E. L. The congruency of adolescent self-perceptions with those of parents and best friends. *Adolescence,* 1974, **9,** 299–303.

Green, C. P., and Lowe, S. J. Teenage pregnancy: a major problem for minors. *Zero Population Growth National Reporter,* 1975, **7,** 4–5.

Greenberg, D. J.; Hillman, D.; and Grice, D. Perceptual incongruity and social interaction as determinants of infants' reaction to novel persons. *Journal of Genetic Psychology,* 1975, **127,** 215–222.

Greenberg, D. J.; O'Donnell, W. J.; and Crawford, D. Complexity levels, habituation, and individual differences in early infancy. *Child Development,* 1973, **44,** 569–574.

Greene, T. M. (Ed.) *Kant selections.* New York: Scribners, 1957.

Grobstein, P., and Chow, K. L. Receptive field development and individual experience. *Science,* 1975, **190,** 352–358.

Gruen, G. E. Experiences affecting the development of number conservation in children. *Child Development,* 1965, **36,** 963–979.

Grusec, J. E., and Skubiski, L. Model nurturance, demand characteristics of the modeling experiment, and altruism. *Journal of Personality and Social Psychology,* 1970, **14,** 352–359.

Guardo, C. J., and Bohan, J. B. Development of a sense of self-identity in children. *Child Development,* 1971, **42,** 1909–1921.

Haaf, R. A., and Bell, R. Q. A facial dimension in visual discrimination by human infants. *Child Development,* 1967, **38,** 893–899.

Haan, N. Personality development from adolescence to adulthood in the Oakland growth and guidance studies. *Seminars in Psychiatry,* 1972, **4,** 399–414.

Haan, N.; Smith, M. B.; and Block, J. Moral reasoning of young adults: political-social behavior, family background and personality correlates. *Journal of Personality and Social Psychology,* 1968, **10,** 183–201.

Hale, J. R. *Renaissance Europe: individual and society, 1480–1520.* New York: Harper & Row, 1971.

Halperin, M. S. Developmental changes in the recall and recognition of categorized lists. *Child Development,* 1974, **45,** 144–151.

Halverson, C. F., and Waldrop, M. F. Relations between preschool barrier behaviors and early school-age measures of coping, imagination, and verbal development. *Developmental Psychology,* 1974, **10,** 716–720.

Harlow, H. F. *Learning to love.* San Francisco: Albion, 1971.

Harrison, C. W.; Rawls, J.; and Rawls, D. Differences between leaders and nonleaders in six- to eleven-year-old children. *Journal of Social Psychology,* 1971, **84,** 269–272.

Harrison, M. J., and Tennent, T. G. Neurological anomalies in XYY males. *British Journal of Psychiatry,* 1972, **120,** 447–448.

Havighurst, R. J. A cross-cultural view. In J. F. Adams (Ed.), *Understanding Adolescence.* 3rd Ed. Boston: Allyn & Bacon, 1976.

Head Start data analysis, final report. Triangle Park, N.C.: Research Triangle Institute, 1972.

Heafford, M. *Pestalozzi: his thought and relevance today.* London: Methuen, 1967.

Heald, F. P., and Kahn, M. A. Obesity. In J. R. Gallather, F. P. Heald, and D. C. Garell (Eds.), *Medical care of the adolescent.* 3rd ed. New York: Appleton-Century-Crofts, 1976.

Heber, R., and Garber, H. The Milwaukee project: a study of the use of family intervention to prevent cultural-familial mental retardation. In B. Z. Friedlander, G. M. Sterritt, and G. E. Kirk (Eds.), *Exceptional infant: assessment and intervention,* Vol. 3. New York: Brunner/Mazel, 1975.

Hersov, L. A. Persistent non-attendance at school. *Journal of Child Psychology and Psychiatry,* 1960, **1,** 130–136.

Hess, E. H. Ethology and developmental psychology. In P. H. Mussen (Ed.), *Carmichael's manual of child psychology,* Vol. 1. 3rd ed. New York: Wiley, 1970.

Hess, R. D., and Shipman, V. C. Early experience and the socialization of cognitive modes in children. In N. S. Endler, L. R. Boulter, and H. Osser (Eds.), *Contemporary issues in developmental psychology.* New York: Holt, Rinehart & Winston, 1968.

————. Maternal influences upon early learning: the cognitive environments of urban preschool children. In R. D. Hess and R. M. Baer (Eds.), *Early education.* Chicago: Aldine Press, 1968.

Hess, R. D., and Torney, J. *The development of political attitudes in children.* Chicago: Aldine Press, 1967.

Hetherington, E. M. The effects of familiar variables on sex-typing, on parent-child similarity, and on imitation in children. *Minnesota Symposium on Child Psychology,* 1967, **1,** 82–107.

————. Effects of father absence on personality development in adolescent daughters. *Developmental Psychology,* 1972, **7,** 313–326.

Hetherington, E. M., and Deur, J. L. The effects of father absence on child development. In W. W. Hartup (Ed.), *The young child: reviews of research.* Washington, D.C.: National Association for the Education of Young Children, 1972.

Hettlinger, R. F. *Human sexuality: a psychosocial perspective.* Belmont, Calif.: Wadsworth, 1974.

Hicks, J. Imitation and retention of film-mediated aggressive peer and adult models. *Journal of Personality and Social Psychology,* 1965, **2,** 97–100.

Higgins, E. T. Social class differences in verbal communicative accuracy: a question of "which question?" *Psychological Bulletin,* 1976, **83,** 695–714.

Hockett, C. F., Logical considerations in the study of animal communication. In W. E. Lanyon and W. M. Tavdga (Eds.), *Animal sounds and animal communication.* Washington, D.C.: American Institute of Biological Sciences, 1960.

Hoffman, M. L. Moral development. In P. H. Mussen (Ed.), *Carmichael's manual of child psychology,* Vol. 2. New York: Wiley, 1970.

Holden, C. Drug abuse 1975: the "war" is past, the problem is as big as ever. *Science,* 1975, **190,** 638–641.

Holland, J. L. *Making vocational choices: a theory of careers.* Englewood Cliffs, N.J.: Prentice-Hall, 1973.

Holstein, C. The relation of children's moral judgment level to that of their parents and to communication patterns in the family. In R. C. Smart and M. S. Smart (Eds.), *Readings in child development and relationship,* pp. 484–494. New York: Macmillan, 1972.

Honzik, M. P.; MacFarlane, J. W.; and Allen, L. The stability of mental test performance between two and eighteen years. *Journal of Experimental Education,* 1948, **18,** 309–324.

Hook, E. B., and Kim, D. Height and antisocial behavior in XY and XYY boys. *Science,* 1971, **172,** 284–286.

Hoppock, R. *Occupational information.* 3rd Edition. New York: McGraw-Hill, 1967.

Horney, K. *Feminine psychology.* New York: Norton, 1967.

Hoy, E. A. Predicting another's visual perspective: a unitary skill? *Developmental Psychology,* 1974, **10,** 462.

Hume, D. *An enquiry concerning human understanding.* (1758) LaSalle, Ill.: Open Court, 1966.

Hunt, E. E. The developmental genetics of man. In F. Falkner (Ed.), *Human development,* pp. 76–122. Philadelphia: Saunders, 1966.

Hunt, J. McV. *Intelligence and experience.* New York: Ronald Press, 1961.

————. The impact and limitations of the giant of developmental psychology. In D. Elkind and J. H. Flavell (Eds.), *Studies in cognitive development.* New York: Oxford U. Press, 1969.

Hunt, M. *Sexual behavior in the 1970s.* New York: Dell, 1974.

Illingworth, R. S. *The development of the infant and young child.* 6th Ed. London: Churchill Livingstone, 1975.

Illingworth, R. S. *The development of the infant and young child.* 6th Ed. London: Churchill Livingstone, 1975.

Imamoglu, E. O. Children's understanding of intentionality from 5 to 12. In C. F. M. Van Lieshout and D. J. Ingram (Eds.), *Stimulation of social development in school*, pp. 115–135. Amsterdam: Swets & Zeitlinger, 1977.

Inhelder, B., and Piaget, J. *The growth of logical thinking from childhood to adolescence.* New York: Basic Books, 1958.

Inhelder, B., and Sinclair, H. Learning cognitive structures. In P. H. Mussen, J. Langer, and M. Covington (Eds.), *Trends and issues in developmental psychology.* New York: Holt, Rinehart & Winston, 1976.

Inhelder, B.; Sinclair, H.; and Bouet, M. *Learning and the development of cognition.* Cambridge, Mass.: Harvard U. Press, 1974.

Irwin, M.,; Engle, P. L.; Yarbrough, C.; Klein, R. E.; and Townsend, J. The relationship of prior ability and family characteristics to school attendance and school achievement in rural Guatemala. *Child Development,* 1978, **49,** 415–427.

Irwin, O. C. Infant speech: variability and the problem of diagnosis. *Journal of Speech and Hearing Disorders,* 1947a, **12,** 287–289.

——. Infant speech: consonant sounds according to place of articulation. *Journal of Speech and Hearing Disorders,* 1947b, **12,** 397–401.

——. Infant speech: consonant sounds according to manner of articulation. *Journal of Speech and Hearing Disorders,* 1947c, **12,** 402–404.

——. Acceleration of infant speech by story-reading. In Y. Brackbill and G. C. Thompson (Eds.), *Behavior in infancy and early childhood.* New York: Free Press, 1948.

Jackson, J. C.; Kantowitz, S. R.; and Graham, F. F. Can newborns show cardiac orienting? *Child Development,* 1971, **42,** 107–121.

Jacobs, B. S., and Moss, H. A. Birth order and sex of sibling as determinants of mother-infant interaction. *Child Development,* 1976, **47,** 315–322.

Jacobs, J. *Adolescent Suicide.* New York: Wiley, 1971.

Jacobson, L. I., and Greeson, L. E. Effects of systematic conceptual learning on the intellectual development of preschool children from poverty backgrounds: a follow-up study. *Child Development,* 1972, **43,** 1111–1115.

Jakobson, R. *Child language, aphasia, and phonological universals* (Trans. by A. Keiler). The Hague: Mouton, 1968.

James, W. *The principles of psychology.* 2 vols. New York: Henry Holt, 1890. (Reprinted in one volume by Dover Publications, Inc.)

Jensen, A. R. How much can we boost IQ and scholastic achievement? In Reprint Series No. 2, *Environment, heredity, and intelligence.* Cambridge, Mass.: Harvard Educational Review, 1969.

Jessor, S. L., and Jessor, R. Transition from virginity to non-virginity among youth: a social psychological study over time. *Developmental Psychology,* 1975, **11,** 473–484.

Johnson, A. Juvenile delinquency. In S. Arieti (Ed.), *American handbook of psychiatry.* New York: Basic Books, 1959.

Johnstone, J. W. C. Juvenile delinquency and the family: a contextual interpretation. *Youth and Society,* 1978, **9,** 299–313.

Jolly, A. Hour of birth in primates and man. *Folia Primatologica,* 1972, **18,** 108–121.

Jones, M. C. The later careers of boys who were early or late maturing. *Child Development,* 1957, **28,** 113–128.

Jones, M. C., and Mussen, P. H. Self-conceptions, motivations, and interpersonal attitudes of early and late maturing girls. *Child Development,* 1958, **29,** 491–501.

Jost, A. D. Development of sexual characteristics. *Science Journal,* 1970, **6,** 67–72.

Kagan, J. Acquisition and significance of sex typing and sex role identity. In M. Hoffman and L. Hoffman (Eds.), *Review of child development research.* Vol. 1, pp. 137–167. New York: Russell Sage, 1964.

——. Reflection-impulsivity and reading ability in primary grade children. *Child Development,* 1965, **36,** 609–628.

——. Reflection-impulsivity: the generality and dynamics of conceptual tempo. *Journal of Abnormal Psychology,* 1966, **71,** 17–24.

——. *Change and continuity in infancy.* New York: Wiley, 1971.

——. *Understanding children: behavior, motives, and thought.* New York: Harcourt, Brace, Jovanovich, 1971.

——. Do infants think? *Scientific American,* 1972, **226,** 74–82.

——. Cross-cultural perspectives on early deprivation. *American Psychologist,* 1973, **28,** 947–961.

Kagan, J., and Kogan, N. Individual variations in cognitive processes. In P. H. Mussen (Ed.), *Carmichael's manual of child psychology.* 3rd ed., Vol. I. New York: Wiley, 1970.

Kagan, J., and Tulkin, S. R. Social class differences in child rearing during the first year. In H. R. Schaffer (Ed.), *The origins of human social relations.* London: Academic Press, 1971.

Kamin, L. *The science and politics of IQ.* Potomac, Md.: Erlbaum Associates, 1974.

Kandel, D. B. On variations in adolescent subcultures. *Youth and Society,* 1978, **9,** 373–384.

——. Inter- and intra-generational influences on adolescent marihuana use. In V. Bengston and R. Laufer (Eds.), Special issue on generations and social change, *Journal of Social Issues,* 1974, **50,** 107–135.

——. Adolescent marihuana use: role of parents and peers. *Science,* 1973, **181,** 1067–1070.

Kandel, D.; Single, E.; and Kessler, R. The epidemiology of drug use among New York State high school students: distribution, trends, and change in rate of use. *American Journal of Public Health,* 1976, **66,** 43–53.

Kanter, J., and Zelnich, M. Contraception and pregnancy: experience of young married women in the United States. *Family Planning Perspectives,* 1973, **5,** 11–35.

Kantor, D., and Lehr, W. *Inside the family: toward a theory of family process.* New York: Harper & Row, 1976.

Kaplan, E., and Kaplan, G. The prelinguistic child. In J. Elliot (Ed.), *Human development and cognitive processes.* New York: Holt, Rinehart & Winston, 1971.

Karniol, R. Children's use of intention cues in evaluating behavior. *Psychological Bulletin,* 1978, **85,** 76–85.

Kasper, J. C., and Lowenstein, R. The effect of social interaction on activity levels in six- to eight-year-old boys. *Child Development,* 1971, **42,** 1294–1298.

Katz, P. A. Stimulus predifferentiation and modification of children's racial attitudes. *Child Development,* 1973, **44,** 232–237.

Katz, P. A., and Zalk, S. R. Modification of children's racial attitudes. *Developmental Psychology,* 1978, **14,** 447–462.

Kavanaugh, R. D. On the synonymity of *more* and *less:* comments on a methodology. *Child Development,* 1976, **47,** 885–887.

Kearsley, R. B. The newborn's response to auditory stimulation: a demonstration of orienting and defensive behavior. *Child Development,* 1973, **44,** 582–590.

Keasey, C. B. Experimentally induced changes in moral opinions and reasoning. *Journal of Personality and Social Psychology,* 1973, **26,** 30–38.

——. Young children's attribution of intentionality to themselves and others. *Child Development,* 1977, **48,** 261–264.

Keeney, T. J.; Cannizzo, S. R.; and Flavell, J. J. Spontaneous and induced verbal rehearsal in a recall task. *Child Development,* 1967, **38,** 953–966.

Keller, M. F., and Carlson, P. M. The use of symbolic modeling to promote social skills in preschool children with low level skills of social responsiveness. *Child Development,* 1974, **45,** 912–919.

Kendler, T. S. Development of mediating responses in children. In J. C. Wright and J. Kagan (Eds.), Basic cognitive processes in children. *Monographs of the Society for Research in Child Development,* 1963, **28** (No. 6), 33–51.

Kendler, T. S., and Kendler, H. H. An ontogeny of optional shift behavior. *Child Development,* 1970, **41,** 1–27.

Keniston, K. *Youth and Dissent.* New York: Harcourt Brace Jovanovich, 1971.(a)

——. *Youth and Identity.* New York: Harcourt Brace Jovanovich, 1971.(b)

Kenniston, K. Prologue: youth as a stage of life. In R. J. Havighurst and P. H. Dreyer (Eds.), *Youth.* Chicago: U. of Chicago Press, 1975.

Kerckhoff, A. C. Social class differences in sexual attitudes and behavior. *Medical Aspects of Human Sexuality,* 1974, **8**, 10.

Kessel, F. S. The role of syntax in children's comprehension from ages six to twelve. *Monographs of the Society for Research in Child Development,* 1970, **35** (No. 6).

Kessen, W.; Haith, M. M.; and Salapatek, P. H. Human infancy: a bibliography and guide. In P. H. Mussen (Ed.), *Carmichael's manual of child psychology.* Vol. I. New York: Wiley, 1970.

Kessen, W.; Salapatek, P.; and Haith, M. The visual response of the human newborn to linear contour. *Journal of Experimental Child Psychology,* 1972, **13**, 9–20.

Kety, S. S. Psycho-endocrine systems and emotion: biological aspects. In D. C. Glass (Ed.), *Neurophysiology and emotion.* New York: Rockefeller U. Press, 1967.

King, M. The development of some intention concepts in young children. *Child Development,* 1971, **42**, 1145–1152.

Kirkendall, L. Can premarital intercourse be healthy? In W. B. Frick (Ed.), *Explorations in healthy personality.* Fort Collins, Col.: Shields, 1974.

Klaus, H. M.; Kennel, J.; Jerauld, R.; Kreger, N.; McAlpine, W.; and Steffa, M. Maternal attachment: importance of first post-partum days. *New England Journal of Medicine,* 1972, **286**, 460.

Klaus, R. A., and Gray, S. W. The early training project for disadvantaged children: a report after five years. *Monographs of the Society for Research in Child Development,* 1968, **33** (4, Serial No. 120).

Klima, E. S., and Bellugi, U. Syntactic regularities in the speech of children. In J. Lyons and R. J. Wales (Eds.), *Psycholinguistic papers.* Edinburgh: Edinburgh U. Press, 1966.

Kodroff, J. K., and Roberge, J. J. Developmental analysis of the conditional reasoning abilities of primary-grade children. *Developmental Psychology,* 1975, **11**, 21–28.

Koff, E.; Rierdon, J.; and Silverstone, E. Changes in representation of body image as a function of mencheal status. *Developmental Psychology,* 1978, **14**, 635–642.

Kohlberg, L. The development of children's orientations towards a moral order. I: Sequence in the development of moral thought. *Vita Humana,* 1963, **6**, 11–33.

————. Relationships between the development of moral judgment and moral conduct. Paper presented at Biennial Meeting of the Society for Research in Child Development, Minneapolis, Minn., 1965.

————. A cognitive-developmental analysis of children's sex-role concepts and attitudes. In E. E. Maccoby (Ed.), *The development of sex differences.* Stanford, Calif.: Stanford U. Press, 1966.

————. Stage and sequence: the cognitive-developmental approach to socialization. In D. A. Goslin (Ed.), *Handbook of socialization theory and research.* Chicago: Rand-McNally, 1969.

————. Moral stages and moralization: the cognitive-developmental approach. In T. Lickona (Ed.), *Moral development and behavior.* New York: Holt, Rinehart & Winston, 1976.

Kohlberg, L., and Gilligan, C. The adolescent as a philosopher: the discovery of the self in a postconventional world. *Daedalus,* 1971, **100**, 1051–1086.

Kohlberg, L., and Kramer, R. Continuities and discontinuities in childhood and adult moral development. *Human Development,* 1969, **12**, 93–120.

Korner, A. F., and Thoman, E. B. The relative efficacy of contact and vestibular-proprioceptive stimulation in soothing neonates. *Child Development,* 1972, **43**, 443–453.

Krause, C. A. *Guyana massacre.* New York: Berkley Publishing, 1978.

Kravitz, H., and Boehm, J. J. Rhythmic habit patterns in infancy: their sequence, age of onset, and frequency. *Child Development,* 1971, **42**, 399–413.

Kroll, A. M.; Dinklage, L. B.; Lee, J.; Morley, E. D.; and Wilson, E. H. *Career development: growth and crisis.* New York: Wiley, 1970.

Krone, W., and Wolf, U. Chromosomes and protein variation. In D. J. H. Brock and O. Mayo (Eds.), *The biochemical genetics of man,* pp. 71–127. London: Academic Press, 1972.

Kuhn, D. Short-term longitudinal evidence for the sequentiality of Kohlberg's early stages of moral judgment. *Developmental Psychology,* 1976, **12**, 162–166.

Kuhn, D.; Langer, L.; Kohlberg, L.; and Haan, N. S. The development of formal operations in logical and moral judgment. *Genetic Psychology Monographs,* 1977, **95,** 97–188.

Kurtines, W., and Grief, E. B. The development of moral thought: review and evaluation of Kohlberg's approach. *Psychological Bulletin,* 1974, **81,** 453–470.

LaBarbera, J. D.; Izard, C. E.; Vietze, P.; and Parisi, S. A. Four- and six-month-old infants' visual responses to joy, anger, and neutral expressions. *Child Development,* 1976, **47,** 535–538.

Lamb, M. E. Father-infant and mother-infant interaction in the first year of life. *Child Development,* 1977, **48,** 167–181.

Lamper, C., and Eisdorfer, C. Prestimulus activity level and responsivity in the neonate. *Child Development,* 1971, **42,** 465–473.

Lamprecht, S. P. (Ed.) *Locke, selections.* New York: Scribner's 1928.

Langer, J. *Theories of development.* New York: Holt, Rinehart & Winston, 1969.

———. Werner's comparative organismic theory. In P. H. Mussen (Ed.), *Carmichael's manual of child psychology.* Vol. I. New York: Wiley, 1970.

Langmeier, J., and Matejcek, Z. *Psychological deprivation in childhood.* New York: Wiley, 1975.

Lasko, J. K. Parent behavior toward first and second children. *Genetic Pyschology Monographs,* 1954, **49,** 97–137.

Lawrence, E. (Ed.) *Froebel and English education.* New York: Schocken, 1969.

Lee, C. B. T. *The campus scene: 1900–1970.* New York: McKay, 1970.

Lee, L. C. The concomitant development of cognitive and moral codes of thought: a test of selected deductions from Piaget's theory. *Genetic Psychology Monographs,* 1971, **83,** 93–146.

LeFurgy, W. G., and Woloshin, G. W. Immediate and long-term effects of experimentally induced social influences in the modification of adolescents' moral judgments. *Journal of Abnormal and Social Psychology,* 1969, **12,** 104–110.

Leifer, A. D.; Leiderman, P. H.; Barnett, C. R.; and Williams, J. A. Effects of mother-infant separation on maternal attachment behavior. *Child Development,* 1972, **43,** 1203–1218.

Lenneberg, E. H. A biological perspective of language. In E. H. Lenneberg (Ed.), *New directions in the study of language.* Cambridge, Mass.: MIT Press, 1964.

———. The natural history of language. In F. Smith and G. A. Miller (Eds.), *The genesis of language.* Cambridge, Mass.: MIT Press, 1966.

———. *Biological foundations of language.* New York: Wiley, 1967.

Lerner, R. M. Nature, nurture, and dynamic interactionism. *Human Development,* 1978, **21,** 1–20.

Lerner, R. M., and Korn, S. J. The development of body-build stereotypes in males. *Child Development,* 1972, **43,** 908–920.

Lesser, G. S.; Fifer, S. G.; and Clark, D. H. Mental abilities of children from different social-class and cultural groups. *Monographs of the Society for Research in Child Development,* 1965, **30** (Serial No. 102).

Levine, M. *A cognitive theory of learning research on hypothesis testing.* Hillsdale, N.J.: Lawrence Erlbaum Associates, 1975.

Levy, B. B. Dialect proficiency and auditory comprehension in standard and black nonstandard English. Paper presented at Meeting of American Educational Research Association, Chicago, 1972.

Lewin, K. Field theory and experiment in social psychology. In D. Cartwright (Ed.), *Field Theory in Social Science.* London: Tavistock, 1959.

———. *Resolving social conflict.* New York: Harper & Row, 1948.

Lewis, M. Cross-cultural studies of mother-infant interaction: description and consequence. Introduction. *Human Development,* 1972, **15,** 73–76.

Lewis, M.; Goldberg, S.; and Campbell, H. A developmental study of information processing within the first three years of life: response decrement to a redundant signal. *Monographs of the Society for Research in Child Development,* 1969, **34** (9, Serial No. 133).

Lewis, M., and Weinraub, M. Sex of parent X sex of child: socio-emotional development. In R. C. Friedman, R. M. Richart, and R. L. Van de Wiele (Eds.), *Sex differences in behavior,* pp. 165–190. New York: Wiley, 1974.

Lewis, M.; Wilson, C. D.; Ban, P.; and Baumel, M. H. An exploratory study of resting cardiac rate and variability from the last trimester of prenatal life through the first year of post-natal life. *Child Development*, 1970, **41**, 799–811.

Liben, L. The facilitation of long-term memory improvement and operative development. *Developmental Psychology*, 1977, **13**, 501–508.

Liberty, C., and Ornstein, P. A. Age differences in organization and recall: the effects of training in categorization. *Journal of Experimental Child Psychology*, 1973, **15**, 169–186.

Lieberman, J. N. Playfulness and divergent thinking: an investigation of their relationship at the kindergarten level. *Journal of Genetic Psychology*, 1965, **107**, 219–224.

Liebert, R. M., and Baron, R. A. Some immediate effects of televised violence on children's behavior. *Developmental Psychology*, 1972, **6**, 469–475.

Linden, R. Myths of middle-class delinquency: a test of the generalizability of social control theory. *Youth and Society*, 1978, **9**, 407–432.

Lipsitt, L. P., and Jacklin, C. N. Cardiac deceleration and its stability in human newborns. *Developmental Psychology*, 1971, **5**, 535.

Lipsitt, L. P., and Kaye, H. Conditioned sucking in the human newborn. *Psychonomic Science*, 1964, **1**, 29–30.

Lipsitt, L. P.; Kaye, H.; and Bosack, T. N. Enhancement of neonatal sucking through reinforcement. *Journal of Experimental Psychology*, 1966, **4**, 153–168.

Lipsitt, L. P., and Levy, N. Pain threshold in the human neonate. *Child Development*, 1959, **30**, 547–554.

Locke, J. *The works of John Locke.* Vols. I & II. Freeport, N.Y.: Libraries Press, 1969.

London, P., and Robinson, J. P. Imagination in learning and retention. *Child Development*, 1968, **39**, 803–816.

Lonky, E., and Reihman, J. The cognitive-developmental approach to political development: a review and analysis of current research. Unpublished paper, U. of Wisconsin, Department of Educational Psychology, Madison, 1978.

Looft, W. R. Egocentrism and social interaction in adolescence. *Adolescence*, 1971, **6**, 485–494.

Lorenz, K. (1935) Companionship in bird life. In C. H. Schiller (Ed.), *Instinctive behavior.* New York: International Universities Press, 1957a.

———. (1937) The nature of instinct: the conception of instinctive behavior. In C. H. Schiller (Ed.), *Instinctive behavior.* New York: International Universities Press, 1957b.

———. *Civilized man's eight deadly sins.* New York: Harcourt Brace Jovanovich, 1974.

———. *Behind the mirror: a search for a natural history of human knowledge.* New York: Harcourt Brace Jovanovich, 1977.

Lubshenko, L. O.; Horner, F. A.; Reed, L. H.; Hicks, I. E., Jr.; Metcalf, D.; Cohig, R.; Elliott, H. C.; and Bourg, M. Sequelae of premature birth. In Y. Brackbill & G. C. Thompson (Eds.), *Behavior in infancy and early childhood,* pp. 70–85. New York: Free Press, 1967.

Luckey, E., and Nass, G. A comparison of sexual attitudes and behavior in an international sample. *Journal of Marriage and the Family*, 1969, **31**, 364–379.

Lunzer, E. A. Formal reasoning: a reappraisal. In B. Z. Presseisen, D. Goldstein, and M. H. Appel (Eds.), *Topics in cognitive development.* Vol. 2, pp. 47–76. New York: Plenum Press, 1978.

Luria, A. R. *The role of speech in the regulation of normal and abnormal behavior.* New York: Liveright, 1961.

Lynn, D. B. *The father: his role in child development.* Monterey, Calif.: Brooks-Cole, 1974.

Lynn, D. B., and Sawry, W. L. The effects of father-absence on Norwegian boys and girls. *Journal of Abnormal and Social Psychology*, 1959, **59**, 259–262.

McCall, R. B.; Appelbaum, M., II; and Hogarty, P. S. Developmental changes in mental performance. *Monographs of the Society for Research in Child Development*, 1973, **38** (3, Serial No. 150).

McCall, R. B.; Hogarty, P. S.; Hamilton, J. S.; and Vincent, J. H. Habituation rate and the infant's response to visual discrepancies. *Child Development*, 1973, **44**, 280–287.

McCall, R. B.; Hogarty, P. S.; and Hurlburt, N. Transitions in infant sensorimotor development and the prediction of childhood IQ. *American Psychologist*, 1972, **27**, 728–748.

McCall, R. B., and Kagan, J. Attention in the infant: effects of complexity, contour, perimeter, and familiarity. *Child Development,* 1967, **38,** 939–952.

McCall, R. B., and Melson, W. H. Amount of short-term familiarization and the response to auditory discrepancies. *Child Development,* 1970, **41,** 861–869.

McCandless, B. R. *Adolescents: behavior and development.* Hinsdale, Ill.: Dryden Press, 1970.

McCarthy, D. Language development in children. In L. Carmichael (Ed.), *Manual of child psychology.* 2nd Ed. New York: Wiley, 1954.

McClearn, G. E. Genetic influences on behavior and development. In P. H. Mussen (Ed.), *Carmichael's manual of child psychology,* pp. 39–76. New York: Wiley, 1970.

Maccoby, E. E., and Feldman, S. S. Mother-attachment and stranger-reactions in the third year of life. *Monographs of the Society for Research in Child Development,* 1972, **37,** (1, No. 146).

Maccoby, E. E., and Jacklin, C. N. *The psychology of sex differences.* Stanford, Calif.: Stanford U. Press, 1974.

Maccoby, E., and Masters, J. C. Attachment and dependency. In P. H. Mussen (Ed.), *Carmichael's manual of child psychology.* 3rd ed., Vol. 2. New York: Wiley, 1970.

McDougall, W. (1908) On the nature of instinct. In D. Bindra & J. Stewart (Eds.), *Motivation.* Baltimore: Penguin, 1966.

––––––. *An introduction to social psychology.* 8th Ed. Boston: Luce, 1914.

McGaugh, J. L. *Learning and memory.* San Francisco: Albion, 1973.

McGurk, H. Infant discrimination of orientation. *Journal of Experimental Child Psychology,* 1972, **14,** 151–164.

Macklin, E. D. Heterosexual cohabitation among unmarried college students. *Family Coordinator,* 1972, **21,** 463–472.

––––––. Cohabitation in college: going very steady. *Psychology Today,* 1974, **8,** 53–59.

MacNamara, J. Cognitive basis of language learning in infants. *Psychological Review,* 1972, **79,** 1–13.

McNeill, D. *The acquisition of language: the study of developmental linguistics.* New York: Harper & Row, 1970.

––––––. The capacity for the ontogenesis of grammar. In D. I. Slobin (Ed.), *The ontogenesis of grammar.* New York: Academic Press, 1971.

Maddi, S. R. *Personality theories.* 3rd Ed. Homewood, Ill.: Dorsey, 1976.

Maddox, G. L. Drinking prior to college. In G. L. Maddox (Ed.), *The domesticated drug: drinking among college students,* pp. 107–120. New Haven, Conn.: College and University Press, 1970.

Madsen, K. B. Theories of motivation. In B. B. Wolman (Ed.), *Handbook of general psychology.* Englewood Cliffs, N.J.: Prentice-Hall, 1973.

Mahler, M. S.; Pine, F.; and Bergmann, A. *The psychological birth of the human infant.* New York: Basic Books, 1975.

Maier, H. W. *Three theories of child development.* Rev. Ed. New York: Harper & Row, 1969.

––––––. *Three Theories of Child Development.* 3rd Ed. New York: Harper & Row, 1978.

Marcus, D. E., and Overton, W. F. The development of cognitive gender constancy and sex-role preferences. *Child Development,* 1978, **49,** 434–444.

Maresh, M. M., and Beal, V. A. A longitudinal survey of nutrition intake, body size, and tissue measurements in healthy subjects during growth. In J. Brozek (Ed.), *Physical growth and body composition: papers from the Kyoto Symposium on anthropological aspects of human growth. Monographs of the Society for Research in Child Development,* 1970, **35** (7, Serial No. 140).

Martin, C. D. Psychological problems of abortion for the unwed teenage girl. *Genetic Psychology Monographs,* 1973, **88,** 23–110.

Martorano, S. A developmental analysis of performance on Piaget's formal operations tasks. *Developmental Psychology,* 1977, **13,** 666–672.

Masangkay, Z. S.; McCluskey, K. A.; McIntyre, C. W.; Sims-Knight, J.; Vaughn, B. E.; and Flavell, J. H. The early development of inferences about the visual percepts of others. *Child Development,* 1974, **45,** 357–366.

Matteson, R. Adolescent self-esteem, family communication, and marital satisfaction. *Journal of Psychology,* 1974, **86,** 35–47.

Maurer, D., and Salapatek, P. Developmental changes in the scanning of faces by young infants. *Child Development*, 1976, **47**, 523–527.

Mead, M. *Sex and temperament in three primitive societies.* New York: Morrow & Co., 1935.

———. Coming of age in Samoa. In M. Mead, *From the South Seas.* New York: Morrow, 1939(a).

———. Growing up in New Guinea. In M. Mead, *From the South Seas.* New York: Morrow, 1939(b).

Meissner, J. A. Judgment of clue adequacy by kindergarten and second grade children. *Developmental Psychology*, 1978, **14**, 18–23.

Melear, J. D. Children's conceptions of death. *Journal of Genetic Psychology*, 1973, **123**, 359–360.

Meltzoff, A. N., and Moore, M. K. Imitation of facial and manual gestures by human neonates. *Science*, 1977, **198**, 75–78.

Mendlewicz, J.; Fliess, J. L.; and Fieve, R. R. Evidence for X-linkage in the transmission of manic-depressive illness. *Journal of the American Medical Association*, 1972, **222**, 1624–1627.

Meredith, H. V. Body size of contemporary groups of one-year-old infants studied in different parts of the world. *Child Development*, 1970, **41**, 551–600.

———. Somatological development. In B. B. Wolman (Ed.), *Handbook of General Psychology.* Englewood Cliffs, N.J.: Prentice-Hall, 1973.

Merelman, R. M. Moral development and potential radicalism in adolescence: a reconnaissance. *Youth and Society*, 1977, **9**, 29–53.

———. Political reasoning in adolescence: some bridging themes. *Sage Professional Papers in American Politics.* Beverly Hills, Calif.: Sage, 1976.

Mermelstein, E., & Shulman, L. S. Lack of formal schooling and the acquisition of conservation. *Child Development*, 1967, **38**, 39–52.

Merton, R. K. *Social theory and social structure.* 3rd Ed. New York: Free Press, 1968.

Messer, S. B.; Kagan, J.; and McCall, R. B. Fixation time and tempo of play in infants. *Developmental Psychology*, 1970, **3**, 406.

Milgram, S. Behavioral study of obedience. *Journal of Abnormal and Social Psychology*, 1963, **67**, 371–378.

———. *Obedience to authority.* New York: Harper & Row, 1974.

Millar, S. Effects of instructions to visualize stimuli during delay on visual recognition by preschool children. *Child Development*, 1972, **43**, 1073–1075.

Millar, W. S. A study of operant conditioning under delayed reinforcement in early infancy. *Monographs of the Society for Research in Child Development*, 1972, **37** (Serial No. 147).

Miller, D. *Psychology, psychopathology, and psychotherapy.* New York: Jason Aronson, 1974.

Miller, D. J. Visual habituation in the human infant. *Child Development*, 1972, **43**, 481–493.

Miller, L. B., and Dyer, J. L. Four preschool programs: their dimensions and effects. *Monographs of the Society for Research in Child Development*, 1975, **40** (5–6, Serial No. 162).

Miller, N. E. The frustration-aggression hypothesis. *Psychological review*, 1941, **48**, 337–342.

———. Theory and experiments relating psychonalytic displacement to stimulus-response generalization. *Journal of Abnormal and Social Psychology*, 1948, **43**, 155–178.

Mims, R. M., and Gohlson, B. Effects of type and amount of feedback upon hypothesis sampling systems among seven- and eight-year-old children. *Journal of Experimental Child Psychology*, 1977, **24**, 358–371.

Mischel, T. Cognitive conflict and the motivation of thought. In T. Mischel (Ed.), *Cognitive development and epistemology.* New York: Academic Press, 1971.

Mischel, W. Sex-typing and socialization. In P. H. Mussen (Ed.), *Carmichael's manual of child psychology.* 3rd Ed., Vol. II. New York: Wiley, 1970.

Mitchell, J. J. Adolescent intimacy. *Adolescence*, 1976, **11**, 275–280.

Moffitt, A. R. Consonant cue perception by twenty to twenty-four-week-old infants. *Child Development*, 1971, **42**, 717–731.

Moore, T. Language and intelligence: a longitudinal study of the first eight years. *Human Development*, 1967, **10**, 88–106.

Moran, J. J., and Joniak, A. J. The effect of language on preference for responses to a moral dilemma. *Developmental Psychology*, 1979, **15**, 337–339.

Morris, C. *The discovery of the individual 1050–1200.* New York: Harper & Row, 1972.

Morse, P. A. The discrimination of speech and nonspeech stimuli in early infancy. *Journal of Experimental Child Psychology,* 1972, **14,** 477–492.

Moynahan, E. D. The development of knowledge concerning the effect of categorization upon free recall. *Child Development,* 1973, **44,** 238–246.

Munn, N. L. *The growth of human behavior.* 3rd Ed. Boston: Houghton Mifflin, 1974.

Murray, J. B. The generation gap. *Journal of Genetic Psychology,* 1971, **118,** 71–80.

Muus, R. E. Puberty rites in primitive and modern society. In R. E. Muus (Ed.), *Adolescent behavior and society,* pp. 468–480. New York: Random House, 1975.(a)

———.*Theories of Adolescence.* New York: Random House, 1975.(b)

Nadelman, L. Sex identity in American children: memory, knowledge, and preference tests. *Developmental Psychology,* 1974, **10,** 413–417.

Nash, D. J. Influence of genotype and neonatal irradiation upon open-field locomotion and elimination in mice. *Journal of Comparative & Physiological Psychology,* 1973, **83,** 458–464.

Neimark, E. D. Intellectual development during adolescence. In F. D. Horowitz (Ed.), *Review of Child Development Research.* Vol. 4. Chicago: U. of Chicago Press, 1975.

Nelson, K. Structure and strategy in learning to talk. *Monographs of the Society for Research in Child Development,* 1973, **38** (1–2, Serial No. 149).

———. Some evidence for the cognitive primacy of categorization and its functional basis. *Merrill-Palmer Quarterly,* 1973, **19,** 21–39.

Nummendal, S. G., and Bass, S. C. Effects of the salience of intention and consequences on children's moral judgments. *Developmental Psychology,* 1976, **12,** 475–476.

Odom, P. B., and Nesbitt, N. H. Some processes in children's comprehension of linguistically and visually depicted relationships. *Journal of Experimental Child Psychology,* 1974, **17,** 399–408.

Odom, R., and Guzman, R. D. Development of hierarchies of dimensional salience. *Developmental Psychology,* 1972, **6,** 271–287.

Osgood, C. E. *Method and theory in experimental psychology.* New York: Oxford U. Press, 1953.

Owen, G. M., and Brozek, J. Influence of age, sex, and nutrition on body composition during childbirth and adolescence. In F. Falkner (Ed.), *Human development.* Philadelphia: Saunders, 1966.

Palermo, D. More about less: a study in language comprehension. *Journal of Verbal Learning and Verbal Behavior,* 1973, **12,** 211–221.

———. Still more about the comprehension of less! *Developmental Psychology,* 1974, **10,** 827–829.

———. *The psychology of language.* Glenview, Ill.: Scott, Foresman, 1978.

Papousek, H. Conditioning during early postnatal development. In Y. Brackbill and G. C. Thompson (Eds.), *Behavior in infancy and early childhood.* New York: Free Press, 1967.

Paris, S. G. Integration and inference in children's comprehension and memory. In F. Restle, R. Shiffrin, J. Castellan, H. Lindman, and D. Pisoni (Eds.), *Cognitive theory.* Vol. I. Hillsdale, N.J.: Lawrence Erlbaum Associates, 1975.

Parke, R. D., and Collmer, C. W. Child abuse: an interdisciplinary perspective. In E. M. Hetherington (Ed.), *Review of Child Development Research.* Vol. 5. Chicago: U. of Chicago Press, 1975.

Parten, M. B. Social participation among preschool children. *Journal of Abnormal and Social Psychology,* 1932, **27,** 243–269.

Parten, M., and Newhall, S. M. Social behavior of preschool children. In R. C. Barker, J. S. Kounin, and H. F. Wright (Eds.), *Child development and behavior.* New York: McGraw-Hill, 1943.

Pavlov, I. P. (1904) *Conditioned reflexes.* London: Oxford U. Press, 1927.

———. (1904) Conditioned reflexes. In R. J. Herrnstein and E. G. Boring (Eds.), *A source book in the history of psychology.* Cambridge, Mass.: Harvard U. Press, 1965.

———. *Lectures on conditioned reflexes.* Translated by W. H. Gantt. New York: Liveright, 1928.

———. Nobel Prize address. In M. Kaplan (Ed.), *The essential works of Pavlov.* New York: Bantam Books, 1966.

Pederson, D. R., and Ter Vrugt, D. The influence of amplitude and frequency of vestibular stimulation on the activity of two-month-old infants. *Child Development,* 1973, **44,** 122–128.

Penfield, W. Some mechanisms of consciousness discovered during electrical stimulation of the brain. *Proceedings of the National Academy of Sciences,* 1959, **44,** 51–66.

Peterson, J. (1926) *Early conceptions and tests of intelligence.* Westport, Conn.: Greenwood Press, 1969.

Phillips, J. L. *The origins of intellect: Piaget's theory.* 2nd Edition. San Francisco: Freeman, 1975.

Phillips, M. M. *Erasmus on his times.* Cambridge, Eng.: Cambridge U. Press, 1967.

Phillips, S.; Levine, M.; and O'Brien, J. T. Transfer in discrimination learning. *Journal of Experimental Child Psychology,* 1977, **24,** 358–371.

Piaget, J. *The language and thought of the child.* New York: Harcourt Brace & World, 1926.

————. (1930) *The child's conception of physical causality.* Paterson, N.J.: Littlefield, Adams, 1960.

————. (1947) *Psychology of intelligence.* Totowa, N.J.: Littlefield, Adams, 1972.

————. *The origins of intelligence in children.* New York: International Universities Press, 1952.

————. *The construction of reality in the child.* New York: Basic Books, 1954.

————. *The stages of the intellectual development of the child. Bulletin of the Menninger Clinic,* 1962, **26,** 120–145.

————. *Play, dreams and imitation in childhood.* New York: Norton, 1962.

————. *The moral judgment of the child.* New York: Free Press, 1965.

————. *The child's conception of number.* New York: Norton, 1965.

————. (1947) *The psychology of intelligence.* Totowa, N.J.: Littlefield, Adams, 1966.

————. *Six psychological studies.* New York: Random House, 1967.

————. *The mechanisms of perception.* New York: Basic Books, 1969.

————. Piaget's theory. In P. H. Mussen (Ed.), *Carmichael's manual of child psychology.* 3rd Ed., Vol. 1. New York: Wiley, 1970.

————. *Biology and knowledge.* Chicago: U. of Chicago Press, 1971.

————. Intellectual evolution from adolescence to adulthood. *Human Development,* 1972, **15,** 1–12.

————. *The child's conception of physical causality.* Totowa, N.J.: Littlefield, Adams, 1972.

————. *The child's conception of the world.* Totowa, N.J.: Littlefield, Adams, 1975.

Piaget, J., and Inhelder, B. (1948) *The child's conception of space.* New York: Norton, 1967.

————. *The child's concept of space.* London: Routledge, 1956.

————. *The psychology of the child.* New York: Basic Books, 1969.

————. *Memory and intelligence.* New York: Basic Books, 1973.

Pick, A. D., and Frankel, G. W. A developmental study of strategies of visual selectivity. *Child Development,* 1974, **45,** 1162–1165.

Pick, A. D.; Frankel, D. G.; and Hess, V. L. Children's attention: the development of selectivity. In E. M. Hetherington (Ed.), *Review of Child Development Research.* Vol. 5. Chicago: U. of Chicago Press, 1975.

Pietrofesa, J. J., and Splete, H. *Career development: theory and research.* New York: Grune & Stratton, 1975.

Place, D. M. The dating experience for adolescent girls. *Adolescence,* 1975, **10,** 157–174.

Poenaru, S.; Stanesco, V.; Poenaru, L.; and Stoian, D. Electroencephalographic study of Turner's syndrome. *Acta Neurologica Belgica,* 1970, **70,** 509–522.

Pomerleau-Malcuit, A., and Clifton, R. K. Neonatal heart-rate response to tactile, auditory, and vestibular stimulation in different states. *Child Development,* 1973, **44,** 485–496.

Porges, S. W.; Arnold, W. R.; and Forbes, E. J. Heart-rate variability: an index of attentional responsivity in human newborns. *Developmental Psychology,* 1973, **8,** 85–92.

Posner, M. I. *Cognition: an introduction.* Glenview, Ill.: Scott, Foresman, 1973.

Poteat, B. W. S., and Kasschau, R. A. Generalization in short-term recognition of auditory verbal stimuli. *Psychonomic Science,* 1969, **17,** 358–359.

Poznanski, E. O. Children with excessive fears. *American Journal of Orthopsychiatry,* 1973, **43,** 428–438.

Prendergast, T. J., and Schaefer, E. S. Correlates of drinking and drunkenness among high-school students. *Quarterly Journal of Studies on Alcohol,* 1974, **35** (March), 232–242.

Proskauer, S., and Rolland, R. S. Youth who use drugs: psychodynamic diagnosis and treatment planning. *Journal of the American Academy of Child Psychiatry,* 1973, **12,** 32–47.

Provence, S.; Naylor, A.; and Patterson, J. *The challenge of daycare.* New Haven, Conn.: Yale U. Press, 1977.

Radke-Yarrow, M. International dynamics in a desegregation process. *Journal of Social Issues,* 1958, **14,** 3–63.

Ramey, C. T.; Heiger, L.; and Klisz, D. Synchronous reinforcement of vocal responses in failure-to-thrive infants. *Child Development,* 1972, **43,** 1449–1455.

Ramey, C. T., and Ourth, L. L. Delayed reinforcement and vocalization rates of infants. *Child Development,* 1971, **42,** 291–297.

Ramirez, M., and Castaneda, A. *Cultural democracy, bicognitive development, and education.* New York: Academic Press, 1974.

Rebelsky, F., and Hanks, C. Fathers' verbal interaction with infants in the first three months of life. *Child Development,* 1971, **42,** 63–68.

Reese, H. W., and Lipsitt, L. P. *Experimental child psychology.* New York: Academic Press, 1970.

Reihman, J. M. The cognitive-developmental approach to moral education: a description and methodological analysis of Kohlbergian training studies and implications for future directions. Unpublished paper, Department of Educational Psychology, U. of Wisconsin, Madison, 1978.

Report of two national samples of Head Start classes: some aspects of child development participants in full year 1967–68 and 1968–69 programs. Research Triangle Park, N.C.: Research Triangle Institute, 1972.

Rest, J.; Turiel, E.; and Kohlberg, L. Relations between level of moral judgment and preference and comprehension of the moral judgment of others. *Journal of Personality,* 1969, **37,** 225–252.

Rewey, H. H. Developmental change in infant heart rate response during sleeping and waking states. *Developmental Psychology,* 1973, **8,** 35–41.

Rheingold, H., and Cook, K. The contents of boys' and girls' rooms as an index of parents' behavior. *Child Development,* 1975, **46,** 459–483.

Rheingold, H., and Eckerman, C. O. The infant separates himself from his mother. *Science,* 1970, **168,** 73–83.

———. Fear of the stranger: a critical examination. In H. W. Reese (Ed.), *Advances in child development and behavior.* Vol. 8. New York: Academic Press, 1973.

Rheingold, H.; Gewirtz, J. L.; and Ross, H. Social conditioning of vocalizations in the infant. *Journal of Comparative and Physiological Psychology,* 1959, **52,** 68–73.

Rieber, M. Hypothesis testing in children as a function of age. *Developmental Psychology,* 1969, **1,** 389–395.

Riegel, K. F. History as a nomothetic science: some generalizations from theories and research in developmental psychology. *Journal of Social Issues,* 1969, **25,** 99–128.

Robinson, I. E.; King, K.; and Balswick, J. O. The premarital sexual revolution among college females. *Family Coordinator,* 1972, **21,** 189–194.

Robinson, J. P., and London, P. Labeling and imaging as aids to memory. *Child Development,* 1971, **42,** 641–644.

Roff, M.,; Sells, S. B.; and Golden, M. M. *Social adjustment and personality development in children.* Minneapolis: U. of Minnesota Press, 1972.

Rogers, C. R. *On becoming a person,* Boston: Houghton Mifflin, 1961.

———. Toward becoming a fully functioning person. In A. W. Combs (Ed.), *Perceiving, behaving, becoming.* Washington, D.C.: Association for Supervision and Curriculum Development, 1962.

———. Toward a modern approach to values: the valving process in the mature person. *Journal of Abnormal and Social Psychology,* 1964, **68,** 160–167.

Rogers, D. (Ed.) *Issues in adolescent psychology.* New York: Appelton-Century-Crofts, 1969, 60–61.

———. *The psychology of adolescence.* Englewood Cliffs, N.J.: Prentice-Hall, 1977.

Rohwer, W. D. Images and pictures in children's learning: research results and instructional implications. In H. W. Reese (Chairman), *Images in children's learning: a symposium. Psychological Bulletin,* 1970, **73,** 393–403.

Roodin, P. A.; Broughton, A.; and Vaught, G. M. Birth order of volunteers for group and individual psychological experimental participation: a negative note. *Perceptual and Motor Skills,* 1978, **42,** 575–580.

Roodin, P. A., and Vaught, G. M. Birth order, volunteering, and status of the experimenter: a negative note. *Journal of Psychology,* 1974, **87,** 119–122.

Rosch, E. On the internal structure of perceptual and semantic categories. In T. E. Moore (Ed.), *Cognitive development and the acquistion of language.* New York: Academic Press, 1973.

Rosch, E.; Mervis, C. B.; Gray, W. D.; Johnson, D. M.; and Boyes-Braem, P. Basic objects in natural categories. *Cognitive Psychology.* 1976. **8,** 382–439.

Rosekrans, M. A. Imitation in children as a function of perceived similarities to a social model of vicarious reinforcement. *Journal of Personality and Social Psychology,* 1967, **7,** 307–315.

Rosen, C. E. The effects of sociodramatic play on problem-solving behavior among culturally disadvantaged preschool children. *Child Development,* 1974, **45,** 920–927.

Rosenhan, D. L., and White, G. M. Observation and rehearsal as determinants of prosocial behavior. *Journal of Personality and Social Psychology,* 1967, **5,** 424–432.

Rosenthal, R., and Rosnow, R. L. *The volunteer subject.* New York: Wiley, 1975.

Rostand, J., and Tetry, A. *An atlas of human genetics.* Translated by K. McWhirter. London: Hutchinson & Co., 1964.

Rothbart, M. K., and Maccoby, E. E. Parents' differential reactions to sons and daughters. *Journal of Personality and Social Psychology,* 1966, **4,** 237–243.

Rothenberg, M. B. Effect of television violence on children and youth. *Journal of the American Medical Association,* 1975, **234,** 1043–1046.

Rovee, C. K. Olfactory cross-adaptation and facilitation in human neonates. *Journal of Experimental Child Psychology,* 1972, **13,** 368–381.

Rubenstein, J. A. concordance of visual and manipulative responsiveness to novel and familiar stimuli in six-month-old infants. *Child Development,* 1974, **45,** 194–195.

Rubin, K. H., and Schneider, F. W. The relationship between moral judgment, egocentrism, and altruistic behavior. *Child Development,* 1973, **44,** 661–665.

Rubin, K. H., and Trotter, K. T. Kohlberg's moral judgment scale: some methodological considerations. *Developmental Psychology,* 1977, **13,** 535–536.

Rugh, R., and Shettles, L. B. *From conception to birth.* New York: Harper & Row, 1971.

Russell, C., and Russell, W. M. S. Language and animal signals. In N. Minnis (Ed.), *Linguistics at large.* New York: Viking, 1971.

Russell, R. W., and Warburton, D. M. Biochemical bases of behavior. In B. B. Wolman (Ed.), *Handbook of general psychology.* Englewood Cliffs, N.J.: Prentice-Hall, 1973.

Rutter, M. *Maternal deprivation: reassessed.* Baltimore: Penguin, 1972.

Rybash, J. M., and Roodin, P. A. A reinterpretation of the effects of videotape and verbal presentation modes on children's moral judgments. *Child Development,* 1978, **49,** 228–230.

Rybash, J. M.; Sewall, M. B.; Roodin, P. A.; and Sullivan, L. Effects of age of transgressor, damage, and type of presentation of kindergarten children's moral judgments. *Developmental Psychology,* 1975, **11,** 874.

Sadava, S. W., and Forsyth R. Person environment interaction and college student drug use: a multivariate longitudinal study. *Genetic Psychology Monographs,* 1977, **96,** 211–245.

Salapatek, P. H., and Kessen, W. Visual scanning of triangles by the human newborn. *Journal of Experimental Child Psychology,* 1966, **3,** 155–167.

Salk, L. Mothers' heartbeat as an imprinting stimulus. *Transactions, New York Academy of Science,* 1962, **24,** 753–763.

————. *What every child would like his parents to know.* New York: Warner Books, 1972.

Sampson, E. E., and Hancock, F. R. An examination of the relationship between ordinal position, personality, and conformity: an extension, replication, and partial verification. *Journal of Personality and Social Psychology,* 1967, **5,** 398–407.

Sapir, E. Language and environment. In D. G. Mandelbaum (Ed.), *Selected writings of Edward Sapir in language, culture, and personality.* Berkeley: U. of California Press, 1958.

Scarlett, H. H.; Press, A. N.; and Crockett, W. H. Children's descriptions of peers: a Wernerian developmental analysis. *Child Development,* 1971, **42,** 439–453.

Scarr-Salapatek, S., and Williams, M. L. The effects of early stimulation on low-birth-weight infants. *Child Development,* 1973, **44,** 94–101.

Schaefer, E. S. A circumplex model for maternal behavior. *Journal of Abnormal and Social Psychology,* 1959, **59,** 226–235.

———. Converging conceptual models for maternal behavior and for child behavior. In J. C. Glidewell (Ed.), *Parental attitudes and child behavior.* Springfield, Ill.: Charles C. Thomas, 1961.

———. A configurational analysis of children's reports of parental behavior. *Journal of Consulting Psychology,* 1965, **29,** 554–557.

Schaeffer, H., and Emerson, P. The development of social attachments in infancy. *Monographs for the Society for Research in Child Development,* 1965, **29** (3, Serial No. 94).

Schaffer, H. R.; Greenwood, A.; and Parry, M. H. The onset of wariness. *Child Development,* 1972, **43,** 165–176.

Scheinfeld, A. *Why you are you: the story of heredity and environment.* Rev. Ed. New York: Association Press, 1971.

———. *Heredity in humans.* Rev. Ed. Philadelphia: Lippincott, 1972.

Schlesinger, I. M. Production of utterances and language acquisition. In D. I. Slobin (Ed.), *The ontogenesis of language acquisition.* New York: Academic Press, 1971.

Schooler, C. Birth order effects: not here, not now. *Psychological Bulletin,* 1972, **78,** 161–175.

———. Birth order effects: a reply to Breland. *Psychological Bulletin,* 1973, **80,** 213–214.

Schwartz, A.; Rosenberg, D.; and Brackbill, Y. Analysis of the components of social reinforcement of infant vocalization. *Psychonomic Science,* 1970, **20,** 323–325.

Sears, R. R. Nonaggression reactions to frustration. *Psychological Review,* 1941, **48,** 343–346.

———. Attachment, dependency, and frustration. In J. L. Gewirtz (Ed.), *Attachment and dependency.* Washington, D.C.: Winston, 1972.

———. Your ancients revisited: a history of child development. In E. M. Hetherington (Ed.), *Review of child development research.* Vol. 5. Chicago: U. of Chicago Press, 1975.

Sears, R. R.; Maccoby, E. E.; and Levin, H. *Patterns of child rearing.* Evanston, Ill.: Row, Peterson, 1957.

Sears, R. R.; Rau, L.; and Alpert, R. *Identification and child rearing.* Stanford: Stanford U. Press, 1965.

Selby-Bigge, L. A. (Ed.) *Hume's treatise on human nature.* Oxford, Eng. Clarendon Press, 1967.

Self, P. A.; Horowitz, F. D.; and Paden, L. Y. Olfaction in newborn infants. *Developmental Psychology,* 1972, **7,** 349–363.

Selman, R. L. Social-cognitive understanding: a guide to educational and clinical practice. In T. Lickona (Ed.), *Moral development and behavior.* New York: Holt, Rinehart & Winston, 1976.

Senn, M. J. E. Insights on the child development movement in the United States. *Monographs of the Society for Research in Child Development,* 1975, **40** (Serial No. 161).

Serbin, L. A., and O'Leary, K. D. How nursery schools teach girls to shut up. *Psychology Today,* 1975, **9,** 56–58.

Serra, J. A. *Modern genetics.* Vol. I. New York: Academic Press, 1965.

Shantz, C. The development of social cognition. In E. M. Hetherington (Ed.), *Review of child development research.* Vol. 5, Chicago: U. of Chicago Press, 1975.

Shatz, M., and Gelman, R. The development of communication skills: modifications in the speech of young children as a function of listener. *Monographs of the Society for Research in Child Development,* 1973, **38** (5, Serial No. 152).

Sheldon, W. H. *The varieties of human physique.* New York: Harper, 1940.

Sheppard, J. L. Compensation and combinatorial systems in the acquisition and generalization of conservation. *Child Development,* 1974, **45,** 717–730.

Sherman, M., and Key, C. B. The "intelligence" of isolated mountain children. *Child Development,* 1932, **3,** 279–290.

Shertzer, B. *Career planning: freedom to choose.* Boston: Houghton Mifflin, 1977.

Shirley, H. F. *Pediatric psychiatry.* Cambridge, Mass.: Harvard U. Press, 1963.

Siegel, A. W.; Kirasic, K. C.; and Kilburg, R. R. Recognition memory in reflective and impulsive preschool children. *Child Development,* 1973, **44,** 651–656.

Siegler, R. S.; Liebert, D. C.; and Liebert, R. M. Inhelder and Piaget's pendulum problem: teaching pre-adolescents to act as scientists. *Developmental Psychology,* 1973, **9,** 97–101.

Sigel, I. E. The Piagetian system and the world of education. In D. Elkind and J. H. Flavell (Eds.), *Studies in cognitive development.* New York: Oxford U. Press, 1969.

Simner, M. L. Newborn's response to the cry of another infant. *Developmental Psychology,* 1971, **5,** 136–150.

Siqueland, E. R. Reinforcement patterns and extinction in human newborns. *Journal of Experimental Child Psychology,* 1968, **6,** 431–442.

Siqueland, E. R., and DeLucia, C. A. Visual reinforcement of non-nutritive sucking in human infants. *Science,* 1969, **165,** 1144–1146.

Siqueland, E. R., and Lipsitt, L. P. Conditioned head-turning in human newborns. *Journal of Experimental Child Psychology,* 1966, **3,** 356–376.

Skinner, B. F. *Contingencies of reinforcement: A theoretical analysis.* New York: Appleton-Century-Crofts, 1969.

Slob, A. K.; Snow, C. D.; and de Natris-Mathot, E. Absence of behavioral deficits following neonatal undernutrition in the rat. *Developmental Psychology,* 1973, **6,** 177–186.

Slobin, D. I. Cognitive prerequisites for the development of grammar. In C. A. Ferguson and D. I. Slobin (Eds.), *Studies of child language development.* New York: Holt, Rinehart & Winston, 1973.

Smart, M. S., and Smart, R. C. *Adolescents: Development and relationships.* 2nd Ed. New York: MacMillan, 1978.

Smiley, S. S. Optional shift behavior as a function of dimensional preference and relative cue similarity. *Journal of Experimental Child Psychology,* 1972, **14,** 313–322.

Smith, D. F. Adolescent suicide: a problem for teachers? *Phi Delta Kappan,* 1976, **57** (No. 8), 539–541.

Smith, N. K. (Trans.) *Immanuel Kant's Critique of Pure Reason.* New York: St. Martin's Press, 1968.

Smith, R. M., and Walters, J. Delinquent and non-delinquent males' perception of their fathers. *Adolescence,* 1978, **13,** 21–28.

Sontag, L. W.; Baker, C. T.; and Nelson, V. L. Mental growth and personality development: a longitudinal study. *Monographs of the Society for Research in Child Development,* 1958, **23** (2, Serial No. 68).

Sorenson, R. C. *Adolescent sexuality in contemporary America.* New York: World, 1973.

Spitz, R. A. Hospitalism: A follow-up report on the investigation described in Vol. 1, 1945. In O. Fenichel, et al. (Eds.), *The psychonalytic study of the child.* New York: International Universities Press, 1946.

————. *The first year of life: a psychoanalytic study of normal and deviant development of object relations.* New York: International Universities Press, 1965.

Sroufe, L. A. Wariness of strangers and the study of infant development. *Child Development,* 1977, **48,** 731–746.

Staffieri, J. R. Body build and behavior expectancies in young females. *Developmental Psychology,* 1972, **6,** 125–127.

Stahl, F. W. *The mechanics of inheritance.* Englewood Cliffs, N.J.: Prentice-Hall, 1964.

Staub, E. A child in distress: the influence of nurturance and modeling on children's attempts to help. *Developmental Psychology,* 1971, **5,** 124–132.

Stenhouse, D. *The evolution of intelligence.* New York: Harper & Row, 1974.

Stern, D. *The first relationship: infant and mother.* Cambridge, Mass.: Harvard U. Press, 1977.

Stern, D. N.; Jaffe, J.; Beebe, B.; and Bennet, S. L. Vocalizing in unison and in alternation: two modes of communication within the mother-infant dyad. *Annals of the New York Academy of Sciences,* 1975, **263,** 89–100.

Sternglanz, S. H., and Serbin, L. A. Sex-role stereotyping in children's television programs. *Developmental Psychology,* 1974, **10,** 710–715.

Stevenson, H. W. Studies of racial awareness in young children. In W. W. Hartup and N. L. Smothergill (Eds.), *The young child.* Washington, D.C.: National Association for the Education of Young Children, 1967.

————. Learning in children. In P. H. Mussen (Ed.), *Carmichael's manual of child psychology*. Vol. 1. New York: Wiley, 1970.

Stratton, P. M., and Connolly, K. Discrimination by newborns of the intensity, frequency, and temporal characteristics of auditory stimuli. *British Journal of Psychology,* 1973, **64,** 219–232.

Suchman, R. G., and Trabasso, T. Color and form preference in young children. *Journal of Experimental Child Psychology,* 1966, **3,** 177–187.

Super, C. M.; Kagan, J.; Morrison, F. J.; Haith, M. M.; and Weiffenbach, J. Discrepancy and attention in the five-month infant. *Genetic Psychology Monographs,* 1972, **85,** 305–331.

Super, D. E. *The psychology of careers: an introduction to vocational development.* New York: Harper & Row, 1957.

Super, D. E.; Starishevsky, R.; Matlin, N.; and Jordaan, J. P. *Career development: Self-concept: Self-concept theory.* New York: College Entrance Examination Board, 1963.

Surgeon General's Scientific Advisory Committee. *Television and growing up: the impact of televised violence.* Washington, D.C.: U.S. Government Printing Office, 1972.

Suter, B. Suicide and women. In B. B. Wolman and H. H. Kraus, (Eds.), *Between survival and suicide.* New York: Gardner Press, 1976.

Sutton-Smith, B. The role of play in cognitive development. *Young Children,* 1967, **22,** 361–370.

Sutton-Smith, B., and Rosenberg, B. G. Modeling and reactive components of sibling interaction. In J. P. Hill (Ed.), *Minnesota Symposia on Child Psychology.* Vol. 3. Minneapolis: U. of Minnesota Press, 1969.

Tanner, J. M. *Education and physical growth: implications of the study of children's growth for educational theory and practice.* London: University Press, 1961.

————. Physical growth. In P. H. Mussen (Ed.), *Carmichael's manual of child psychology.* 3rd Ed., Vol. 1, pp. 77–155. New York: Wiley, 1970.

————. Growing up. *Scientific American,* 1973, **229,** 35–43.

Tapp, J., and Kohlberg, L. Developing senses of law and legal justice. *Journal of Social Issues,* 1971, **27,** 65–91.

Tavris, C., and Offir, C. *The longest war: sex differences in perspective.* New York: Harcourt, Brace, 1977.

Taylor, C. What is involved in a genetic psychology. In T. Mischel (Ed.), *Cognitive development and epistemology.* New York: Academic Press, 1971.

Templin, M. C. *Certain language skills in children: their development and interrelationships.* Minneapolis: U. of Minnesota Press, 1957.

Terman, L. M. *The measurement of intelligence.* Boston: Houghton Mifflin, 1961.

Terman, L. M. and Merrill, M. A. *Stanford-Binet intelligence scale.* Boston: Houghton Mifflin, 1960.

Thiessen, D. D., and Rodgers, D. A. Behavior genetics as the study of mechanism-specific behavior. In J. N. Spuhler (Ed.), *Genetic diversity of behavior,* pp. 61–71. Chicago: Aldine, 1967.

Thomas, A., and Chess, S. *Temperament and development.* New York: Brunner/Mazel, 1977.

Thomas, A.; Chess, S.; and Birch, H. C. The origin of personality. *Scientific American,* 1970, **223,** 102–109.

Thomas, R. M. *Comparing theories and child development.* Belmont, Calif.: Wadsworth, 1979.

Thompson, C. R. (Trans.) *The colloquies of Erasmus.* Chicago: U. of Chicago Press, 1965.

Thompson, W. R. Development and the biophysical bases of personality. In E. F. Borgatta and W. W. Lambert (Eds.), *Handbook of personality theory and research.* Chicago: Rand McNally, 1968.

Thompson, W. R., and Grusec, J. Studies of early experience. In P. H. Mussen (Ed.), *Carmichael's manual of child psychology.* New York: Wiley, 1970.

Thompson, W. R., and Wilde, G. J. S. Behavior genetics. In B. B. Wolman (Ed.), *Handbook of general psychology,* pp. 206–229. Englewood Cliffs, N.J.: Prentice-Hall, 1973.

Thomson, K. S. H. M. S. Beagle, 1820–1870. *American Scientist,* 1975, **63,** 664–672.

Thorndike, E. L. (1913a) *Educational psychology. Vol. I: The original nature of man.* Reprint (3 vols. in 1). New York: Arno, 1969.

————. (1913b) *Educational psychology. Vol. II: The psychology of learning.* Reprint (3 vols. in 1). New York: Arno, 1969.

Tinbergen, N. *The study of instinct.* London: Oxford U. Press, 1951.

Tizard, J., and Tizard, B. The social development of two-year-old children in residential nurseries. In H. R. Schaffer (Ed.), *The origins of human social relations.* London: Academic Press, 1971.

Tolor, A. The generation gap: fact or fiction. *Genetic psychology monographs,* 1976, **94**, 35–103.

Tomlinson-Keasey, C., and Keasey, C. B. The mediating role of cognitive development in moral judgment. *Child Development,* 1974, **45**, 291–298.

Toulmin, S. The concept of "stages" in psychological development. In T. Mischel (Ed.), *Cognitive development and epistemology.* New York: Academic Press, 1971.

Tracy, R. L.; Lamb, M. E.; and Ainsworth, M. D. S. Infant approach behavior as related to attachment. *Child Development,* 1976, **47**, 571–578.

Trehub, S. E. Infants' sensitivity to vowel and tonal contrasts. *Developmental Psychology,* 1973, **9**, 91–96.

————. The discrimination of foreign speech contrasts by infants and adults. *Child Development,* 1976, **47**, 466–472.

Trehub, S. E., and Abramovitch, R. Less is not more: further observations on nonlinguistic strategies. *Journal of Experimental Child Psychology,* 1978, **25**, 160–167.

Trehub, S. E., and Rabinovitch, M. S. Auditory-linguistic sensitivity in early infancy. *Developmental Psychology,* 1972, **6**, 74–77.

Triplett, D. Language patterns of elementary school children. In A. R. Binter and S. H. Frey (Eds.), *The psychology of the elementary school child.* Chicago: Rand McNally, 1972.

Tulkin, S. R., and Kagan, J. Mother-child interaction in the first year of life. *Child Development,* 1972, **43**, 31–41.

Turiel, E. An experimental test of the sequentiality of developmental stages in the child's moral judgments. *Journal of Personality and Social Psychology,* 1966, **3**, 611–618.

Ullian, D. Z. The development of conceptions of masculinity and femininity. In B. Lloyd and J. Ascher (Eds.), *Exploring sex differences.* London: Academic Press, 1976.

Uzgiris, I. C., and Hunt, J. M. *Assessment in infancy: ordinal scales of psychological development.* Urbana: U. of Illinois Press, 1975.

Vaughn, V. C. Developmental pediatrics. In V. C. Vaughn and R. J. McKay (Eds.), *Nelson's textbook of pediatrics.* 10th Ed. Philadelphia: Saunders, 1975.

Verner, A. M., and Stewart, C. S. Adolescent sexual behavior in Middle America revisited: 1970–1973. *Journal of Marriage and the Family,* 1974, **36**, 728.

Verville, E. *Behavior problems of children.* Philadelphia: Saunders, 1967.

Villee, C. A. Biologic principles of growth. In F. Falkner (Ed.), *Human development,* pp. 1–9. Philadelphia: Saunders, 1966.

Vygotsky, L. S. *Thought and language.* Translated by E. Hanfmann and G. Vakar. Cambridge, Mass.: MIT Press, 1962.

Wadsworth, B. J. *Piaget's theory of cognitive development.* New York: David McKay, 1971.

Walker, R. N. Body build and behavior in young children. I: Body build and nursery school teachers' ratings. *Monographs of the Society for Research in Child Development,* 1962, **27** (3, Serial No. 84).

Wallach, L.; Wall, J.; and Anderson, L. Number conservation: the roles of reversibility, addition, subtraction, and misleading perceptual cues. *Child Development,* 1967, **38**, 425–442.

Walters, R. H., and Willows, D. C. Imitative behavior of disturbed and nondisturbed children following exposure to aggressive and nonaggressive models. *Child Development,* 1968, **39**, 79–89.

Warren, J. Birth order and social behavior. *Psychological Bulletin,* 1966, **65**, 38–49.

Wasserman, M. Stokely's speech class. Recorded by Jane Stembridge, *This Magazine is About Schools,* 1970. In *Readings in Human Development,* Annual Editions, pp. 142–143. Guilford, Conn.: Dushkin Publishing.

Waterman, A. S.; Geary, P. S.; and Waterman, C. K. Longitudinal study of changes in ego identity status from the freshman to the senior year at college. *Developmental Psychology,* 1974, **10**, 387–392.

Watson, J. B. (1924) *Behaviorism*. Chicago: U. of Chicago Press, 1957.
――――. *The ways of behaviorism*. New York: Harper, 1928a.
――――. *Psychological care of infant and child*. New York: Norton, 1928b.
Watson, J. S. Operant conditioning of visual fixation in infants under visual and auditory reinforcement. *Developmental Psychology*, 1969, **5**, 508–516.
Webster, R. L.; Steinhardt, M. H.; and Senter, M. G. Changes in infants' vocalizations as a function of differential acoustic stimulation. *Developmental Psychology*, 1972, **7**, 39–43.
Wechsler, D. *Wechsler preschool and primary scale of intelligence manual*. New York: Psychological Corporation, 1967.
――――. *Wechsler intelligence scale for children —revised manual*. New York: Psychological Corporation, 1974.
Weitz, S. *Sex roles: biological, psychological, and social foundations*. New York: Oxford U. Press, 1977.
Wellman, H. M. Knowledge of the interaction of memory variables: a developmental study of metamemory. *Developmental Psychology*, 1978, **14**, 24–29.
Werner, H. *Comparative psychology of mental development*. Rev. Ed. Chicago: Follett, 1948.
Wessman, A. E., and Ricks, D. R. *Mood and personality*. New York: Holt, Rinehart & Winston, 1966.
White, B. L. *Human infants —experience and psychological development*. Englewood Cliffs, N.J.: Prentice-Hall, 1971.
White, C. G.; Bushnell, N.; and Regnemer, J. Moral development in Bahamian school children: a three-year examination of Kohlberg's early stages of moral judgment. *Developmental Psychology*, 1978, **14**, 58–65.
White, E.; Elsom, B.; and Prawat, R. Children's conceptions of death. *Child Development*, 1978, **49**, 307–310.
White, S. Evidence for a hierarchical arrangement of learning processes. In L. P. Lipsitt and C. C. Spiker (Eds.), *Advances in child development and behavior*. Vol. 2. New York: Academic Press, 1965.
Whorf, B. L. *Language, thought, and reality*. Cambridge, Mass.: MIT Press, 1956.
Wildman, T. M., and Fletcher, H. J. Developmental increases and decreases in solutions of conditional syllogism problems. *Developmental Psychology*, 1977, **13**, 630–636.
Williams, J. E., and Morland, J. D. *Race, color, and the young child*. Chapel Hill: U. of North Carolina Press, 1976.
Witkin, H. A.; Goodenough, D. R.; Hirschorn, K. XYY men: are they criminally aggressive? *The Sciences*, 1977, **17**, 10–13.
Wohlwill, J. *The study of behavioral development*. New York: Academic Press, 1973.
Woodward, K. L.; Hager, M.; Huck, J.; Reese, M.; Mark, R.; and Marbach, W. D. The world of cults. *Newsweek*, December 4, 1978 (No. 23), 38–83.

Yando, R., and Kagan, J. The effect of teacher tempo on the child. *Child Development*, 1968, **39**, 27–34.
Yang, R. K., and Douthitt, T. C. Newborn responses to threshold tactile stimulation. *Child Development*, 1974, **45**, 237–242.
Yankelovich, D. *The changing values on campus*. New York: Simon & Schuster, 1972.
Yarrow, L. J.; Rubenstein, J. L.; and Pedersen, F. A. *Infant and environment*. Washington, D.C.: Hemisphere, 1975.
Yarrow, M. R.; Scott, P. M.; and Waxler, C. Z. Learning concern for others. *Developmental Psychology*, 1973, **8**, 240–260.
Yendovitskaya, T. V.; Zinchenko, V. P.; and Ruzskaya, A. G. Development of sensation and perception. In A. C. Zaporozhets and D. B. Elkonin (Eds.), *The psychology of preschool children*. Cambridge, Mass.: MIT Press, 1971.
Young, F. W. The function of male initiation ceremonies: a cross-cultural test of an alternative hypothesis. *American Journal of Sociology*, 1962, **67**, 379–391.

Zajonc, R. B. Family configuration and intelligence. *Science,* April 1976, **192,** 227–236.

Zajonc, R. B., and Marcus, G. B. Birth order and intellectual development. *Psychological Review,* 1975, **82,** 74–88.

Zax, M., and Cowen, E. L. *Abnormal psychology.* New York: Holt, Rinehart & Winston, 1976.

Zigler, E.; Abelson, W. D.; and Seitz, V. Motivational factors in the performance of economically disadvantaged children on the Peabody Picture Vocabulary Test. *Child Development, 1973,* **44,** 294–303.

Zupnick, J. J., and Forrester, W. E. Effects of semantic and acoustic relatedness on free recall in normal children and retardates. *Psychonomic Science,* 1972, **26,** 188–190.

Index of Names

Aaron, R. I., 9
Achenbach, T. M., 263
Adelson, J., 403
Adler, A., 310
Aiken, H. D., 9
Ainsworth, M. D. S., 161
Alexander, T., 230, 320
Allen, J. P. B., 218
Altkin, W. J., 271
Altus, W. D., 310
Amatea, E. S., 405, 406, 409
Anastasi, A., 197
Anastasiow, N. J., 232
Andersen, H., 91
Anderson, B. F., 278
Anisfeld, M., 216
Anthony, E. J., 261
Apgar, V., 86 *Box*, 96 *Table*
Appel, L. F., 276
Arbuthnot, J., 351
Aronfreed, J., 327
Asher, S. R., 226
Ashton, P. T., 395
Austin, V. D., 348
Axline, V., 244

Baer, D. M., 104
Baggett, A. T., 309
Bailey, K. V., 302
Bakan, D., 358
Baldwin, A. L., 300, 363
Baltes, P. B., 379
Bamber, J. H., 367
Bandura, A., 37, 244–246, 248, 251, 253–254, 280, 327–328, 351, 359–360, 401
Barker, R. G., 299
Barnes, K. E., 241
Baron, R., 252, 253–255
Barrett-Goldfarb, M. S., 139

Bart, W. M., 395
Bauer, D. H., 260
Baumrind, D., 305, 308–309, 314, 321, 412–413
Bawkin, 95, 260
Bayley, N., 113, 192–193, 194, 301
Becker, W. C., 305–306
Bee, H. L., 314
Bell, R. Q., 308
Belmont, T., 310
Benedict, R., 365–366
Berecz, J. M., 261
Berg-Cross, L., 350
Berko, J., 136, 215–216
Berkowitz, 253
Bernard, J., 137
Bernstein, B., 229–230
Berzonsky, M. D., 390, 395, 399–400
Bettleheim, B., 361
Beyer, B., 351
Bijou, S. W., 100, 164–165
Binet, A., 14, 51, 184–185, 187–188, 192
Birch, H., 159, 160
Birns, B., 109, 316
Blakney, R. B., 10
Blanton, M. G., 108
Blatt, D., 351
Block, J., 263–264
Blood, R. O., 305
Bloom, L., 135, 138, 221
Blos, P., 398
Blurton-Jones, N., 58
Bodemann, Y. M., 418
Boehm, J. J., 101
Bogartz, G. A., 323
Bohan, J. B., 318–319
Boll, E. S., 312–313
Bolles, R. C., 39
Borke, H., 201
Bossard, J. H. S., 312–313

455

Index of Subjects